WEST VANCOUVER MEMORIAL LIBRARY

P9-AFZ-960

Withdrawn from Collection

WEST VANCOUVER MEMORIAL LIBRARY

Before
CALIFORNIA

An Archaeologist Looks at
Our Earliest Inhabitants

Brian Fagan

ROWMAN & LITTLEFIELD PUBLISHERS, INC.
Lanham • Walnut Creek • New York • Oxford
An AltaMira Press book

ROWMAN & LITTLEFIELD PUBLISHERS, INC.
Published in the United States of America by Rowman & Littlefield Publishers, Inc.
4501 Forbes Boulevard, Suite 200
Lanham, MD 20706

PO Box 317
Oxford
OX2 9RU, United Kingdom

ALTAMIRA PRESS
1630 North Main Street, #367
Walnut Creek, CA 94596
www.altamirapress.com

Copyright © 2003 by Rowman & Littlefield/AltaMira Press

All rights reserved. No part of this publication may be reproduced,
stored in a retrieval system, or transmitted in any form or by any
means, electronic, mechanical, photocopying, recording, or otherwise,
without the prior permission of the publisher.

British Library Cataloguing in Publication Information Available

Library of Congress Cataloging-in-Publication Data

Fagan, Brian M.
    Before California : an archaeologist looks at our earliest inhabitants /
Brian Fagan.
        p. cm.
    Includes bibliographical references and index.
    ISBN 0-7425-2794-8 (alk. paper)
    1. Indians of North America—California—Antiquities. 2. California—
Antiquities. I. Title.

E78.C15 F34 2003
979.4'01—dc21   2002015917

Printed in the United States of America

⊗™ The paper used in this publication meets the minimum requirements of
American National Standard for Information Sciences—Permanence of Paper for
Printed Library Materials, ANSI/NISO Z39.48–1992.

To

Shelly Lowenkopf

with gratitude

And when they'd put aside desire for food and drink,
The Muse inspired the bard
To sing the famous deeds of fighting heroes—the song whose fame had
reached the skies these days.

— Homer *The Odyssey,* Book 8: lines 85–88.
[Robert Fagles, *Homer: The Odyssey.*
New York: Penguin Books, 1996]

Contents

CONTENTS

Preface

Before California began when the Executive Board of the Society for California Archaeology asked if I would be interested in writing a book about the archaeology of the state for the general public. In a rash moment, I accepted the invitation.

Two years later, after countless drafts, prolonged hours of wading through often-confusing academic literature, and frequent moments of literary despair, I have produced this book. This, quite simply, has been the toughest archaeological and writing project I have ever undertaken.

The society's charge was a simple one: write a book for the broadest possible audience. This meant a minimum of archaeological jargon, as few laundry lists of artifacts as possible, and a constant focus on the larger issues rather than the arcana of archaeological research. It also meant wrestling with a suitable narrative style for the book. In the end, I decided that this was as much a personal journey as anything else, for I found myself developing opinions about an archaeology that is often obscure, frequently virtually unintelligible, and always incomplete. There were times when I despaired of ever making a story out of it. But I think that I have succeeded. I think it is generally accurate. Of course, experts are bound to disagree with various interpretations. I was unable to locate, far less read, all the literature, especially those works in progress and the often-unavailable cultural resource management reports.

The Organization of the Story

Before California consists of four parts. Part I, "The Archaeologist's Tale," a single chapter entitled "A Stream of Time," is a general overview of what happened in the 13,000 years or more of California's early past.

Part II, "Beginnings," carries the story forward from first settlement (chapter 2) through the earliest colonization of the coast, describes the Milling Stone Horizon, a little-known period in California history, then moves the island story forward to about 2500 B.C.

Part III, "The Web of Interconnectedness," begins in about 2500 B.C., when acorns and hunting assumed great importance in California life, and people began to exploit the seacoasts more intensively. "A Changing World" describes acorn harvesting and other major changes that took hold in California societies after 2500 B.C., followed by "The Seductive Glass," which surveys the obsidian trade and ranges more widely over ancient interconnectedness generally, paying attention to social organization and the role of individuals in promoting trade. "The Realm of the Supernatural" sets forth what we know about ritual beliefs and shamanism, while "Art on the Rocks" describes the controversies surrounding California's rich archives of rock art.

Part IV, "A Crowded World," carries the story forward from about 2000 B.C. We work our way southward through the state, starting with the salmon fishers of the north coast and extreme northwest. "A Landscape of Mounds" covers San Francisco Bay, while "Realm of the Rivers" describes what we know about the Central Valley and Sierra foothills. "Coast, Hinterland, and Desert" takes up the archaeology of the desert regions of the southeast, then on to the Santa Barbara Channel region with its sophisticated maritime societies. The book ends with a brief summary of the European arrival.

"Notes and References" provides an annotated excursion through what is one of archaeology's most complex and obscure academic literatures. This makes no claims to be even slightly complete, but it will allow interested readers to delve more deeply into various aspects of the subject if they desire.

It's worth mentioning that this book is concerned with *ancient* California, the long history of native Californians before the Spanish *entrada* of the sixteenth century. Consequently, there is no coverage of the tragic history of native American societies after European contact, which is a subject unto itself. I have confined coverage of native societies at contact to the minimum, except for descriptions of general life ways where appropriate. By the same token, I have deliberately omitted anything but passing references to linguistic differences and oral history, which are, to put it mildly, complex subjects, mainly of interest to academic experts. (You will find maps of California societies at contact and of the main language groups, in chapter 1.)

European contact was a momentous event, with terrible consequences for California's native peoples. You'll notice that I refer to them in the past tense, NOT because they no longer exist, but simply because the traditional societies, which flourished at contact, have either vanished or been transformed beyond recognition. Some anthropologists wrongly refer to "the ethnographic present," as if there were a moment frozen in time when native Californian societies ceased to change, stopped adjusting to ever-changing climatic conditions, and become fossilized for the delectation of scholars, as a baseline for looking back at the societies of the remoter past. No human society, let alone those of the Californians at contact, has *ever* remained static.

This book is written from *published research* only, except where I have received specific permission by researchers to quote their latest, unpublished work. This means that I am working with the accessible literature. An enormous amount of California archaeology is embedded in what is often called the "gray literature," publications of limited circulation resulting from cultural resource management projects. This makes it very hard for a general work to be up-to-date, especially on the more subtle nuances of the field. I have done my best to work with the best and highest-quality sources available, but there are obvious limitations.

Finally, I wish to make it clear that I am not a California archaeologist, nor have I ever conducted original field research in the state. I was asked to write this book by experts in California archaeology, who flattered me by considering me qualified for the job. My qualifications are those of both a professional archaeologist with extensive fieldwork experience, and of a generalist and archaeological writer, with expertise in the broad issues of the human past and North American archaeology. As an outsider, I can perhaps take liberties with my account that would not sit well with fellow specialists. Nevertheless, I have attempted to navigate through the treacherous shoals of controversy as even-handedly as I could. Inevitably, I have had to gloss over major debates, to generalize in the interests of brevity. I have taken a few liberties with the ethnographic record in the interests of writing a vivid and interesting narrative. Of course, there have been the inevitable murmurs in the background to the effect that, as a non-California archae-ologist, I am not qualified to write this book. Why, ask these folk, did the Board not ask one of us? To which there can only be one response. Sit down and write one of your own! Goodness knows we need not one book on ancient California, but at least half a dozen. Enough said. I am honored to have been asked to undertake the job.

Brian Fagan
Santa Barbara, California
August 2002

Author's Note

The following conventions have been adopted in this book, either as a result of common usage, or because they are the most convenient.

- All measurements are in miles, yards, feet, and inches, these being the units most commonly used in public life. Readers should be aware that archaeologists commonly work in the metric system.
- Dates in calendar years are expressed as A.D./B.C., following common convention. Years before present are used occasionally, when stylistic needs demand it.
- Please be aware that radiocarbon dates are statistical approximations. Where possible, and unless otherwise stated, they have been calibrated against tree-ring chronologies.
- All modern place names are in accordance with contemporary usage. I have used Native American spellings commonly used in the literature. I have used the *Handbook of North American Indians,* volume 8: *California* (Robert F. Heizer, ed., Washington, D.C.: Smithsonian Institution, 1978) as an authoritative source.
- Any technical archaeological terms used in the text are defined (by notes at the back of the book) on first occurrence in the narrative, but are kept to an absolute minimum.

Acknowledgments

I AM GRATEFUL TO THE PRESIDENT AND EXECUTIVE BOARD of the Society for California Archaeology for their invitation to write this book and for their constant support. I also owe a great debt to Malcolm Margolin of Heyday Books, who was instrumental in initiating the project and obtaining commitments of financial support for the writing and research. Without his encouragement, this project would never have got off the ground. Mitch Allen of AltaMira Press has given invaluable advice and frank criticism of the kind one gets from old friends. I am proud that he is publishing the book.

Many colleagues and friends have given advice, shown me sites or collections, provided references, and offered stimulating encouragement and discussion. It's impossible to name them all, but among them were: Linda Agren, Jeffrey Attschul, Jeanne Arnold, Jim Cassidy, Lynn Gamble, Michael Glassow, Donn Grenda, William Hildebrand, John Johnson, Terry Jones, Russell Kaldenburg, Roger La Jeunesse, Kent Lightfoot, Ed Luby, Dana McGowan, Mark Raab, Jim Pearson, Judy Porcasi, John Pryor, Jan Timbrook, Claude Warren, David Whitley, and Diane Winslow. If your name is omitted, please accept my apologies! Thank you one and all.

My greatest debt is to Shelly Lowenkopf, who has seen me through many books, and was at my side throughout the long gestation period of this one. An editor of vast experience, his insights were—quite literally—priceless. In many respects, this is as much his book as mine. He has been my mentor in the writing world for many years: the least I can do is to dedicate this book to him. Steve Cook, "Mr. Prez," has been a wonderful source of wisdom during the project.

Steve Brown drew the line drawings and maps with his customary skill.

Finally, it may be a cliché, but my grateful thanks to Lesley and Ana, also our cats and rabbits, who have lived with this book from Day 1 and are very glad to see the back of it!

I also acknowledge, with gratitude, financial support for the research and writing of this book from:

USDI Bureau of Land Management, California

USDA Forest Service, Pacific Region

The California State Office of Historic Preservation (National Park Service Heritage Preservation Fund).

This publication has been financed in part with Federal funds from the National Park Service, Department of the Interior. However, the contents and opinions do not necessarily reflect the views or policies of the Department of the Interior.

This program receives Federal financial assistance for identification and protection of historic properties. Under Title VI of the Civil Rights Act of 1964, Section 504 of the Rehabilitation Act of 1973, and the Age Discrimination Act of 1975, as amended, the U.S. Department of the Interior prohibits discrimination on the basis of race, color, national origin, disability, or age in its federally assisted programs. If you believe you have been discriminated against in any program, activity, or facility as described above, or if you desire further information, please write to: Office of Equal Opportunity, National Park Service, 1849 C Street, NW, Washington, DC 20240

PART I

The Archaeologist's Tale

"Eastward the dawn rose, ridge behind ridge
into the morning, and vanished out of eyesight
into guess; it was no more than a glimmer
blending with the hem of the sky, but it spoke
to them, out of memory and old tales, of the
high and distant mountains."

[J.R.R. TOLKIEN, *Lord of the Rings*][1]

A Stream of Time

(Before 11,200 B.C. to A.D. 1542)

EARTHMAKER CREATED THE UNIVERSE FOR THE MAIDU of northeastern California. Floating on the primordial waters, he imagined the world and brought it into being with the aid of a meadowlark's nest, Coyote, and much singing. He stretched the nest out "to where the day breaks," to the south and the west, to "the North Country" and the "rim of the world." Earthmaker fashioned creatures of all kinds in pairs, then "two people, then two more and then two more." "You will live here," he proclaimed. "You and your country will have a name. Living in a country that is little, not big, you will be content." When he had created humankind and the world, Earthmaker "went past the middle of the world, built a house, and lived there."[2]

"A country that is little." "You will be content. . . ," These few words define the ideal of ancient California life. The ancient Californians lived in familiar places, often no more than five to ten miles across. Everyone knew the boundaries of their territory, the creeks, canyons, boulders, and conspicuous springs that marked their land. They shared their homeland with animals, endowed in their myths with human speech, powerful emotions, and the capacity to create and destroy. Rich legends and oral traditions

3

defined familiar surroundings, lands where the living and supernatural realms came together and lived in a carefully nurtured harmony.

Most people rarely strayed far from their birthplace, except to hunt, harvest plants, or sometimes to trade. Even highly mobile desert bands rarely moved outside their homelands. In 1918, anthropologist E. W. Gifford interviewed an old Monache woman named Wiinu who lived west of the Owens Valley in Central California. She was about ninety-five years old. During her long life, she had lived all her years, except for one winter as a child, in an area six miles across and seven and a half miles wide. Over nine decades she had lived in no less than fourteen camps within this small territory, moving for all manner of reasons—marriage, the birth of a son, the passing of her husband, then the death of her son, and to live among close relatives.

Her experience was typical of most people, who never traveled far from family and close kin. They lived in small, seemingly unchanging worlds, aware of others living nearby or at a distance, their lives defined by the endless cycles of the changing seasons.

Over three hundred thousand people lived in what is now California when the first Europeans arrived in the sixteenth century A.D. They formed a dense network of groups, large and small, speaking more than sixty languages, occupying about 256,000 square miles of varied terrain. The population density was about one person per two square miles, a higher figure than average for the North America of five centuries ago. They had adapted to coastlines teeming with fish and sea mammals, to sluggish estuaries, lakeside environments, and marshes, to thick redwood forests and open grasslands alive with acorn-rich oaks. Many groups flourished in harsh deserts, living off plants and small rodents. Yet they all shared a belief in an unchanging, cyclical world (see figures 1.1 and 1.2).[3]

The Unchanging Verities

A Sierra Miwok creation story says: "Before the people, there was only water. Coyote looked among the ducks and sent one particular kind to dive. It went down, reached the bottom, bit the earth, and came up to the surface. Coyote took the earth and sent the duck to dive for seeds. He mixed the earth and seeds into a ball, which swelled until the water disappeared and the earth came into existence . . . ."[4]

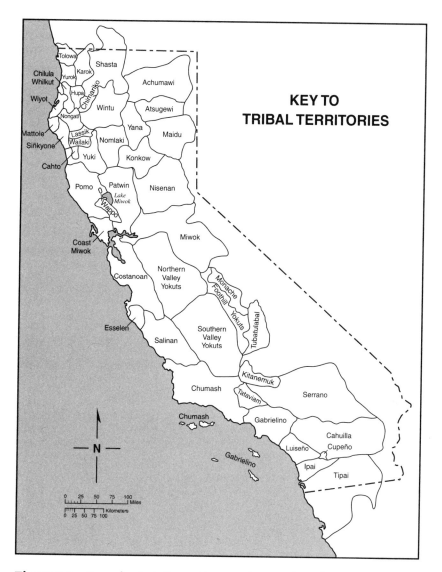

Figure 1.1. Some basic information on the peoples of California.
(a) The distribution of all known groups inhabiting the state in the fifteenth century
A.D. As such, it is a convenient reference for the narrative in this book. The information comes from Robert F. Heizer, ed., *The Handbook of North American
Indians,* Volume 8: *California* (Washington, D.C.: Smithsonian Institution Press,
1978), p. ix, arguably the most authoritative source on the subject.

(Continued)

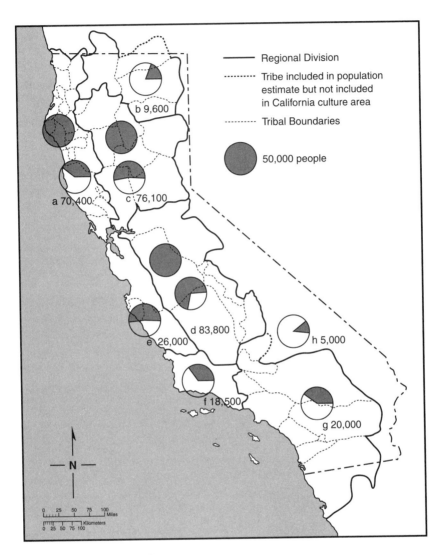

Figure 1.1. Continued.

(b) Demographer/anthropologist Sherburne F. Cook spent much of his career studying pre-European populations in California. This map, compiled from his many publications on the subject, gives the estimated population by broad regions. The densest populations were in the food-rich Central Valley, with much lower densities in the southern deserts and northeast. Cook's best population estimate for California's population in A.D. 1542 was 310,00 ± 30,000 people, which is probably as reliable a calculation as we will ever get. Data compiled from the *Handbook of North American Indians*, Volume 8: *California*.

The ancient Californians lived in a living, vibrant world, carefully defined by myth, oral tradition, and ritual. Creatures like Coyote and Deer had occupied the world before humankind, prepared it for them. The mythic creator beasts had helped them obtain the first acorns, salmon, and other foods—to say nothing of creating fire and ensuring death. As a Wintun man from the west bank of the Sacramento River once said to an ethnographer: "Everything in this world talks, just as we are now—the trees, rocks, everything."

This world was eternal, unchanging. Songs and chants of the creation, of a familiar, ageless world, defined by sea, mountains, forests, and the heavens, a cosmos where the living and spiritual domains passed seamlessly one into the other—the native Californians dwelt in a world of cyclical time, the passage of the seasons measured by the movements of the heavenly bodies. Each generation lived with a legacy of knowledge passed down to them by their ancestors, which they expected to pass on to their children and grandchildren in due time. The world was always the same, a place where the verities of life unfolded for each generation; birth and new growth in spring; youth and adulthood in the warm days of summer; plenitude, old age, and then death with the fall nut harvests and the coming of the cold weather.

The passing of the generations, age-old chants, and rituals defined the world—comforting, exhorting, warning, and validating human existence at every turn. It could not be any other way in societies where all knowledge was passed from father to son, from mother to daughter, by example and by word of mouth. The oldest members of a family of a hunting band were the most experienced, the most honored, and most valuable people, for they were the repositories of knowledge, of hard-won experience. In a world where rainfall was unpredictable, droughts and hunger were commonplace, and survival depended on flexibility and opportunism, the elders and shamans, individuals with unusual spiritual powers, were an anchor to history, the ancestors, and the forces that controlled human destiny.

Such a past offers reassurance that life will continue in an unchanging pattern, measured by the movements of heavenly bodies, by the routines of birth, growth, old age, and death—spring, summer, fall, and winter. Animals and plants, the cosmos, and the passage of the seasons, defined human experience, all part and parcel of present, past, and future. The future was always uncertain, but would always be the same. Life would continue as it

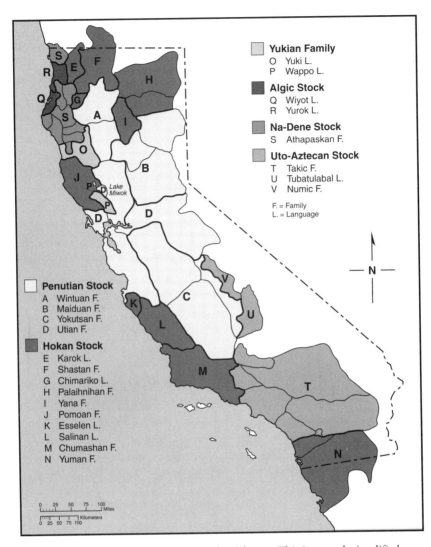

Figure 1.2. Major language groups of California. This is a much simplified map for the purposes of this book. Data compiled from the *Handbook of North American Indians*, Volume 8: *California*.

BOX 1.1 The Languages of California

William Shipley, writing in *The Handbook of North American Indians* (1978), estimated that there were between sixty-four and eighty native Californian languages at European contact. These were mutually unintelligible, without taking dialects into account. Only about two dozen of these languages survived into the mid-twentieth century and these were in danger of extinction, being spoken only by older people. The map shows the distribution of the major language groups. While the experts disagree on some of the details, it gives a general impression sufficient for this book.

Linguistic history is a dauntingly complex enterprise, a mixture of detective work and specialized knowledge that requires infinite patience and a gift for detail. Even the basic summaries have me calling for restoratives! It is almost impossible to date the moments when different language families arrived, while the relationships between them challenge even experts. For the purposes of this book, I summarize the major linguistic families, as we refer to them occasionally in the narrative. Interested readers will find some standard references on ancient California's languages in the Guide to Further Reading.

Here's a general summary of the main language families, which are shown in figure 1.2 (see page 8).

The oldest language group still found in California is *Hokan*, probably spoken over much of California (perhaps alongside other now vanished language families that have left no trace), but was broken into smaller units by the spread of *Penutian* languages. Penutian spread through the Central Valley, forcing Hokan to the edges.

Yukian, an isolated family of languages, appeared mainly in Mendocino and Lake and Napa counties. There were originally about two thousand Yukian speakers, but the relationships of this family are a mystery, perhaps lying with Hokan or Penutian, but this is uncertain.

Algic was confined to extreme northwestern California, comprising both Wiyot and Yurok, languages spoken along the coast. The *Na-Dene* languages of California belong to the Athapaskan family and were also confined to the northwest.

(Continued)

BOX 1.1 Continued

Uto-Aztecan speakers thrust into southern California, further isolating the Hokan-speaking Yumans of the south from their linguistic relatives. There are three branches, of which Numic was spoken over a vast area of the west, but only by the Mono in eastern California. The Takic branch was spoken by several important southern California groups, among them the Gabrieleño, the Luiseño, and the Cahuilla and Serrano.

always had been, and always would be. This was a complete antithesis to the linear history of Western society.

Many of today's native Californians still have no interest in a linear history of their remote ancestors. They believe that their ancestors have lived in their homeland since the beginning of time. Their cultural identity is anchored in cyclical history. Tragically, nearly all the oral records of this history vanished in the aftermath of European contact. Only smatterings remain in occasional Spanish chronicles, in ethnographic accounts collected long afterward, in the nineteenth and twentieth centuries, and in a few carefully preserved oral traditions kept quietly by survivors, only now coming to light. Most of the traditional record of the past has gone. Only Western science remains to fill the vacuum.[5]

In dramatic contrast, archaeologists armed with all the elaborate panoply of modern science proclaim that humans have lived in California for more than 13,000 years.

Two apparently incompatible pasts, or are they? Anthropologists refer to "emic" histories, which construct both world views and visions of the past firmly embedded in the cultural and social traditions of which the tellers are part. These contrast with the "etic" histories, constructed from science and dispassionate observation by outsiders such as archaeologists and ethnohistorians.[6] The two histories tell quite different tales and are seemingly incompatible. But since neither completely reflects what actually happened in the past, this incompatibility does not matter that much. The past is a synthesis of different approaches, different perspectives, filtered through our individual, idiosyncratic minds. In a real sense, it is what we make it.

If you want to be technical about it, then this is an etic history, the story of ancient California told from an archaeologist's perspective.

A Past from the Spade

I am an archaeologist, trained in the traditions of Western science to look back at human existence on a long, linear time scale. Archaeology tells a different story of humanity, which begins with the earliest tool-making humans in eastern Africa over two and a half million years ago, and encompasses everything that has happened to humanity since then.

Archaeology's story telling comes not from oral traditions, but from stone artifacts and animal bones, pot fragments, village sites, and minute seeds and ornaments—the material remains of humanity's past. We unfold a tale on a global canvas, of modern humans first emerging over 100,000 years ago, of a great diaspora of *Homo sapiens* across Europe and Asia. And we show how small handfuls of Stone Age people crossed from Siberia into Alaska and a hitherto uninhabited continent some time after about 15,000 years ago.[7]

It also tells us that the remote ancestors of the native Californians settled in their homeland before 11,000 B.C. Unfortunately, most of the thirteen millennia since then still remain veiled in historical obscurity.

Archaeology is always a frustrating arena of shreds and patches, tiny morsels of information about ancient societies extracted from the destructive forces of history. We are at the mercy of the vagaries of soil chemistry and the environment. California archaeology is one of the most frustrating mazes of all.

When told that I was writing this book for the public, more than a few of my California colleagues laughed and wished me luck. Some flatly declared the task impossible. There were many times when I wondered if they were right. Time and time again, I found myself seeking answers to the most fundamental of questions. Almost immediately, I came up against a dead end, smothered in a meaningless goulash of projectile points, bead styles, and other obfuscations. Many times, I despaired of ever telling a coherent story.

The record of more than 13,000 years of ancient California comes down to us in a confusing jumble of stone artifacts, animal bones, seashells and shell beads, and the occasional bone artifact. Only in the arid landscapes of the interior do perishable artifacts survive—basketry, bows and arrows, netting, seeds, and shaman's paraphernalia. But even there, little has survived, thanks to the destructive hands of early archaeologists and nineteenth-century collectors. We have, at best, an incomplete jigsaw puzzle of California's past, with many missing pieces.

Unfortunately, the puzzle will always have gaps. There are thousands of archaeological sites in the state, many of them still undiscovered. There are even more that have fallen victim to the inexorable forces of destruction—by looters out for salable items or museum specimens, by developers building new suburban tracts, by industrial agriculture, huge water control systems, mining, highway construction, and every form of day-to-day activity possible. Much of California's past is gone forever, vanished into an oblivion from which it can never be recovered.

Archaeological excavations began in the late nineteenth century, when inexpert excavators like government surveyor Carl Schumacher descended on California and shipped literally tons of artifacts and skeletons from shell mounds and cemeteries back east to the Smithsonian Institution and other museums.[8] Private collectors ransacked sites into the 1920s, doing incalculable damage to the archaeological record. Serious investigations began with the founding of the Department of Anthropology and University Museum at the University of California, Berkeley, a century ago. The pioneer anthropologist Alfred Kroeber encouraged professional archaeologists like Nels C. Nelson to survey and excavate shell mounds in the San Francisco Bay Area. This work began as Kroeber and others made Herculean efforts to study surviving native groups before traditional cultures vanished.

During the 1920s and 1930s, excavations in many parts of the state resulted in the first chronological sequences of ancient societies, identified from changes in artifact styles in stratified occupation layers of shell mounds and caves. Large numbers of site reports and dreary monographs saw the light of day, complete with arid, labored descriptions of stone projectile points, shell beads, and other artifacts, remarkable for their proliferation of artifact types and cultural labels, many of them completely meaningless except to those who formulated them. Right up to the 1970s, and still today, much of the literature of California archaeology was, and is, a potpourri of obscure papers and proliferating reports on excavations that were often hastily conducted, of poor standard, and never described in full. Even the most distinguished California archaeologists of the day, like Robert Heizer, rarely ventured beyond artifacts into the realm of human behavior.

BOX 1.2 Dating California's Past

Archaeologists are obsessed with dating. Small wonder, for they know how hard it is to date archaeological sites of any kind, especially shell mounds and the kinds of inconspicuous sites that occur throughout California.

Here are the major dating methods used today, which we refer to at intervals during the narrative:

Historical Records provide very limited dating information, as they do not extend back further than Juan Cabrillo (A.D. 1542) and only become more plentiful after the founding of the missions in the late eighteenth century. European imports such as coins, glass beads, and other exotica can sometimes provide dates for sites occupied at about the time of European contact or thereafter, as is the case in the Bay Area, the Sacramento Delta, and the Santa Barbara Channel region—to mention only a few instances.

Dendrochronology (tree-ring dating) (present day to c. 8000 B.C.), from the Greek, *dendros*, tree. The annual growth rings of long-lived trees such as sequoias, bristlecone pines, and European oaks provide an accurate master chronology for much of the past 10,000 years. Tree-ring dating began in the Southwest, where it was used to date wooden beams in ancient pueblos. In California, tree-ring dates are especially important for dating climatic events. They are also used to calibrate radiocarbon dates.

Radiocarbon dating (c. A.D. 1500 to 40,000 years ago). Radiocarbon dating is based on the measurement of the decay rates of C14 atoms in organic samples like charcoal, shell, wood, hair, and other materials. When combined with accelerator mass spectrometry, it can produce dates from tiny samples such as single seeds, which are then calibrated, if possible, against tree-ring dates to provide a date in calendar years. Radiocarbon chronologies give us the time scale of ancient California with reasonable accuracy but should always be thought of as statistical estimates as they have margins of error attached to them. In recent years, accelerator mass spectrometry (AMS) radiocarbon dating has become the method of choice. AMS dating allows the use of tiny samples, even a single seed.

There are other dating methods, notably obsidian hydration, which provide limited chronologies. These are described in the narrative, where appropriate. But radiocarbon dating remains the staple chronological method used in California.

California's past was dehumanized, a thing of artifacts and, after the 1950s, radiocarbon dates, all-too-often stitched together in meaningless, jargon-riddled summaries that treated artifacts just like postage stamps. Fortunately, field training has improved in recent years (figure 1.3).

Then came Cultural Resource Management (commonly known as CRM). Until the 1960s, California archaeology was almost entirely an academic pursuit, bolstered by a long tradition of amateur involvement. Very often, the avocational archaeologists were better than the professionals. Since then, federal, local, and state legislation have mandated archaeological investigations in advance of development or other activity on publicly owned lands and many other properties. Within a few years, archaeology mushroomed from being a small, somewhat haphazardly planned activity into a statewide enterprise, all of it directed to complying with legal requirements, to mitigating the effects of disturbing archaeological sites, large and small. Academia trains the archaeologists, but, increasingly, they find employment with the federal and state government or with private-sector companies, engaged in administering CRM law or in fieldwork (see box 1.3).[9]

With the frenzied pace of development across the state, excavation and survey proceed everywhere at a dizzying pace, work aimed at complying with legal requirements, usually confined to small areas such as a single lot or a pipeline corridor, with work now conducted outside the contracted area. Some of these projects last for many years and produce major results, like the Playa Vista and Ballona Wetlands projects in west Los Angeles (figure 1.4). But, for the most part, CRM projects are short-term, small-scale research designed to satisfy legal requirements. There are some glowing examples of CRM research, where the investigators have made fine efforts to address broader questions, and they are quoted in these pages. Unfortunately, however, many surveys and excavations appear in publications of limited circulation, and are often inaccessible to the broader audience.

Inevitably, the story of ancient California is a fractured portrait, much of it created by generations of mindless archaeology, widespread destruction, a confusing, and often effectively inaccessible literature, and poor preservation.

Back in 1984, a distinguished California archaeologist, Michael Moratto, wrote a vast tome entitled *The Archaeology of California*. His book is a gallant attempt to make sense of this confusion, a confusion so profound that he was forced to bring in co-authors to help him with some regions. Moratto did a fine job, but the book in all its mind-numbing and inevitable

Figure 1.3. CRM archaeology requires lengthy field training. Here, an archaelo-
gist measures the boulders of a plant processing platform at the
Skyrocket site in the Sierra foothills. Courtesy of Mark Raab.

Figure 1.4. CRM in action. A crew at site LAN-63 on the Westchester Bluffs overlooking the Ballona Wetlands in west Los Angeles excavate a concentration of ground stone artifacts. (a) The feature is exposed and plotted in the ground. (b) The exposed feature. (c) A plan of same, showing the different artifacts and other remains in the concentration. Courtesy of Statistical Research, Inc.

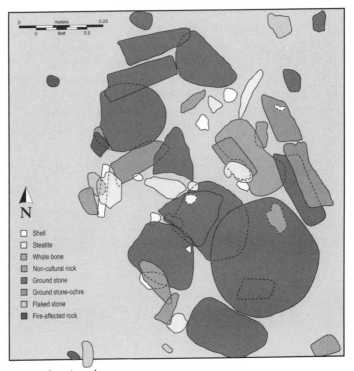

Figure 1.4. Continued

BOX 1.3 Cultural Resource Management

Cultural Resource Management (CRM), now the dominant form of archaeology in California, stems from a series of historic preservation laws and other mandates, which began with the National Historic Preservation Act (NHPA) of 1966. NHPA was the culmination of over a century of legislation and court rulings, beginning with the Antiquities Act of 1906. The Reservoir Salvage Act of the 1930s provided a mandate for large amounts of archaeological work in areas to be flooded by massive water projects. The WPA did a great deal of work in the Midwest and Southeast and some in Orange County under this legislation. NHPA mandated that archaeological work be carried out whenever federal funds, lands, or permits were needed to alter the land. The legislation requires that a federal agency must check to see if any archaeological sites or other cultural resources of national importance would be lost or impacted during the project. California, like other states, also has equivalent legislation, as do many counties and local governments.

Section 106 of the NHPA requires that a federal agency must take into account the effects that land modification activity will have on anything in the project area that could be listed in the National Register of Historic Places. This "Section 106 process" is intended to ensure compliance with the law and lies at the core of CRM. NHPA also required each state governor to appoint a State Historic Preservation Officer (SHPO), to develop state preservation plans and coordinate historic preservation activities throughout the state.

The Section 106 process does not stop construction or development. Rather, it offers an opportunity for the assessment of cultural resources and for their proper recording *before* they are damaged or destroyed. The process involves not only the responsible federal agency, but also the SHPO, local government, and any native or other group that attaches ceremonial or religious importance to a property eligible for the National Register. In California, the SHPO and his or her staff are responsible for reviewing and keeping a list of register-eligible properties. They review the reports and recommendations of the archaeologist or archaeological organization contracted to carry out the 106 process within a specific area, like, for example, the Ballona wetlands in west Los Angeles. In most CRM projects, the archaeologist in charge deals not only with the federal agency and the SHPO, but also with other consulting parties with an interest in the process.

CRM primarily revolves around compliance with Section 106, using well-established procedures to make recommendations for preservation or "mitigation" of damage to cultural resources. This can mean rerouting a highway, completely excavating a site to collect as much information as possible before it is destroyed, covering a settlement with a layer of sterile overburden, and so on. The process has a set of built-in checks and balances and requires that the work be done by a professionally qualified archaeologist. So far, archaeologists are not professionally certified, but it is only a matter of time before it becomes routine.

Every CRM project involves a series of well-defined stages—comprehensive background research, identification of possible sites and other historic properties through survey and reconnaissance, then testing and evaluation. If the work so far determines that a site is eligible for listing in the National Register, then a process of mitigation begins, which involves input from the involved parties and the public, development of a Memorandum of Agreement specifying the mitigation, and the actual mitigation itself, which may involve excavation to recover archaeological data or avoidance of the location all together. If data recovery is involved, then the project moves on to the last stage—processing and analysis of the recovered materials and writing and submitting the project compliance report. The report is thoroughly reviewed before final approval, at which point it is an official compliance document. It's safe to say that most California archaeology today exists in the form of hundreds, if not thousands, of compliance reports. Part archaeological monograph and part official document, they are now the central archive of California's early past.

The Native American Grave Protection and Repatriation Act (NAGPRA) of 1990 requires all federal agencies and museums receiving federal funds to inventory their holdings of Indian human remains and associated funerary objects. A second requirement protects all Indian graves and other cultural objects found within

(Continued)

BOX 1.3 Continued

archaeological sites on federal and tribal land. NAGPRA requires consultation with affiliated or potentially affiliated Indian groups when human remains are discovered, either by accident or in an excavation. In California, Indian monitors are present on all excavations to oversee the treatment of any burials. NAGPRA makes sure that California archaeologists work closely with Indians, something that was uncommon even a generation ago.

CRM projects can vary in size from a single city lot to a huge, multiyear project involving hundreds of sites and multimillion dollar budgets. Today, most cutting-edge advances in surveying and excavating technology are coming from CRM research, where issues of cost effectiveness and limited time to complete large-scale research are the realities. Such projects are revolutionizing our knowledge of California archaeology, with a flood of new data, which it will take generations to digest. But the important thing is that much of the finite, and very precious, archaeological record of California's early past is being recovered for more leisurely study in future generations.

detail is monstrously difficult to grapple with—through no fault of the author.[10]Fortunately, I found some salvation in the work of a small number of archaeologists, many of them trained in the 1970s. They are asking broader questions, looking beyond the small universe of a single excavation, and undertaking thoughtful and provocative research. So much has vanished that it's a challenging form of detective work, much of it focusing on broad regions rather than single excavations, involving data from obscure CRM investigations, the analysis of museum collections untouched since the 1920s, even tracing important baskets and other artifacts to institutions as far afield as in St. Petersburg, Russia. Sound archaeological theory enriches this new work, which draws from many academic disciplines. The latest work melds climatology with zoology, subsistence with ritual usages, rock art with ancient shamanism. I only wish these perspectives had been around a half century ago, when there was so much left undestroyed.

Unfortunately, so much is lost that California's earlier past is a frustrating will-'o-the-wisp, never to be grasped in its entirety, never to be fully understood. All I can offer is an incomplete story.

This book tells the story of the first Californians, as we know it from the testimony of anthropology, history, the trowel, the spade, and the very latest in scientific technology.[11] It is not a book about archaeology, but a narrative of people, individuals and groups, going about their daily business—hunting and foraging, living and dying, loving, raising children, living in plenty and in hunger, negotiating and quarreling, pondering their cosmos, and facing the unpredictable challenges of drought and El Niños. (For the benefit of those who are not familiar with El Niños—and they cannot possibly live in California—this irregularly occurring phenomenon, caused by higher sea surface temperatures in the tropical Pacific, brings warmer water, tropical fish, and heavy, potentially destructive winter rainfall to California.)

This book is about people, not artifacts, for, as the great British archaeologist Mortimer Wheeler reminded us many years ago: "archaeology is the driest dust that blows." Regrettably, and unnecessarily, California archaeology has been unspectacular, very dry dust indeed. This is also a book about interconnectedness and interdependence, about the challenges of survival in a fractured, demanding landscape, where the sheer unpredictability of rainfall, El Niños, and drought cycles, to mention only a few events, forced people to live conservatively and worry constantly about hunger.

The remainder of this chapter summarizes the story and discusses the major themes. It's a narrative marked by continuity and interconnectedness, and by sudden bursts of innovation and change—what I call two major changes, one in about 2000 B.C., the other at the end of the first millennium A.D.

When I took a long view of ancient California, I was struck by the important changes in ways of making a living or of organizing society, which took hold at moments when growing populations outstripped available food supplies. In themselves, the changes do not seem earth shattering, but I felt they were profound changes in human life, sudden shifts in direction preceded and followed by long periods of continuity. They were times when people changed direction and adapted to new environmental and social realities, important landmarks in over thirteen millennia of an unfolding past. For example, acorns became a staple and the hunting of larger mammals became important in about 2500 B.C. Major social changes reduced the level of violence in some societies 1,500 years later. The effects of these shifts rippled through ancient California societies for centuries.

And now the story. . . .

The Story Begins (Before 11,200 to c. 9000 B.C.)

We do not know exactly when the first human settlers entered California, but it was certainly before 11,200 B.C., possibly as much as a thousand years earlier. They probably arrived from the north or east, perhaps down the natural corridor of the Central Valley or from the Great Basin, fanning into coastal regions. No one believes that they paddled down the inhospitable, and often windy Pacific coast, simply because there were no suitable watercraft for doing so.[12]

The newcomers found themselves in a very different land from the California of today—colder and wetter, the snow levels on the Sierras lower than in modern times. Redwood forests grew much further south than their present-day limits; thick pine forests mantled much of the southern coastal zone. Shallow freshwater lakes fed by glacial meltwater and local rainfall abounded in the Central Valley and in the southern deserts, then semi-arid, better-watered lands. But the most dramatic difference was along the coast, where the Pacific lay about three hundred feet below modern levels. Extensive continental shelves stretched westward from today's shoreline. The Golden Gate was a river estuary; the four northern Channel Islands were a single landmass, only six miles from the nearest mainland. Low-lying coastal plains bounded the Santa Barbara shore and filled San Pedro Bay (see figure 1.5).

This was no land of plenty. The most abundant food supplies lay along the edges of major lakes and rivers, with seemingly inexhaustible shell fish and sea mammal colonies along rocky shores. When the first humans arrived, large Ice Age animals such as wild horses and camelids still roamed the landscape. They abruptly became extinct after 11,000 B.C., casualties of increasing aridity and warmer temperatures. Human predators may have accelerated the extinction of these animals with their hunting, especially slow breeding animals such as mammoth. We simply do not know.

We do know that the descendants of the first settlers settled in every part of the state, especially along the shores of lakes in the rapidly drying

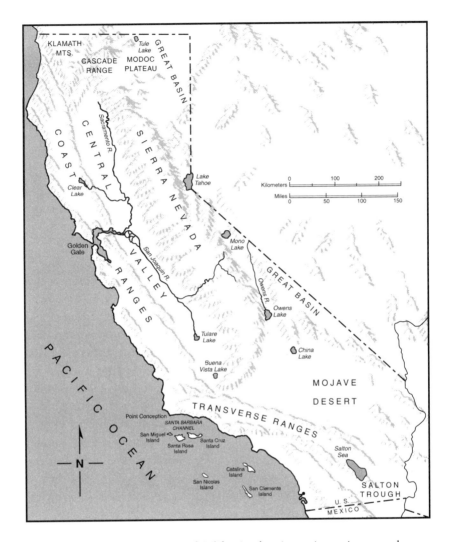

Figure 1.5. Topographic map of California, showing major environmental zones.

interior. Fortunately, these hunter-gatherer groups used highly distinctive stone spear points with thinned bases known as Clovis points, after the first site where they were discovered in New Mexico (see figure 2.2). Clovis points occur throughout the lower forty-eight states, and turn up throughout California in widely separated locations, except along the coast, where they are rare indeed. Judging from radiocarbon dates from a few sites, and from Clovis settlements further east, these early settlers flourished between about 11,200 and 10,900 B.C. Then their characteristic spear points vanish, never to return.

As far as we can tell, the Clovis people were never just big-game hunters, but highly mobile hunter-gatherers who also relied heavily on both smaller animals and a wide variety of edible plant foods, and perhaps on mollusks at the coast.

In the millennia that followed, the still sparse hunter-gatherer population increased slowly. Population growth continued slowly, and at times rapidly, albeit with stops and starts, right up to the Spanish *entrada*. As the climate warmed rapidly and lakes shrank in the increasing dry interior, local environmental diversity intensified, triggering much greater cultural variation from one group to another, even if basic tool kits and technology remained simple and highly portable. The key to survival was mobility, the foraging of food supplies scattered widely over large hunting territories, but a mobility anchored to permanent water supplies such as lakes and wetlands.

Even as early as 11,000 B.C., the densest populations flourished near lakes and rivers, where fish were abundant and migrating waterfowl could be netted in spring and fall. But most groups lived in isolation for most of the year, with only sporadic contacts with neighbors in neighboring territories. And sometime during this period of early settlement, a few hunter-gatherer bands reached the coast.

The First Coastal Settlement
(? Before 11,000 to 7000 B.C.)

Unfortunately, the coastline of 13,000 years ago is now submerged, so we can only guess when people first settled along the Pacific. No question: they were there early on, for human activity on Santa Rosa Island, one of the northern Channel Islands in southern California, may date to as early as 11,000 B.C. The first coastal settlement was probably entirely casual. As we shall see in chapter 3, the first coastal residents may simply have included the coast in their annual movements through large territories inland. Shellfish were there for the taking in winter; the hunters used clubs to take sea mammals in their rookeries. Intensive exploitation of the coast was a phenomenon of much later millennia, but one should never think of the coast and interior as two separate worlds. They were interconnected and indivisible from the earliest times, for the inhabitants of the one depended on the denizens of the other for food and other commodities and they shared a basically common culture.

Some people settled on the offshore islands surprisingly early, which means that they had effective watercraft. Controversy swirls around these vessels, for no traces of them survive. Many experts believe that simple tule reed canoes crossed the then much narrower Santa Barbara Channel on calm days. In the closing centuries of ancient times, the Chumash of the region used highly developed planked canoes, the famous *tomol*, which, so archaeological writ informs us, was invented comparatively late, by A.D. 650. But with rapidly rising sea levels and much longer open waters across to Santa Catalina and San Clemente Islands in the south, I believe that planked canoes, albeit in simpler forms, were in use many of thousands of years earlier. This could have been as early as 7000 B.C, when the longer distances between islands and mainland made easily waterlogged reed canoes impracticable. Whatever the watercraft, we do know that shellfish collectors and fisherfolk flourished on San Clemente Island, a full twenty-four miles from the nearest landmass, and forty-five miles from the mainland, as early as 6500 B.C. And they were not visitors but permanent residents.

Rising sea levels rushed into the Golden Gate about 9000 B.C., forming the San Francisco Bay, a great intersection of rivers from the interior. However, large-scale settlement of the marshy shores of the bay did not take hold until after 3000 B.C. By the time of Christ, local populations along the northern bay shore reached impressive densities, forming a landscape of shell mounds, which may have served as cemeteries, as villages, and as ritual centers. Tragically, most of the large mounds were quarried away or have vanished under urban sprawl since the late nineteenth century, so they remain somewhat of an enigma.

Even during the early centuries of coastal settlement, edible plant foods assumed overwhelming importance in daily life.

A Past Writ in Milling Stones
(? 9000 to 2000 B.C. and Later)

The extinction of the megafauna came at a time when California's sparse hunter-gatherer population diversified its food quest even more. We know little of the California of 9000 B.C., but we know that edible plants, especially grasses, formed important staples; so did small mammals like rabbits, a trend that was to endure into historic times. Why plants? CO_2 levels in the atmosphere climbed to higher levels than at any time during the past 120,000 years after the Ice Age. Plant productivity soared throughout the world and people were quick to exploit them.

Whatever their surroundings, every band lived from year to year, ranging over large territories, anchoring their movements to permanent water supplies. The densest populations lived by lakes and marshlands, as they did throughout ancient times. Everywhere, the rhythm of life varied from year to year. In drought cycles, people congregated near springs and water holes and fell back on less desirable plant foods such as acorns when the usual staples such as chia and goosefoot were in short supply. In good rainfall years, they would move out and exploit the full range of their territories. One survived by being flexible, by seizing every opportunity, and by having an adequate cushion of supplementary, famine foods.

I mentioned earlier that populations rose gradually, but not continually, throughout ancient times. I should amend this statement to read "local populations," for densities varied enormously from one area to another. Deserts like the Mojave could only support a miniscule, highly mobile population, whereas the shores of Tulare Lake or the banks of the San Joaquin River in the Central Valley were home to much higher numbers of people, often living more-or-less permanently at the same location. But, wherever people lived, the sheer unpredictability of the environment meant that one or two dry years resulted in food shortages and hunger, even with mechanisms to exchange food stuffs with neighbors.

After 6500 B.C., the climate became warmer and considerably drier and remained so for four thousand years.

Many years ago, an eminent geologist, Ernst Antevs, identified this four-thousand-year-long "Altithermal" dry period from lake deposits in the Great Basin. Like so many other such terms, the Altithermal came into wide use, then went out of fashion, but now enjoys a new respectability. Much more sophisticated observations, including numerous tree-ring samples, have proved that Antevs was correct. A prolonged period of much drier conditions descended on California and the west about 6500 B.C.—during a time when human populations were on the rise. This period of increasingly scarce water supplies and reduced, widely scattered plant foods lasted until about 2000 B.C.

Even before the Altithermal, wild grasses were a, if not *the*, staple of both inland and coastal diet. The drier and warmer conditions made grasses growing near lake margins and in river valleys even more desirable at a time of seriously reduced food supplies. Traditionally, men were hunters, women plant gatherers (see figure 1.6). But we believe grasses now became so important that both men and women harvested them. Unfortunately, grass harvesting leaves little for us to study. All we have to identify these still little-known societies are the distinctive flat milling stones they used to process the seeds. So widespread are these artifacts that many archaeologists refer to a Milling Stone Horizon, for there is little else left to identify what once must have been very diverse, small-scale societies.

The Milling Stone Horizon is a black hole in California's past, 7,000 years when almost nothing survives of what must have been highly mobile, expert hunter-gatherer societies. Then, about 2000 B.C., the people turned to new staples, to hitherto underexploited foods.

The First Major Change: Acorns (c. 2500 B.C.)

The Altithermal was the driest and warmest period since the end of the Ice Age. After four and a half millennia, its arid harshness became a catalyst for some centuries, in about 2500 B.C., when California's sparse, but growing population may have exceeded the ability of the arid environment to feed it. The carrying capacity of California environments was never high, except in the most favored areas, where fish and other marine foods made all the difference. Inland, in semi-arid areas, and in regions away from major rivers and lakes, the margin between enough food and too little was thin indeed. Food shortages and hunger may have become endemic among the often isolated and widely scattered hunter-gatherer population. This was the first of our major changes, when groups in many areas intensified their exploitation of a wider range of plants, some of them requiring much more preparation. Above all, they turned to acorns as a staple.

Figure 1.6. Women gathering grass seed in the San Joaquin Valley. From H. R. Schoolcraft, *Indian Tribes of the United States* (Philadelphia: Lippincott, 1858).

Fifteen species of oak flourish in California. Each fall, they produce bountiful harvests, which vary from year to year and from species to species. But in a good year, California oaks would produce enough nuts to feed fifty to sixty times more people than lived in California at Spanish contact. Furthermore, they are easily stored in such numbers that they provide food for an entire year. But acorns have disadvantages. They are inedible without lengthy processing because of the bitter-tasting tannic acid in them, which has to be leached out before they can be eaten. And this leaching process is very labor intensive. This may be why acorns were only a supplementary food for many thousands of years.

Once people accepted the labor of processing acorns, they had a highly nutritious, easily storable food, which could feed people year-round. And the number of mouths a good acorn harvest could feed was far larger than wild grasses, reliable as they were as a staple.

It's tempting to talk of an acorn "revolution" akin to that elsewhere in the world, when people turned from foraging to agriculture. This grossly overstates the case. All that happened was an intensification of acorn harvesting and an acceptance of the greatly increased effort required to process food, a task that fell to women. By harvesting fall acorn crops, groups living in oak areas acquired enormous quantities of easily stored food, more than enough to tide them over until the bounty of spring and summer.

Both men and women harvested acorns in fall, but there was now a sharper division of labor. The women shouldered the burden of processing acorns and gathered other plant foods. Meanwhile, hunting once again assumed greater importance, not of smaller animals like rabbits, which were always taken, partly to keep their numbers down before they consumed all the plants in the landscape, but of larger animals like deer, tule elk, and bighorn sheep. We know this because many more bones of such larger prey occur in sites of this period. Taking such animals would have required lengthy expeditions, often into hilly terrain, perhaps for weeks on end. But they were highly prized and prestigious quarry because of their high meat yield.

Along the southern coasts, food supplies were always more reliable, the ever-predictable shellfish and sea mammals, as well as inshore fishing in the kelp beds that abounded close inshore. During periods of colder sea surface temperatures, natural upwelling in the Santa Barbara Channel brought up plankton from deep water, and a bounty of anchovies and other fish to the coast. Over many centuries, local populations rose, especially at estuary mouths and in coastal sloughs, where marshlands provided plant foods year round, mollusks were available for the taking, and waterfowl teemed. But, for all their dependence on maritime foods, the people still harvested acorns, hunted deer, and traded foodstuffs with their land-based neighbors.

North of Monterey, and especially along the rugged north coast, coastal settlement came late, for the real bounty lay along the fast-flowing rivers with their spring and fall salmon runs. North of San Francisco, migrating (anadromous) fish such as salmon and steelhead ruled, a staple so reliable that people lived upstream from the Pacific, in the same riverside settlements close to rapids and river confluences for many generations.

Aggrandizers, Big Men, and Men of Power (after 1000 B.C.)

Acorns and a generally intensified food quest restored the balance between people and the environment. Populations rose still further and the landscape filled up. The isolation of earlier times gave way to a more crowded world, where group territories became smaller and more tightly drawn.

Two thousand years ago, a bewildering diversity of hunter-gatherer societies flourished throughout California. In the northwest, the salmon reigned. The great rivers of the Central Valley and the Sacramento Delta now supported permanent communities on the edge of waterways and wetlands. Away from the water, population densities were much lower in environments where food was scarce and widely scattered. There were growing populations in the Bay Area, where mollusks abounded. And in southern California, especially between Point Conception and Point Mugu, burgeoning coastal groups lived off plentiful fisheries, nourished by natural upwelling of cold water from the Pacific seabed. Only in the desert interior were populations sparse and widely scattered, a vast region peopled, for the most part, by small, highly mobile bands.

At the time of Christ, most California societies were basically egalitarian, with leadership in the hands of respected elders, people with long experience or with unusual spiritual powers. From the earliest times, the spiritual and supernatural worlds intersected in societies where an unpredictable climate of extremes unleashed powerful dangerous forces. Those with the ability to intercede with the spiritual world acquired considerable power in both coastal and interior societies. This was the realm of the shaman, the Man of Power, who traveled freely through the cosmos in hallucinogenic trances derived from plants like datura and native tobacco (see chapter 8). Shamans were respected and feared; they were curers, sometimes astronomers or rainmakers. The continuity of human life was in their hands. But they were spiritual forces in the community, not secular leaders.

Rising populations, finite food supplies, much more confined hunting territories, and increasing interconnectedness—all the ingredients for conflict and competition were there. Inevitably, some individuals became community or kin leaders in a world where kin ties and reciprocal obligations were all-important. California society was changing. Egalitarian bands gave way to societies with distinct social ranks.

There are signs of social ranking in village cemeteries as early as 1000 B.C., marked by obsidian objects, shell beads, and other distinctive grave offerings. Who were these people? We do not know for sure, but it seems unlikely that at first they inherited rank at birth. More likely, they acquired status through decisive leadership, but also through their abilities at fostering exchange with neighbors, at acquiring much-needed foodstuffs and wealth, and at redistributing food to their loyal followers or fellow kin. Charisma and personal skills counted for everything, for the loyalty of one's followers depended on one's ability to satisfy their needs and desires. This loyalty could evaporate in a moment, and vanished once one's grave was sealed. The followers moved on and transferred their loyalties to someone else.

These were "Big Men," perhaps better called "Aggrandizers." They were gifted not only with exceptional ability, but with a competitive, self-aggrandizing personality, an urge to acquire wealth and power. At first, their leadership endured only for their lifetimes, but, inevitably, the office began to transcend the life span of a single individual. In time, the power became hereditary, but exactly how and why we do not know. The aggrandizers became chiefs, heads of chiefly families, members of prestigious king groups, who passed their office to their sons at death. This meant that infants acquired the privileges and ornaments of rank at birth. Inherited social rank now separated commoners from the more elite, skilled artisans and members of secret societies from ordinary office. A chief's power was not absolute; his succession could be blocked by popular opinion on occasion, and a council of headmen or elders advised him. But the very existence of the office, of privileged families and formal office holders, quite apart from shamans, meant that the reins of control passed into fewer hands.

Control of trade, control of food stuffs, control of wealth of all kinds was in the hands of chiefs and a few families. These were the people who maintained contacts with their fellow kin and other important people in neighboring and more distant communities. These were the war leaders who planned hostilities against neighbors for control of food stuffs, to expand territorial boundaries, or to right perceived insults and interpersonal disputes. These were competitive individuals, who blended personal gain with the common interest, men and women to whom personal prestige was important, who presided over societies where most people rarely traveled over distances of more than a few miles. They presided over communal rituals, which reinforced the need for social conformity and cooperation, validated human existence, and ensured the continuity of human existence.

Violence and Competition (First Millennium A.D.)

Chieftainship flourished in an increasingly unpredictable and competitive world. Populations were rising fast in areas where food supplies were relatively abundant, but deep sea cores and tree rings reveal rapid and unpredictable climatic fluctuations over the past two thousand years. Long drought cycles, especially at the end of the first millennium A.D., strong El Niño events with violent rainfall, and constant changes in sea surface temperatures—all these climatic fluctuations brought even more uncertainty into an already competitive world. For generations, warmer sea temperatures suppressed natural upwelling. The productivity of coastal fisheries in the Santa Barbara Channel fell. Year after year of drought along the coast and inland played havoc with acorn and grass seed harvests. And with so many more people to feed, the cushion of famine foods and game was inadequate to take up the slack.

Inevitably, there were food shortages; telltale signs of malnutrition appear on the bones of the dead in cemeteries in several parts of the state.

People moved into larger, crowded settlements closer to reliable water supplies. Inevitably, too, the resulting poor sanitation brought disease, again to be discerned in the skeletal remains of the day. And food shortages brought conflict—raids for food, over ownership of food supplies. People died from head injuries and arrow wounds, buried in cemeteries with arrowheads still in their wounds. Signs of such violence are not universal, but have come to light in cemeteries in the Bay Area, in the Central Valley, and in southern California.

Sporadic violence continued into Spanish times, but, about a thousand years ago, profound changes came over some California societies.

Second Major Change: Interdependence (A.D. 900 to 1542)

Somewhere around A.D. 1100, there came another major change, a realization that food shortages and violence went hand in hand, that society, whether in the Central Valley or along the Pacific, was breaking down. The delicate balance between mouths to feed and food supplies had been upset. Then, suddenly, the spiral of violence slowed; war casualties are much rarer in village cemeteries. And, at about the same time, the volume of exchange, in foodstuffs and exotic ornaments like shell beads, explodes. Something happened that revived and expanded the ancient web of interconnectedness that had quietly sustained California life for thousands of years. In many places, chiefs and communities realized that interdependence was as important as competition, that everyone was in the same situation, and that the continuity of life depended on cooperation as much as competition. We know this because the volume of local and middle distance trade expands exponentially in many areas, to the point that such activities as bead production consumed a great deal of time.

No one knows what the catalyst for change was, but it must have involved profound changes in society and in social values, toward a much greater appreciation of the finite nature of food supplies. There are hints from archaeological sites on the northern Channel Islands and along the mainland of overfishing, which may have sent wealthy men's canoes into deeper water in search of larger, often prestigious fish like tuna and swordfish. Shellfish stocks in some long-exploited areas no longer yielded the mature mollusks of earlier times. And the vagaries of climate change added another value to an already complex equation. We know that the social changes involved rank and hereditary chieftainship. In many groups, wealth, and presumably the responsibility for distributing food supplies, was in those hands. The wealth and chiefly authority were individual, but the underlying philosophy was one of communal welfare, of interconnectedness. Some profound, and compelling, religious ideologies, now lost to us, must have formed a catalyst for the new societies.

The solution to the immediate and long-term problem varied greatly from one area to another. For example, Chumash chiefs in southern California developed a massive trade in acorns and other foodstuffs with their opposite numbers on the Channel Islands. Their island neighbors, in turn, controlled large-scale production of shell beads, which passed in the tens of thousands to groups on the mainland. Obsidian exchange was important in the far northwest, where more prestigious people lay in graves literally paved with volcanic glass. They exchanged dried salmon from the rivers at their doorsteps for the precious stone. In the Central Valley, the Yokut traded foodstuffs and ornaments with coastal groups, with whom they had many material and ritual ties.

Powerful, and now largely forgotten, religious beliefs, and a complex realm of the intangible lay behind all these changes and activities.

The World of the Intangible

In the regions most affected, the changes resulted in more complex social organization, a much elaborated ritual life, and, perhaps, in a greater preoccupation with the passage of the seasons, the prediction of rainfall, and the harmony of the cosmos.

California is justly famous for its ancient rock art, most of which dates to the past two thousand years. This may be due in part to the inevitable effects of weather and erosion on the rock faces of caves and rock shelters. But there does seem to have been an efflorescence in such paintings and engravings. As we will see in chapter 9, some of this art is associated with hunting, and some of it with shamans, who painted animals and signs to record their dreams. The stress of constant climatic shifts, of increased crowding and more complex world, may have triggered an intensification of ritual activity, of shamanistic visions, such as occurred later, after the stress of European contact. These activities revolved around the relationship between people and the cosmos that surrounded them.

For thousands of years, the ancient Californians regarded the universe as a complex network of interactions between humans and spirit beings, which controlled the movements of heavenly bodies, the changing seasons, and the living things that inhabited the earth. They believed that people could deal with the uncertainties of human existence by performing the proper rituals and correctly using the power acquired from the supernatural. This involvement with the supernatural brought understanding of the cosmos, of a complex, cyclical world. From the very beginning, the living and spiritual worlds intersected in a seamless human existence, a masterly synthesis of myth, legend, and storytelling that defined the world, validated chiefly authority, and proclaimed another web of interconnectedness between living people and the demanding territories in which they lived. Mountain ranges, conspicuous peaks, a spring, or a lake—the familiar landscape served as a memnonic peg for legend and oral tradition.

This oral synthesis provided a conceptual framework for all of human existence, the flexibility and mobility essential to survival in the desert, for the brash individualism of northwestern salmon fishers, and for the entrepreneurship of valley and Chumash chiefs, who adjusted society to reflect new realities. Always, ritual and the visions of shamans strove for an equilibrium in the cosmos, the completion of the annual cycle.

For thousands of years, the ancient Californians achieved this equilibrium with a combination of pragmatic opportunism, technological skill, an intimate knowledge of their environments, and by melding the spiritual with the material, the world of the supernatural with that of everyday life.

Three Underlying Currents

Like the shamans and storytellers of old, archaeologists try to tell a story. Their narratives are not of Coyote and mythic beasts behaving like humans, but rather of material things, of ways of making a living in a harsh environment. The chants and recitations of yore have long vanished on the wind, like all the intangibles of the past. This means that we will never fully comprehend what happened at those memorable turning points of ancient

California history when growing populations and moments of hunger or strife led to new directions, to technological innovations, and to supplementary foods becoming staples. All we can do is monitor the changes from broken bones, shells, and humble artifacts. We will never discern the twists and turns of ritual, the unspoken and acted-out rationales that defined these moments in terms of restoring order to worlds out of balance. But we know that these rituals and rationales worked astoundingly well, simply because ancient California societies changed, survived, and thrived when they changed direction, refining their relationships with one another, the environment, and the cosmos.

They were often brilliantly successful. We have only to look at the example of the Chumash, one of the best-known native societies of ancient California. After A.D. 1150, both island and mainland chiefs turned away from violence and adjusted their world to enhance interconnectedness and interdependence, while following their own individual aspirations. They ruled over a complex society redefined by new metaphors and allegorical meanings. These meanings were known to a limited few, those who had access to dream helpers through datura and other hallucinogenic substances. But the wisdom of these few provided the sense of equilibrium and purpose that gave the Chumash four centuries of comparative prosperity before Juan Cabrillo's caravels shattered their world forever (see chapter 15, *Entrada*).

Three underlying currents drive our story. The first is a continuity of culture. We see cultural adaptations to a rapidly changing and challenging world, which adjusted and adjusted again over many millennia. I believe that the biological and cultural roots of the California societies of the fifteenth century A.D. go back thousands of years into the remote past; that the story of ancient California is one of lasting continuity and continual adjustment to changing times. This continuity involved constant mobility, not so much large migrations or major population movements, but the natural ebb and flow of hunter-gatherer life, triggered by drier and wetter centuries, drought cycles and periods of higher rainfall. These population shifts brought new languages into California and saw people retreat to lakes and estuaries where food was more abundant and then advance into better watered territories when conditions were more favorable.

Continuity is the backbone of our story, a continuity reflected, also, in gradual population growth from the earliest times up to the fifteenth century A.D. This growth was never a smooth curve, for there were pauses, sometimes declines, along the way. There was a close relationship between population densities and the ability of California's diverse environment to support them—which is why there were significant turning points when I believe that people faced a stark option: change or perish.

The second current to our story is interconnectedness. California is an environmentally fractured land, more so than many other more uniform environments in North America. Except in unusually well-favored areas, human populations were often sparse, increasingly hemmed in by rugged topography, arid lands, neighbors, and more circumscribed territorial boundaries as numbers increased. From the very beginning, every group, however isolated, however small, relied on neighbors for critical food stuffs in times of shortage, for exotic ornaments, or for tool-making stone (see figure 1.7). This web of interconnectedness, of interdependency, was a reality throughout ancient California's history.

Figure 1.7. The French artist Louis Choris drew these San Francisco mission Indians wearing ceremonial shell headdresses in 1822. Courtesy of Davidson Library, University of California, Santa Barbara.

Informal exchange networks linked camp with camp, the coast with the interior, desert peoples with lake peoples. We find traces of it in Pacific shell beads that traveled as far as the Great Basin, volcanic glass flakes appearing hundreds of miles from their source. Interconnectedness ebbed and flowed over the millennia, before exploding in many areas in the challenging centuries at the end of ancient times. At that point, the web became so central to life, such an important part of food distribution and the acquisition of wealth, that many groups relied on a form of shell bead currency as a mechanism of exchange.

The third underlying current is inchoate, difficult for archaeologists to reconstruct. It is the strong underpinnings of supernatural belief that underlay all ancient California existence. We obtain glimpses of these undercurrents from the notes of nineteenth-century anthropologists who interviewed survivors from earlier times and from the researches of John Peabody Harrington, one of the most remarkable twentieth-century scholars of ancient California society. They enable us to attempt an interpretation of rock paintings and engravings, of ancient astronomy, and of knowledge restricted to a few and jealously guarded, shared unwillingly with outsiders. This is the great lacuna in our story, for we are humbled in the face of a remote, now vanished world, whose vast bodies of lore and knowledge are lost to us.

The great nineteenth-century German statesman Otto von Bismarck once described human history as a "Stream of Time," on which all humanity floats and attempts to navigate, where people follow the footsteps of God with greater and lesser success. This is the story of how the ancient Californians navigated this stream with brilliance and panache for more than 13,000 years. Had it not been for the destruction wrought by Cabrillo and his successors, they would be navigating it to this day.

We have placed the players in the wings, the stage is set. Let Act 1 of the play begin: the first settlement of California described in chapter 2.

PART II

Beginnings

(Before 11,200 to C. 2500 B.C.)

In the beginning, there was no earth or sky or anything or anybody; only a dense darkness in space. This darkness seemed alive. Something like lightnings seemed to pass through it and meet each other once in a while. Two substances which looked like the white of an egg came from these lightnings. . . . Two boys emerged: Mukat and Tamaioit. . . . As they lay there, both at the same time heard a noise like a bee buzzing. It was the song of their mother, Darkness.

[CAHUILLA CREATION EPIC,
part of a song cycle][1]

First Footprints
(Before 11,200 B.C. to c. 9000 B.C.)

I ONCE SPENT FIVE YEARS WRITING A BOOK ON THE FIRST
human settlement of the Americas. At the end, I wrote that
"anyone studying the first Americans sets sail in hazardous
academic seas, beset on every side by passionate emotions and contradic-
tory scientific information."[2] How right I was! The passing years merely
add fuel to the controversies.

Hypothetical scenarios abound: (1) big-game hunters moving into an
uninhabited continent, slaughtering large animals as they traveled south;
(2) theories of settlement as early as 40,000 years ago based on handfuls of
dubious artifacts in South America; (3) visions of bold mariners in skin
boats skirting Alaskan shores to settle in the Pacific Northwest.

Generations of scientists have woven what amounts to little more than
fairy tales, because we have almost no archaeological finds to work with.[3]
The same controversies wash into California, where even claims of first settlement as early as a quarter of million years ago have their devoted followers, despite firm (and definitive) scientific rebuttals.

I ignore these bankrupt theories here, as they have no scientific legs to
stand on. In any case, the real quest is far more interesting—for people who
arrived in the Americas, and California, somewhere around 15,000 years
ago, perhaps somewhat earlier.

The search is challenging, often frustrating. We are looking for an archaeological equivalent of a moving target—people who were small in numbers, constantly on the move, and possessed of simple, usually perishable artifacts and weapons. They were, ultimately, of Siberian origin, with a short life expectancy—for most people, in their twenties. Even after more than a century of intensive archaeological research in many parts of California, they remain a scientific willow wisp—virtually invisible, their signature on the land transitory at best.

The primordial Californians are still an almost mythic presence, known from a scatter of distinctive projectile points and little else, haunting the land as early as 13,000 years ago, perhaps earlier. Most likely, they arrived during the first flurry of global warming after the Ice Age ended about 15,000 years ago. And we know that they entered a place where no other humans had trodden before.

A Pristine Land (16,000 B.C.)

Eighteen thousand years ago, the Santa Barbara Channel, southern California. The Pacific is mirror-still, the ridges of the snow-capped mountains razor-sharp against the deep blue sky of the winter morning. No haze obscures the lines of the deep valleys, the sandy beaches at the coastal plain's edge. Silence is absolute—just the gentle sloughing of tiny waves rippling on the fine sand. A few miles offshore another coastline, again low lying, this time more rocky, rises in ridges and hummocks to a rugged mountain chain running parallel to the mainland.

Three mammoths feed on the green sedge and grass close to water's edge, browsing slowly among the sand dunes and windswept brush. Their long coats brush the ground. A family of wolves crouches in a thicket close by, eyes casting for prey, oblivious to the large beasts. A narrow game path twists and turns across the low-lying coastal shelf, passes through a narrow defile in the steep ridge that bounds the higher ground inland. The air is cool, with a sharp bite when an occasional gust of wind wafts off higher ground. A few hundred yards inland, the heavily trodden path passes through a gurgling stream, the water cold from snow melt. Two deer start up nervously from their feeding among the pine trees at water's edge. Away from the stream, the path passes imperceptibly into a rolling plain covered with pine forest.

The rains have been plentiful, so the ground is damp underfoot. Lush, green grass carpets the forest clearings. In six month's time, in full summer, the grass will be stunted, yellow, and dry. The occasional ponds of standing water will be gone, the animals that once fed at water's edge will be elsewhere. Summers are short and warm, times of aridity and food shortages for animals of every size. Winters are long and cool, sometimes intensely cold, with rainfall as unpredictable and widely spaced as it is today. But when the wind fills in from the north and blows at storm strength, then the full fury of an Ice Age winter descends on the coast. Rain mingled with snow blusters horizontally as gray scud on the wings of the arctic gale. Salt spray flies far inland on the wind. The churning roar of the Pacific erodes the beaches and the wind chill factor brings temperatures to near-zero. Sometimes thick snow mantles the coastal plain. Ice covers shallow ponds and water holes. Everything soon melts as the wind drops and temperatures rise.

Eighteen thousand years ago, California enjoys a generally temperate climate, but one colder and wetter than today. Chilly seas lap the coast, where, as always, the climate is mildest, less seasonally extreme. Far to the north and east, the Central Valley lies under snow, its rivers frozen over despite the bright sunshine. Gray clouds from the departing storm hide the high peaks of the Sierras. Flocks of waterfowl twist and turn low above the ice, searching for open water. Deer pick through the snow cover with their hooves at the edge of now-frozen swamps. Beaver dams huddle at strategic narrows. Stark, bare pine trees stand motionless in the cold morning air.

Much of late Ice Age California is dry and cold, seemingly lifeless, for its deserts have always been arid lands, despite numerous lakes, large and small. The tree levels on the surrounding mountains are hundreds of feet lower than they are today, rainfall is higher on the lower foothills. In the hot, dry summers, vast natural brush fires, started by lightning strikes, burn for weeks, even months on end, devouring thick chaparral and pine forests, part of the natural ecological order of things.

This rugged land of dramatic contrasts offers many environments: low-lying coastal plains and offshore islands, dense redwood forests and extensive wetlands, steep mountain ranges and sheltered valleys in every configuration imaginable, millions of acres of semi-arid land. One foothill valley teems with bird life and deer, attracted by the small lake nestling between mountain sides. Only a few miles away, another defile is arid and waterless, separated by a high ridge from yet another microenvironment where oak trees flourish in sheltered terrain and acorn harvests are abundant in the fall.

Apart from the colder, damper climate, the greatest differences are on the coast. Sea levels are as much as three hundred feet lower than today. Rivers are faster moving and descend into the Pacific through narrow valleys, cutting down to the much lower Pacific. California's coastline is still rugged and exposed to the full drift of westerly gales, but the configuration is very different. A continental shelf extends offshore, not far off rugged northern coasts, but nearly joining southern California's Channel Islands to the mainland. San Pedro Bay is dry land. San Diego's magnificent natural harbor and San Francisco Bay are narrow river valleys leading to the continental shelf. Staggering environmental diversity unfolds within short distances. Even at the height of the late Ice Age, temperatures can vary by twenty degrees on either side of a mountain range, or between coast and interior.

California is alive with animals of every kind, among them herds of large Ice Age species like the long-haired mammoth, the cold-loving elephant, wild horses, and several forms of camels—the celebrated "megafauna" soon to become extinct. Familiar creatures can be seen on every side. Numerous bears and dire wolves lurk in forest and lowland. Deer abound in foothills and on coastal plains.

But there are no human beings.

Late Ice Age California is a pristine world, where humans have never trod. No wisps of camp fire smoke rise into the air from lake- or riverside encampments. No canoes ply the inshore waters of the Pacific. No human footprints mark narrow game paths on the coastal shelf. No stealthy figures flit from tree to tree stalking deer and other prey. California is still a virgin land, as is all of North America. Several thousand years will pass before the first humans set foot in the uninhabited lands, and then only during dramatic environmental changes at the end of the Ice Age.

Beringia and Beringians (c.16,000 to 11,700 B.C.)

The story of ancient California began far to the north and west, in a bitterly cold Ice Age world. All the experts agree on one point: that the original settlers of the New World originated in northeast Asia. Archaeology, genetics, and linguistics all point in the same direction—to Siberia. Whether these primordial colonists were coastal peoples or dwelt in the frigid interior of Siberia is still unknown.

Whoever they were, and whenever they lived there, everyone also agrees that the remote ancestors of the North American Indians and of the ancient Californians were tiny in number, living in a very inhospitable environment, indeed, in a world very different from our own.

The earliest known traces of human settlement in extreme northeast Siberia date to about 14,000 B.C. They comprise unspectacular scatters of stone tools, lying in the occasional cave or rock shelter or in the much-disturbed sand and gravel layers of the river valleys that once intersected the bitterly cold, treeless steppe-tundra.

Beyond Siberia, the seemingly endless scrub passed eastward onto a wide, low-lying shelf of land that then joined Asia to Alaska's higher ground. Dense ice pack bordered the shores of this land bridge, breaking up only during the short arctic summer, if then. Winter lasted some nine months a year, with subzero temperatures for weeks on end. Geologists call this now-sunken Ice Age continent Beringia, after the Russian explorer Vitus Bering, who discovered the strait that bears his name in 1726.

We know nothing about the few human groups who hunted and foraged on the now-submerged land bridge, or who fished and hunted sea mammals along its shores. All we can do is speculate about them. But such speculations are important and have a direct bearing on the question of the first human settlement of California.

If there were humans on the Bering Land Bridge after 16,000 B.C., then they were Stone Age hunter-gatherers, people without metals, who were not afraid to tackle even large animals like the mammoth. Some experts call them big-game hunters, a misleading label, for, like all hunter-gatherers, they would take advantage of seasonal plant foods in the short Beringian summer and hunt many small animals, also birds. Their larger and more spectacular prey included mammoth, musk ox, saiga antelope, and reindeer.

These people were expert arctic hunters, completely at home in an environment of long, frigid winters and months without daylight. They wore tailored, layered clothing, fashioned with bone needles and fine thread, which enabled them to work outside in the harshest temperatures. Judging from Stone Age sites in the Ukraine and elsewhere far to the west, the ancient Beringians lived in domelike semisubterranean houses built of mammoth bones or driftwood and covered with hide or sod.

The population of the land bridge was at most several hundred people who lived in small bands, their winter camps anchored to the shallow river valleys that crisscrossed the windy land bridge. Each band was aware of its neighbors, occasionally trading or intermarrying with them. As time went on, sons would split off from their fathers and colonize an empty valley nearby. Families would quarrel, men would be killed in hunting accidents, women would perish in childbirth, and bands would splinter and coalesce through the natural events of Stone Age hunting life. And, in time, a sparse population of hunting bands spread across the desolate land bridge and into the higher ground of Alaska to the east, perhaps during the period of rapid global warming and rising sea levels after 13,000 B.C.

This global warming was spectacularly rapid by geological standards. Fossilized beetles found in the sediments at Windmill Lake in central Alaska chronicle dramatic environmental changes in Beringia. In 12,000 B.C., beetles characteristic of herbaceous, arctic tundra flourished around the lake. By 10,500 B.C., temperatures had soared to near modern levels and much warmer-loving beetle species flourished. Fifteen hundred years later, rising sea levels severed the Bering Land Bridge, at first with a narrow strait, then with a rapidly widening defile as the waters of the Pacific and Arctic Oceans mingled for the first time in millennia. As the land bridge vanished, its animal and human inhabitants must have moved onto higher ground.

The first settlement of the Americas was not a simple migration in which people set off on a long, deliberate journey to colonize a virgin continent. Rather, it was the result of repeated small-scale population movements over many thousands of years, which followed one upon the other, sometimes occurred simultaneously, then often ceased for centuries.

Some experts believe that the Americas were settled not only by land, but along the shores of Beringia as well, by people who moved eastward in skin boats, exploiting sea mammals and living by hook, net, and line. Once again, there is absolutely no evidence for such activities, in part because their sites, if any, are deep below the Bering Strait.

The earliest known human occupation of interior Alaska dates to about 11,700 B.C., over two thousand years before the land bridge was severed. Unfortunately, any contemporary (or earlier) coastal occupation lies below modern sea levels.

By Land or Sea? (Date Unknown. ?c. 11,500 B.C.)

The first Alaskans found themselves in a glacier-free land, hemmed in to the east and south by icy mountains and the enormous Cordilleran and

Laurentide ice sheets, which covered the Rockies and Canada as far south as Seattle. Like their Beringian ancestors, they must have settled in sheltered river valleys, by glacial lakes, and by the rugged coastline.

By 11,500 B.C., they were living in dramatically changed terrain, with much warmer temperatures. The great ice sheets were melting rapidly. The Cordilleran and Laurentide ice had parted east of the Rockies, opening up a widening, rugged corridor to the south, which led to the heart of an uninhabited continent.

At some point, and at a still unknown date, small groups of Stone Age hunter-gatherers moved southward from Alaska. Herein lies one of the great controversies of California archaeology, which pits advocates of inland settlement against those who believe the first migrants came by sea (see figure 2.1).[4]

Did handfuls of these Stone Age hunter-gatherers make their way between the retreating ice sheets in pursuit of animals, large and small, then explode into the vastness of the Great Plains?

Or did the first settlers move along the coast, exploiting fish and sea mammals, making their way southward from sheltered bay to sheltered bay along the still-exposed continental shelf off coastal Alaska, then to British Columbia's fjords and to the Queen Charlotte Islands, and southward into the Pacific Northwest and then California?

For generations, archaeologists assumed that the first Americans used an overland route between the retreating ice sheets. They also assumed that the first Paleo-Indian settlers were "Clovis" big-game hunters, who preyed off the large Ice Age animals that roamed the Great Plains (see figure 2.2).[5] Their base-thinned stone projectile points occur throughout the United States and in California.

All we knew of the first settlers comes from big-game kill sites and scatters of distinctive Clovis points from throughout North America. Under this scenario, the Clovis people epitomized the first Americans—rapacious hunters, who exploded into an uninhabited continent and spread rapidly to all corners of North America. Some of them were thought to have spread westward from the Plains and Great Basin into California.[6]

This is a completely misleading portrait of the first Paleo-Indians—and of the first people to settle in California. Even the term Clovis is confusing, for it really only refers to a readily identified form of projectile point, which was widely used by hunters over an enormous area of North America between 11,200 and 10,900 B.C.

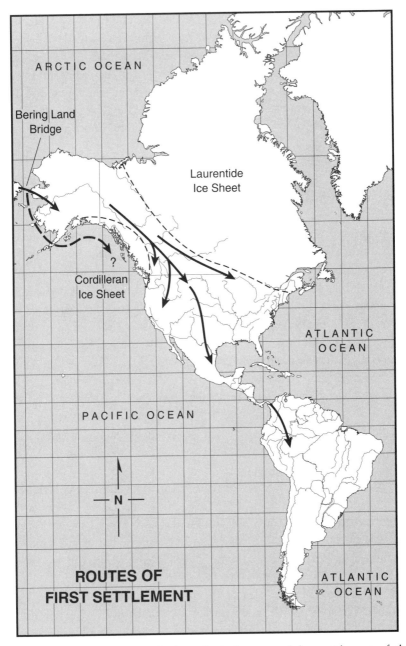

Figure 2.1. Map showing the hypothetical routes of first settlement of the Americas, including California. The routes are, at best, speculative.

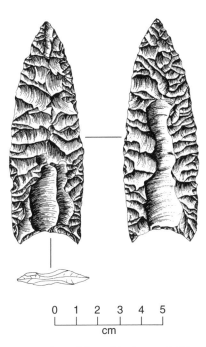

Figure 2.2. A Clovis point from Schonchin Butte, California. Note the characteristic longitudinal thinning flake detached from the base. Such projectile point heads are found in all fifty states. Drawing by Randall Engle. Courtesy of Michael Moratto.

In fact, Clovis points and other traces of human settlement dating to as much as one thousand years earlier occur in extremely diverse environments throughout North America. No question, they adapted at once to a remarkable diversity of environments soon after their arrival. Many of them never hunted a large animal in their lives. Clovis points and early Paleo-Indian sites occur in woodland and desert settings, near rivers, estuaries, and lakes, and on open plains and near-glacial landscapes.

The big-game hunter scenario is intellectually bankrupt.

How, then, did Paleo-Indians reach California?

Most experts believe that some early Paleo-Indian groups using Clovis points drifted westward from the Plains and Great Basin and into California, where they settled by lakes and perennial streams in the interior valleys. In time, some of them hunted and gathered their way into territories on or near the coast, where they simply collected shellfish and perhaps hunted sea mammals using familiar tools and weapons long employed inland. Such foods were plentiful in winter, when edible plants were in short supply.

When they arrived remains a complete mystery, but, since Clovis points are dated on the Plains to between 11,500 and 11,000 B.C., first settlement cannot have been much earlier than that.

This scenario is appealingly vague and fits such evidence as there is, which is not much.

But . . . could sea mammal hunters and fisherfolk have moved into California before anyone lived in the interior, pushing southward from the north along a now-submerged coast? What are the realities of this scenario?

Sea levels rose rapidly along the California coast after 10,000 B.C. The continental shelf vanished, drastically affecting the configuration of the shoreline, especially in the San Francisco Bay Area and parts of southern California. Theoretically, at any rate, the flooded estuaries and coastal marshes created by the rising Pacific could have acted like a magnet to Paleo-Indians—if they had the technology, watercraft, and knowledge to exploit sea mammals, birds, and fish. In later times, the ancient Californians exploited marine resources of every kind intensively, to the point that some groups occupied quite large, permanent settlements. But when did their predecessors first take up fishing and sea mammal hunting? Did remote Paleo-Indian ancestors in the far north use canoes and skin boats on the rugged, windswept shores of Alaska and the Pacific Northwest, then move southward in small numbers into California's warmer, but still formidable, waters?

In recent years, a number of archaeologists both in California and in the Pacific Northwest have begun studying the notion of such migrations, but, so far, have not been able to marshal any solid evidence in favor of it. There are some serious problems with a coastal hypothesis.

As we shall see in chapter 3, some of the earliest archaeological sites in California lie on the northern Channel Islands of southern California, dating to around 9000 B.C., perhaps even earlier. However, the existence of these sites does not necessarily prove that first settlement was along the coast. Once again, we are faced with the reality that most, if not all, of the sites needed to prove such migrations lie below modern sea level.

Any hypothesis that argues for first settlement via a coastal route has to take account of two realities—the seafaring abilities of the first settlers and their watercraft, and conditions off the California coast at a time of lower sea levels and much cooler temperatures.[7]

All kinds of craft are bandied around in discussion, even in the literature, with dugouts and skin boats the favorites. Some scholars are particularly mesmerized by the Eskimo *umiak,* the whale boat and load carrier used for many centuries in the far north. In theory, such boats offer seductive possibilities for coastal voyaging to the south, but the fact remains that no large skin boats were ever built by historic groups in California. On these grounds alone, they are unlikely to have been used in earlier times.

Then there are the coastal waters themselves. As any small boat sailor will tell you, these waters are no maritime picnic ground, especially north of Point Conception or the Bay Area, where the open Pacific breaks on a steep and merciless coast. Safe beaches are rare, and were probably even rarer when sea levels were much lower.

I do not doubt for a moment that Paleo-Indians were familiar with simple watercraft such as dugouts and tule reed boats, which worked well on lakes and rivers, and in calm inshore waters. But there is a great difference between voyaging along a coast and merely launching canoes to fish or hunt sea mammals close inshore. Coasting, even in fine weather and in modern small craft along rugged coasts like those around Cape Mendocino or Big Sur, requires constant watchfulness, keeping far enough offshore to avoid being swept onto the rocks, and steady bailing to keep the boat dry.

It must be no coincidence that the greatest concentration of fishing and sea mammal hunting communities in later times were in bays, estuaries, and other sheltered waters, or in areas like the Santa Barbara Channel, where natural upwelling brought millions of fish close inshore.

We should also remember that the Chumash of southern California, the most skilled of all California maritime peoples, never took their canoes offshore when even moderate westerlies blew, or when northeasterly Santa Ana winds swept down mountain canyons on the mainland far offshore.

Over the past few centuries, we know that no California groups ever went on long voyages down the northern and central California coast on the wings of the prevailing summer winds. They lacked the watercraft to do so. We cannot assume that their remote ancestors did either.

In later times, the sheer bounty of coastal fisheries saw the development of elaborate maritime societies along the Pacific, especially in areas of natural upwelling. Did coastal upwelling provide such a bounty in early millennia, especially during the critical centuries of first settlement?

We still have little insight. A deep sea core taken seventy-five miles off the southern Oregon coast provides a fleeting snapshot of environmental conditions over the past 30,000 years. Minute fossil diatoms from the Cascade mountains far inland occur in the late Ice Age section of the core, carried there by persistent strong easterly winds blowing from the dry continental interior. From these clues, we know that 18,000 years ago, the late Ice Age climate was cold and dry, with none of the modern-day summer coastal fog produced by upwelling of cold water. For these cold millennia, atmospheric models predict strong easterly winds during the winter months and weak westerlies during the summer. As a result, downwelling was as much as two-thirds less than during later times, making for less productive coastal fisheries.[8]

As warming accelerated after 12,000 B.C. and the ice sheets retreated, the pollens of fossil trees appear in the core, with a full expansion of redwood forest, which is nourished by coastal fog, after 7000 B.C.[9] Winter westerlies now blew across the shore, while summer northwesterlies swept southward parallel to the coast, just as they do today. The warming atmosphere brought persistent summer fogs and rising temperatures throughout the Pacific Northwest. Upwelling was still minimal at first. By 7000 B.C., it was vigorous and commonplace in some years and not in others. Sometimes the coastal winds were weaker than today, so the nutrient-rich coastal waters were not transported far out to sea.

Pacific coastal waters may not have been as productive as they are today.

There is no question that human populations could have flourished along the Pacific coast once the ice retreated, but how productive a maritime environment they enjoyed is questionable.

I believe that coastal settlement resulted not from epic voyages from the north, but from Paleo-Indian groups settling in areas like San Francisco or Estero Bay in the Cayucos area of central California, the Santa Barbara Channel, and southern lagoons and sloughs, where they adapted rapidly to a life based on fishing, hunting sea mammals and water fowl, and plant collecting. The artifacts to spear fish or hunt sea mammals are basically the same as those used by terrestrial hunters.

Like other Paleo-Indians, the first Californians were opportunists, who settled in areas where food was abundant, and close at hand. In a way, the seashore or an estuary is little different than a lake in terms of the simple methods used to exploit its wildlife.

The First Californians
(Before 11,200 B.C. to c. 9000 B.C.)

Hundreds of ducks crowd the calm lake waters, swimming in closely packed quarters, feeding, grooming their plumage. The calm water ripples with their passing, darkening as the sun moves to the western horizon. A hunter crouches in the shallows, his head adorned with a startlingly realistic duck mask. He stands absolutely still, head barely above the surface, birds cascading around him, just out of reach. He waits and waits, oblivious to the cold as the ducks settle down for the night. Then he moves infinitely slowly, a waterfowl swimming gently toward shore. Instinctively, the birds nearby swim with him toward a gap in the reeds. He stops short, but his feathered neighbors swim ahead toward the reeds. Suddenly, a fine fiber net flies across the inlet and lands on top of the unsuspecting birds, gathered together and clubbed with lightning speed by men and women hiding at water's edge. In the confusion, the hunter in the water grabs two birds by the legs as they skelter by. He wrings their necks in seconds and helps haul the laden net ashore. . . .

The first Californians were few in number and constantly on the move. They cast an elusive shadow in the archaeological record. Their archaeological signature is so faint as to be almost unrecognizable, and is known to archaeologists as the "Fluted Point Tradition," after the distinctive Clovis-like projectile heads used by some of the first settlers.

A scatter of Clovis-like points marks their passing, almost invariably found by the shorelines of long dried-up bodies of water, in ancient grassland areas, and in mountain passes between higher altitude lakes. Only two fluted points have come from in sight of the coast, but we can be sure that Paleo-Indians foraged along the Pacific. They certainly did not take up shellfish collecting and other coastal hunting strategies out of desperation when global warming decimated large animals, as was once suspected. From the moment people settled at the shore, they took advantage of what it had to offer—just as they had in every other environment they encountered.

The transition from a diet that was wholly terrestrial to one that also used kelp fish, mollusks, sea mammals, and other maritime foods was no big deal.

All major fluted-point sites in California have also produced another distinctive artifact—the eccentric crescent, a useful hunting knife used until at least 5000 B.C., long after fluted points had vanished (see figure 2.3).

Judging from radiocarbon dates for Clovis sites on the Plains and in the Great Basin, Paleo-Indians had arrived in California by at least 11,000 B.C., perhaps as much as a thousand years earlier. Their "Fluted Point Tradition" lasted until about 9000 B.C.[10]

From the very beginning, the Paleo-Indians exploited a broad range of animals and plants and were not just the stereotypical big-game hunters beloved of earlier archaeologists. Some groups may indeed have exploited the large, now extinct animals like camels and wild horses that abounded in some areas at the time of first settlement, but even they also relied heavily on smaller animals and plant foods.

All of them, whether coast or interior dwellers, probably anchored their nomadic wanderings to permanent water sources such as estuaries, perennial streams, and pluvial lakes, both much more abundant than today. As archaeologist Terry Jones has pointed out, such environments offered much the same food patches wherever they were located, so highly mobile Paleo-Indian groups could assess their value at a glance. Such areas, with their high-yielding foods, provided the focus for the enormous ranges of Paleo-Indian territories and gave some structure to their random movements within them (see figure 2.4).[11]

Some of the densest Paleo-Indian populations may have been along the shores of interior lakes, such as those that flourished in the then much wetter

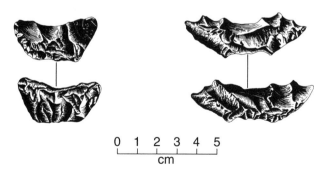

0 1 2 3 4 5
cm

Figure 2.3. Stone crescents from the shoreline of Lake Mojave. Drawing by Randall Engle. Courtesy of Michael Moratto.

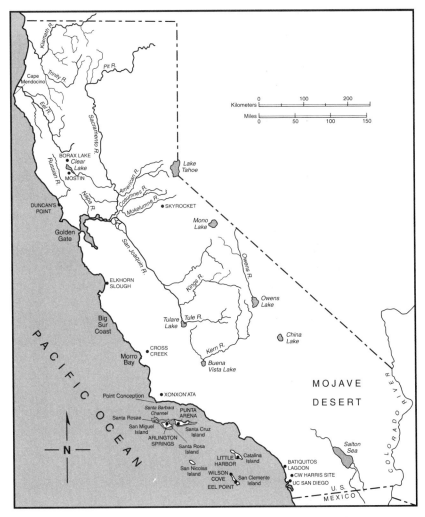

Figure 2.4. Map showing the sites mentioned in chapters 2–5. The Xonxon'ata site is included for convenience (see chapter 6).

and marshier Mojave Desert. Fluted points come from the ancient shores of China Lake and Lake Mojave in the southern interior. Unfortunately, all of them come from the surface and cannot be dated accurately. At Basalt Ridge on China Lake that once overlooked a marshy bay, fluted points and the bones of camel, horse, and mammoth come from above two tufa (volcanic) layers, which mark high stands of the lake. These are radiocarbon dated to about 11,000 B.C., but no one knows if the points killed the animals.[12]

Tulare Lake in central California was a large body of water in 11,000 B.C. Numerous fluted points, many of them Clovis-like, come from its shores, together with scrapers, bifaces (tools flaked on both sides), and smaller stone artifacts. At one location, many horse, bison, and ground sloth bones come from the surface of the high lake shore within an area about one and a half miles long by half a mile wide. These fossils are undated and are not, for sure, associated with human artifacts. Both stone tools and animal bones may date to the time of high water.

Almost all human settlement of the day was near permanent water supplies, perhaps to the point that some groups lived a sedentary life, rarely moving from exceptionally rich marsh, lake, or riverain environments. A short distance south of Clear Lake in northern California, the Mostin site lies along a low terrace in the bed of Kelsey Creek.[13] The site was occupied over a long period, with the earliest horizon dating to about 9250 B.C. The people took waterfowl in nearby Clear Lake, relied heavily on freshwater mollusks, and gathered plant foods, at a time when pollens show a transition from pine to oak forests in the area.

Mostin was ultimately occupied over a period of about three thousand years and incorporates a cemetery, one of the earliest in the western United States. The location may have been occupied continually—because of its unusually diverse and rich environment.

The Borax Lake site lies in the heart of the Coast Ranges, nine miles east of Mostin, on the edge of a dry lake bed in a confusion of freshwater deposits. It is a place visited by hunter-gatherer groups over many centuries as they collected obsidian locally to make into stone tools. The earliest occupation may be a variant of the Clovis culture, dating to about 11,000 B.C. or earlier (see figure 2.5).[14]

These few sites and a wide scatter of Clovis-like points throughout the state chronicle a nomadic population that never numbered more than a few thousand.

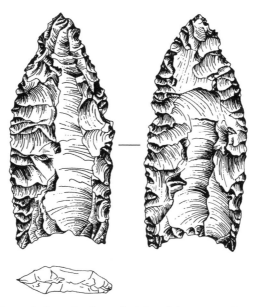

Figure 2.5. Borax Lake point from the lake of that name. Drawing by Randall
Engle. Courtesy of Michael Moratto.

Over a period of some two thousand years, perhaps longer, the descendants of the first settlers adapted to the diverse environments of a California
considerably cooler and wetter than today.

The Megafauna Vanishes (c. 10,900 B.C.)

The first Californians lived in a land where large animals abounded—
camels, horses, mammoths, sloths, and other now long-extinct species. This
megafauna was a zoological holdover from the Ice Age, prey that Paleo-
Indians exploited, just as they foraged for other foods. But the large animals
vanished over a period of more than 1,000 years and were extinct by about
10,000 B.C., leaving a much impoverished fauna in their train.

This extinction coincides, in general terms, with a massive decimation
of Ice Age animals of all kinds throughout the world, notably in northern
latitudes. Scientists disagree profoundly as to whether this was the result
of environmental change and global warming, or the consequence of
human predation.

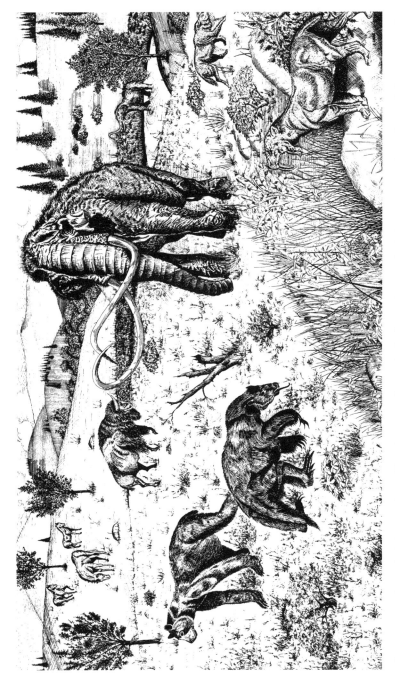

Figure 2.6. An artist's impression of Ice Age megafauna, including saber-toothed tiger, mammoth, and camelids. Drawing by Randall Engle. Courtesy of Michael Moratto.

Back in the 1960s, Paul Martin of the University of Arizona painted a vivid scenario of rapacious Clovis hunters bursting into the heart of a North America teeming with large animals. The ruthless human predators spread rapidly across a broad front, killing off the megafauna as they advanced. Vance Haynes of the same university challenged Martin's theory, arguing that the founder population was small, crashed soon after arrival, then only grew slowly over the millennia. Other experts argue that increased aridity and warmer temperatures imposed severe stress on the megafauna, which perished gradually, perhaps assisted on its way by human hunting of slower breeding species. But the human impact on the extinction process was probably minimal.[15]

A somewhat similar situation unfolded in Australia, where mass extinctions of Ice Age game coincided, in general terms, with first human settlement. There, scientists now favor a combination of changing environmental conditions combined with opportunistic human hunting of animals that yielded the most meat per kill. In time, a combination of these two factors caused impoverishment of the Australian fauna. The Aborigines adjusted to scarcer big game by diversifying their diet and focusing more on small prey and plant collecting. The same may have happened in North America, where Paleo-Indians may have accelerated the demise of an already-vanishing bestiary.

The extinction seems to have occurred relatively rapidly, over a period of a few centuries. In California, big-game hunting was never a major part of Paleo-Indian subsistence, in a world where the hunter-gatherer could draw on a broad range of food resources without the dangers inherent in big-game hunting with stone-tipped spears (see box 2.1).

As the game vanished, and Paleo-Indian groups preyed on the last mammoth and horses, the ancient Californians had already adapted to the full range of coastal and inland environments in their rapidly changing homeland. Many groups now broadened and diversified their diet still further, drawing on a huge cushion of edible foods in their world.

Some of these foods required much more effort to harvest and process, but, as we shall see, the technology needed for this already existed. From the very beginning, the earliest Californians survived comfortably by exploiting a wide range of foods, and knowing of many others as well.

The quest for the first Californians is reminiscent of Captain Ahab's search for the Great White Whale. Occasionally we get a glimpse of the first

BOX 2.1 Hunting Game with Spears

Imagine trying to hunt a tule elk, let alone a mammoth, with nothing but your two legs, a stone-tipped wooden spear, and, perhaps, a throwing stick, or *atlatl*. The only way you can make a kill is by getting up close, so close that you can literally touch your prey.

Throughout their long history, ancient Californians hunted on foot. Once the megafauna vanished, they could prey on such animals as the bighorn sheep, deer, and tule elk, as well as smaller animals like rabbits, which they took by the hundred.

Hunting on foot requires an intimate knowledge of your prey, infinite patience, and the ability to blend in with your surroundings. Many years ago, I went hunting antelope in central Africa with a man armed with nothing but a flintlock musket of dubious accuracy. We were hunting a medium-sized antelope, the impala, which likes long grass. The first day, we got within twenty feet of a male, fired, and missed. The second day, we wounded another male, having taken six hours to get within the same distance, crouching absolutely still for minutes on end as the suspicious impala looked in our direction. This time, my companion scored a hit and wounded the beast. We tracked it for three hours, only to be beaten to the punch by a lion, which killed the crippled antelope effortlessly. I learned the hard way that everything depended on patient stalking, on knowing the habits of your quarry as well as you knew your own, and on getting close enough to inflict a fatal wound.

The ancient Californians faced the same challenge, without firearms. Sometimes, they could run down a disabled animal or younger beast and wrestle it to the ground, a hazardous pastime at best. Sometimes they dug pit traps or set snares, especially for smaller animals. They drove rabbits into nets, where they speared them at leisure, and sometimes stampeded larger animals into swamps or places where one could get close and kill immobilized beasts.

But, for the most part, the hunter had to rely on sheer stalking ability and field skills. Such hunting was a solitary pastime, possibly hazardous, and often considered prestigious. And, like all skilled hunters, the ancient Californians were opportunists, never missing a chance to anticipate their prey's behavior. For instance, deer loved to feast on the rich acorn droppings of ripe oaks. Without fail, the hunters were there.

The technology was lethal when used right, but everything depended on the knowledge, patience, and stalking ability of the hunter.

settlers, like the fluke of a diving whale—a scatter of artifacts, a thin line in an ancient lake bed. Even more rarely, there is a dark shadow in the water, a fleeting view of the wider picture, a site with animal bones or other telling clues to Paleo-Indian behavior.

To catch our archaeological whale, we will need large data sets, excellent preservation, and sophisticated theoretical models. The pursuit is often frustrating, and relies heavily on a broad range of scientific disciplines—everything from tree rings to nuclear physics. Our fleeting glimpses are but a momentary reflection of a complicated reality, of a process of first settlement that took centuries, perhaps millennia. Complex, natural population movements brought people into a rugged, environmentally diverse land where their successors flourished and developed a remarkable variety of hunter-gatherer societies over more than 11,000 years.

We must now explore the first settlement of the southern California coast, where offshore islands beckoned and shellfish offered a reliable winter food source.

The First Coastal Settlement
(C. 11,000 to 6500 B.C.)

THICK FOG SWIRLS OVER THE PACIFIC BREAKERS, HUG-
ging the gray, oily water and the kelp-mantled rocks
close inshore. The fur seals lie on them, just clear of the
water, bodies touching, asleep.

Duncans Point, near Bodega Bay, 6000 B.C.: the hunters sidle ever
closer, moving quietly on the slippery rocks, spears and heavy wooden clubs
in hand. Well spread out, sure of foot, and carefully downwind, they move
in so close that they can literally touch their prey. Then the killing begins.
Quick spear thrusts, brutal blows with the wooden clubs as the men set
about them left and right, trying to kill every seal in reach. Many of the nim-
ble adult males escape quickly, wriggling to safety in the breakers. The
hunters take the mothers and their young, also older beasts, which wake up
confused, to stare death in the face.

A few hectic moments and the hunt is over. The men club any dying
beasts, then carry and drag away the fresh carcasses. They skin and butcher
them on the low cliff above the rookery. Back at camp, they hang strips of
meat out to dry in the afternoon sun, while the women peg out the seal skins
and scrape them clean. . . .

Elkhorn Slough, central California, 6000 B.C.: the shell mound sprawls
across the low promontory, freshly consumed clams spilling down the slope
toward water's edge. Men and women crouch over rocky outcrops, newly

uncovered by the falling tide. They search the rocks, prying off mollusks with deft movements of stone choppers. Two men wade in the shallow water, waves washing around their waists. They reach below the water, their fingers feeling for the telltale curve of an estuary clam shell, guiding the chopper to the edge of the mollusk, throwing their catch into a carrying basket within close reach.

Three women sit upwind of the odiferous mound, shelling the clams, casting the empty shells onto the nearby heap. The fresh meat lies in a shallow basket, ready for the evening meal at the simple camp inshore, away from the smell of rotting shellfish. . . .

In 11,000 B.C., humans were rare animals, clustering in small bands, flitting from place to place through environments where dangerous predators like grizzly bears and saber-toothed cats lurked and winters were much harsher than today. You could have traveled for days without seeing a human being, the smoke of camp fires, or the rotting uprights of crude brush dwellings. An occasional well-trodden path across a clearing, a fresh scar on a tree trunk, or the bones of a recently butchered elk were the only human imprints on the primordial landscape.

Some of these people visited the coast. In chapter 2, I theorized that some Paleo-Indian groups included the coast in much larger hunting territories and visited the Pacific shoreline as part of their seasonal round. I also argued against a first settlement of California by canoe. Now we must look more closely at the archaeological evidence for the first, more sustained exploitation of the coastline, which began as early as 9500 B.C., perhaps even earlier.

The first hunter-gatherers to visit the Pacific inhabited a very different world than the familiar coastline of today.

A Changing Coastline (13,000 to 6000 B.C.)

Fifty-five feet, sixty-five feet, eighty feet . . . the depth meter on my boat tracks the seabed as I head offshore. Plenty of water to sail in, and it's easy to forget that this was dry land in 7000 B.C. Sometimes I imagine myself sailing over the former grazing grounds of mammoth and tule elk, over huge stands of wild rye grass, over shallow ponds and long sandy beaches—a vanished world.

When Paleo-Indians wandered on the exposed continental shelf just after the Ice Age, sea levels were more than three hundred feet lower than today.[1]

Dense redwood and pine forests grew close inland. San Francisco Bay was a river valley, opening onto a wide coastal plain. The four familiar northern Channel Islands of today formed a single, mountainous landmass known to geologists as Santarosae. Only six miles from the nearest mainland. San Pedro Bay, now a huge artificial harbor, did not exist (see figure 3.1).

The environmental changes began before 13,000 B.C. Over the next seven thousand years, about 95 percent of the water that was trapped in continental glaciers melted into the oceans. Sea levels rose rapidly throughout the Pacific; low coral reefs were submerged, continental shelves and estuaries were flooded. Entire continents were separated by the deluge. Even as late as 6000 B.C., the sea level off North American coasts stood about thirty-three to sixty-five feet below modern levels. After 5000 B.C., when ancient Egypt was nothing more than a series of small, competing kingdoms and the Polynesian islands were still uninhabited, the rate of glacial melting and crustal adjustment declined.[2] Sea level rise slowed dramatically.

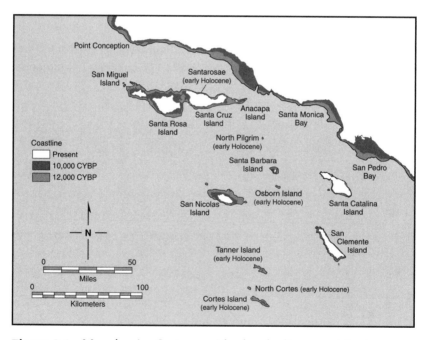

Figure 3.1. Map showing Santarosae island and adjacent mainland coast, c. 13,000 B.C. Courtesy of The Pacific Coast Archaeological Society and Judy Porcasi.

Only a few thousand people dwelt along California's changing coast-line during these seven millennia out of the estimated ten thousand or so living throughout the state at the time. These coastal dwellers experienced remarkable environmental changes, which varied greatly from one location to the next.

North of Cape Mendocino, where even inshore the waters are deep, the northern California shoreline merely shifted closer to higher ground. This may have led to more crowding, but it did not have radical effects on food supplies or territorial rights. The greatest changes came in areas with a broad and gradually sloping continental shelf, such as extended seaward off the Golden Gate and parts of southern California. Here, rising sea levels inundated enormous acreages of land.

California has lost about 7,700 square miles over the past 15,000 years. Off San Francisco Bay, the shoreline moved between twelve and sixteen miles eastward toward the modern coastline, turning the granitic peaks of the Farallons into rocky islands. Rising sea levels soon covered the rocky base of the Golden Gate, some 220 feet below modern sea level. Between 9000 and 8000 B.C., the rising Pacific flowed inexorably into what was then a convergence of large river valleys. The northern arm of the bay drained the Sacramento and San Joaquin Rivers, the southern arm received water from Coyote Creek and the Coast Ranges. The bay filled rapidly over the next 3,000 years, as the local sea level rose by about three-quarters of an inch a year—a horizontal movement of up to a hundred feet over this time in some areas. As the sea level rise slowed, extensive marshes formed in many places, ideal environments for mollusks and shallow-water fish (for map, see chapter 11, page 246).[3]

Along the central California coast, rising sea flooded deep indentations in the coast, forming productive estuaries and wetlands like Elkhorn Slough in Monterey Bay and Morro Bay in San Luis Obispo County. Here fresh and sea water met. Ebbing and flooding tides stirred the minerals and nutrients in the water, creating highly productive estuaries that abounded in fish and mollusks.

In southern California, the coastline moved shoreward an average of three miles, once again flooding estuaries and coastal lagoons. The rising Pacific formed paradisal environments for fish, mollusks, and waterfowl—and for the humans who preyed on them.

Imagine a world in which your homeland is vanishing rapidly under water. Sea levels rose so rapidly over these seven thousand years that hunting territories changed considerably within the memory of a generation. A family could look out from a low ridge on the coastal plain and see the remains of brush shelters used only a few years earlier exposed at low tide. The effects were even more marked in confined waters. The rising water could inundate a prized sea lion rookery within living experience, depriving the people of a vital food source. High waves from storm surges could destroy a shore-side freshwater pond in a few hours.

Within the span of a single generation, a shoreline group would have had to shift their camps, adjust their territorial boundaries. With less and less area to share between neighboring groups, there would have been constant social and political adjustments to be made in areas where food supplies were always distributed unevenly across the coastal landscape, in places where the land could support very few people per square mile.

Except in the most productive estuaries and coastal areas close to natural ocean upwelling, shoreline populations remained sparse throughout the Early and Middle Holocene (see box 3.1).

How Did the First Coastal People Live? (?11,000 to 6000 B.C.)

The blueprint for coastal settlement over the first seven thousand years came into being at the very beginning, before 11,000 B.C., long before sea levels rose rapidly. For these seven millennia, most people considered the coast part of their annual round, a part of much wider foraging territories, even if they spent long periods of time there.

Apart from the abundant plant foods on the continental shelf, the coast had two valuable and easily acquired foods—sea mammals and mollusks. Neither of them required elaborate technology or watercraft for harvesting.

Seals and sea lions breed on land. Females and pups spend many weeks on land in well-established rookeries. Basking animals also haunt rocky outcrops close to shore. During breeding season, it was a simple matter for terrestrial hunters to stalk sleeping sea mammals and then club or spear them in short order—as happened at Duncans Point over many centuries. The hunting technology was on hand anyhow, and the prey far easier to bag than deer.

Mollusks abounded in tidal pools and on rock-bound shores, where they could be found in abundance for the taking during much of the year. Only the red tides of summer turned them toxic and inedible.[4] It's easy to

BOX 3.1 The Holocene

The Greek word *"holos"* means "recent"—whence the Holocene, the most recent of all geological eras, which began with the global warming at the end of the Ice Age 15,000 years ago and continues until today. (There are those who argue that the Holocene is actually part of the Ice Age, as we will, one day, return to another glacial period, but the argument is for purists.)

Conventionally, both paleoclimatologists and archaeologists subdivide the Holocene of California into three arbitrary parts, subdivisions I use in these pages.

Early Holocene (12,700 to 6500 B.C.)

The Early Holocene encompasses the most dramatic and rapid environmental changes after the Ice Age, with rapid sea-level rise everywhere and deglaciation in northern latitudes. Coastal forests shifted north. Freshwater lakes persisted over much of the interior, rainfall was higher, and temperatures somewhat cooler than today.

Middle Holocene (6500 to 2000 B.C.)

Sea levels still rose, but more slowly, reaching near-modern levels by six thousand years ago. California's climate grew drier and warmer, at times hotter than today. Many pluvial lakes in the interior dried up.

Late Holocene (2000 B.C. to today)

Basically, modern climatic conditions prevailed, with somewhat wetter cycles than the Middle Holocene, also prolonged drought periods. The climate continued unpredictable, with irregular El Niños and other short-term climatic events.

Climatic changes were never uniform throughout California; they varied greatly from one location to another, and from sea level to inland. But this tripartite subdivision serves as a useful, general framework.

think of mollusks as food to be eaten when other food sources were in short supply, but fresh- and saltwater mollusks were a reliable food source in environments where people were constantly on the move and heavily dependent on seasonal plant foods like wild grasses. Their sheer availability, especially in the lean winter months, made mollusks a near staple.

A skilled free diver could have harvested shellfish underwater with little more than a casually sharpened rock and a simple fiber net bag. Sharp-edged cobbles and crude picks sufficed to knock and lever abalone, limpets, and other mollusks in tide tools or rocky outcrops in shallow water.

Ancient mollusk collectors all over the world used the same basic shellfish-collecting technology of stone choppers and scrapers. In South Africa, northern Europe, and eastern North America, to mention only a few locations, they used casual tools to knock the mollusk off their perches and then to open them.

But it's important to understand that for seven thousand years, the California shoreline, with its shellfish and sea mammals, was part of a much larger hunter-gatherer world, not a maritime universe unto itself.

Those who frequented the coast during these seven millennia were familiar with estuaries and inland lakes, and may, at first, have thought of the Pacific as nothing more than an enormous lake. Certainly, they exploited the foods on the coast just as they took animals and mollusks inland. Sea mammals and mollusks—living by the ocean—were but one facet of hunter-gatherer lives that were firmly anchored on land, as much to game and plant foods as to the resources of the Pacific. From the very beginning, any visitation and settlement of the offshore islands was part of a much larger world on the mainland. No one could live completely isolated on such botanically impoverished land masses.

Santarosae and the Earliest Coastal Sites (?11,000 to 6000 B.C.)

The waterway is glassy calm at summer's dawn, the sun a red disk on the eastern horizon. Two small tule reed canoes, their hulls sealed with bitumen, venture into open water. The two-men crews paddle strongly, dipping deep into the water, aiming at the island shoreline a short distance away. Small waves from their passing ripple far across the flat water. Sea lions bask in the morning sunlight, flippers in the air. As the men approach land, a light breeze from the west riffles the channel. They ground on a sandy beach and haul their light craft clear of the breakers, turning them over to dry in the hot sun. . . .

Surprising although it may seem, some of the earliest human settlements in California lie on the northern Channel Islands, the then-single landmass, Santarosae. Today, the Channel Islands form the southern boundary of the Santa Barbara Channel. In 11,000 B.C., they were a far larger frontier, only six miles from Point Hueneme, the nearest promontory on the mainland.

Very soon after the first humans appeared at the coast, some of them paddled across to Santarosae, the island close offshore like those on familiar pluvial lakes inland. They built simple tule reed canoes and paddled across. The crossing was a mere hop, skip, and a jump compared with the open water passage of today (see box 3.2).

Back in the 1930s, Phil Orr, a Santa Barbara archaeologist, caused quite a stir when he announced that he had found human hearths associated with the bones of pygmy mammoths on Santa Rosa Island at the outer reaches of the Santa Barbara Channel. (The Santa Rosa mammoths were a unique Channel Islands form, which stood about six feet high. Their ancestors had swum over from the mainland during the earlier Ice Age and evolved to a diminutive size in complete isolation.)

Orr claimed that the hearths were over 40,000 years old.[5]

Pygmy mammoths did indeed flourish on the Channel Islands, but the reddened earth "hearths" have proven to be of natural origin. Orr's claims of 40,000-year-old settlement have long been discredited.

Despite his preoccupation with the hunting of pygmy mammoth, Orr was a perceptive observer of archaeological sites. He located and sampled a series of what he considered to be early shell middens on Santa Rosa's rocky northwestern shore.[6] Orr carried out most of his fieldwork before radiocarbon dates came along. His suspicion was correct. Four of them date to somewhat later than 7400 B.C., a very early date for archaeological sites in the region.

Both these middens and his mammoth hearths convinced Orr that his theory was correct: people had settled on Santa Rosa Island in very early times. Then, in 1959, Orr unearthed the thigh bones of a woman that had eroded from deep in the walls of an arroyo at Arlington Springs, also on the northern coast. He proclaimed the Arlington Springs woman to be one of the oldest known Californians.

Orr may have been right. A team of experts has recently investigated the Arlington Springs arroyo with the full panoply of modern science (see figure 3.3). They have radiocarbon dated arroyo deposits similar to those from which the woman is said to have come to at least 11,000 B.C., perhaps earlier—to a time when the landscape in the area was marshy. But is the Arlington woman

BOX 3.2 Tule Canoes

Tule canoes, constructed of bundles of tule reeds, probably date from as early as Paleo-Indian times. This is only a guess, of course, but they are so simple and effective on lakes and rivers that it seems a logical hypothesis. Small tules, when dry and newly constructed, are buoyant and easily handled, ideal for fishing.

Tules were simple to build from readily available raw materials. There were, as an indication, more than 1,800 acres of tule-producing estuary along the mainland coast in Chumash country as recently as 1980 and many more on the continental shelf of earlier times. (Tule reeds are much scarcer on the Channel Islands.)

The smaller tules were "three-bundle" craft, stiffened with a willow pole, which allowed them to carry a load. One bundle served as the bottom of the canoe, the other two as the sides. The tied ends of all three bundles formed a pointed bow and stern. Such canoes were wide enough to allow a paddler sitting on the bottom bundle to propel them easily with a double-bladed paddle (see figure 3.2).

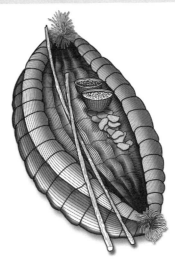

Figure 3.2. Artist's impression of a Chumash tule canoe. Original from *The Origins of a Pacific Coast Chiefdom* (Salt Lake City, Utah: University of Utah Press, 2001). Original drawing by Jeanne Arnold.

According to nineteenth-century Chumash Indian informants, a three-bundle tule could venture out on the Pacific and carry one or two passengers, provided they did not mind getting wet and the canoe stayed close inshore. Some three-bundlers may have been as much as fourteen feet long.

"Five-bundle" tules were more substantial vessels, with a chunky bottom pallet of thick reeds forming the bottom. The remaining four bundles were smaller and formed the side "planks." These planks were thinner bundles than the base, only the lowermost ones being tied to the bottom, while the uppermost ones were secured to their neighbors alone. This provided a flexible and durable hull with more above-water height than the three-bundled version. The builders sometimes inserted as many as three driftwood seats or braces between the reeds.

At European contact, Chumash tules were coated with natural bitumen to prevent the reeds from becoming waterlogged. Presumably, this coating was also applied in earlier centuries.

Like their three-bundle cousins, the larger tules were light and buoyant, easily carried and launched. Chumash informants reported that some larger tules journeyed to the Channel Islands, but they had serious limitations. Even a lightly burdened five-bundle tule was laborious to paddle in any sea and leaked copiously. Speed over the water was of the essence, lest one got caught out in afternoon breezes and wind waves. According to Chumash canoe builder Fernando Librado, interviewed by anthropologist John Harrington, five-bundlers became waterlogged and useless after only four days in the water, which inhibited a great deal of longer distance paddling. Even after short journeys, their owners were careful to dry them in the sun as often as possible.

For the most part, tules were used for inshore fishing, often with a large basket set amidships for the catch. You were certain to get wet. But this did not matter when fishing in the kelp, as you would probably get wet in the surf anyhow and you were never afloat for more than a few hours. Nor would it matter if the crossing to the islands was a mere six miles or so, as it was before 8000 B.C.

Figure 3.3. Excavations at Arlington Springs, Santa Rosa Island. Courtesy of Santa Barbara Museum of Natural History.

really that early? Unfortunately, the meticulously collected radiocarbon dates do not come from the exact location where the skeleton was found, which has long eroded away. For this reason, there will always be a question mark about the precise date of the burial (see figure 3.3).[7]

If the Arlington Springs woman is indeed twelve millennia old, then people were at least visiting Santarosae very soon after first settlement indeed.

San Miguel Island lies to the west of Santa Rosa, a bleak and arid landmass exposed to the full strength of the northwesterly winds that sweep down the coast past Point Conception. I have lain at anchor here on many occasions for days on end, listening to the northwesterly wind howl in my rigging, sweeping down the steep cliffs at Cuyler Harbor on the north coast of the island. Two anchors lay at 45 degrees to the bow; 150 feet of line and chain on each. The boat heeled to the gusts and the anchor lines vibrated in the wind. Strong winds can blow for weeks, cascading banks of fog close to the stunted vegetation. This is an inhospitable place to live, with water in short supply, yet we have evidence of it being visited early on because of its rich mollusk beds and sea mammal colonies.

In 9000 B.C., what is now San Miguel Island was the westernmost extremity of Santarosae, even then exposed to the full strength of strong westerly winds. The continental shelf off the island was narrow, so rising sea levels caused relatively few changes in the configuration of the shoreline. From the earliest times, human visitors camped in deep canyons and rock shelters, close to scarce water supplies and away from the windy, often waterless shore.

Daisy Cave at the eastern end of the island once lay within two hundred yards of the ocean. Early Holocene people camped there as early as 9000 B.C., perhaps considerably earlier, living off mollusks, fish, and sea mammals (see figure 3.4). We know this occupation was a seasonal one, because thin layers of bird guano interrupt the archaeological deposits.[8]

Archaeologist Jon Erlandson has combed San Miguel Island for traces of early human settlement. With infinite patience he has focused his search on rock shelters and areas close to freshwater springs, looking for what he calls "low density sites"—small scatters of shells, stone tools, and hearths, the only archaeological signature left by transitory visitors taking shellfish or hunting sea mammals.

He concentrated on the northwestern coast, where overgrazing by sheep in historic times has exposed an ancient land surface known as the Simonton Soil. Erlandson found eleven early mounds, nearly all of them

Figure 3.4. Daisy Cave, San Miguel Island. Courtesy of Michael Glassow.

close to fresh water springs, all of them dating to before 6000 B.C., at least one to 7300 B.C. At most sites, the abalone, limpet, and mussel shells were of considerable size, suggesting that the visitors were exploiting rich shellfish colonies previously untouched by humans.[9]

A single early shell mound on the southern shore of Santa Cruz Island to the east also provides evidence of intensive shellfish exploitation in early times.

For all these finds, few, if any, people lived on Santarosae permanently, or the three islands that followed it, until after about 3000 B.C., when fishing assumed greater importance in local economies. Whether one landmass or three, the islands were biologically impoverished, except for sea mammal rookeries, the rich kelp fisheries close inshore, and the dense shellfish colonies that thrived on the rocky coasts. Shellfish were an easily collected food, so much so that mollusk populations on the mainland soon came under pressure, leaving few larger shellfish within easy reach. These may have been one of the circumstances that turned the mainlanders' eyes offshore.

After some cautious and well-rewarded visits, probably in small tule canoes, visitations across the narrow channel became more regular—during periods of prolonged calm weather between storms in winter and during the quiet hours of summer days. But the initiatives must have always come from the mainland, where many more foods were to be found.

Santarosae was a source of shellfish, and perhaps dried kelp fish like sheephead, a place visited for a few weeks a year, on the frontiers of the mainland world. But, as sea levels rose and distances across the channel increased, tule canoes could no longer make the passage safely, nor could they be relied on to transport large loads. Permanent settlement of the northern Channel Islands awaited new, more efficient and safer watercraft—planked canoes.

The Mainland: Duncans Point, Elkhorn Slough, and Cross Creek (? 11,000 to 6000 B.C.)

Between about 11,000 and 6000 B.C., the population of the mainland coast was so sparse that its human occupants left few traces of their presence behind them. Again, one hears the familiar archaeological litany: "almost nothing is known." In this case, it's hardly surprising, thanks to two other archaeological laments: many settlements lie deep below modern sea levels on the now-submerged continental shelf, or, alas, they are submerged under today's urban sprawl. Only a scattering of inconspicuous sites tell the story, most of them dating from about 6000 B.C.

As far as archaeologists know, coastal settlement began considerably earlier in the south, perhaps as early as 11,000 B.C., and certainly by 9000 years B.C. In contrast, there are no known traces of human settlement along the north coast earlier than about 6000 B.C., perhaps the consequence of narrower continental shelves and more rugged coastlines. As we shall see in chapter 10, salmon and other migrating fish were the key to riverine and coastal settlement north of San Francisco.

For convenience, however, let's travel in search of early settlement from north to south along the mainland coast.[10]

The Duncans Point site of about 6000 B.C., near Bodega Bay on the northern California coast, is among the earliest-known human settlements along the modern shoreline north of San Francisco. Here, the people subsisted off sea mammals from the nearby rookeries and from mollusks, which abound along the rocky shoreline.

Elkhorn Slough near Moss Landing in Monterey Bay supported small groups of clam collectors at about the same time. Judging from contemporary sites inland, both the Duncans Point and Elkhorn Slough groups must have ranged far inland as well.

Many such bands would have lived in the lower reaches of coastal river valleys that emptied into the ocean or flowed into the edge of the continental shelf. Winter storms and encroaching sea water must have eroded many of their camps away, or buried them under deep alluvium deposited by increasingly sluggish rivers affected by rising sea levels. For example, virtually all sites earlier than about 5000 B.C. along the shores of the estuary that is now San Francisco Bay are buried deep below many feet of river sediment deposits.

Further south, Cross Creek, a recently discovered site in central California's San Luis Obispo County, gives us a momentary portrait of a community living slightly inland.

The Cross Creek site lies in the Edna Valley, five and a half miles from the coast. When first occupied, the settlement was even further inland—ten and a half miles from the coast and over five miles from a marine estuary. A buried shell mound covered with river silt lies on an ancient terrace overlooking the water. No less than twelve radiocarbon samples from estuarine clam shells dated the occupation to between 8350 and 5670 B.C.—firmly in the Early Holocene.[11]

This was a place where plant foods were important, among them various grasses and the ubiquitous yucca, ground with handstones and milling stones, just as they were elsewhere in California at the time (see chapter 4 and figure 3.5).

But shellfish were a significant part of the Cross Creek diet. The people hauled shallow-water clams by the dozens from a now-extinct estuary that flowed from near the modern San Luis Obispo County community of Halcyon to Pismo Beach. They also took some open-coast mollusks, too, but their main source of supply was the estuary. We know this was an important location, for other groups camped by the estuary between about 7660 and 7000 B.C.

Cross Creek provides convincing proof that the coast was part of much wider hunting territories, even if its inhabitants stayed at the same location fairly close to the shore for considerable periods. They, like other such groups, may have been less mobile than many other bands living in environments with more widely distributed, and less reliable, foods to draw on.

A scatter of early mainland sites occurs further south, in the Santa Barbara and Los Angeles regions and in Orange County.

In the far south, in what is now San Diego County, people exploited the coast by at least 9000 B.C. As sea levels rose over the next 6,500 years, forming coastal lagoons, many seminomadic groups settled in these favored locations. The lagoons were open to the Pacific and formed excellent habitats for shellfish of all kinds.

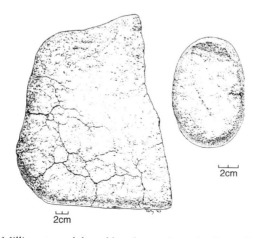

Figure 3.5. Milling stone slab and hand stone from the Cross Creek site near San Luis Obispo. Courtesy of Terry Jones.

Some of the earliest shell mounds come from the University of California campus at La Jolla, where coastal groups camped as early as 6300 B.C. and continued to visit for at least five thousand years. Shellfish were not the only staple. These sites and others have yielded fish bones and the remains of deer and other game, as well as tools for processing plant foods. In some places, the concentration of sites is truly impressive. Over 170 ancient sites have come from within two miles of the banks of Batiquitos Lagoon south of Oceanside, where hunter-gatherers flourished from as early as the seventh millennium B.C.[12]

■   ■   ■

By 7000 B.C., people had been living at, or visiting, the coast for over four thousand years. The population was never large, the shoreline and offshore islands part of a much wider world, of hunting territories that extended far inland, deep into an increasingly arid landscape. One has a sense of cultural continuity, of hunting territories and life ways that changed but little over many thousands of years, a world where populations were sparse and there was plenty of space for everyone. Then, around 6500 B.C., just about when sea levels reached near-modern levels, island colonization became more lasting. Before telling this story, however, I recount developments on the mainland in the next chapter.

The Mainland:
A World of Milling Stones
(9500 to 2500 B.C.)

THE CENTRAL VALLEY. THE PURPLE SALVIA BLOSSOMS have withered in the early summer sun. The chia stems stand dry, the heads bursting with small gray seeds. Flocks of birds dart low over the branching plants, spilling seeds to the ground as they feed off the ripe stems. They take flight as the harvesters approach with their shallow baskets, tapping the stems and heads gently so the seeds cascade into the tightly woven tray.

The men and women work steadily from one end of the densely packed *Salvia* plants to the other, passing laden trays to waiting children, who tip the precious seeds into deep carrying baskets. Across the valley, small parties of harvesters can be seen working through yellowing chia stands as fast as they can. Humans are competing with animals for the harvest, which only lasts a few days. The desiccated seeds soon separate from the stems and fall useless to the ground.

Back at camp, women and girls sit and kneel, crude, flat milling stones between their legs, full baskets of carefully charred seeds close at hand. They scatter seed on the stone, then grind it steadily with a soft scraping sound, adding more seed, sweeping the meal into another basket. Hour after hour they labor, turning the harvest into fine, nourishing meal. Two men come by, hunting spears in hand, in pursuit of the deer feasting on the harvest. They grab a fistful of seeds, mix them with water in a small basket and drink deeply. The nourishing mixture will sustain them for hours.

In chapter 3, I described the first coastal settlement and concluded that Paleo-Indian groups simply incorporated the shoreline, and then the off-shore islands of southern California, into their much larger hunting territories. They may, indeed, have thought of the Pacific as a vast lake, even if its waters were salty. As we headed offshore, we left a tiny mainland population confronting a warmer, drier world almost devoid of large animals—the fabled megafauna. We must now follow their fortunes as they adjusted to thousands of years of much more arid and hotter climate.

Global Warming and a Black Hole

For many years, most archaeologists believed that the extinction of the megafauna, the large Ice Age animals like mastodon and wild camelids, in about 10,900 B.C., was a defining moment in ancient North America. In 1987, I myself wrote that "scattered human populations living in desert and woodland environments . . . learned instead to hunt smaller, more solitary animals like the white-tailed deer and moose, and to exploit a broad spectrum of other foods, among them nuts, fish, and shellfish."[1] I was profoundly wrong. There was no part of North America except, perhaps, parts of the Great Plains, where people could live off big game alone, and certainly not in California, with its diverse landscapes, unpredictable rainfall, and sparse human populations.

Plant foods, especially wild grasses that require relatively little processing, were of as much importance to the first Paleo-Indians as they were to their successors. The fundamental survival strategies for living in ancient California came into being not with the extinction of the megafauna, but with first settlement. These strategies endured for more than 11,000 years. Safety lay in conservative behavior, flexibility, mobility, and opportunism, in an ability to adjust constantly—often at short notice—to unpredictable drought cycles, unusually heavy rains, even earthquakes and fire—the four curses of living in California that afflict us to this day.

As the centuries passed, global warming intensified. Summer temperatures rose, rainfall became sparse and irregular. But there was one inconspicuous, yet all-important environmental difference. Ice core columns from Greenland's interior tell us that the CO_2 level in the atmosphere was now up to a third higher than it had been at any time during the previous 120,000 years. This enrichment increased photosynthesis, biomass, and seed yield, so that Holocene plants were more productive and more drought tolerant than in earlier times. This greater, but inconspicuous, plant productivity was an important asset for hunter-gatherers who'd settled in a diverse and harsh land where food was scattered widely over the landscape.[2]

Edible grasses and tubers were important to ancient Californians from the very beginning of human settlement—far more important than the large game animals, which dominate so much thinking about first settlement. Herein lay the great continuity of mainland life—in a dependence on edible plant foods, especially seeds of many kinds. Despite increasing aridity, virtually all of California was still an edible landscape, with an extraordinary range of vegetable foods, so much so that even groups living in the most arid of lands had a cushion of less palatable foods to fall back on in drought years. The staples varied widely from one end of the state to the other. Unfortunately, we know almost nothing about the people who faced the challenge of this intensified global warming.

The first eight thousand years or so of human history in California are a vast black hole, especially the seven millennia that separate first settlement from the end of a dry and warm period between 6500 and 2500 B.C. The very forces of flooding and erosion that afflicted the few thousand people living in California during these years have decimated the archaeological record of the period, a record that was not particularly conspicuous in the first place. Hunter-gatherers on the move rarely leave much behind them. Their dwellings are transitory, often little more than windbreaks.[3] Their toolkits are light, often perishable, and always portable.

The archaeology of these seven thousand years is wrought in humble milling stones and little else, in large part because seeds and other edible plants assumed overwhelming importance in an arid land with searing temperatures. As a result, we have only a blurred impression of their makers.

Global Warming and the Onset of the Altithermal (9600 to 5000 B.C.)

Like the coast, the interior mainland was a changing world. As we saw in chapter 3, the Pacific rose with dramatic speed after 13,000 B.C., consuming acres of continental shelf and the grassy habitats that flourished along the now-buried shoreline. As we also saw, sea levels were still on average between sixty-five and thirty-three feet below modern levels in 6000 B.C. A thousand years later, the rise slowed, then more or less stabilized at near modern levels. Within a mere seven millennia or so, hundreds, if not thousands, of natural stands of wild grasses vanished under the Pacific, depriving both animal and human predators of a major food source at a time when large game populations had plummeted and the large pluvial lakes of earlier times were drying up rapidly.

In 9000 B.C., a chain of pluvial lakes and marshes covered much of the California interior, from the extreme northeast, through the Central Valley into the Mojave and the deserts of the south.[4] As long as winter rainfall was more abundant than today, lake levels remained high, despite increasingly severe summer evaporation. Summer temperatures were cooler, so evaporation rates were lower and lake levels reasonably stable. Most inland groups hunted and gathered near pluvial lakes, or close to permanent streams, where they found seed-bearing grasses and other plant foods, as well as waterfowl, shallow water fish that could be speared, and large numbers of rabbits.

We know of these people, often grouped into an ill-defined "Western Pluvial Lakes Tradition," from dozens of inconspicuous archaeological sites between Oregon and southern California. All of them share a common toolkit, from the Fort Rock area of Oregon in the western Great Basin in the north, southward along the eastern slopes of the Cascades and Sierra Nevada, and deep into the now-arid lands of southern California. Everywhere, their surviving toolkit was of the simplest—mostly leaf-shaped projectile knives or points, as well as an array of scrapers and woodworking tools. Above all, they used milling stones to process a wide variety of grass seeds and other vegetable foods.[5] Almost none of these groups stayed in one place for any length of time, even if they returned to the same locations repeatedly. And the seeming monotony of projectile points disguises a broad diversity of changing hunter-gatherer societies confronting significant global warming (see box 4.1).

Most of the pluvial lakes were doomed. As summer temperatures rose after 6500 B.C., so evaporation rates accelerated. One by one, most of the ancient lakes vanished, as winter rainfall totals dropped and the climate became somewhat warmer than today. A long dry period known to geologists as the Altithermal ensued.[6] As the interior became hotter and drier,

BOX 4.1 Studying Climate Change in Ancient California

Geologist Ernst Antevs identified the Altithermal from studies of ancient lake shores in the Great Basin, using purely geological methods. Later, more precise research has proven him generally correct. Today, a revolution in paleoclimatology, the study of ancient climate, is transforming our knowledge of the climate of the past 13,000 years. People living in semiarid and desert lands with irregular rainfall are always at the mercy of sudden climatic shifts, but it is only in recent years that we have begun to understand just how important these changes are. For the first time, we are gaining access to extremely fine-grained climatic data gleaned from a number of sources. These include the following:

Ice Cores. Deep cores drilled in the Greenland ice cap and into mountain glaciers in the South American Andes offer a long view of climatic change extending back well into the Ice Age. The cores uncover the annual growth layers of the ice or snow, which can be counted just like the rings on a tree trunk. This seems like an ideal way to study short-term climate change, but much depends on the level of definition in the individual rings, which can currently show climate changes with the resolution of about a century. Chemical analysis of the air caught in the cores also provides valuable climatic data. This is how we know that the Holocene atmosphere contains about a third more CO_2 than that of the previous 120,000 years—a strong influence on plant productivity.

Deep Sea Cores and Lake Cores. These also provide important records of Holocene climate change, especially in circumstances where sea floor deposition conditions are especially even, as is the case in the Santa Barbara Channel. Most deep sea cores do not provide very accurate records of short-term climatic shifts. The latest Santa Barbara Channel core is a notable exception.

Tree-Rings. Tree rings, or dendrochronology, the study of annual growth rings in tree trunks, offers a potentially accurate way of studying such phenomena as drought cycles, major El Niño events, and so on. However, dendrochronology is still in relative infancy

(Continued)

BOX 4.1 Continued

in California. Judging from experience in the Southwest, where tree rings have been studied for nearly a century, you need hundreds of samples to provide accurate information on short-term climatic shifts.

Pollen Analysis (palynology). This is the study of minute pollen grains preserved in waterlogged and marshy deposits, which provide a record of local vegetational changes over long periods of time. Palynology is much used in Europe and in some parts of North America, but is still in its infancy in California.

These are but a few of the methods being used to study ancient climate change. Within a generation, we will likely have a fine-grained portrait of Holocene climate change, which will allow us to better assess the impacts of short-term climatic shifts on California's ancient societies. Stay tuned . . .

people simply followed the same strategies they had pursued for thousands of years. They congregated in places where water supplies could be relied on for much of the year. These places were their "anchors" from which they moved out over the landscape in search of increasingly dispersed food supplies, of which edible seeds and plants of all kinds were now the most important. Increasingly, they found themselves living in circumscribed areas of unusual diversity of food resources. The marshes and shallow rivers of the Central Valley and the San Francisco Bay estuary areas formed by rising sea levels are two examples. We know almost nothing about their lives, as both human activity and natural flooding and erosion have either destroyed or covered their settlements under deep layers of silt.

Rising sea levels had gradually inundated the Golden Gate and San Francisco Bay. As the estuary of earlier times overflowed its banks and formed extensive shallow backwaters, the flat bottomlands of what is now the Sacramento Delta backfilled and flooded, creating massive silting and backing up the great rivers of the Central Valley. The valley became a low-elevation flatland, with millions of acres of alluvial plains, sluggish river channels, marshes, lakes, and sloughs (see chapter 11).

The tidal streams of the newly formed San Francisco Bay ebbed and flowed into the Delta, creating enormous saltwater wetlands. Each spring snow melt from the Sierras backed up and turned thousands of acres into lush wetlands. The San Joaquin Valley alone boasted of about two thousand square miles of lakes, marshes, and sloughs, which teemed with wildlife and plant foods of many kinds (see chapter 12). The largest of these many lakes was Tulare Lake in King County, which flooded a huge natural basin and was in places as much as twenty-eight miles wide. A ridge formed by alluvial fans created a natural ridge that impounded the waters of the lake and its enormous swamps. Tulare and other lakes like Kern fluctuated constantly with short- and long-term climatic shifts, but there was always water in them.

These, and many other lakeside environments through the valley, provided an extraordinary range of food and other staples for hunter-gatherers from Paleo-Indian times until the modern era. The spring floods renewed the wetlands and fostered a lush swamp vegetation of coarse grasses, tule reeds, and cattails, which provided not only food but plant fibers for all kinds of purposes, also building materials.

Everywhere, as the pluvial lakes vanished, so the people living by them adapted easily to a much drier world. They had always been on the move, always exploiting a wide variety of animals and plants, always adapting their diet and their technology to new circumstances. Now survival depended on different foods than before, but it was nothing that the people did not know about. There was always a cushion of plant foods for hungry people to exploit, even if they were less palatable than others.

The Californians of these millennia, faced with an increasingly dry world, simply diversified into the wider universe of plant foods available to them. Processing hard seeds requires work, but not elaborate tools. It is an ancient technology known to plant collectors and sometimes used since the earliest times. To grind these edible seeds, the Paleo-Indians needed milling stones and hand stones, implements as important as the stone projectile points on the tips of their spears.

Only a handful of sites provide any sense of the adaptations people made to a drying and increasingly harsh climate. Even fewer sites possess the stratified layers that chronicle such changes. Of these, the Skyrocket site in the central Sierra foothills is the most informative.[7]

The Skyrocket Site (7200 to 5000 B.C.)

Back in the 1850s, miners flocked to the central Sierra foothills east of Stockton, sinking mine after mine in search of gold. Many of them lived in a town named Hodson, which flourished briefly then faded away as the prospectors and miners departed, usually empty handed. The Gold Rush explorers knew there was gold in the area, but they found little of it with their rough-and-ready conventional methods. A century and a half later, a new gold rush developed in the foothills, using new technology to float out the precious metal chemically.

For some years, the Royal Mountain King Mine operated an open-pit gold mine where Hodson once flourished, the only economic way to extract ore from the ground. (Royal Mountain ceased operations in the early 1990s.) Gold Rush operators just staked a claim and moved in. Today, mine operators have to comply with rigorous environmental laws, avoid archaeological and historical sites, and return the land to its near-original state. As part of their compliance, they paid for the partial excavation of a large archaeological site that lay in the middle of the area to be occupied by their largest pit. The dig revealed an astonishing 9,500 years of virtually continuous human occupation in a foothill valley separated from the Central Valley by a low ridge.

The Skyrocket site, named after a nearby nineteenth-century mine, is that rarity of rarities in California—a stratified settlement occupied again and again over thousands of years. The archaeological deposits extend over six hundred yards and are twelve-and-a-half-feet deep at the center. Excavators Roger La Jeunesse and John Pryor calls this "a wonderful layer cake of soil strata," and with good reason. Skyrocket documents local history from about 7200 B.C. to the mid-nineteenth century A.D., just before direct contact with Europeans. Its earlier layers span the life of the Western Pluvial Lakes Tradition and give us insights into the major adjustments made by people of the time (see figure 4.1).

Many early archaeological sites in California have vanished, victims not only of human activity, but of the forces of flooding and erosion. But at Skyrocket, a natural ridge in the bedrock protected the earliest settlement from massive flooding from about 5000 to 4000 B.C. Layers of gravely clay and thick midden deposits from much later visitors then sealed the rich black soil of the first occupation.

Figure 4.1. General view of the Skyrocket site. Courtesy of Roger La Jeunesse and John Pryor.

Pryor and La Jeunesse brought in a backhoe and exposed a larger area, then carefully dug into the black layer. The earliest settlement lay in rich, black soil, thick with artifacts and well-preserved plant remains, the residue of an ancient marsh fed by artesian springs. These same springs account for the continual use of the site over thousands of years. Even in severe droughts they produce plenty of water. The excellent preservation conditions revealed an environment in transition from the cold, wet landscape of the Ice Age to the oak savanna of today. Acorns, pine nuts, and wild cucumber seeds abounded in the same layers. They also yielded hundreds of flat milling stones. Clearly, plants were of the greatest importance in the Skyrocket diet, perhaps far more so than hunting. Many stemmed projectile points came from the milling stone layer, including a broken Clovis specimen that could, conceivably, have been picked up by the inhabitants as a curiosity.

The mine operators cooperated with the excavating, bringing in heavy machinery to shift overburden from the enormous area of the site. Their Case 235 backhoe exposed a much larger area of the settlement than is normal with a site of this age. Pryor and La Jeunesse uncovered a thirty-three feet by thirty-three feet stone platform, which extended out into the surrounding marsh deposits, originally built around a natural bedrock finger into the waterlogged ground and covering nearly nine hundred square feet. The surface was carefully leveled and occupied by a large hearth built on a baked clay layer. The base of this remarkable structure dated to about 7500 B.C., the level where the Clovis point came to light. It remained in use until about 5000 B.C., some 2,500 years. Generation after generation of visitors camped on the platform, leaving hundreds of milling stones and hand stones behind them together with hundreds of stone tools made from a local greenstone quarried nearby. The wear patterns on the stones are such that Pryor and La Jeunesse suspect that their users crushed nuts as well as seeds with them (see figure 4.3).

The Skyrocket stone platform is unique, not only as a structure, but also because it remained in use, and was presumably maintained in good order, for two and a half millennia. That it was closely associated with the processing of plant foods of many kinds is unquestionable. There is certainly a far greater investment of time in what must have been some form of base camp at this nine hundred to one thousand-year-old settlement than there is at any other known site of this age elsewhere in California. No question—people probably lived at this location for weeks, if not months, on end, simply because

Figure 4.2. CRM at work. The Skyrocket excavations required the careful use of earthmoving machinery to move overburden and to dig carefully monitored trenches. Courtesy of Roger La Jeunesse and Roger Pryor.

Figure 4.3. The stone platform from the lowermost Skyrocket levels. Courtesy of Roger La Jeunesse and John Pryor.

plant foods proliferated nearby. Most likely, the occupation was seasonal, the place used by a band that also moved through the nearby Central Valley, with its lakes, rivers, and marshes, perhaps during the colder winter months.

At the very top of the marshy layers, fire reddened the black deposits, as the ground had dried out enough for the inhabitants of the platform to burn off the grass—the reddish deposits appear to originate there. The end of the first Skyrocket occupation coincided with the onset of the progressively drier and warmer conditions of the Altithermal, a time when plant foods assumed even more importance in California life.

Technically, Skyrocket belongs in the Western Pluvial Lakes Tradition. This was a place where grasses and other plants were all-important, a mirror of a human world where hunting, marked for archaeologists by projectile points, had given way to life ways dominated by harvesting the edible landscape. The numerous milling stones at Skyrocket proclaim that such artifacts, and the activities associated with them, date back to before the onset of the Altithermal, and perhaps to the time of the first settlement of California. Pryor and La Jeunesse also believe that acorns were already a supplementary food.[8]

What Is a Milling Stone?

Just what is so fascinating about a milling stone? They are nothing much to look at—just a crudely shaped rock with a flat surface smoothed by hours of grinding used by ancient people all over the world. I hated constantly lifting them into Land Rovers at the end of a hard day's digging in Central Africa, monotonous, rough artifacts that were ubiquitous wherever Stone Age hunter-gatherers had paused to collect wild grasses. Then, one day, I watched a Toka woman, a farmer's wife from the Zambezi River Valley, preparing dinner from a large pile of mongongo nuts.

She sat on the ground, a hammerstone, milling stone, and grinder close at hand. One by one, she adeptly cracked the nuts on the milling stone with a sharp blow from the hammerstone, sweeping them into a shallow basket alongside. Ten minutes later, she started milling the nuts on the same stone with a coarse grinder, just a convenient, rounded boulder from the nearby river. Scrape, scrape, scrape: The sound filled the clearing for a long time, as she added more and more nut fragments to the coarse meal under the grinder, then sweeping the increasingly fine meal into a convenient wooden tray. A long time passed before she was satisfied with the texture of the milled nuts. Later, we ate a dinner of tasty mongongo porridge with a relish of wild vegetables and guinea fowl meat on the side. Memorable and delicious: I have taken milling stones seriously ever since.

Milling stones were an ancient technology in California, dating back to Paleo-Indian times, perhaps even to the time of first settlement. Like all simple artifacts, they are implements of infinite flexibility, used for all kinds of grinding, including, one can assume, such diverse substances as red ocher coloring or other pigments, grass seeds, some forms of soft-shelled nuts and fibrous roots, and even dried mollusks and animal flesh. Milling stones are universal, and often casual, artifacts, which hardly make sense as accurate chronological markers, for, after all, there are few ways in which one can modify them or improve them. Nor does one need to, for they are astoundingly effective, if labor intensive to use. They had but serious weakness as far as early Californians were concerned. Milling stones work well with grass seeds, but are often ineffective with more oily nuts like acorns or soft tubers, which require pounding in a hollow mortar, otherwise the nuts or roots just slip sideways. I'm sure they were used to process such foods on occasion, but they were impracticable for the truly large-scale processing that became commonplace in later times (see figure 4.4). If there is one artifact that epitomizes the black hole in California's past, it is the milling stone. Inevitably, milling stones have entered the archaeological vocabulary.

The Milling Stone Horizon?
(?Paleo-Indian Times to 5000 B.C. and Later)

When I started to write this book, I soon learned that California archaeologists take milling stones very seriously indeed, ever since an excavator of the 1920s, David Banks Rogers used this most monotonous of artifacts to identify an entire "Milling Stone Horizon" in ancient California in 1929.[9] The label stuck and is with us to this day. By Milling Stone Horizon, he meant a well-defined period of the past when milling stones were *the* most characteristic artifacts to survive through the millennia, and, as such, diagnostic of the time. Find enough milling stones at a site, he and others argued, and one could reasonably place it in the Milling Stone Horizon.

In 1955, the Milling Stone Horizon was so well embedded in the academic literature that William J. Wallace, an expert on southern California

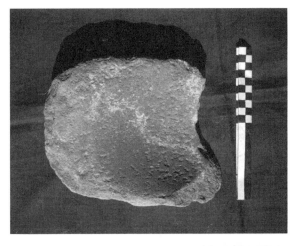

Figure 4.4. Milling stone and hand stone from Skyrocket. Courtesy of Roger La Jeunesse and John Pryor.

archaeology, was moved to write that it was "a culture marked by extensive use of milling stones and mullers [hand stones], a general lack of well made projectile points, and burials with rock cairns."[10] He dated the Horizon to between 5000 and 3000 B.C., the time when the first cities were developing rapidly between the Tigris and Euphrates Rivers in distant Mesopotamia. Wallace noted how, in contrast with later sites, when the food quest became more diversified, plant processing tools outnumbered stone projectile points on Milling Stone sites by over 27:1, with the proportions of milling tools remaining relatively constant from one area to another. He was not deafeningly enthusiastic about a society that apparently did not take projectile point manufacture seriously, when other, later cultures did. Since projectile points are the most fundamental of artifacts for classifying ancient Californian societies, Wallace implied that the Milling Stone people were, by definition, somewhat impoverished folk culturally.

Wallace's ideas caught on. Many people believe that the sheer abundance of milling stones during the Milling Stone Horizon means that hard seeds were of overwhelming importance over much of California around 6000 B.C.—to the point that this is practically archaeological dogma.

Is the Milling Stone Horizon a valid concept? As a generic label, it has some utility, but the term is a totally artificial construct, developed by archaeologists as a convenient way of telling other colleagues what they are talking about. If I describe a near-coastal site in central California to a colleague at lunch as a Milling Stone settlement, he or she knows at once that I am describing a location where I found significant numbers of flat, crude milling stones and the grinders used with them, almost no projectile points, if any, with maybe, also, some mollusks in the site if it's near the coast. My colleague also understands that I am talking about a site that dates to somewhere between 6000 and 3000 B.C., more likely at the later end of this time scale. The Skyrocket levels of 7200 B.C. extend back the chronological bracket even further, and milling stones were certainly used much earlier than this.

Simply put, the term Milling Stone Horizon disguises what must have been a considerable diversity of hunter-gatherer societies, all of which placed great emphasis on plant foods.

There is also information to be had in the sheer number of Milling Stone locations. We do know that sites with significant numbers of milling stones dating to this general time period occur widely through central and southern California, and into the Baja Peninsula. Only a handful have so far come from northern California as far north as Lake County, but this may be more a reflection of a lack of research than cultural reality. This wide distribution and a handful of radiocarbon dates are enough to establish the Milling Stone Horizon as a widespread, observable archaeological phenomenon. But can one claim that, just because stone projectile points are scarce on Milling Stone sites, hunting was less important than plant collecting and, near the coast, mollusks and sea mammals? To argue this way is to argue from the surviving tool kit alone, which is misleading at best.

Every time I examine a Milling Stone collection, I am struck at once by the sheer monotony of the toolkit—little more than large milling stones, made of a wide variety of hard rocks, and small hand stones of many kinds, used for crushing seeds. In many places, the foragers simply used natural stone cobbles, perhaps modified slightly to form pounders, scrapers, or picks, but there are few, if any, formal tools like those used by the earlier Paleo-Indians. It is as if the toolmakers harvested wild seeds, then simply cast around for convenient stone slabs and pounders and then processed their harvest near where it came from. When the job was done, they moved on, leaving their casually chosen artifacts behind them, perhaps to be used some other time, just as they did at Skyrocket. Few Milling Stone tools can be classified accurately or their use be guessed at. The most diagnostic Milling Stone artifact is a crude "scraper-plane," identical to those used by desert groups in the nineteenth century for all kinds of plant processing, most often for preparing agave and yucca plants.

Harvesting wild grasses required exquisite timing, for the ripe seeds only remain on the stalk for a few short days. And a great deal of hard work is involved, milling and milling the seed again, labor-intensive tasks that consumed much more time than had been the case in the past (see figure 4.5).

I suspect the dominance of milling stone technology may be illusory, simply because such artifacts survived the millennia. Nearly everything else more perishable in the toolkit vanished long ago, leaving us with but guesswork to fill in the gaps. But intelligent speculation is legitimate. We can guess, for example, that the men habitually carried hunting spears, even if stone points are rare in the surviving archaeological sites. They would have been dumb not to do so, simply because they might find opportunistic prey such as a solitary deer or a rabbit. No one living in a harsh, unpredictable environment is going to let a walking larder pass by. But the pursuit of this larder does not necessarily leave any durable sign archaeologically. Projectile points are, after all, used in the field, and not back at home, and may well have been manufactured away from the plant-processing areas with their milling stones—hence no trace on site millennia later.

We can also assume that the women wove fine quality baskets for carrying harvested grasses and for use during processing seed, and for storing it. The long tradition of native California basket making goes back much earlier than the last few centuries of ancient times. I suspect that baskets

Figure 4.5. Women in the San Joaquin Valley transporting wild grass seeds. From H. R. Schoolcraft, *Indian Tribes of the United States* (Philadelphia: Lippincott, 1858).

were commonplace in Paleo-Indian societies, simply because they were vital for seed harvests.

I believe that what appears in the archaeological record may be skewed and may give us a totally misleading picture of life in Milling Stone communities. Granted, the Milling Stone Horizon sites document plant-processing activity and the consumption of hard seeds, but this can only have been part of a hunter-gatherer life way that depended on a very broad diet indeed. For example, a small Milling Stone shell mound about three quarters of a mile from the Big Sur coast in southern Monterey

County was used between about 4400 and 3300 B.C. The inhabitants collected California mussels, plucking small specimens from coastal rocks. They also took cabezon (a rock fish) and lingcod, as well as deer and harbor seals. All this suggests a generalized diet, with a heavy emphasis on terrestrial foods. Some human remains from the midden yielded a bone isotopic profile characteristic of a predominantly herbivorous diet.[11]

By no means did all groups have access to a wide variety of foods. In more arid regions such as southeastern California, the agave (*Agave desertii*) was a staple of Milling Stone groups. It can be harvested in early winter and stored for long periods of time, becoming a vital food during lean months. Judging from historical Cahuilla groups in the southern desert, men and boys would travel in groups to harvest the flowers, leaves, and stalks (see chapter 13). The latter were the preferred part of the plant, gathered by the hundreds, roasted with the leaves in rock- and grass-lined pits for up to three days. Among the Cahuilla, cleaning and roasting agave was considered an important male skill. At least one ethnographic study shows how scraper planes served to extract the fiber from the plant, while milling stones and handstones crushed and ground leaves that formed a fibrous plant staple.[12]

A great deal of Milling Stone subsistence appears to have been opportunistic—trapping a lizard or small rodent, using nets and traps to take rabbits. Groups may also have driven jackrabbits and killed dozens of them at one time, while deer were relatively unimportant until late in Milling Stone times. For example, at the Duncans Point site in Sonoma County, rabbits were all-important quarry immediately after 6000 B.C. Over the next five millennia, deer became an increasingly favored quarry.

Native Californians everywhere hunted and ate the ubiquitous rabbit, often hunting them in communal drives, especially in the spring, when a surging lagomorph population threatened to strip the nearby landscape of precious edible foods. Rabbit hunts would have been even more important in drier times, when plant foods were more widely dispersed and in shorter supply. . . .

We can imagine the scene on a quiet spring late afternoon in 6000 B.C., the sun casting long shadows over a lakeshore, where hundreds of rabbits feed in the cool of the late afternoon. The elders have strung long fiber nets between large boulders, where men and women hide, clubs and spears in hand. Several bands have come together for the hunt, encircling the unsuspecting animals, then moving in slowly, waving sticks and deer hides. The rabbits circle and weave in confusion, clubbed down as they panic. Many stampede toward the waiting nets, where clubs and spears fly. Dozens of carcasses litter the ground, piled up to one side quickly as the hunters cast around them in a killing frenzy. As the sun sets, men and women quickly gut and skin the carcasses, cooking many of them in hot ashes for the feast that will follow.

Next day, when the hunters move on, taking their nets with them, all that remains is a scattering of stone tools, abandoned brush shelters, and hundreds of shattered rabbit carcasses. Within a few years, only the stone fragments remain. Every family's possessions and toolkit numbered no more than a few dozen artifacts, all of them light and portable, except hand and milling stones. And, judging from the Skyrocket platform and the widespread distribution of milling stones throughout much of the state, they simply left their grinding equipment behind and used it again the next time they returned to the same location. Indeed, why carry them when mobility was all-important and other stones could be used as needed?

Plant foods were the main staple everywhere. Just how important is clear from the few Milling Stone burials that survive, where there is no differentiation between men and women. Regardless of their gender, all known interments lie in their graves accompanied by milling stones. Later practice finds men with projectile points and bifaces, only women buried with milling equipment. In Milling Stone societies, everyone, male and female, harvested plant foods and processed them. Wild grasses were that important.[13]

Milling Stone societies flourished throughout much of California during the Altithermal, a four-thousand-year-long period of much drier and warmer conditions throughout the American West, which lasted until about 2500 B.C. The impact of this prolonged dry spell on human societies is the subject of much debate. Did, for example, the hot and arid climate mean that much of the Great Basin and the California deserts were abandoned altogether? Or did the sparse human population of the mountains, valleys, and arid lands simply adapt to changing conditions by basing themselves on the few permanent water sources around, and by moving around constantly over large territories? Judging from the experience of historic desert peoples in the Mojave and elsewhere, they simply adjusted to harsher conditions and continued to flourish in a much drier world, where winter rainfall was virtually nonexistent and most precipitation came from summer thunderstorms.

The later levels of the Skyrocket site offer some clues.[14]

Skyrocket II (5000 to 3000 B.C.)

We can see the drastic adjustments to drier, hotter conditions of the later Altithermal at Skyrocket, where the gravelly clay overlying the earliest, marshy settlement reflects a time when thunderstorms brought intense downpours. These eroded nearby dry hillsides where topsoil and vegetation were now virtually nonexistent. Clay and gravel cascaded downslope and flowed out over the ancient marshes until they vanished. The artesian springs vanished. People still came to the area to gather wild grasses, storing their milling stones and other artifacts at the site instead of carrying them over long distances. But their visits were more transitory, reflecting a life on the move that had them covering much larger distances through the year. Instead of lingering by a lush marsh, they now settled by the banks of a small creek, digging pits to obtain subsurface water. These were highly mobile folk, who used a light and simple toolkit, well suited to life on the move. At the same time, they no longer used the fine-grained greenstone so characteristic of the earlier settlement. The outcrops may have been exhausted or buried by gravel and clay. But greenstone was less important anyhow; the visitors no longer used fine projectile points to hunt game, and their major meat source was the ubiquitous rabbit.

Harsh times indeed, but they did not last for ever. By 3000 B.C., the Altithermal had effectively ended, bringing much higher rainfall and cooler temperatures. Oak savanna replaced the arid sagebrush and juniper of the previous four thousand years. This was the moment when life at Skyrocket changed profoundly as it did elsewhere in California, the moment when acorns became a staple. But there is also startling evidence of profound cultural continuity. Four thousand years after the first stone platform into the marsh was abandoned, a new platform came into use, this time built at the confluence of two streams. Now that people did not have to move around so much, they simply resumed their ancient life way in a changed world, melding new foods and carefully elaborated technologies onto hunting and gathering strategies that had worked well for thousands of years.

But, for the first time, they were also part of a more interconnected world. The clay and gravel of their settlement yielded projectile points made from obsidian that came from the Bodie Hills on the eastern side of the Sierras (see figure 4.6). And the first abalone and *olivella* shells from the Pacific coast appear silently in the same levels for the first time.

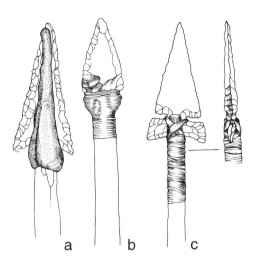

Figure 4.6. Hafting methods used on projectile points: (a) split wooden shaft, sinew wrapping covered with asphaltum; (b) split wooden shaft, sinew wrapping; (c) split wooden shaft, sinew wrapping. From *Handbook of American Indians*, Vol. 8, 68.

The Alithermal was a prolonged period of dry and warm climate, which must have inhibited natural population growth throughout the region. The Milling Stone population in 3000 B.C. cannot have exceeded a few thousand, hardly enough people to fill the landscape. But the arid conditions meant that even the most bountiful environments supported less than a person per square mile. Hunting territories were much larger than in earlier times, mobility the rule of the day. Even in these early millennia, though, there were some constraints apart from neighbors—the distance people could walk and return in a day, the distribution of food and water supplies, and the limitations of local topography. In later times, many tribes lived in territories defined by watersheds or valleys. The same must have been generally true in earlier millennia, even with many fewer people around. You lived where the food was, or where it was within easy distance, anchored, above all, to reliable water supplies or convenient sources of plant foods.

The secrets to survival in early California were very simple: First, exploit as many different ecological zones as you can and keep moving around within your foraging territory. Second, schedule your movements through the landscape with exquisite care, so that you are in the right place at the right moment. To do this, you must know your environment intimately, its animals, plants, and water supplies, especially when you rely on grasses, nuts, and other seasonal plants for much of your food supply. Finally, survival depended on not just one food source, but many, even with relatively few mouths to feed, and even when big-game was there to be taken. There was never a time in early California when as diversified a diet as possible was not the most logical strategy for survival. This is why there was such enduring continuity from before 11,000 to about 3000 B.C., or slightly thereafter.

Then, between 3000 and 2000 B.C., something changed. Perhaps populations in some areas rose to a critical point where many groups experienced regular food shortages, forcing major changes in the ways people lived. Or maybe the end of the Altithermal with its cooler and wetter weather stimulated new directions in California society. Whatever the cause, the changes at Skyrocket in 3000 B.C. signal the appearance of new ideas and a growing web of interconnectedness we'll meet in Part III. But before continuing the mainland story, we must paddle offshore, to chronicle important changes in island life that took hold in southern California after 6500 B.C.

The Dolphin Hunters

(c. 6500 to c. 2500 B.C.)

W E RETURN TO THE OFFSHORE ISLANDS, TO TELL another story of remarkable cultural continuity.

People first crossed to the northern Channel Islands at a time of much lower sea levels, when the mainland was a mere six miles from the island at Point Hueneme. These were transitory, perhaps seasonal visitors, small groups of men and women who crossed to Santarosae as if it were an island in a huge lake—just as others on the mainland ventured out to islands in freshwater lakes. From the beginning, the islands were an extension of mainland hunting territories, just as the coastline was linked closely to the interior.

Judging from the size and simplicity of their tiny sites, the visitors never stayed long on an island whose main attractions were shellfish, some kelp fish, and sea mammals. Such staples as grasses and other edible plants were in short supply when compared with the nearby mainland. They probably made the crossing in tule reed boats, adequate enough watercraft for a six-mile passage.

But then their world changed. Sea levels rose rapidly. Santarosae became three islands, separated by windy defiles. By about 5000 B.C., shorelines along the southern California coast stabilized at near-modern heights. Now the northern Channel Islands were a minimum of twelve miles from the nearest mainland, further isolated by a belt of much stronger westerly winds funneled down from Point Conception along the north coasts of the islands, then between Anacapa Island and Point Mugu.

Inevitably, the northern islands became more isolated from the mainland world. The rising sea levels made little difference to the southern Channel Islands, where the distances were already much larger. But it was a different matter in the north, where the channel between Anacapa Island and the mainland widened century by century. Voyaging by tule must have become more hazardous as shore lines receded.

Then, in about 6500 B.C., before shorelines stabilized at fully modern heights, the first signs of more permanent island settlement appear, not on Santa Cruz Island or one of the other northern landmasses, but on one of the remotest—San Clemente Island, nearly sixty miles off the southern California coast. The nearest land is the southwestern tip of Santa Catalina Island, some twenty-five miles away.

San Clemente is one of those places that lots of people have seen, but few have visited. The island hovers on the horizon, visible from the mainland on exceptionally clear days. From a distance, it looks like a table mountain, with a bold and conspicuous northeastern coast and a more gentle southwestern shore. The federal government has owned San Clemente since 1848; it has been a military installation for years. Fortunately for archaeology, the navy guards its property carefully. Almost no civilians visit the island, which means that San Clemente's archaeological sites are virtually undisturbed by development or illegal looting.

Archaeologist Mark Raab has worked on San Clemente Island for many years. He has located numerous ancient settlements there, including a large village with at least eighteen semisubterranean dwellings dating to about 3000 B.C. But his most important discovery is at Eel Point on the southwestern shore of the island. Here he has unearthed layers of human occupation spanning almost nine thousand years.[1]

Eel Point (The First Settlement: 6558 to 5958 B.C.)

Eel Point is a spectacular site—the eroded remnant of a coastal terrace, capped with no less than sixteen feet of shell-bearing midden, which contains well-stratified layers of human occupation spanning nearly nine thousand years. Such long sequences of human activity are rare anywhere in California. Here, the midden deposits cover nearly five acres, most of them accumulated since 1500 B.C.

Archaeologists have worked on and off at Eel Point for some time, but it is only recently that we have been able to date the site with certainty.

When archaeologist R. A. Salls excavated into the Eel Point midden during the 1980s, he identified three well-defined areas of occupation within the huge mound. Salls obtained a few radiocarbon dates for the earliest settlement that lay between 8000 and 7000 B.C., with extensive later occupation between about 2250 B.C. and A.D. 900 (see figure 5.1).

The Salls excavations gave only a general impression of Eel Point chronology, and tantalizing hints of very early settlement. In the early 1990s, Mark Raab reinvestigated the lowermost levels specifically to date them more accurately, using more accurate accelerator mass spectrometry (AMS) radiocarbon dating (see box 1.2 in chapter 1). He soon obtained a new suite of more accurate radiocarbon dates, which placed the earliest occupation of all to between about 6558 and 5958 B.C., somewhat later than Salls's readings, but still impressively early. Even more important, Raab's digging revealed a well-established early maritime community, a camp that was significantly larger and more intensively used than any of the early sites on San Miguel Island and elsewhere in the northern islands (see box 5.1).

Figure 5.1. Eel Point site, San Clemente Island. Courtesy of Mark Raab.

BOX 5.1 Ethnographic Analogy

In studying the Eel Point dolphin, Judy Porcasi made use of modern-day observations of shallow water dolphin hunting in Polynesia and elsewhere. She drew on archaeology as well. For instance, she noted that prehistoric Japanese fisherfolk from the Hokkaido region of northern Japan were hunting dolphins in large numbers at the same time as the Eel Point and other Channel Island groups were preying on the same animals. She also studied accounts of the "grind," a traditional pilot whale hunt in the Faroe Islands, where a fleet of boats used shouts and noise under water to drive their prey into the shallows. But can Porcasi legitimately use the grind and modern-day Polynesian dolphin hunts to interpret the Eel Point bones? In so doing, she used a common tool in the archaeologist's workshop known as ethnographic analogy—comparisons with living societies to interpret the material remains found in an archaeological site.

Ethnographic analogy is a much debated topic among archaeologists. Of course, no one suggests that you can make direct connections between living Inuit hunters from northern Canada and late Ice Age hunters in Europe, or argue that they had similar societies because they lived in the same kinds of cold environments. Such comparisons are both unrealistic and too simple. Having said that, analogies between the practices of living societies and ancient ones can be made if carefully controlled and highly specific. For example, no one seriously questions that the same simple methods to harvest wild grasses or process acorns used in recent times were not in use much earlier. Carefully thought out comparisons between, say, mortars found in a Sierra foothills site and examples from historic times in the same region are fine—provided, of course, that you carefully spell out the circumstances of the analogy. Although the ethnographic record of native California life is surprisingly complete, much more so than is the case for many other parts of the North America, it still has many gaps. This record has provided a rich fountain of information for establishing the uses of different kinds of stone tools, on hunting and gathering

(Continued)

BOX 5.1 Continued

methods, and on such practices as salmon fishing or deer hunting. Simple ethnographic analogies of this kind occur frequently in these pages and have legitimate credibility.

We tread on thinner ice when working with larger problems, such as Porcasi did with inshore dolphin hunting. She gave legitimacy to her analogy by studying dolphin hunting in a wide range of societies, by consulting fisheries biologists and other experts, and by asking specific questions, like, for example, "How can you hunt dolphin close inshore?" Porcasi's research was an exercise in controlled analogy, which is *not* a direct comparison, but a possible explanation for material remains found in an archaeological site. As such, it has great credibility.

Things become even trickier when you attempt interpretations of rituals, religious beliefs, and other intangibles of ancient life. The interpretation of rock paintings and engravings is a classic example. One school of thought uses ethnographic records of shamanism as well as studies of altered states of consciousness to explain the significance of the art. Other archaeologists disagree violently and argue for many motives behind the same art. There's more on this debate in chapter 9.

Properly used, ethnographic analogy plays a significant role in California archaeology, as it does at Eel Point. But one should never assume that native societies at European contact necessarily reflect much earlier cultures for one good reason. Every human society, however egalitarian, and however simple, changed constantly over the generations and centuries. Neither the past nor the present were or are static.

If you had visited Eel Point in about 6250 B.C., you would not have recognized the place. For a start, there was no midden. The first settlers built a camp in a sheltered natural depression in the lee of a rocky outcrop, which gave them protection from the prevailing winds. The settlement was about a hundred feet across, a jumble of windbreaks, pits, hearths, work areas, and what archaeologist Mark Raab calls "toss zones," a polite term for garbage heaps.

People returned to the same camp site on and off for between three hundred and five hundred years. Then Eel Point was abandoned, to be reoccupied much later, around 4400 B.C.

What attracted people to the Eel Point location? Just like early coastal folk on the northern Channel Islands and the mainland, they subsisted off sea mammals and mollusks, both of which abounded nearby. They also took sheephead, which fed off sea urchins and shellfish close inshore and were readily taken in shallow water with nets, spears, or simple bone gorges on fiber fishing lines.[2] But fishing was of relatively minor importance, as it was elsewhere along the coast at the time. These people were hunters and shellfish collectors more than fisherfolk, practicing a way of life that had taken hold along the coast since Paleo-Indian times, flourishing ever since with relatively little change. The most striking feature of daily life was a recurring opportunism, which had hunters returning to the same locations again and again, to places where predictable food supplies could be found.

Meat was plentiful near Eel Point. All the hunters had to do was to club seals or sea lions in their rookeries. Females and pups comprise over 70 percent of the Eel Point sea mammal remains, as if the hunters were preying on breeding colonies on land. Such hunting required no more than simple wooden clubs, just as it did at Duncans Point near Bodega Bay far to the north. The people regularly took animals weighing between 150 and 450 or more pounds, each a substantial meat package obtained with minimal effort. This was wasteful hunting, which eventually decimated the breeding areas and caused people everywhere to pay closer attention to fishing and to sea mammal hunting from canoes.

But the most startling discovery at Eel Point was dozens of dolphin bones.

Large, fast-swimming, and seemingly deep-water animals, dolphin appear to be an unlikely prey for island people with simple technology. Isn't catching a dolphin a formidable task, requiring seaworthy canoes and much more elaborate fishing gear than just fiber nets and spears? Not if the Eel Point people knew that their settlement lay at a unusual location, where a deep submarine canyon came right up to the shore—far closer than today with its higher sea levels. Dolphin schools could swim and feed close inshore, while still remaining in deep water.[3]

The dolphin bones offer an apparent contradiction. Here are hunter-gatherers subsisting off mollusks and sea mammals, yet taking deep-water animals. To take them offshore would have required very seaworthy watercraft. Even close to shore, the hunters would need fast, maneuverable canoes to chase their quarry.

The archaeologists puzzled over this conundrum, until bone expert Judith Porcasi embarked on a comprehensive study of modern-day, low-tech dolphin hunting. She studied not only the bones from Eel Point and other sites, but also more contemporary accounts of dolphin hunting. To her surprise, she found that even today Pacific Islanders take dolphins close inshore. They do so by exploiting the dolphin's vulnerability to disorienting underwater sounds (see box 5.1).

We cannot prove it, for all we have to go on are the material remains of ancient hunts, but the sheer number of dolphin bones in the lower levels of Eel Point can only be attributed to some form of highly effective, close inshore hunting somewhat similar to that practiced in Polynesia today.

Let's use such accounts to imagine a dolphin hunt at Eel Point. A large school swims into sight close offshore on a calm summer's morning. A watching boy calls out. The village comes alive as the fishermen run down to their canoes and launch them quickly into the bay. They paddle a short distance offshore quickly and silently, watching the unsuspecting school as it feeds in the deep, blue water close to the beach. Piles of large cobbles lie in the bottoms of the canoes.

The boats fan out. Quiet hand signals position the canoes around the unsuspecting beasts. When everyone is in position, the leader of the hunt gives a signal. The crewmen grab pairs of cobbles and knock them together underwater, causing a loud cacophony below the surface. Instantly, the school is thrown into chaos, disoriented by the unfamiliar sound. The dolphin swim to and fro until their leader steers them away from the noise into the narrow bay and the shallows. The canoes follow them inshore, still beating the cobbles, spearmen at the ready.

As the confused animals flounder in the shallows, men, women, and children rush into the water and literally fling the helpless dolphin ashore. They sometimes catch the beasts by holding them softly by the mouth and guiding them ashore or close to canoes, where waiting spears make quick work of them—or the helpless animals are swung alive into the bottom of the boat.

A few hours later, the beach reeks with the stink of drying flesh, as the women hand long strips of fresh dolphin to dry in the sun and wind.

There is an astounding consistency about the accounts of dolphin fishing in shallow water throughout the Pacific. I am certain that the same basic methods worked at Eel Point.

All that was required to hunt dolphin was close observation of their habits and vulnerabilities, some canoes, perhaps fiber nets into which the school might be driven, and no elaborate technology whatsoever.

Until recently, excavators paid little attention to dolphin bones, despite their being easily recognizable, on account of their distinctive skull bones, which have a sandpaper-like structure. But they have turned up at sites on other islands, on the southern coasts of Catalina and Santa Cruz, where submarine canyons come close to shore. At Punta Arena on the southern shore of Santa Cruz Island, for example, a low spit of land once joined what is now off-lying Gull Island to the coast, forming a strategic bay into which dolphin could be driven with ease (see figure 5.2).

Figure 5.2. A place for dolphin hunting. Punta Arena on the southern coast of Santa Cruz Island. In Early and Middle Holocene times, a spit of land joined the point to now-off-lying Gull Island (left), creating an ideal inlet for landing dolphin, which teemed in the nearby submarine canyon.

Dolphin hunting began at Eel Point during the first occupation and continued for thousands of years, just as long as the deep canyons were close enough to shore. Dolphins were serious prey, which had the potential to provide a very stable food source, far more so than sea mammals, which only come to their rookeries at breeding season. No question, they were an important staple for people living in a botanically impoverished environment. What may have begun as opportunistic quarry, perhaps an occasional catch, became a way of supporting much larger, more permanent communities.

For more than six thousand years, dolphin hunting gave remote island communities a relatively predictable food source at a time when sea mammal rookeries were depleted by hunting and mollusk beds suffered from increasingly intense exploitation. Then, about 2000 B.C., the numbers of dolphin bones fall sharply. By now, sea levels had risen to the point where the subterranean canyons were further offshore, dolphin schools were less accessible, and the simple hunting methods of earlier periods no longer worked. This happened at a time when shell fishhooks came into use and fishing assumed overwhelming importance in island life. After thousands of years of exploitation, sea mammal rookeries were depleted and mollusk populations were decimated at the same time, coastal populations were rising steadily. Rising sea levels were putting a stop to once highly productive dolphin fisheries. The emerging maritime societies of the coast had depleted the easier foods, leaving only the potential of much more intensive fishing for the future.

But How Did They Get There?

Dolphins and near-shore submarine canyons may have been a key to Eel Point and other early settlements. The dolphin remained a favorite prey for millennia. The inhabitants of Eel Point, Little Harbor, and other such locations could not have hunted them successfully without tough watercraft, capable of carrying heavy loads. Nor could they have landed the huge sunfish, which can weigh up to nine hundred pounds. Sunfish bones also occur at Eel Point.[4] All of which brings us to the question of questions. How did the Eel Point people and their contemporaries reach San Clemente Island in the first place? Don't forget—this was a nonstop journey of nearly sixty miles from the mainland and about twenty-five often-turbulent open water miles from the nearest landmass—Catalina Island. How indeed? (box 5.2)

BOX 5.2 Navigating across Open Water

The crew kneel on grass pads, their double-ended paddles moving effortlessly from side to side. Their pace never varies, a steady rhythm from stroke to stroke, the work done by the shoulders. The planked canoe glides effortlessly through the calm water, rising and falling gently in the ever-present ground swell. As they paddle, the crewmen sing the same song again and again in an effortless chant: "You have the power to reach the other side, so that you may get where you want to go. . . ."

How did ancient canoe skippers navigate safely across the open waters off the Pacific Coast in canoes with low sides and only a limited ability to travel against even a light wind? Unlike modern sailboat sailors, a canoe captain lived in intimate association with the ocean every day of his life. Almost certainly, navigation and seamanship skills passed from one generation to the next, for, obviously, the inheritance of a canoe involved the possession not only of a valuable artifact, but of arcane skills acquired by hard experience.

Most mainland-to-island navigation was a matter of line-of-sight passage making, using conspicuous peaks and other landmarks. For example, the lowest point of land on Santa Cruz Island lies behind what is now Prisoners Harbor, a major canoe village in later times. And Two Harbors at the western end of Catalina Island can be spotted from miles away, simply by steering for the low ridge between the two bays. Except in foggy conditions, and even then visibility is rarely less than a quarter mile, navigation is straightforward. Any canoe skipper worth his salt would need only a momentary break in the gloom to fix his position along an island or mainland coast. And he would know what approximate course to steer by maintaining a position relative to conspicuous landmarks astern until his destination came in sight or he could use swell patterns or other signs of nearby land to guide him inshore.

The art of navigation off southern California involved predicting the weather and planning one's passage for the calm hours of the day. Canoe paddlers thrive in flat calm weather, when they can

(Continued)

BOX 5.2 Continued

establish a steady rhythm, a cadence maintained with chant and song. The skipper would watch the weather pattern for several days, then, if conditions were settled, leave the island or mainland at the first break of dawn. In this way, he would maximize the calm hours. Within three hours or so of fast paddling, he would be close to his destination.

You can be sure that every skipper learned the telltale signs of weather close to land and offshore. For instance, they would have watched the mountain peaks of the Channel Islands for the streams of white clouds, which warn of strong winds twenty miles offshore. They would be familiar with the razor-sharp visibility and utterly calm seas of Santa Ana conditions of fall, when no one ventures offshore, lest they be caught in a sixty-mph northeast wind. And they would know the signs of impending southeasterly storms—the gray clouds hovering over the ocean, the sloppy waves from the same direction that precede rain and wind, then the sudden swing to a northwesterly gale as the rain passed. Once you knew the general weather patterns of winter and summer, of the wet and dry seasons, you knew when to expect calm weather for long passages.

Even then, there were unexpected hazards, sometimes detectable only once one was at sea. High swells from distant storms far offshore in the Pacific, or from Mexican tropical disturbances can arrive without warning. Even a slight breeze can pile up steep wind waves, which are potentially more hazardous for a low-lying canoe. And beware the skipper who is caught in a cross sea—wind waves from one direction, swells from another.

Everything depended on the skipper's experience and instincts—his ability to gauge the nearness of land from subtle cross swells, from the behavior of land and sea birds, from patches of kelp, and so on. The art of safe passage making was never to take risks and never to be caught out in a rising wind and steep seas. In such conditions, a canoe is a potential death trap, even in the hands of an expert. All the skipper could do was to head into the waves, or at an angle to them, using the paddlers to maintain a constant direction and a stationary canoe. A heavily laden canoe blown sideways to the waves was in grave danger. A capsize was almost inevitable, and usually fatal. Sometimes an expert crew could run before a moderate sea and swell, paddling fast, maintaining a stern-to course, perhaps with some crew members sitting on the edges of the boat to add extra stability, but this was also hazardous. Canoe voyaging was a perilous venture, a matter of conservative judgment and maximal use of the long calms that sink over southern California's benign seas. But we can be sure that hundreds, if not thousands, of people perished over the millennia when caught out on open water.

I would risk a guess that a defining moment came some time before sea levels stabilized at today's heights, an event conventionally dated to about 5000 B.C. Somewhere around this date, I suspect that new canoe designs replaced seagoing tules. Whatever their design, the canoe skippers who first crossed twenty miles or more of the Pacific must have possessed watercraft capable of open water voyages when heavy, and of returning safely not just once, but again and again. They needed canoes with three qualities: seaworthiness, good load-carrying capacity, and an ability at fast passage making.[5]

In historic times, native Californians used three main types of simple watercraft, most of them confined to inland lakes and rivers, sheltered estuaries, or the calm waters inside the near-ubiquitous kelp beds close offshore—dugout canoes, tule reed craft, and planked vessels. According to nineteenth-century informants, people fished in dugouts close to shore, but there were never large canoes, like the large redwood craft of extreme northwestern California, described in chapter 10.

Tules are buoyant enough when dry, but are hard to paddle in any sea or wind, and totally unsuitable for long offshore passages (see box 3.2 in chapter 3). Few people have experience with seagoing reed vessels. The ancient Egyptians used papyrus boats on the calm waters of the Nile; so did the Mesopotamians on the Tigris and Euphrates, but neither of them ventured far from land. There are always the wishful thinkers who envisage bold ocean voyages to America by ancient Egyptians in fleets of reed boats, but such thoughts strain credibility.

Norwegian explorer Thor Heyerdahl tried to cross the Atlantic in a so-called replica of an Egyptian papyrus reed boat, the *Ra*, in the late 1960s.

He built his first *Ra* using African methods and sank two-thirds of the way across the Atlantic when the fairly loosely packed reeds became waterlogged. Undeterred, Heyerdahl turned to Aymara Indians from Lake Titicaca, who produced a tightly packed reed hull made with their traditional methods. This began to sink rapidly when the boat was originally overloaded, but became more buoyant when lightened. A much waterlogged *Ra II* reached Barbados—just. Heyerdahl remarked that the Aymara built a much more sophisticated reed boat, but also observed that he should have covered the hull with pitch to waterproof the papyrus better, as the ancient Egyptians did with their reed vessels. California's tules were unsophisticated craft compared with those of Lake Titicaca. If the *Ra* experience is any indication, then even larger California tules cannot have been effective sea-going boats.

We are left with only one alternative—the planked canoe.

Planked Canoes

Planked canoes like the Chumash *tomol* and the Gabrielieño *tiat* have a distinguished history in southern California, and especially in the Santa Barbara Channel. In much later times, the Chumash fisherfolk of the region were famous for their *tomols*, planked craft that excited the admiration of early Spanish explorers with their speed and maneuverability. The Chumash themselves called the canoe "The House of the Sea," a tribute to its remarkable seaworthiness.

We know from archaeological excavations on the islands and mainland that these distinctive watercraft were in use in the Santa Barbara Channel by as early as A.D. 650. Fragments of planks, asphalt plugs from threaded holes, and canoe builder's drills document these early *tomols* (for *tomol* construction, see box 14.2 in chapter 14). Unfortunately, we have no archaeological clues as to the appearance of the first *tiat*. On the basis of these finds, archaeologists like Jeanne Arnold and Lynn Gamble believe that planked craft appeared around A.D. 650.[6] But I suspect that they may be wrong (see figure 5.3).

While Arnold and Gamble may indeed be correct that the *tomol* in all its elaboration (and the *tiat*) appeared within the past 1,500 years, I am convinced that some form of planked canoe plied southern California waters

Figure 5.3. The *Helek*, a replica of a Chumash *tomol*, sets sail across the Santa Barbara Channel. Courtesy of Santa Barbara Museum of Natural History.

much earlier, from the time, perhaps as early as 7000 B.C., when rising sea levels made offshore travel in a tule reed craft impracticable, even dangerous. Yes, I am guessing, but sheer commonsense and practical seamanship dictate far more seaworthy craft for longer passage making. Planked canoes offer important advantages over tules. Their higher sides make them more seaworthy in rough water. They can carry far heavier loads, and can take infinitely more abuse. Nor do they become waterlogged. Furthermore, one can paddle them much faster and maintain a higher cruising speed over longer distances. It is entirely possible that the first planked canoes appeared in the south, for Catalina Island with its steatite (soapstone) outcrops had more to offer than just mollusks and sea mammals.

Experiments with modern *tomol* replicas show that speeds of eight miles an hour are possible in calm water. Such an average speed would bring even a simpler planked vessel across from, say, the Santa Barbara area of the mainland to Santa Cruz Island just over twenty miles offshore in three hours or so, and allow one to cross from Catalina Island to San Clemente Island in the same time. Three-hour periods of calm weather are commonplace in southern California waters and easy to forecast if one knows local conditions. These calm "windows" were the secret to successful *tomol* passage making. The same passage-making rules must have applied in earlier times.[7]

(However, we should note that oral traditions and historic accounts stress that most crossings were from Point Hueneme to Anacapa Island, with only short stretches of open water to navigate thereafter.)

Here's a theoretical scenario: The first mainland settlers arrived already familiar with dugouts and tules of different sizes. They were aware that dugouts are unsafe in any rough water, whereas the more buoyant tule fared better. At first, they used five-bundled or even larger tules in an attempt to travel further offshore. Even coated with bitumen, and even with shorter distances to travel to the islands at a time of lower sea level, the boats would have been sluggish to paddle and soon became waterlogged.

As sea levels rose and the islands became more inaccessible, canoe builders turned from tules to driftwood, splitting straight-grained logs into planks, woodworking techniques used on land every day. The five-bundled tule was the prototype. The skippers fashioned a simple planked equivalent, forming the outside surface of a split tree trunk as the keel, fashioning the sides with planks split from the trunk with stone or shell wedges. Alternatively, they may have patched together the sides from lengths of driftwood. They caulked the sides with local bitumen and stitched the planks together with the same milkwood fibers used in later times.

While the woodworking skills required were widely used in communities everywhere, the actual canoe-building expertise was another matter, instincts and visualization skills that were far more important than the technology behind them. They came from a mind set passed down from generation to generation, a combination of unhesitating ability at handling simple tools, and, even more important, the art of visualizing a canoe's shape in one's mind without any wood in front of one. The men who built planked canoes, however simple, were the rocket scientists of their time. Without question, they were honored individuals from the day the first planked canoe ventured out on the Pacific, men respected for their skills, the remote predecessors of the elite Brotherhood of the Canoe that lay at the center of Chumash society in later times. The mere presence of such honored people as canoe owners must have caused at least minor ripples of social change.

While an early planked canoe may be a figment of my lively imagination, I believe that the Chumash *tomol* and Gabrielieño *tiat* did not suddenly appear 1,300 years ago. The sophisticated *tiat* and *tomol* were born of thousands of years of simple boat building and inconspicuous passage making—from hard won experience over many centuries of seafaring (see figure 5.4).

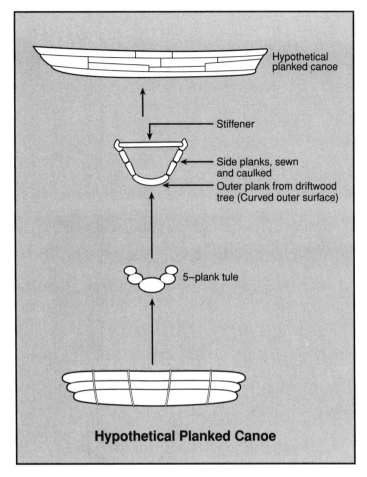

Figure 5.4. The development of a planked canoe from a prototype five-bundle tule (bottom) to a simple planked form (top).

If I am correct, as rising sea levels brought longer distances and more hazardous crossings, planked canoes provided the solution to open water passage. For the first time, canoe skippers could reach the remoter southern Channel Islands and cross the Santa Barbara Channel with relative ease.

Eel Point itself has yielded no canoe planks, asphalt plugs, or other parts of planked canoes. But, interestingly, considerable numbers of stone woodworking tools come from the lower levels of the midden—drills, reamers, wedges, planes, and abraders, all tools that are simple and effective parts of a woodworking technology that relied heavily on splitting and smoothing. Stone wedges are all-important for splitting. One such wedge at Eel Point bears polished high points on both faces. The opposite side is battered from the blows used to drive it into a soft but abrasive material, almost certainly wood. There are also small pieces of a black substance from the same deposits, so far unidentified, which might be imported bitumen, not found on the island (see figures 5.5 and 5.6).[8]

With simple hammers and stone wedges, the Eel Point people could easily have split planks from redwood logs that washed up as driftwood. Large

Figure 5.5. Stone artifacts from the lower levels of the Eel Point site. (a) drills, (b) scraper-planes. Courtesy of Jim Cassidy.

Figure 5.6. Bone implement from the lower levels of the Eel Point site, bearing a black substance, perhaps bitumen. Courtesy of Jim Cassidy.

flakes, sometimes trimmed to a rectangular shape, served as planes. Heavy wear appears on both sides of the longer edges, exactly the kind of abrasion that would result from smoothing timber. A piece of imported sandstone from the mainland served as an abrader. Archaeologist Jim Cassidy, who has studied the artifacts, has replicated the wear patterns on drills and reamers with controlled experiments, showing how a woodworker would begin a hole by rotating the drill by hand. Then he would use a reamer to smooth and enlarge the opening, sometimes using sand as an abrasive. According to Cassidy, these artifacts look remarkably similar to those used by Chumash canoe builders many centuries later.

But perhaps the most compelling argument of all for planked canoes comes from the mere presence of an archaeological site at Eel Point on San Clemente as early as 6500 B.C. No one in his or her sane mind would have taken even a large tule that far offshore.

New Island Communities (c. 4500 to 1500 B.C.)

For five hundred years or so, people visited Eel Point for short periods of time. Then they stopped coming, for reasons that are unclear. Perhaps San Clemente was even uninhabited for some time. In about 4400 B.C., a new community flourished on the ancient midden, with occupation intensifying between about 3800 and 1400 B.C.

The newcomers still took dolphin, mollusks, and sea mammals, but fishing gradually assumed greater importance, as sea levels continued rising. The same simple maritime culture persisted virtually unchanged, based on the same staples, and on the same annual routines. The population of San Clemente was never large, but it was greater than in earlier millennia, with people living in more substantial, even permanent settlements. Eel Point was one such location. Mark Raab excavated another such community, the Nursery site (also known as SCL 1–1215), where he located no less than eighteen house pits. He excavated four of them, dating to around 2800 B.C., the remains of dome-shaped houses with rafters made from stranded whale bones. The dwellings lie close to a large midden, clear evidence of a lengthy occupation and reasonably large village population. And with greater permanence of settlement must have come changes in society itself, and a greater level of interaction with the mainland and communities on other islands (see figure 5.7).[9]

Figure 5.7. An excavated dwelling from the Nursery site, San Clemente Island. Courtesy of Mark Raab.

By 3000 B.C., there were longer-term settlements on other islands as well, notably at Little Harbor on the southwestern shore of Catalina. Today, Little Harbor is a small boat sailor's favorite, for it offers excellent anchorage in summer weather. Just like Eel Point, the site, overlooking a bowl-shaped bay, lies at the head of a submarine canyon, which brings deep-water fish like tuna very close to shore—and the dolphins and other sea mammals that feed on them.[10]

Clem Meighan of UCLA, a veteran archaeologist, excavated at Little Harbor between 1953 and 1955, but he was unable to obtain a satisfactory radiocarbon chronology for the large middens there. Mark Raab has re-excavated the site, identified five possible phases of ancient occupation, and dated the second one to about 3328 B.C., contemporary with the later Eel Point settlement.

We still do not know when Little Harbor was first occupied, but, again, sea mammals taken from shore were very important, many of them slain with the heavy stone projectile points found in the middens.

Some canoes ventured even further afield in search of rock fish and abalone, even as far offshore as remote and windy eight-mile-long San Nicolas Island, fifty-four miles west of Point Hueneme on the mainland. Eight sites dating to between 3450 B.C. and about 950 B.C. document brief visits, perhaps for fishing and abalone collecting.

By this time, there were more people living on the southern islands, more contacts with the mainland, and larger, more permanent settlements. No one could ever have lived in complete isolation on the southern islands; food supplies were far from diverse, water often in short supply. Every band must have maintained social and economic ties with communities on the mainland, but whether the major settlements were offshore or there is unknown. This was why seaworthy canoes were of such vital importance. They were the lifelines that linked relatives, seasonal camps, and larger settlements, the vehicles that carried people, food, and more exotic items far offshore and in the opposite direction. And the individuals who built, owned, or skippered these canoes assumed an ever-greater importance in a slowly changing world.

Now, for the first time, we find evidence of some form of trading activity, of interconnectedness, in the form of rare, rectangular *olivella* shell beads, made from an uncommon purple shell. Such beads occur over an enormous area of southern California—on the Orange County mainland

and far inland, even into the Great Basin, as well as in southern Santa Barbara County. Most important of all, they come from the southern Channel Islands, from Little Harbor on Catalina, from the Nursery site on San Clemente, and on San Nicolas, all from sites in the 3800 B.C. range. Such beads do not occur on the northern Channel Islands. This handful of exotic finds links even remote islands to a developing web of interconnectedness that was to expand greatly in later centuries (see figure 5.8a and b).

■ ■ ■

Seven thousand years had passed. The southern islands were familiar territory to mainland communities, linked to them by ancient social ties and continual, if irregular canoe traffic across open water. Island populations were rising, but their way of life remained largely the same, except to reflect the realities of overexploitation of sea lions and intensive culling of mollusk beds. Life was exactly as it had been seven millennia before—an annual round of opportunistic fishing, mollusk collecting, and sea mammal hunting with little variation from year to year, century to century, millennium to millennium. Human technology was of the simplest, with few imperatives to develop more elaborate tools or weapons. Such changes that did take hold represented miniscule shifts in hunting or gathering driven by rising or falling water temperatures or shifts in game or mollusk populations.

I believe that some simple form of planked canoe lay at the very core of early island existence—the lifeline to the mainland, a platform for inshore dolphin hunting, and, above all, an agent not only for survival but for social change. By 3000 B.C., we can see the first signs of such change in the form of exchange of seemingly prestigious shell beads. Such exchange would not have been possible without canoes and their owners, the individuals who controlled the ebb and flow of traffic across open water, between mainland and islands. The canoe and ocean travel had become part of the ancient California world thousands of years before the Chumash perfected "The House of the Sea" and surrounded it with all the ritual and mystique of the Brotherhood of the Canoe.

The Channel Islands were never a world apart, just as the mainland coast was never isolated from the interior with its deserts, pluvial lakes, and mountains. Better than anyone else, canoe skippers had some knowledge of

Figure 5.8. (a) Excavations on a shell midden on San Nicolas Island. (b) All the deposit is carefully screened for such small artifacts as shell beads and for seeds and other food remains. Courtesy of Statistical Research, Inc.

the world on the mainland, where important changes were taking hold, linking community to community as never before. Apparently, there were periodic food shortages, too, as the number of people exceeded the ability of the environment to feed them in some places.

Then, between 3000 and 1500 B.C., all these still little known circumstances came together, in one of the major changes of California's history.

PART III

The Web of Interconnectedness

(C. 2500 to 1500 B.C.)

In the beginning there was no sun, no moon,
no stars. All was dark, and everywhere there
was only water. A raft came floating on the
water. It came from the north, and in it were
two persons—Turtle and Pehe-ipe. . . . Then
from the sky a rope of feathers, called *pokelma*,
was let down, and down it came Earth-Initiate.
When he reached the end of the rope, he tied it
to the bow of the raft and stepped in. His face
was covered and was never seen, but his body
shone like the sun. . . .

—A MAIDU CREATION LEGEND[1]

A Changing World

(c. 2500 to 1500 B.C.)

THE NEWLY RISEN SUN SLANTS LONG, GOLDEN BEAMS through the dense oak leaves, leaving patches of red and orange on the dusty soil. A few men flit from tree to tree through the shadows, bow and arrows in hand, stalking the deer they had heard feeding by night. Closer to camp, families gather below the oaks, empty carrying baskets stacked nearby. The young men climb high into the branches, shaking the boughs gently. A shower of acorns cascades downward, showering their wives and the elders with ripe acorns. Everyone laughs, as they gather the plump, ripe acorns into the waiting baskets, combing the ground carefully, quickly discarding cracked or rotten nuts, keeping only those that will store well. As the men move to another tree, the women carry the laden baskets back to the nearby camp and stack the harvest carefully on dry skins. Hour after hour, the backbreaking work of collecting and carrying goes on, for time is short and acorns will prevent hunger in the winter months ahead.

The labor has hardly begun, for it is a long way back to base camp from the temporary settlement near the oaks. As soon as much of the harvest is gathered, women and girls start work with hammer stones, shelling the acorns, then pounding the nuts with pestles and mortars and turning them into meal, thereby reducing the weight of the loads to be carried away.

Meanwhile, the men stalk and hunt as many deer as they can, for this is a time of year when the shy animals are close at hand and easier to hunt than they are in the height of summer or during the colder months.

We see the change at Skyrocket in the Sierra Nevada foothills, where the carbonized remains of acorns and the mortars used for pounding them suddenly appear in about 2500 B.C. At about the same time, we can track significant changes on the southern California coast, where fishing assumes ever greater importance. Acorns and sea-mammal hunting and mollusks are no longer as important as they once were. Now the first large shell mounds appear on the marshy shores of San Francisco Bay and in the Sacramento Delta. Suddenly, within that time frame around 2500 B.C., ancient California societies altered course quite independently of one another in a subtle paroxysm of economic, political, and social changes. These changes took hold rapidly and laid the foundations for the events of the next four thousand years. The ancient societies took up serious acorn processing, tended to live in the same places for longer periods of time, and maintained much closer trading ties with their neighbors.

The droughts of the Altithermal were remote history by 2500 B.C. California's climate now closely resembled today's weather menu—the same unpredictable rainfall and somewhat cooler temperatures than those of the preceding four thousand years. One would have thought this would have brought bounty to people who had lived for thousands of years in a harsh, much drier world than today. But there's now a veritable explosion in the number of archaeological sites, especially in regions like the Bay Area, Sacramento Delta, and favored coastal locations in the south. The Californians of the Altithermal adapted so successfully to much drier conditions that they seem to have lived to the maximum carrying capacity of the drought-prone landscape. Now the good times returned, as one archaeologist remarked to me, but there were many more mouths to feed in a world that could not support many more.

This, then, was the first great watershed moment of ancient California, the centuries when the population growth curve went one way and the staple food supplies of many millennia were inadequate to feed them. There was hunger in a more crowded land. In many areas, people could no longer hunt and gather over huge, poorly defined territories. Now many more families lived off the same area, which shrank rapidly to become, instead of one large tract, several, even dozens of them, confined by the boundaries of watersheds, small river valleys, or several coastal bays and a couple of canyons inland.

In chapter 4, we noted the vital cushion of less palatable or harder-to-process foods that hunter-gatherers fall back on in lean years, when staples are insufficient. When the world becomes more crowded, the first logical strategy is to anchor oneself to a lake, an estuary, or a marsh—somewhere where many foods can be found—a strategy not open to everyone. The second strategy is to make staples of hitherto supplementary foods. There's a third strategy, too—exchange food stuffs with neighbors, using ties of kin and reciprocal obligations as the mechanism for doing so.

Like so many watershed moments, these changes were not so momentous in their adoption, for all of them, whether settling near lakes, acorn processing, ocean fishing, elk hunting, or trading with neighbors, are simply logical extensions of ancient subsistence strategies that would have come to people as naturally as harvesting grasses at the right moment. From the earliest Paleo-Indian times, the ancient Californians dwelt in an edible landscape, where every animal, plant, and tree was as familiar to them as the faces of their relatives. But the watershed moment of 2500 B.C. had long-term consequences that changed California society in fundamental ways and linked neighbors near and far in webs of interconnectedness that would have been unimaginable in earlier times.

Acorns at Skyrocket (3000 to 1000 B.C.)

Because the Skyrocket site in the central Sierra foothills is, quite simply, one of the most complete early archaeological sites anywhere in California, let's return there to map out some of the changes.[2]

By 3000 B.C., the inhabitants of Skyrocket were living once again in an oak savanna, staying near the stream somewhat longer, building a new stone platform for plant processing. But the postholes from their temporary shelters probably come from a seasonal camp, where the inhabitants hunted large numbers of rabbits, whose bones abound in the middens of the time. As early as 2500 B.C., they also harvested acorns on a large scale. We know this because carbonized acorns came from the middens, as did stone bowl mortars, some located by the stream. Excavators John Pryor and Roger La Jeunesse also unearthed what they think is a pit used to leach acorns of their tannic acid from the nuts. This is the oldest example of such a pit, where the meal was ground first and water poured over it to remove the tannins. The profile of the Skyrocket pit is quite similar to that described by many early California ethnographers.

Acorns now loomed large in Skyrocket diet. The human skeletons of the time reveal a much lower infant mortality rate and longer life expectancy, as well as better health than any population that lived at the site over nine thousand years. (Specifics on the population remain unpublished.)

These were prosperous times at Skyrocket; it was also the moment when the inhabitants developed more regular contacts with neighbors. The hunters used large projectile points made of obsidian that came all the way from the Bodie Hills on the eastern side of the Sierras. For the first time, abalone shell beads and pendants appear in the middens, as do *olivella* seashell beads, described in more detail in chapter 7.

Skyrocket was a seasonal camp, probably for people with a territory along the Stanislaus River, the nearest large body of water, where they resided for much of the year exploiting a wide range of animal and plant foods, as their predecessors had done for thousands of years. But, for the first time, the group lived in a far more interconnected world, where the acorn was a staple, stored for winter use. Judging from historical records, ground acorn meal also changed hands for other foodstuffs. The acorn was now at the center of human life.

Acorns: The Staff of Life

Acorn consumption was big business in ancient times, and not only in California. In fact, Californians were surprisingly late in exploiting them intensively. Fourteen thousand years ago, the oak forests of Syria produced such bountiful harvests that entire villages lived mostly off acorns and rarely moved from one place. Ancient and medieval European farmers consumed bushels of acorns; so did North American Indians in the Midwest. As late as the nineteenth century A.D., acorns provided about 20 percent of the rural diet in Italy and Spain. Balanophagy is an ancient tradition and by no means unique to ancient California.[3]

What is balanophagy? The word defeated even my faithful *Shorter Oxford Dictionary*. I turned to the full-length version and was stumped again. The ultimate arbiter of the English language had never heard of the word. But I managed to glean enough information from a Latin dictionary to establish that balanophagy is acorn eating. Then I went to the Web, typed the word out of curiosity into the Google search engine, and was astounded to find more than fifteen entries on this seemingly obscure subject. Acorn eating is a serious field of study for more than a few people, archaeologists among them, many of them working in California.

Nowhere did acorns assume such great importance as in California. They became a mainstay of native diet before 1500 B.C. As local populations grew after A.D. 500, the acorn fed more and more people and may have contributed to this growth. At Spanish contact, the 300,000 native Californians were harvesting more than 60,000 tons of them a year—more than the sweet corn harvest in the state today. By then, acorns formed as much as half the diet of many groups.

Here is one of the fascinating mysteries of early California history. Why did ancient Californians subsist quite happily off almost every other edible plant food for thousands of years and neglect acorns? The changeover has been likened by archaeologist Mark Basgall and others to a near-revolution, a Californian equivalent of the switchover from foraging to farming in other parts of the world, although this may be somewhat of an overstatement.[4]

The solution to the mystery involves, among other things, pestles, mortars, and population.

California, however cool and wet, low or high, or hot and dry, has always been a palimpsest of edible landscapes. The endless rotation of the seasons brought a vast constellation of plant foods, which grew, flowered, or ripened in different months, in a kaleidoscope of potential diet. Late spring and early summer was a special time, when fresh greens abounded and people could feast off miner's lettuce, the unrolled fronds of bracken ferns, wild pea leaves, and many more wild vegetables. Next, wild flowers burst into vibrant color, then into seed for the all-important grass harvest. By late summer and during early fall, blue elderberries, manzanita berries, and other fruit reached perfection. Fall was the time of the nut harvests—hazel, piñons, and, above all, oak acorns. The plants varied from altitude to altitude, location to location, but there was always a wide cushion of edible forms. For example, in the southern deserts, agave and mesquite were favored staples, but the people would move to higher elevations for piñons, and knew of many alternatives even in the driest locations.

But, for some reason, the acorn did not figure large in native diet—at first.

Fifteen species of oak grew from southern California to Oregon, except in some parts of the Central Valley, where they were confined to river banks. In a good year, California oaks brought forth enough acorns to feed birds, deer, humans, and rodents, with plenty left over. In the north coast ranges, yields as high as 1,300 to 1,750 pounds/two and a half acres were not uncommon. Such a yield could have supported *fifty to sixty times more people* than lived in the area at the time of European contact. A reliable food supply, one would have thought, but one with the disadvantage that the harvest fluctuates considerably from grove to grove, and even from one tree to another. Most oak species produce a good crop once every two to three years, although the yields vary from one oak species to another. The harvesters were well aware of varying yields. They anticipated them by collecting in several areas and gathering from different species, if more than one grew in the same place. People living in mountainous areas like the north coast ranges and the Sierras simply climbed to higher elevations where yields were quite different.

Acorns are not only plentiful, but have excellent nutritional value. Once processed into meal before cooking, they have between 4.5 and 18 percent fat, as high as 70 percent carbohydrates, and about 5 percent protein, the proportions varying with the species. Compare this food value with maize and wheat, which contain about 1.5 percent fat, 10.3 percent protein, and 73 percent carbohydrates.

Add to these stellar nutritional qualities a tolerance for storage, and acorns are an ideal food. Some groups stored acorns for up to two years, to compensate for crop fluctuations. They kept them in baskets inside their houses or in large raised outdoor granaries, carefully insulated against moisture and protected against predatory rodents.

Acorns were the ideal staple, once one decided to undertake the work involved. And, above all, they could be stored, if necessary for more than a year.

Oak acorns have two serious drawbacks. They are a labor-intensive crop, not so much to harvest as to process. Shelling and pounding them takes hours, far longer than milling grass seeds. Even then, the meal is inedible, for acorns contain bitter-tasting tannic acid, which has to be leached away with time-consuming care before consumption (see figure 6.1).[5]

This may be why Paleo-Indian and Milling Stone people never ate large quantities of acorns. They had plenty of other foods and may have eaten

Figure 6.1. Northern or central Pomo woman using a stone pestle to pound acorns in a basketry mortar. Photographed near Ukiah, California, by H. W. Henshaw, 1893. Reproduced with the permission of the National Anthropological Archives, Smithsonian Institution, negative no. 47,750-A.

acorns only in lean times. Given their intimate knowledge of plants, we can be sure that they worked out simple ways of leaching out the tannic acid to make them palatable. But, when local populations rose and there were periodic food shortages, they then assumed the extra labor of harvesting, storing, and processing acorns in enormous numbers.

Like agriculture in the eastern Mediterranean world ten thousand years ago, acorn consumption gradually became a cornerstone of ancient California diet throughout the oak belt. Grinding and cooking acorn meal became one of the central activities of family life, a skill passed from mother to daughter down many generations.

Westerners have little concept of acorns as a food, which is a pity, because they are a palatable dish when properly prepared or made into bread. I make no apologies for the fairly extended discussion that follows of how the acorn goes from tree to pot.

From Harvest to Meal

The work began with the harvest. These were the two or three busiest weeks of the year. As with grass seeds, the harvest required exquisite timing, reaching the trees before the acorns fell off into the mouths of waiting deer feeding on the nut-rich mast as it rotted on the ground. At harvest time, entire families would camp close to the oaks, the men taking advantage of the rich acorn droppings to hunt deer feasting under the oaks.

Acorn harvesting took days. Back in the 1930s, anthropologist Charles Du Bois observed acorn collecting by the Wintu of far northern California.[6] They could harvest a large tree or two small ones in the course of a day's work. The yield from a single tree could be as high as fifty-five pounds or more. But this work paled into insignificance beside the necessary processing to make even a small number of the nuts suitable for consumption. We have few estimates as to how long this process took. UCLA anthropologist Walter Goldschmidt once observed a woman grind up six pounds of dry, shelled acorns in three hours.

Harvesting the acorns was time consuming enough, but then they had to be brought back to camp, a job that fell to the women. Archaeologist Martin Baumhoff once theorized that the reason that tribal territories in California were so small was because of the heavy labor involved in hefting loaded acorn baskets over rugged terrain. He may have had a point.[7]

Acorns have to be kept dry and safe from rodents. Building and maintaining granaries also took days. Some groups stored them in baskets, mixed with bay leaves, which gave off a pungent aroma and discouraged insects. On the northern California coast, historic groups often smeared the trunks of oaks supporting their granaries off the ground with pine pitch for the same reason.

The largest granaries stood in winter camps, in the Sierras at lower elevations, and close to perennial water supplies. These were the stockpiles used year-round, while smaller outlying granaries could feed hunters and others in the early spring.

The Sierra Miwok built some of the largest and most elaborate granaries, up to 12 feet high and 5 feet across, with a capacity of between 95 to 196 cubic feet—space for a lot of acorns. They would drive a circle of saplings into the ground above a boulder or tree stump, then weave grapevines or willow branches around them to form a roughly twined open container. Next, they thatched the walls with carefully tamped brush, adding more and more leaves until the interior was dark. Finally, they would line the inside with pungent, minty wormwood to repel insects and worms. Pine needles kept the acorns from falling through the bottom. Once the granary was finished, the women piled basketfuls of unshelled acorns inside, climbing higher and higher atop the nuts until there was no room for them. Finally, a wormwood-and-pine-needle layer sealed the precious harvest, and the outside of the granary were rain- and snow-proofed with a cap of incense cedar bark combined with thatch to keep out animals (see figure 6.2).[8]

A large Miwok granary would hold enough acorns to feed a family of six people for a year. Many granaries held two years' supply or more of nuts; some acorns were even stored for as long as four years.

Then came the processing.

Until I started delving into the literature and talked to some colleagues, I had no idea that acorn processing was such an arduous and careful business.[9] Details varied greatly from group to group, but the general sequence

Figure 6.2. Acorn granaries from the Central Valley. Stephen Powers, *Tribes of California* (Berkeley, Calif.: University of California Press, 1976; reprinted edition edited by Robert F. Heizer), fig. 42.

of events was the same. First, crack the shells with a hammer stone, then inspect and winnow them, finally pound them into meal. But the entire process would be impossible without a pestle and mortar.

In chapter 4, I pointed out that milling stones were a simple and ancient technology that was ideal for crushing seeds and less oily nuts. The acorn is far more demanding, requiring a bowl-shaped depression to catch and hold the shelled nut and prevent it from slipping away from the pestle. You do not grind an acorn, you pound it. Expert pounders used several shapes and grades of depression to achieve a fine-grained acorn meal.

Mortars are very different from milling stones, which are little more than flat surfaces. You can identify a stone mortar in an archaeological site with ease, because of its hollow center, laboriously pecked out with a hammer stone, then smoothed by constant use. Pestles are easily identified, too—long, easily held rocks of varying weight with worn ends. Many women also used wooden mortars, often prized artifacts passed down from mother to daughter.

Pestles and mortars are hardly spectacular artifacts, but they have become an archaeological barometer. They are so closely identified with acorn processing in many archaeologists' minds that they are almost universally agreed to be a reliable indicator of such activity, even when no acorns are found in the same occupation deposits. One should be careful about this, for we know that pounders served many other purposes in historic times, for crushing berries, even processing red ocher pigment for paint. It is probably safer to say that the appearance of numerous pestles and mortars as opposed to milling stones means a significant increase in the *intensive* exploitation of acorn crops. This intense exploitation was certainly a turning point in early California history.

Most mortars were portable, often carefully buried at harvest spots and used year after year. In the Sierras, many women pecked out depressions in natural rocky outcrops, where they would gather to pound acorns in company and to gossip with one another. The flat surface of the rock provided a comfortable place to sit as well as a clean area for the flour. Some of these mortar sites remained in use for many generations and are surrounded by extensive midden deposits resulting from cooking acorns and other foods. They became important economic and social focus points, as much part of group territories as the groves of oak trees that provided the harvest.

Nearly everywhere, the toolkit for acorn processing was simplicity itself: a set of baskets and basketry trays, one or more soaproot brushes, mortars, and pestles. The technology was an ancient one, perhaps as ancient as the milling stone, like all native Californian technologies—simple and highly effective. The work, like milling and canoe building, was highly labor intensive.

You shell the acorns with a hammer stone, then inspect the nuts carefully, rejecting those that show any signs of rot. Next, you winnow the nuts in a scoop-shaped basket to remove the rusty-colored skin that adheres to them, a process much harder than it sounds. Then you pound them, wielding the pestle in a regular up-and-down motion, starting with a small batch of nuts, adding more as the crush continues. The heavier the pestle, the quicker the flour forms, so an experienced pounder usually changes pestles several times, sometimes using some already crushed "starter" to aid in the initial crush. Different mortars can be used at different stages in the pounding, too, their different qualities providing finer meal at the end (see figure 6.3).

Figure 6.3. "Woman pounding acorns." Powers, *Tribes of California* (Berkeley, Calif.: University of California Press, 1976; reprinted edition edited by Robert F. Heizer), fig. 32.

Acorns are crushed, not ground, the secret to the process being an effortless rhythm of up-and-down movement that goes on without a break. Extreme care is necessary to maintain a layer of flour between pestle and mortar, to prevent minute rock chips from entering the mix.

Once pounded to a fine consistency, the flour is sifted through a tightly woven basket and is ready for leaching.

You can leach acorns in various simple ways. The simplest, and perhaps the earliest, much used by northern groups, required immersing them in water or mud for weeks, even months before pulverizing. This technique sweetened the acorns, but removed only a fraction of the tannins and involved a high spoilage rate. Soaking was an inefficient method, which did not produce enough treated acorns to support a large number of people. It also required ample water, so many base camps were located close to streams.

Soaking was probably the original way of processing acorns, used when acorns were just an occasional supplemental food. Just soaking them involved little labor once they had been collected, especially if the people were foraging other staple foods at the same time.

Once acorns became a staple in their own right, many groups switched to a more labor-intensive processing system. Once pounded, the meal was spread in a porous depression in the ground. Leaching took between two and six hours, carried out by flushing water repeatedly through the meal into the soil below. This long, tedious process consumed enormous amounts of time. For example, Goldschmidt's 6 pounds of pounded acorns became 5.3 pounds of meal. Leaching this sample took just under four hours, about one and three-quarter hours per 2 pounds.[10]

Acorn meal made excellent bread and a variety of soups and gruels. The nuts or processed flour were easily carried on long trading expeditions across the Sierras, or offshore in planked canoes to the Channel Islands, where acorns were scarce (see chapter 14).

Large-scale harvesting, transportation, and processing of acorns were a very labor intensive way of feeding people, something to be avoided when there was no necessity for it. We can be sure that the earliest Californians were well aware that acorns were edible and nutritious and that they were toxic if unleached. We can be sure, too, that they ate them occasionally when hungry and other foods were in short supply. But apparently acorns were not a staple at first, simply because they were too time consuming to prepare.

The Archaeology of Acorns
(c. 2500 B.C. to 1000 B.C. and Later)

The earliest record of acorn processing on any scale inland comes from Skyrocket. Another site, Llano Seco in Butte County, yielded acorns alongside milling stones, in a level dated to about 2300 B.C. A cache of charred acorns came from the Fish Camp Slough site in the San Joaquin Valley, radiocarbon dated to just after 1000 B.C. Only in later sites do acorns become abundant.[11]

Acorn processing seems to have begun about 2500 B.C., perhaps earlier in some coastal estuaries like the Goleta Slough, now the site of Santa Barbara Airport, where mortars appear as early as 3000 B.C. The meal would have added a carbohydrate element to a protein-rich diet, but the mortars may, in fact, have been used to process roots and other pulpy foods on a large scale, especially in marshland areas like the Goleta Slough. In the far south, coastal lagoons with their abundant plant foods and kelp beds close offshore (perhaps more abundant than today) provided long-term habitats for coastal groups, who had no need of the planked canoes that may have linked the southern Channel Islands with the Orange County mainland.[12]

The mortar and pestle did not appear suddenly, as they would have had a sudden revelation about the nutritional value of acorns come to grass seed users. Rather, they trickled into use over many centuries, as acorns assumed greater importance in local diets. Working from north to south, we find them as early as 2000 B.C. in the San Francisco Bay Area, in sites in north-central Sonoma County by about 1000 B.C. The new technology is commonplace in the central north coast ranges by 500 B.C. Mortars and pestles were in use in the Central Valley in some numbers by the time of Christ, and in the central and southern Sierra Nevada at about the same time. Here rocky outcrops abound, providing ideal surfaces for women to pound acorns together; such communal pounding areas are commonplace in the Sierras. By 2000 B.C., mortars and pestles were widespread through the southern San Joaquin Valley, throughout interior southern California, and in the Santa Barbara Channel region.

As pounding technology came into use, the ancient milling stone methods faded away; they were still used occasionally and always useful, but were no competition for the efficient and versatile mortar.

There's another change, too. Nearly everywhere projectile points reappear in much greater numbers than in previous millennia, as if hunting had assumed a renewed importance. Highly distinctive stemmed and side-notched points come into use at the same time as mortars and pestles. As we shall see in chapter 7, these artifacts may reflect a new trend toward hunting larger mammals, a phenomenon that affected the intensity of obsidian trading.

The Nature of the Changeover

The changeover to acorns was no revolution, as has sometimes been suggested. What little archaeological evidence there is hints at a more gradual change, during centuries when plant foraging economies changed dramatically.[13]

All kinds of arguments surface to explain the change. One hoary favorite is environmental change. Under this rubric, conditions during the Middle Holocene became warmer and drier, to the point that grass seeds and other long-utilized plant foods became scarce. Unfortunately for these theorists, the change over to more acorns actually took place after the Altithermal, when the climate was cooler and slightly wetter than during preceding millennia.

Human skeletons provide an excellent, and dispassionate, chronicle of individual medical histories, and of injuries suffered in war. In many cases, we know more about an individual's health in death than they knew in life. Signs of malnutrition are familiar in ancient skeletons from many parts of the world—the telltale Harris Lines, which appear etched onto bones, are a clear sign of severe dietary deficiencies. So is dental hypoplasia.[14] Both conditions appear frequently on Middle Holocene individuals, the result of episodes of dietary stress during lean months and drought years

Both Harris Lines and dental hypoplasia are much more common on human remains dating to before 1000 B.C., when acorns were only an occasional food than afterward, when they were a staple. Furthermore, signs of dental caries, often caused by carbohydrate consumption, are more common after 1000 B.C.—acorns are rich in carbohydrates, which lead to caries (more discussion on this in chapter 14).

The changeover to more intensive acorn consumption may have resulted from more frequent episodes of malnutrition at a time when California's population was rising considerably. It's interesting to note that the Skyrocket skeletons of this period display exceptionally good health, in levels where acorns are abundant.

But Why Acorns?

In Milling Stone times, most Californians survived by exploiting a broad spectrum of different foods—everything from deer meat and grass seeds to mollusks, sea mammals, and fish. They survived because they lived in edible landscapes where many different foods were there for the taking, many more labor intensive in their collection than others. What happens, however, if the number of people living off these edible landscapes rises slowly but surely, until they begin to exceed the carrying capacity of their homelands—the number of people per square mile that they can support?

First, growing populations and increased fecundity from more reliable food supplies and sedentary settlement mean more people living off a finite amount of land, which only supports a few individuals per square mile. The landscape is more crowded, territorial boundaries become more circumscribed and more carefully policed, and there is greater competition for food, perhaps even fighting over natural grass stands or mollusk beds.

Second, for thousands of years, these peoples' ancestors subsisted comfortably by moving around freely over loosely defined territories. Now the presence of others circumscribes their mobility. They tend to settle in more permanent base camps, then move out from there in search of food at different seasons of the year.

Third, people crowded into smaller territories encounter periodic food shortages, which are accentuated by droughts and other natural climatic fluctuations. When this happens, they follow a logical strategy, which has always been their standby in lean times. They eat less-favored foods, those that they would only use occasionally. Perhaps such foods were less palatable, or more expensive to collect and process, conceivably only available at some distance.

Among them, perhaps, were acorns.

It's easy to visualize what happened. Acorns were always eaten, perhaps as a famine food, when it was worthwhile processing some with milling stones or with simple mortars to ease a food shortage, or to amplify a sparse diet of game meat, grass seeds, or shellfish on a short-term basis. Once the food crisis was over, the acorn receded into the dietary background until it was needed again.

By 2500 B.C., circumstances changed considerably. There were many more people foraging over the landscape, crowded into increasingly more circumscribed territories. The cushion of alternative foods was under considerable pressure year after year. This was the point where people turned to more expensive, labor intensive foods—just as foragers in the Near East took up the vastly more laborious task of agriculture in 10,000 B.C. It was a logical move, not even a major stretch, of survival strategies that had been in place for thousands of years. The changeover was a patchwork, combined with a move, where possible, to areas with more predictable and abundant foods. There was nothing new in this strategy of flexible mobility, which had governed hunter-gatherer life for thousands of years.

This time there was one difference. Once the changeover was made, the labor involved accepted as part of daily and seasonal routine, the technology of processing and storage in place, group after group realized that they now had more to eat, a much more reliable food supply, and a staple food that could be stored in quantities so large that many harvesters collected two year's food supply in a few weeks.

Another solution would have been to start farming maize and beans, just as they did in the Southwest in the second millennium B.C. But why should people with abundant acorns at hand go to all the trouble of clearing fields and planting crops? The ancient Californians were well aware of agriculture and of maize through sporadic contacts with farmers living near the Colorado River and in the Southwest, but, except for some desert groups, they stuck to their acorns.

Within a millennium or so, perhaps faster, the acorn became a vital staple of California life from Oregon to the southern deserts.

Consequences

It would be a mistake to claim that the acorn revolutionized life in ancient California. This humble nut did not trigger a subsistence revolution on the scale of that produced by the shift to agriculture in many parts of the world. But it certainly made food supplies more predictable for people living in a much more crowded and territorially circumscribed world.

Mobility was one of the foundations of early California existence and a deep part of local ritual and tradition, for everyone knew they would move when drought or other events threatened their livelihood. Now there were fewer places to move to, smaller scale ties of kin scattered over much smaller areas. The widely spread intelligence gained from vast networks spread over hundreds of square miles now shrunk to a smaller compass, where one's world was a single watershed, a small stretch of open coastline, or a desert landscape endowed with a handful of perennial springs. Before 1000 B.C., most California societies had moved constantly, exploiting foods that were the least trouble and "cost" to collect and process. Now many of them settled down in a few base camps, occupied for months on end, a more sedentary existence made possible in large part by the intensive harvesting of acorns, which supported many more people within much smaller territories.

As acorns became the staple, the realities of the harvest, of the work involved, began to dictate other aspects of group life. Territories shrank, as people stored the harvest and moved around less. Their homelands encompassed oak groves, the distance needed to carry loaded baskets, and not the much larger tracts of land used in earlier times when life was more oriented toward highly mobile gathering and hunting. At the same time, the number of archaeological sites dating to after 1500 B.C. rises rapidly, a sure sign of population increases.

Burials from the Central Valley reveal some remarkable health changes after about 800 B.C. and confirm what we know from the Skyrocket population. A larger proportion of the later population survived to adulthood as the population increased, the rate of increase accelerating as time went on. Many experts believe that this rise in population, and the gradual adoption of acorn-based economies, were closely connected.

Acorns are only harvested once a year, and then in enormous numbers. It is all very well collecting them in bulk, but you then have to store them and monitor the precious stocks. Now there were schedule conflicts between the demands of acorn harvests and stored food and those of food resources scattered in clusters over large territories. To harvest, say, wild grasses, means being at the location where natural stands occur during the few days when the seeds are ripe enough to be knocked off the stem. Instead of camping by the ripe stands, parties of harvesters would move out to gather the seed, then return to base. Mobility gave way to highly organized collecting, a kind of foraging that required careful orchestration and new forms of leadership to oversee it.

At first, the changeover may have caused conflict between different factions within a group, but, for all the hard work they require, acorns were a much more reliable food. The acorn offered a logical solution, which brought greater dietary reliability, enough food to feed more people crowded into much smaller foraging territories, and both improved health and longer life expectancy.

Acorn foraging contributed to the viability of smaller territories, and to the increasing diversity of the ancient and tiny tribelet system that flourished in California at European contact (see chapter 7). Small homelands also meant less self-sufficiency and greater dependence on others. In drought years, or at times of failed acorn crops, neighboring kin in different territories may have exchanged food stuffs and other commodities in increasingly formalized systems of exchange that were universal in historical times.

Simultaneously, the dynamics of human society may have become more complex, closely tied to the need to manage relationships between individuals and their groups, and with neighboring groups, in situations where people stayed in one place for much longer periods of time. Inevitably, ceremony, ritual, trade, and the management of stored food resources assumed much greater importance in societies where people moved around much less. Most people spent their entire lives within a narrow compass of watershed or valley terrain no more than about five miles across. Inevitably, too, some members of society—kin leaders, individuals perceived to have exceptional supernatural powers—acquired better access to food and other commodities than others, and became the leaders of far more complex societies, especially in areas where food resources were diverse and exceptionally abundant.

Large-scale acorn harvesting was a turning point in California history, which had an impact akin to that of agriculture in other parts of North America. Acorn harvesting, like intensive fishing, brought permanent settlement, more complex social organization and ritual life, and constant interaction with neighbors near and far.

Men and Women

Acorns did not necessarily mean greater social and political elaboration, nor were they a simple response to rising population densities. Rather, they were a catalyst behind much of the greater complexity of California society after 1500 B.C. The sheer amount of time required to process them had a profound effect on the roles of men and women in ancient California society.

In earlier Milling Stone times, both men and women gathered and probably processed plant foods. Now, women shouldered the entire burden of pounding, storing, and cooking acorns. During the critical weeks of harvest, everyone—men, women, and children—worked flat out. But, once the harvest was over, acorns were women's work. Survival literally depended on their balanophagous activities.

Meanwhile, the men engaged in two now much expanded subsistence activities—fishing and hunting—as well as in war. With the growing population and much greater definition of group territories, fighting became more common, as neighbors poached harvests from ripe oaks and killed women's foraging parties.

"The women stayed at home and looked after the children" is one of the constant refrains of archaeology when confronted with interpreting male/female roles in ancient societies. There is some truth in this statement, although there are many exceptions. Acorn processing is a sedentary activity carried out close to home, hours of grinding allowing plenty of time to keep an eye on young children, as well as interaction between the women of the community at a level more like that found in a sedentary village farming community than in a nomadic foraging group.

Acorns were social instruments in the sense that they kept women home, busy with processing them. A month or so of hard work at harvest season yielded food for the entire year, which immediately removed the stress of day-to-day survival and cut down dramatically on the amount of time spent foraging for plants away from camp. A day's hard pounding could provide food for a family for two or three days without moving from camp. The women could now forage when they felt like it, to introduce some variety into the diet, or simply when plants came into season, so that meals changed with the seasons. Archaeologist Thomas Jackson believes that women's mobility may have been reduced as much as a third by acorns.[15]

Acorn harvesting, like intensive fishing, brought permanent settlement, more complex social organization and ritual life, and constant interaction with neighbors near and far. It also brought quite rapid population growth in many areas.

The changeover to acorns may be historically significant, but what may be even more significant is the increased processing labor required to produce the new foods. This gave women an added importance in society and the arranging of strategically advantageous marriages became a matter of considerable significance in more sedentary societies, surrounded by neighbors and operating within confined territories.

With food surpluses commonplace for the first time, the control of these surpluses in acorns must have become a major social issue. In historic times, men dominated intergroup exchange and trade, but they could never have done so without negotiating for access to full granaries, an activity in which male rituals probably played an important part. As we shall see, the great sophistication of many later California societies was as much in the spiritual arena as it was in the domestic and material, where men and women each had well-defined roles.

With much smaller territories and a much higher degree of inter-dependence on others, trade and exchange became a major factor in human life. For example, archaeological sites along the coast contain more sea otter bones, animals prized for their pelts, which were traded over considerable distances in historical times. Fragments of obsidian, volcanic glass much prized for tool making, now appear in many places, traded from considerable distances away in the interior. To participate in the exchange of valuable commodities means intensifying the labor to prepare otter pelts, process acorns, and other trade goods. This means that women's labor became ever more important, resulting in an institution that was widespread at the time of European contact—social alliances fabricated by marriages between members of different lineages living at some distance.

A colleague once described the emergence of the acorn as a staple food to me as a moment when ancient California lost its innocence. He has a point, because things changed when the pounder and the acorn brought a measure of dietary stability unknown in earlier millennia. A more crowded world, smaller territories, less ability to move—the thousand years between 2500 B.C. and 1500 B.C. was a time when new social institutions, more elaborate rituals, and much more intensified hunting and gathering emerged for the first time in California. And, in the long term, the greatest changes came in social and political organization.

A Jigsaw of Tribelets

When the first Spaniards arrived, the native Californians lived in a bewildering array of small political and social groups. Some were tiny bands, no more than a few families occupying part of a river valley or a lakeside canyon.[16] Many were seemingly egalitarian, with no obvious leaders, except the most experienced individuals. In some areas, people lived in much larger, often permanent settlements headed by wealthy and powerful leaders, in societies where social ranking based on kin ties and personal qualities was all-important. Ancient Californian societies formed a continuum from tiny, nomadic bands, to groups like the coastal Chumash of the south, who lived in village societies that approached the elaboration of farming cultures in other parts of North America (see chapter 14).

California societies seemed unique to the pioneer anthropologists who encountered them. These early scholars often didn't have sufficient ways of describing the social order they observed. The ubiquitous Alfred Kroeber made a lasting contribution to the debate when he pointed out that political life in ancient California was so different from that in other parts of North America that one needed an entirely new model. Kroeber pronounced the term "tribe," used elsewhere, meaningless in California. Tribes were much larger social and political units covering many communities with a much more specific identity. Such identities did not exist here in California, so Kroeber coined the term "tribelet" instead. The nomenclature has endured as a useful one, despite much criticism on the grounds that one cannot compare tribelets to societies elsewhere.

Kroeber's tribelet was a village community, the largest group over which one person could exercise authority. It was autonomous, self-governing, and independent. Tribelets comprised people who shared a common language and culture, and a common history. Kroeber himself estimated that there were as many as five hundred tribelets in California, with between one hundred and five hundred people in each. Modern estimates place the figure at nearer a thousand. The total number in each may be smaller than Kroeber calculated.

The population density of Kroeber's tribelets varied greatly from one environment to another. Densely populated areas with varied food resources, say the Yokut territory in the Central Valley or the Chumash homeland in southern California, may have supported densities of up to ten people a square mile. In such areas, tribelet territories may have been as little as fifty square miles, which was the case with the Miwok of Central California. This contrasts dramatically with the six thousand square miles or more required by some desert tribelets in the southeast.

The tribelet usually had a principal base settlement or major seasonal camp where council meetings were held, treasures maintained, and food caches stored. Everywhere, a complex set of economic and social checks and balances maintained an approximate equilibrium between the population and available food resources, and fostered relationships with neighbors. Food and other essentials were the catalysts for political and social interconnectedness, for ceremonies and rituals, trade feasts, and trade. And the lasting ties of kin and lineage provided the links that made these connections function.

Tribelets flourished in various forms right across ancient California, with a few exceptions. In the far northwest, groups living along the Klamath River shared forms of social organization with people living in the Pacific Northwest. Here the individual reigned supreme; society was highly fractured. People lived in clusters of settlements that were technically tribelets, but really little more than loosely connected sets of settlements. There was not the sense of close-knit cohesiveness, which was such a marked feature of tribelets elsewhere. Personal status, prestige, and wealth were all-important in societies where everyone strove for themselves and their families. Competition and individualism won out against communal ownership and cooperation, although even in these groups, outright excess was kept in check by ritual observance.

The Aggrandizers

Kroeber's tribelets are a useful conceptual framework for envisaging the mosaic of ancient groups in California. But, like all such classifications, they fall down in the details. The tribelet is a tiny social grouping, flexible, very localized, and, as such, basically egalitarian, with none of the social ranking that is a marked feature of many later ancient California societies. As we shall see, people like the Chumash of southern California and the Yokut of the Central Valley lived under wealthy, hereditary chiefs. The great shell mounds of the San Francisco Bay shoreline were a landscape presided over by powerful individuals, who were far more than experienced elders or tribelet headmen. The chiefs of all these groups often inherited their rank, but their effectiveness depended on their personal qualities, their entrepreneurship, and their ability to command loyalty from their followers. In short, they were Big Men, with a capital B and a capital M, or, to use a more contemporary title, Aggrandizers.[17]

The term "Big Men" came to anthropology from Marshall Sahlins of the University of Michigan, who studied Pacific Island chiefdoms. His Big Men were aggressive, entrepreneurial individuals, who initiated trading contacts and developed friendships and alliances with their opposite numbers in other groups. They acquired wealth, attracted loyal followers, and redistributed the food and other commodities through their communities via feasts and other such social mechanisms.

Big Men acquired economic and political power through sheer ability, through personal initiative and charisma, and through their skill at maintaining the loyalty of those who benefited from their largess. They became chiefs, but, unless the chiefdom was hereditary, their power evaporated at their deaths unless inherited by their descendants.

Such individuals were aggrandizers: entrepreneurs, expert at fostering personal relationships, confident in their leadership skills. They knew how to retain followers and how to interact with key individuals in neighboring communities. Like shamans, who communicated with the supernatural, they listened carefully to the eddying cross-currents of public opinion and exploited it to their advantage.

Aggrandizers were the catalysts for social ranking, for a greater elaboration of society. They flourished in some parts of California as early as 1000 B.C., a product of a changing world where rising population densities and more restricted tribelet territories made interaction with neighbors necessary. And, in some areas, they became hereditary chiefs (see figure 6.4).

Social Ranking, Chiefs, and Friends

Early observers frequently commented on the prevalence of social "classes" in many, but not all, native Californian societies. Generalizations are always dangerous, but we can divide society in the centuries before Europeans arrived into three broad categories. The first was an elite of chiefly families, often about a quarter of the population. These controlled distribution systems by virtue of their control of political and ritual privilege, or food and

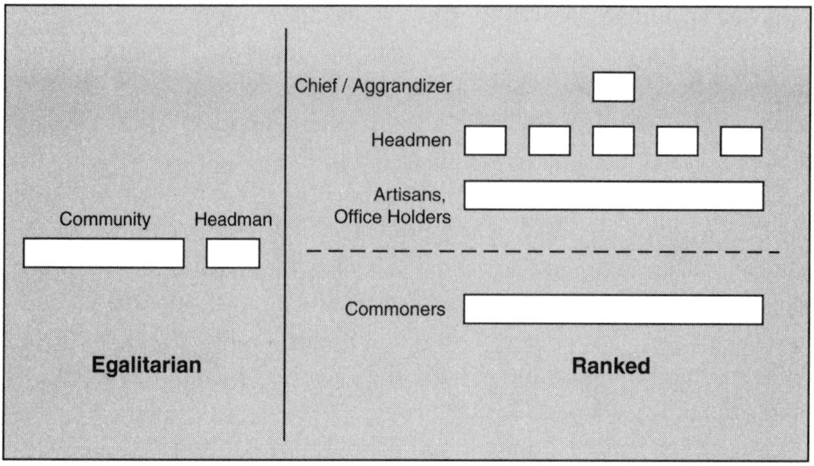

Figure 6.4. Egalitarian and ranked societies. A hypothetical diagram contrasts the two general forms of society.

other commodity surpluses. They maintained carefully nurtured, often secretive, ritual knowledge; sometimes used a special language among themselves; and tended to marry one another.

Then there were members of the chief's extended family, who held special offices as assistants or religious specialists. Their tasks usually revolved around the organizing of ritual observances, for economic and political matters were articulated in this way. Older, experienced officials formed the chief's council of advisers in smaller tribelets comprising subchiefs from smaller communities. Some younger chief's assistants served as messengers or reporters, aiding communication between the leader and the people, listening to the thrust of public opinion, relaying information and gossip. One anthropologist was moved to refer to them as "native gossip columnists."

Yet other members of the elite were especially gifted artisans such as bow makers, canoe builders, or basket makers. Below this broadly defined elite were commoners, men and women without any special skills, then the poor, outlaws, and sometimes slaves.

Most people inherited their social ranking. We know this from differences in burial adornment in ancient cemeteries, where enough has survived for a study of social ranking. This ranking was generally a rigid and authoritarian structure, which endured for generations. Commoners lived within the confines of their tribelet territory and did not enjoy the mobility of the elite, artisans, ritual specialists, and traders.

Travelers were only safe in areas where the prestige of their village and its chiefs extended. Much depended, also, on the status of their own kin or formal trading partners in more distant communities, who protected them when they visited. Most people lived out their lives within the narrow compass of a few square miles. People of higher rank were the experts in interacting with the world without.

Under such circumstances, the trading partner or special friend was of vital importance. This was the mechanism by which a chief or member of the elite could extend his social, economic, and political networks to much larger universes. The Pomo and other central California groups recognized special friends, who were individuals in outside communities who were bonded in friendship by ritual ceremony. The friends then reinforced the relationship with a valuable gift such as a feathered basket. Such friendships were always ones of great trust and reciprocal obligation, sometimes even cemented by marriage. They were especially important in those many California societies where the family, extended family, or lineage were the primary means of defining social relationships, and where trust rarely extended far beyond them. The special friend was bound to one by ritual ties and reciprocal economic ties, a way of facilitating activities of all kinds, even making a profit.

Such networks of friendship and reciprocal observation were the cement that held hundreds of small tribelets together in relationships of interdependency that were essential for their survival in harsh, highly localized environments.

Trading feasts also cemented exchanges between politically separate areas to each side's advantage. And always, food of all kinds could serve as a community of exchange, which was often transformed into prestigious objects, shell money, or craft items like obsidian knives or charm stones, or the materials to manufacture them.

Throughout California, chiefs were administrators, who managed the production, distribution, and exchange of goods. The post involved the maintenance of gift-giving relationships, ritual alliances, and intermarriages with other groups, the kinds of acts that sealed agreements between kin leaders living in different communities. Chiefs were economic administrators, perceived as wealthy, sometimes living in relative luxury in a larger dwelling, and supported by their communities. They had enough obligations without engaging in ordinary labor. Their signs of office were conspicuous and exotic—formal regalia, shell bead money, or obsidian knives, displayed on important occasions.

Chiefs were prestigious individuals, respected and feared; they were usually married to several women from the elite of different tribelets. Such strategies provided children and kin ties with close and distant neighbors. Since a chief's role involved bringing together larger numbers of people for communal work and important ritual events, such ties were in constant use.

In each of these usually densely populated areas, and others, we find developing hierarchies of settlements: a major village with hundreds of inhabitants surrounded by, and linked by economic and kin ties to lesser camps and hamlets in the surrounding territory. Elsewhere, such hierarchies develop in farming societies. Here they developed among people who harvested food in the wild, and who never domesticated crops and animals, although they were well aware of maize agriculture.

We have only a dim understanding of the internal organization of tribelets, which varied considerable from one area to the next. But you cannot think about individual tribelets in isolation without considering their alliances.

Alliances and Exchange Networks

Everywhere in ancient California, political and social relations were in a constant state of flux. They depended, to a great degree, on the competence and expertise of individual chiefs and other leaders. A maze of ever-shifting alliances created economic and ritual networks linking tribelets in entirely different environments, often people of varying nationalities, separated by considerable distances. There was a constant ebb and flow of military, ritual, and trading alliances, which often reflected the realities of ecological constraints and local population densities.

In northern California, such alliances often involved at least three tribelets, each of them living in a different ecological zone. For example, groups living on the coast maintained ongoing alliances with people living by rivers inland, or with neighbors at higher elevations. These were usually over relatively short distances—from the Pacific shore inland to the coastal ranges.[18]

In southern California, equivalent relationships extended over much larger areas—from the Pacific coast across deserts and mountain passes, even into Arizona and New Mexico. We know that east-west alliances linked the Chumash with the Yokuts of the Central Valley and the Mojave of the desert; the Gabrielieño of the modern-day Los Angeles area with the Cahuilla and other desert groups into the Southwest; and the Diegueño of the far southern coast and interior with the Yuma of the lower desert.

By no means were all the alliances east-west. The Gabrielieño allied themselves with the Chumash and traded soapstone with them and with the Salinan further north. The Miwok of the Bay Area and southwestern Pomo to the north also enjoyed an alliance.

Political confederations and economic alliances went hand-in-hand with ritual congregations, many of them revolving around the jimsonweed cult, which linked southern California tribelets with one another. In central and northern California, the Kuksu and World Renewal rituals had the same effect. Major rituals brought together neighboring tribelets within fifty- to seventy-five-mile radiuses, to the point where several hundred, even a thousand people would congregate for a mourning ceremony or a World Renewal. Major ritual centers in Yokut territory or among southern California groups like the Chumash or San Diegueño could attract as many as three thousand people—opportunities for intensive trading as well as for social and political dealing.

Xonxon'ata: Interconnectedness in Action

I think of a wonderful example of economic alliances from a more recent site every time I leave Highway 101 for California 154, which crosses the San Ynez Mountains north of Buellton. The old T-junction at the freeway was dangerous and the scene of a growing number of serious accidents. Before construction on a new interchange was begun, an archaeological survey of the area turned up an important Chumash village known as Xonxon'ata right at the intersection. In a farsighted move, the Santa

Barbara Association of Governments rerouted the interchange at considerable additional expense. The surviving parts of the site remained intact. The association also commissioned further excavations, which revealed an ancient Chumash community, Xonxon'ata, closely interconnected with the coast, about seventeen miles away.[19]

Xonxon'ata lies along the east side of Zaca Creek, on a natural corridor, which links the Santa Ynez Valley, Gaviota Pass, and the Santa Barbara Channel. A substantial community flourished at the site from A.D. 1300 until as late as 1806. This was no isolated village: the mollusks and fish bones from its middens reveal a great dependency on the coast.

As always, the clues came from careful attention to the humblest of finds. Seventy percent of the shellfish from Xonxon'ata were mussels, which were not used for bead making. Almost certainly, they arrived at the village live. Mussels, being intertidal zone dwellers, can survive for long periods of time out of the water. Thus, one can trade them as food over reasonably short distances without them going bad. Another telltale clue: 83 percent of the fish at the site were small schooling species like anchovies and sardines. Anyone who has eaten canned sardines can tell you that they are consumed whole without gutting or filleting. And they are easily dried: I have eaten delectable dried sardines in Portugal (but, not, alas, in California). Such fish were a wonderful food for exchange purposes, because they were light, required little processing, and could be harvested in enormous numbers. There is no question that these fish were traded inland. Contrast the fish bone counts from inland Xonxon'ata with a coastal site at Cañada del Corral, some eighteen miles away, where small schooling fish are only 43 percent of the total catch, much of which was inshore rock fish. Mussels were less than half of the shellfish collected.

Mussels and small fish passed inshore, but what did coastal people receive in return? Acorns and pine nuts are the obvious candidates, for acorn-bearing oaks abound near Xonxon'ata. But, with so much food nearby, why did the inhabitants trade with the coast at all? The answer may lie in the animal bones. Today, deer are plentiful near the site, but there are few bones of these animals in the site middens, just numerous rabbits. William Hildebrandt and the other archaeologists who excavated Xonxon'ata believe that there came a point when hunting had seriously depleted deer populations in the interior—some time after A.D. 380. This may have been when exchange of marine products for acorns and other plant foods accelerated—to balance out food shortages resulting from overhunting of deer. By the time local Chumash settled at Xonxon'ata, such exchanges with the coast were routine, allowing this inland village and others to achieve far larger sizes than would otherwise have been the case.

Food and social relationships go together, as Raymond Firth pointed out in the South Pacific. John Johnson of the Santa Barbara Museum of Natural History has spent much of his career analyzing mission records of Chumash marriages and baptisms from the historic period and proved Firth correct. He has shown that marriages between mainland and interior Chumash helped maintain vital exchange relationships. Of nowhere was this truer than Xonxon'ata, where mission records reveal extensive marriage ties with other communities, not only within a few miles, but also with distant villages deep in San Luis Obispo County. This was an important and strategic settlement in terms of interconnectedness. For example, at least 118 people from the first generation born at the local missions and 10 from other villages had at least one parent from Xonxon'ata.

The Xonxon'ata case shows us how mutual obligations and rights developed between widely separated communities, all of which intensified their exploitation of resources that were abundant within their local territories. And in times of need, these reciprocal ties ensured that food went to areas where supplies were short, thereby protecting more than one community from food shortages. Moreover, villages like Xonxon'ata, situated as they were on strategic corridors for exchange, assumed considerable importance. Their chiefs enhanced their wealth, prestige, and authority by virtue of their involvement in exchange. A complex web of interconnectedness linked dozens of local communities and the individuals that presided over them.

While the commodities trade may have changed as fashions shifted, or economic needs varied, the reality of human existence never changed on offshore island, coast, or in the interior—a reality that centered on interconnectedness. One could not survive in California's highly localized and varied environments without the help of others and without the intricate social ties that linked individual to individual, kin group to kin group. These ties had assumed increasing importance during the past two thousand years.

In chapter 7, we examine what may have been the earliest exchange of all, the first element in the web of interconnectedness—the obsidian trade.

CHAPTER 7

The Seductive Glass

T HE SHORES OF A SMALL LAKE IN THE SIERRA NEVADA foothills on a summer's day, 11,000 B.C. An Indian hunter sits on a low boulder at water's edge in the late afternoon sun.[1] Nearby, two women scrape an elk skin stretched out to dry, using stone-scraping tools. A pile of long bow staves lie at the hunter's side. He turns a large biface of lustrous volcanic rock to and fro in his hands, and then strikes a carefully chosen spot with a small hammer stone. A sharp-edged flake falls onto the sand at his feet. Putting the biface aside, the hunter turns the new flake over and around, feeling the thin fragment, visualizing the lethal weapon in his mind.

Minutes pass as he contemplates the flake. Then he picks up a rounded length of deer antler, grinds the perimeters of the stone, and deftly applies pressure to one edge. Thin flake after thin flake flies softly off the edge as he works one side to a curved point. The hunter turns the flake over, repeats the process on the other side, and then starts on the second edge. Within a few minutes, the flake becomes a razor-sharp point. But the base is too thick. Again, the man weighs the flake in his hands, turning it back and forth, feeling the stone. Finally, he places it on end on a log, takes an antler punch, and strikes off a longitudinal flake from the base. Many times, the punch has shattered the new head. But this time, the thinning works. The stoneworker holds up the point to the sun. The black tool glistens translucently. He looks at it with profound satisfaction. . . .

In ancient California, stone tool making and the manufacture of hunting weapons was no luxury. It was a survival skill. Deadly, highly effective stone spear points required the best possible raw material. The most treasured stone for such weapons was obsidian, the finest of volcanic glasses. Hunting and obsidian went hand in hand, not only among Paleo-Indians, who preyed on occasion on very large animals, but among their successors, many of whom hunted nothing larger than a deer, duck, or rabbit. People cherished obsidian, traveled long distances to obtain it, passed the shiny stone from hand–to hand over hundreds of miles. And when hunting larger animals became more commonplace after 2500 B.C., obsidian became a fabric of interconnectedness that linked hundreds of isolated communities in subtle ways.

Obsidian and Tool Making

I love handling obsidian. The feel is sensuous, soft, and buttery to the touch, the rock fine grained and often translucent at the edges, formed by long-forgotten volcanic eruptions. Obsidian has been famous since the days of Roman author, Pliny the Elder. He recounted its discovery by one Opsius in Ethiopia—a miracle rock that "reflects shadows instead of images."

The sensuous feel comes from a violent past. Obsidian forms when molten lava flows into a lake or the ocean and cools rapidly. The cooling produces a glassy rock. Iron and magnesium give the stone a dark green-to-black hue. A rich, reddish brown hue is extraordinarily beautiful and much prized. Sometimes, ancient air bubbles created distinctive gold, green, or yellow sheens in the molten rock. Obsidian outcrops are rare, their cobbles highly prized for their brilliant sheen and superb tool-making qualities. California is blessed with more than its share of obsidian sources.

This rare and exotic volcanic glass has an unusual quality. Obsidian fractures conchoidally. In other words, when you strike a piece of it, shock waves ripple through the stone and form a distinctive cone. If you strike the rock at the edge, a flake forms. The stone fractures along the edge of the ripple. This fracture quality, combined with the fine grain of the rock, makes obsidian ideal for use as projectile points (see figure 7.1).

I have never been able to master stone tool making, even after spending several days some years ago at a lithic technology camp under the tutelage of a master like Jeff Flenniken, who makes Clovis points as easily as other peo-

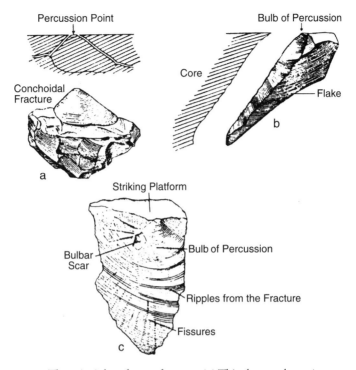

Figure 7.1. The principles of stone fracture. (a) This shows a lump (or core, to use technical parlance) of obsidian or other fine-grained stone, struck with a hammer stone. (b) A flake falls from the core, displaying the characteristic "bulb of percussion," and shock rings resulting from the blow. The technical terms are used to describe features of the flake, some of which are referred to in these pages.

ple strike matches. The skill, once learned, is like riding a bicycle—something that becomes second nature.

Skill was one thing, and, had I persisted, I would probably have acquired a basic proficiency in a few weeks. I learned from Jeff that the greatest expertise lies not in the fashioning of the artifact, but in knowing the "feel" of the stone, predicting how it will flake. This is akin to splitting planks from a log, where an experienced woodsman listens to the noises coming from the cracks his wedges generate and knows when to hammer more.

I also learned that a great deal also depends on the qualities of the tool-making stone. Conchoidal fracturing is essential, a fine-grained, glassy rock ideal. And obsidian is the most desirable raw material of all. Apart from being gorgeous to behold and possessing of all the desirable technological qualities, obsidian is wickedly sharp. The late Don Crabtree of Idaho was a maestro of stone tool manufacture and could replicate any prehistoric artifact ever fashioned in rock. He even made the surgical tools for his own cataract surgery—the cutting edges were sharper than the finest stainless steel.

Ancient Californians prized obsidian for projectile points, and, later, for much smaller arrowheads. In later times, exotic obsidian bifaces and blades became symbols of wealth and prestige, displayed in public on ceremonial occasions.[2]

Obsidian outcrops in relatively few places. Some of the finest North American deposits lie in California and the western Great Basin, especially in the northeast of the state, where people quarried, used, and traded the lustrous rock for well over 11,000 years. Small fragments of obsidian from the Clear Lake and Mountain Lake highlands regions of northern California, and from the Casa Diablo and Coso volcanic areas on the eastern slopes of the Sierras, as well as other locations, turn up in archaeological sites of all periods many miles from their original sources (see figure 7.2).

Thanks to some remarkable high technology science, we can use obsidian as a measure of interconnectedness between different groups thousands of years ago. From spectrographic analysis, we can identify the actual source of many of the obsidian artifacts manufactured in ancient times. Each source has its own distinctive combination of trace elements in the obsidian, making it possible to link artifacts hundreds of miles from their point of origin with a specific location. Such sourcing enables us to trace dramatic changes in the ways obsidian changed hands over the millennia.

Sourcing research began in the eastern Mediterranean during the 1960s. Some contemporaries of mine at Cambridge University used spectrographic analysis to identify important obsidian sources in Turkey, Iran, and elsewhere. Then they traced the distributions of these obsidians in the form of artifacts from village to village over hundreds of miles. Since then, obsidian sourcing has become big business. There is even an International Association for Obsidian Studies.[3]

The sourcing problem is enormous in California. I was astounded to learn from the Web that there are at least fifty-five obsidian sources within the borders of the state, each with its own distinctive signature of trace elements. Such elements are invisible to the naked eye: minute amounts of

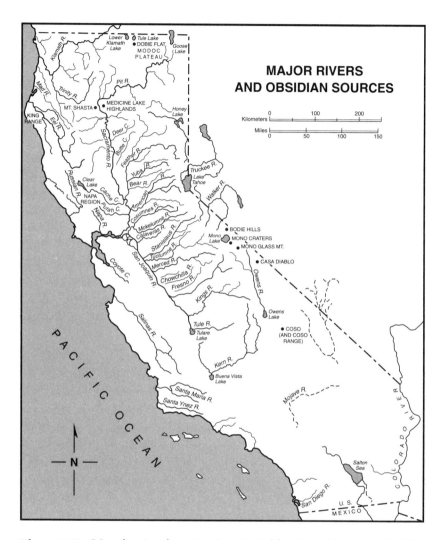

Figure 7.2. Map showing the major rivers in California and the principal obsidian sources mentioned in this book.

chemical elements in the obsidian. However, they emit characteristic wavelengths of light when heated to incandescence and viewed with a spectrometer. After thousands of analyses, we can begin to discern the vast extent of California's ancient obsidian exchange.

We cannot rely on trace element analysis alone, which merely provides information on the source. As archaeologists we have more profound questions. To what extent did a group living in, say, the Central Valley, make use of exotic as opposed to local stone? Did these proportions change over time? Was obsidian used for specific types of ceremonial or utilitarian artifacts and not for others? Did people obtain volcanic glass by going to the source and collecting it, or did they exchange it hand to hand over long distances? These questions are just as important as plotting sources on a map and then reconstructing trading networks from them.

Obsidian Exchange

The Clovis people blazed the obsidian trail. Paleo-Indian and other early hunter-gatherer groups around Tule Lake in northeastern California made extensive use of local obsidian. In this region, populations were so sparse that they almost certainly traveled to the nearest outcrop and quarried the stone for themselves. A visit to the obsidian quarries was part of the annual round for people who moved over long distances throughout the year.

We know this because of studies of such groups on the Great Plains, where people would travel more than 150 miles to obtain good quality toolmaking stone for their projectile heads. Plains people tended to use fine-grained cherts and chalcedonies, but their distant relatives in the west had access to basalt, obsidian, and other good quality volcanic rock in much greater abundance.[4] No one "owned' the outcrops, so far as we can tell; most groups simply visited quarries and obtained lumps of tool-making stone when they needed it. These lumps were fashioned on the spot into large blanks that were easily carried.[5]

I have always thought of Paleo-Indian stone technology as operating somewhat like a savings account. The accounts were large nodules of obsidian and other tool-making stone, usually flaked on both sides and often called "bifaces," collected or exchanged from known outcrops, then carried around for use as needed. Clovis projectile points are sophisticated-looking artifacts, but were simple enough that an expert artisan could turn one out in short order. The finished heads came from thin flakes carefully struck off from the biface, which became smaller and smaller as the weeks and months passed. Much the same principle operated in later times, when people used every lump of precious volcanic rock to the fullest. Everyone was careful with their projectile points, modifying and resharpening them for reuse to save raw material. Inevitably, the "savings account" of raw stone eventually ran low and had to be replenished with a fresh biface from the Paleo-Indian equivalent of an ATM.

Paleo-Indian and Milling Stone groups were small and isolated, with only sporadic contact between neighbors. This meant that the greatest use of obsidian was among those living closest to the natural outcrops, where stone was to be found for the picking up. Obsidian was highly valued, but the tentacles of the trade were small and highly localized, with the greatest use always being within a few days' journey of the source. We know this from the Modoc Plateau in northeastern California, where archaeologists working on a pipeline project extending over Idaho, Oregon, Washington, and California discovered thousands of obsidian artifacts and fragments in the sites along the pipeline corridor. Between 90 and 100 percent of the tool-making stone on the plateau was obsidian, testimony to the abundance of the rock in that region within a twenty- to thirty-mile radius. Far south in the Sacramento and Delta areas, raw materials were far more diverse, with obsidian forming 41 percent of the stone, most of it from sources in the Napa region.

The Medicine Lake highland region around Mount Shasta was the richest source anywhere in northern California. People living all the way from Tule Lake to the Pit River area made use of this fine obsidian, an expanse of more than seventy miles. The pipeline study found that some exotic obsidians traveled an average distance of ninety-four miles from their original source.

Throughout ancient times, obsidian exchange operated most intensively within a reasonable distance of the source. The Medicine Lake highland and extreme northeastern California sources, for instance, are commonplace over a radius of about seventy miles, but fall off sharply thereafter. Oregon and Blue Mountain obsidian from far northeastern California do not appear south of the Modoc Plateau. Nearly all Sacramento and Delta area obsidian came from the Clear Lake and Napa regions.

How, then, did these obsidians travel? The easiest way is for their owners to journey to the source and collect it themselves. Such a strategy operated well in Paleo-Indian times, when population densities were small and people traveled long distances in the course of their seasonal rounds. The obsidian trade began with this simple collecting strategy and probably operated this way for thousands of years. Even distant groups organized special detours, or even expeditions to acquire obsidian from its source, just as they did plant foods and other commodities.

But when populations rose and mobility became more circumscribed in some areas, as they did after about 2500 B.C., the issue of access became more complex. Then obsidian became an item of exchange. A day's walk was the magic bullet, for beyond that radius an exotic commodity like obsidian became an item of exchange. This highly prized glass became the catalyst for the extensive trade in all manner of exotic and prosaic objects and raw materials of later millennia. Tool-making stone was probably the first commodity exchanged between neighbors in California. Fortunately, hundreds of sourcing samples allow us to study the trade.

In 1994, Pat Mikkelsen, William Hildebrandt, and Deborah Jones compiled a survey of the distribution and changing use of Medicine Lake Highlands obsidian in northern California.[6] They used a large database of obsidian artifact data from eleven adjacent regions in northern and northeastern parts of the state. Using this information, they plotted the percentage of obsidian as opposed to other tool-making materials in sites across northern California. As one might expect, the percentage drops sharply as one moves south from the Medicine Lake region into the Central Valley, and travels west of the coast ranges and Klamath Mountains. Medicine Lake obsidian in the form of projectile points and bifaces moved in relatively large quantities within about fifty miles of its source to the south and west. Then it thinned out rapidly (see figure 7.3).

But were there changes in obsidian use through time? Did later people use the glass for the same purposes as Paleo-Indians? Fortunately, you can date obsidian samples, as well as source them. A newly made obsidian surface absorbs water from its surroundings, forming a measurable hydration layer that is invisible to the naked eye. The freshly exposed surface has a strong affinity for water and keeps absorbing it until it is saturated with a layer of water molecules. These molecules slowly diffuse into the body of the obsidian. This hydration zone contains about 3.5 percent water, increasing the density of the layer and allowing it to be measured accurately under polarized light. The depth of the hydration layer represents the time since the object was manufactured or used. Obsidian hydration is not the most

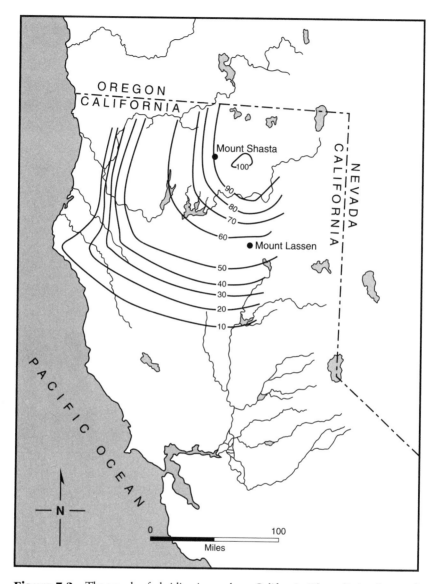

Figure 7.3. The travels of obsidian in northern California. The radiating lines and numbers indicate the percentage fall off from source. Courtesy of William Hildebrandt, Far Western Anthropological Research Group, Inc.

accurate of dating methods, one problem being that hydration rates tend to be site-specific and to depend on temperature. But it does allow the development of "hydration profiles" extending over many centuries. Thus, one can assess the maximum periods of use of particular obsidians.

We know from obsidian hydration tests that the Medicine Lake profiles peak long after Paleo-Indian times, between 1500 B.C. and A.D. 650. The same peak occurred at Dobie Flat and Tule Lake to the east, also to the south and west in the Pit River and Upper Sacramento Valley areas, where Medicine Lake obsidian was still dominant. Then, after A.D. 650, the use of obsidian tailed off considerably.

I find this fascinating. Until about A.D. 650, the people living over this large area were still highly mobile. Many groups could visit the obsidian sources and collect the material for themselves. Hunters carried projectile points far and wide as they pursued their quarry; other artifacts and bifaces changed hands as part of a system of informal exchange. But, by the first millennium A.D., California's population had risen to the point where people lived in more circumscribed territories and moved around a lot less. The entire dynamics of obsidian exchange altered dramatically. Obsidian use tapered off sharply in many areas, as people turned to local rock such as chert or quartzite for their projectile points.

Along the King Range area of the northwestern coast, Medicine Lake obsidian continued to be popular right into near-historical times. Here, the people rarely used volcanic glass in day-to-day life, but reserved obsidian for ceremonial use. Almost all the obsidian found along the coast consists of angular fragments buried with the dead. Their bodies lay on beds of obsidian debris, created deliberately at the time of burial. Wiyot people displayed black or red finely made obsidian blades like jewelry at major ceremonies, a practice known to have flourished in earlier centuries (see chapter 10).

The same decline in obsidian exchange occurred in the south, where the Coso and Casa Diablo sources east of the Sierras were in peak use between 1000 B.C. and A.D. 1000. How these obsidians reached the groups west of the mountains is a matter for discussion. The people living west of the Sierras were highly mobile hunter-gatherers, occupying large territories in dry terrain. They were hardly in a position to organize large-scale trade networks across the mountains. Many archeologists believe that people simply traveled to the source and collected what they needed. Other authorities, like Michael Moratto, theorize there were large-scale exchange systems in operation across the Sierras at the time, organized by sedentary communities living at some distance from one another on each side of the mountains.

Then, around A.D. 550, much warmer and drier conditions settled over the region for two centuries, disrupting sedentary life and long-established obsidian trade networks. There are signs, however, that the trade continued on a large scale. For example, obsidian and other imports such as shell beads abound at Little Lake, on the extreme westernmost edge of the Great Basin, in east-central California, where late occupation abounds.[7]

There are other potential explanations, too—volcanic eruptions in the area of the Casa Diablo quarries around A.D. 1300 may have limited access. Technological changes resulting from the introduction of the bow and arrow may have caused demand for fine-grained rock to plummet. At the same time, the obsidian trade became more costly in terms of effort and organization, at a time when movement across the Sierras was constrained by territorial boundaries and when arrows with much smaller stone tips became more important than spears.

As we saw in chapter 1, population densities throughout California remained relatively low until about 2500 B.C., when the frequency of archaeological sites increases dramatically, presumably a reflection of growing population. And, as we saw in chapter 6, these population increases stimulated more intensive hunting and gathering, among them the widespread processing of acorns.

As I was doing research for this chapter, the latest issue of *American Antiquity*, the national journal for American archaeologists, arrived. In it, I found a fascinating paper by William Hildebrandt and Kelly McGuire in which they question the commonly held assumption that the hunting of larger animals declined over the millennia from Paleo-Indian times.[8] They point to the rising counts of larger animals after 2000 B.C. throughout the state, where the men, once heavily engaged in plant gathering during Milling Stone times now turned to the hunting of more prestigious animals, prized for their high meat yield and difficulty of slaying. In the Coso Range of the southern interior, for one example, bighorn sheep, deer, and pronghorn increase threefold relative to rabbits and other small animals from earlier sites. They do so precisely during the centuries when obsidian exchange spikes in the north and south (for more discussion on this point, see chapter 9).

Herein may lie the explanation for the popularity of obsidian in earlier times—it was used to make the lethal projectile points and bifaces hunters carried as they pursued their elusive prey. Obsidian's desirability fluctuated through the centuries according to need, passing from hand to hand in exchanges driven by both pragmatic, and, later, ceremonial concerns.

Here, as elsewhere in the world, interconnectedness meant relying on others to provide commodities and exotic items that you needed. And when such materials and finished artifacts were no longer needed, the demand fell. Then as now, fashion, and the simple laws of supply and demand, shaped contacts between near and distant neighbors.

The ancient traffic in obsidian was one of the catalysts for an explosion in interconnectedness among ancient California societies after 1500 B.C. So was that in shell beads.

Intelligence and Interdependency

If obsidian was a catalyst, what, then, were the political and social realities behind this growing interconnectedness? Two words provide the context: food and survival.

Many years ago, the great anthropologist Raymond Firth wrote of the Tikopia people of Polynesia in the South Pacific: "Food serves as a most important manifestation of social relationship, and through it kin ties, political loyalty, indemnity for wrong, and the canons of hospitality are expressed."[9] I thought about and reread Firth's classic work on Polynesian economies early on in my research for this book. Polynesia is a long way away from the western United States, but I realized that Firth had hit on a fundamental reality of life at the subsistence level. The close ties between food supplies and social relationships of all kinds observed by Firth applied with equal force in ancient California. If anything, they were even more pressing in a land of unpredictable rainfall and profound environmental contrasts.

Myths abound about California's past, romanticized tales of golden, cloudless days, never too warm, never too cold, with plentiful food on every side.[10] Wrote Alfred Kroeber in 1925: "The food resources of California were bountiful in their variety rather than in their overwhelming abundance. If one supply failed there were a hundred others to fall back upon. . . . Downright mortal famine had been less than often the portion of the Californian tribes than of those in most other regions of the continent."[11]

Reality was very different. There was never a golden age in California when there was always enough to eat and people could gather food effortlessly without relying on others. Theirs was a world of uncertain rainfall and dramatic temperature gradients, of patchy food supplies widely scattered over the landscape. In most places, the landscape could only support at most a handful of people per square mile, and when populations rose beyond the ability of the environment to support them, they were in trouble.

For thousands of years, California's population was highly mobile and thinly scattered over large territories. Such mobility provided some protection against food shortages and a level of self-sufficiency. To survive and remain self-sufficient required an encyclopedic knowledge of less commonly eaten animals and plants. You also had to know where food was to be found.

Today, almost no hunter-gatherers still live off the land. The San of the Kalahari Desert in southern Africa (often still called Bushmen) are some of the most intensively studied hunter-gatherers on earth. They still retain many of their institutions, but have been in touch with cattle herders and farmers for centuries. Richard Lee and the other anthropologists who lived among them observed how the San spent enormous amounts of time talking to others, gathering information about water supplies, game, and plant foods over large areas beyond the horizon. Carefully gathered intelligence was the language of interaction, and of survival in the San's arid world. Undoubtedly, the same held true in ancient California.[12]

The Paleo-Indians and their successors must have spent a great deal of time on intelligence—finding out from neighbors where patches of food plants were to be found, where water still remained in times of drought, tracking the movements of game animals across their territory. Information was survival, obtained from kin in neighboring bands, from visitors to camp from nearby areas, from hunters from other groups encountered by a water hole. The language of survival was intelligence, and the instrument of its acquisition the kin ties that linked families and bands over hundreds of square miles. Individual talked to individual, bartered an obsidian biface for some seeds. Fellow kin arranged marriages and exchanged food or tool-making stone.

There was never complete self-sufficiency nor complete isolation: every band had a mental map of its territory and land beyond. But the world was a small one, and the interconnections between neighbors at best sporadic, and always informal. There was no need for anything else.

We know that populations rose sharply after 3000 B.C., at the end of the dry and warm Altithermal period. Within a thousand years or so, much of

California was full. The carrying capacity of the land could no longer support many local populations. Tribal territories became much smaller, mobility increasingly circumscribed. Few groups could now feed themselves, living as they were in local environments, which might be abundant, say, in seed plants, but not in deer. Basket-weaving materials were plentiful in one band's territory, but unavailable over the hill, where their neighbors needed baskets to process acorns. The language of survival changed, from intelligence to interdependence, from self-sufficiency to a new social and political world, where alliances, individual ability, and kin ties counted for much more—and for food.

Beads and Sundries

As I started to write this book, I found myself wading through pages of site inventories and through report after report that mentioned obsidian, seashells, and other exotic imports. The catalogs were endless, but what did they mean in human terms? We archaeologists study the material remains of ancient societies. Only the most durable artifacts survive; there is virtually no information about such intangibles as kin ties, social organization, and political structure. I remember many years ago finding a solitary red glass Indian Ocean trade bead in a remote African farming village of 1,500 years ago, no less than 600 miles from the Indian Ocean. I wondered what stories this tiny bead could tell about its long journey from the Indian Ocean shore, about the people who carried it, and about the African farmer who once wore it then lost it in the dust of the village. Alas, the bead was silent, but just the fact that it was in such a place was an important scientific fact.

I've had the same feeling as I look over California museum collections, with their boxes of shell beads and simple ornaments. What stories these unspectacular beads could recount: of long-forgotten relationships between people in neighboring villages and between chiefs and their opposite numbers inland, who offered acorns for beads; of the prideful display of bead necklaces and shell ornaments at trade feasts; or of the adorning of a woman in her finery as she is laid in her grave. But the beads are silent. All that remain are the material artifacts of intricate and ever-changing human relationships.

Objects like beads, or, for that matter, obsidian points, tell us little of the subtle interplay between people on either sides of an exchange, of the often complex social mechanisms, which helped pass exotica from one household to another. They cast no light on the deeds of the more aggressive members of society, who initiated trade with neighbors, channeled it through their hands, or organized the trading feasts and elaborate ceremonies that passed their wealth to others. The artifacts are silent, it is only the impressive ingenuity of the archaeologist, often extrapolating from historic times, which draws aside the curtain and moves us from the material to the ancient intangible.

The range of artifacts and commodities exchanged by ancient Californians was truly remarkable. *The Handbook of North American Indians*, volume 8 surveys the peoples of California. In its magisterial pages, I found a list of the artifacts and commodities exchanged by native Californians in recent times, compiled by anthropologist James Davis in 1961.[13] The list took my breath away. Foods alone covered the whole spectrum of what was available in the environment—acorns, berries, fish, game meat, mollusk flesh, pine nuts, salt, and seeds of all kinds. Then there were essential commodities: asphaltum, basketry materials, bow wood, obsidian, and steatite (a massive talc)—to mention only a few. Finished artifacts and ceremonial objects changed hands: bows and arrows, dugout canoes, stone pestles and mortars, tule mats, and all manner of ceremonial regalia, as well as shell and stone beads of all kinds. Of course, not all of these commodities or objects changed hands at the same time, for fashions and needs ebbed and flowed over the centuries.

Only a fraction of this trade survives for the archaeologist, most notably the traffic in shell beads.

Let me admit at once that I have an aversion to beads. This dates back to my early archaeological career, when I excavated burials festooned in thousands of freshwater and ostrich eggshell beads and others adorned with imported Indian Ocean glass trade beads carried hundreds of miles into the heart of tropical Africa. Sorting them for weeks on end was not a stimulating experience.

But beads are deceptive. They may be monotonous to gaze on, but, in California, beads are a mine of information on ancient exchange, and on the fleeting, and sometimes lasting, ties, which linked coastal groups to people living in the interior. Changing bead fashions also serve as chronological markers. Like stone spear heads, they are the potsherds of ancient California, substituting for the clay vessels used over the rest of North America for the same purpose (see figure 7.4).

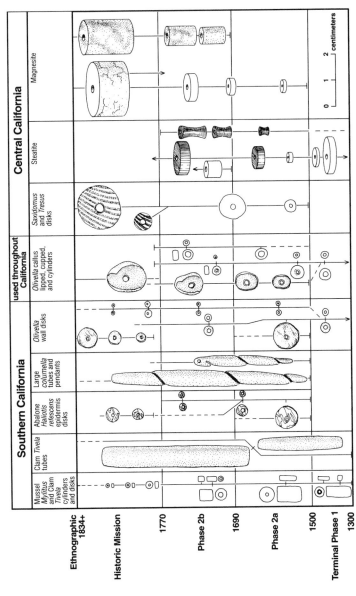

Figure 7.4. A wide variety of shell beads were manufactured in central and southern California during later times. This drawing displays some of the different forms used by archaeologists to date sites. Data are from the *Handbook of North American Indians*, Volume 8, 59.

I have an even stronger aversion to literature on shell beads, which often means almost nothing except to the handful of specialists who study such artifacts. I confess that I skated over the complex, and often ponderous, bead literature with almost indecent haste. What follows are some general comments on beads as a historical phenomenon.[14]

Millions of shell beads circulated through California in ancient times, most of them during the past five hundred years, when some shell beads became a form of currency, with recognized value. This obsession with bead money persisted into historic times. Long after Europeans arrived with their money economy, some older Pomo from northern California used cash to purchase clamshell beads, their ancient wealth, to be buried with them. The Chumash and the Miwok, among other groups, manufactured enormous numbers of beads in the centuries immediately before Europeans arrived. Bead making had become a specialized craft.

Shell bead exchange began as early as Milling Stone times, but never on a large scale. We know for certain that some *olivella* shell beads were in circulation as early as 6000 B.C., and probably considerably earlier, but there were never large numbers in circulation until later times (see box 7.1).

After A.D. 1000, at a time of rising populations and rapidly expanding trade, shell beads became a major exchange commodity, to the point that some shells, like the Pismo clam, became a form of informal currency and a source of individual wealth.

Of all shell beads, the abalone and *olivella* were the most popular. *Olivellas* document hand-to-hand exchanges involving marine shells far into the desert interior and northeast into the Great Basin over many centuries. In the second millennium A.D., the ancient Mojave Trail extended from southern Chumash territory deep into the Southwest and carried both abalone and *olivella* into that region, although the Gulf of Mexico was another source. But, for the most part, the millions of shell beads made by the Chumash, Miwok, and other groups stayed closer to home, consumed by island and mainland communities, used in funerary rites, and in ceremonial life. The volume of truly long-distance exchange was very small indeed when compared with the constant movement of commodities and prestigious artifacts within tribelet territories and between neighbors, the level at which most interconnectedness operated.

For all the trade activity along the innumerable trails that linked all parts of ancient California, few people traveled long distances. Rather, strings of

BOX 7.1 The Common Trade Beads
of Ancient California

The *olivella* was the most common trade shell. It is a small bivalve commonly found along the Pacific coast. This seemingly unimportant shell assumed great importance as an ornament, as a source of small beads, and as currency. Generations of archaeologists have created elaborate typologies of *olivella* beads, which reflect changing fashions and the use of different parts of the shell. We know most about them from the Santa Barbara Channel region, where a major *olivella* bead industry developed after A.D. 1000 (see chapter 14).

The earliest *olivella* beads came from grinding the spire of the shell, then punching or abrading small holes in them. Another simple method involved punching a small hole in a thin, carefully shaped fragment. The dead wore the end products—square and rounded disk beads from the walls of the shells, barrel-like beads, and ground spires. Such simple beads come from graves or were scattered in residential middens; they were manufactured on a modest scale for local use and sometimes exchanged with neighbors and passed from hand to hand over considerable distances (see figure 7.5).

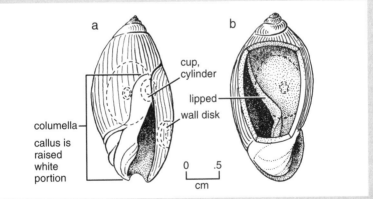

Figure 7.5. Component parts of an *olivella* shell. Redrawn from the *Handbook of North American Indians*, Volume 8, 60.

Strings of *olivella* traveled long distances inland, passing from hand to hand, from individual to individual, even as far as the Great Basin. A string of about fifty *olivellas* passed hand to hand as far east as Leonard Rockshelter in Pershing County, Nevada, in about 6600 B.C., 250 miles from the coast.

Olivellas were the most common shell beads for thousands of years. Disk beads came from the wall of the shell, more lipped and cupped beads from the shell's callus, the edges chipped to form a curved edge. We know most about *olivellas* in southern California, where earlier bead makers produced disk beads made almost entirely from the wall of the shell, which largely gave way to the callus form after A.D. 900, when disk beads shrank to less than a third of the total production. Bead manufacture continued after European contact, when the wall bead came back into fashion alongside the callus.

Haliotis rufescens (red abalone) were prized for display purposes. These mollusks flourish at depths where it is necessary to dive to acquire them for food. So they were in shorter supply and the available shell heavily exploited. But the shells made attractive ornaments, with their reddish, rough outer surface, and shiny mother of pearl interior. Bead makers used the epidermis of the shell, separating it from the nacre before shaping their bead blanks. They would sometimes grind the surface smooth before breaking it into bead-sized fragments. Then they drilled a hole in the shell. After stringing the blanks, the bead maker ground them to the desired shape on a slab of sandstone or some other abrasive rock. Abalone beads were uncommon before A.D. 1000, when production increased considerably, accelerating even further in historic times. Both black and red abalones provided the raw materials for oblong and rectangular pendants and other ornaments in many areas.

The Pismo clam (*Tivela stultorum*) thrives on sandy beaches. This mollusk has a tough shell, which was prized by some groups and frequently made into beads during the past thousand years.

California mussels (*Mytilus californianus*) were commonplace, but rarely made into beads, except as dark purple specimens used to accent strands of white *olivellas*.

Dentalium beads were popular in northwestern California, and occur very rarely further south.

beads, Southwest Pueblo stone axes and cotton blankets, and many other items passed from hand to hand, often over hundreds of miles. Like obsidian, shell beads served as a familiar medium of exchange. In the centuries before Spanish contact, shell beads were of standardized size, exchanged in measured lengths of bead strands, and used to cement exchange relationships and to validate social status.

With more circumscribed territories, higher population densities, and much greater challenges in extending exchanges of exotic commodities beyond local boundaries, interconnectedness was ultimately a local phenomenon. Less mobile groups depended on one another for different kinds of food and other materials in a world where there was intense competition for food and the rainfall was highly unpredictable. This is why ritual, social, and political institutions were all-important.

In Part IV, we describe the diverse societies that flourished in ancient California after 1500 B.C., over three and a half millennia when ritual came to assume an increasingly significant role in human existence, as we will see in chapter 8.

The Realm of the Supernatural

T HE DANCER'S HEADDRESS AND CAPE SHIMMERED IN THE firelight, a cascade of abalone shell fragments glittering down his back. He wore a swordfish skull complete with beak, which projected out from his forehead, the great eyes depicted in abalone fragments set in asphalt. Feathers and breast ornaments replicated the fins. The dancer mimicked the movements of the swordfish as it leaped from the water. Tonight, the swordfish is the ritual guest, honored for bringing ample whale meat to the people.

The pursuit of the swordfish in deep water involved risk and skill as well as prestige. Numerous Chumash myths identify the great fish as their marine allies, who drove whales ashore for humans to feed on. Elaborate costumes, dances, and feasting honored this most formidable of prey, an equal in the complex world of his hunters. The swordfish were people. "They had a house at the bottom of the ocean, but there was no water inside." A fisherman once glimpsed one, a squat man. "On his head was a long bone, his instrument of attack. The fisherman threw a rock and the *'elye'wun* jumped far out into the water and disappeared."[1]

The Challenge of the Intangible

In chapters 6 and 7, we witnessed the gradual major change that spread through a more densely populated California after 2500 B.C., the more

177

intensive focus on acorns and other foods, and the growing interconnectedness linking communities and kin groups. We mentioned the ambitions of aggrandizers, individuals of ability and unusual skills, who became major players in a changing world where wealth and prestige, and the ability to attract loyal followers counted for more and more. Some of them became hereditary chiefs.

Like ambitious, powerful people everywhere, ancient California's aggrandizers needed far more than food and lavish gifts to foster loyalty and exercise authority over the people who fed them, paddled their canoes, or fabricated shell beads or ceremonial ornaments. In a world without writing, they needed the validation of ritual.

The relationship with the supernatural world was always important in ancient California life, even as early as Paleo-Indian times. Creation legends, chants, and dances validated human existence and the familiar world order, the passing of the seasons and the continuity of life. But, as the world became more crowded, relationships with others more important, and the need for cooperation more pressing, so formal ritual moved to center stage both as a setting for human life and as a mechanism for validating chiefly authority.

We know a great deal about ancient California society after 1500 B.C., when the world became even more crowded, the landscape of daily life more political. But scientists have tended to ignore the central role that rituals of all kinds played in these changing cultures. Even the humblest aggrandizer learned early on that to control ritual activity was to control people, a way of ensuring conformity, of reinforcing collective identity, and, above all, of justifying the exercise of chiefly authority.

But how do we study long-vanished rituals in societies that flourished centuries before the brief time span covered by oral tradition?

Archaeologists converse with "material voices" from ancient California's past—with stone artifacts like Clovis points and Windmiller charmstones and with shell beads, animal bones, seeds, and mollusk shells. These voices are the durable legacies of long-forgotten human behavior, made and used by the tribelets of centuries and millennia past. Our finds tell tales, but, as previous chapters have made only too clear, the narratives are incomplete and unsatisfying. For the most part, they describe only the business of daily life. The real storytellers are long silent.

This is the most tantalizing, nay frustrating, part of archaeology, which I have regretted ever since I met the Greek poet and epic storyteller Homer for the first time. Homer's *Iliad* and *Odyssey* are heroic adventure stories, written down sometime in the ninth century B.C. But what is not often realized is that Homer set down rich oral traditions, recited for hundreds of years by itinerant singers and storytellers. Try reading the following aloud, and you will get the point:

> Here young boys and girls, beauties courted
> With costly gifts of oxen, danced and danced,
> Linking their arms, gripping each other's wrists . . .
> And now they would run in rings on their skilled feet,
> Nimbly, quick as a crouching potter spins his wheel,
> Palming it smoothly, giving it practice twirls
> To see it run, and now they would run in rows,
> In rows crisscrossing rows—rapturous dancing.[2]

I was blessed with a wonderful Classics teacher in high school, who lived and breathed Homer. He recited the *Iliad* and *Odyssey* like living epics, with all the subtle nuances of good and evil, joy, pathos, and tragedy. When Homer was read aloud at the teacher's funeral, there was not a dry eye in the place. But of all the verses he recited, the lively dancers have always stuck in my mind, both because you are literally watching the dance, and because they strike at the very core of what archaeologists try to do—reconstruct the intangible from the most prosaic of material objects. The oral traditions Homer used are a similar genre to the rich stories and legends of ancient California. And these are almost all lost to us.

We work with a very incomplete record and can only use indirect methods to infer the ancient intangible. Chant and dance, narrative, and performance and ritual defined the ancient California world. We cannot witness them in person, only study them remotely, impersonally, from scatters of artifacts and rock art (see box 8.1).

The intangible was the realm of the storyteller, lived on long winter nights by the fireside, when such gifted people held sway. Flickering firelight, a rapt audience watching intently as the story unfolds with delicate nuance and careful orchestrated expressions. The listeners have heard the story before, but it is never exactly the same. They laugh, fall silent, wait for the punch line, living with the storyteller in a world peopled by good and bad animals, by spirits and mythic beings, where the forces of the natural world

BOX 8.1 Studying the Ancient Intangible

For years, archaeologists threw up their hands in despair when confronted with the ancient intangible. There was a category for unexplained artifacts and structures labeled "ritual." Today, some of the best intellects in archaeology are grappling with scientific methodologies for studying ancient religion and belief. There is a very fine line between science and bold flirtation with the speculative, "a kind of bungee jump into the Land of Fantasy," as archaeologists Kent Flannery and Joyce Marcus called it.

Today, California archaeologists use a variety of methods to study ancient belief and ritual. These include:

Historical records and oral tradition, also early anthropological observations are an important source of information about the intangible as it existed at the time of European contact and thereafter. How much time depth such records give us is a matter for discussion, for both beliefs and rituals changed profoundly over many centuries. But these sources provide an invaluable baseline, especially the records collected by such scholars as Harrington, Kroeber, and others.

Ethnographic analogies—comparisons between historic and ancient institutions, practices, and artifacts—are a useful way of interpreting archaeological finds, and especially for identifying sacred motifs or ceremonial objects. This approach is especially useful when there is evidence of cultural continuity from the time of European contact deep into the past, as was the case in many areas.

Rock art, in the form of engravings and paintings, is a potentially fruitful source of information on the intangible, provided it is securely dated and its context well established. The engravings found in the Coso Range, described in chapter 9, are an excellent example.

Artifacts, architecture, and art set in precise contexts of time and space are significant sources of information on the intangible. The shaman's regalia found in Newberry Cave in the Mojave Desert, described in the next chapter, are an excellent example. The distinctive architecture of sweat houses is another.

Exotic artifacts, such as the fine obsidian bifaces so highly prized in northwestern California, are distinctive objects known from historical records to be symbols of wealth, displayed at important ceremonies.

Landscape and settlement archaeology place archaeological sites and hierarchies of larger and smaller archaeological sites in their environmental context. Sometimes, the distribution of these sites on the landscape and in relation to one another can speak volumes about ancient beliefs and religious observances, witness the clusters of ancient shell mounds in the San Francisco Bay Area.

In studying the ancient intangible, much depends on the skill and imagination of the archaeologist, as well as sheer luck. For instance, the chance find in 1923 of an elaborate swordfish costume with a burial in the Santa Barbara region dating to about 100 B.C. proved that the historic dance in honor of the swordfish was at least two thousand years old (see figure 8.1).

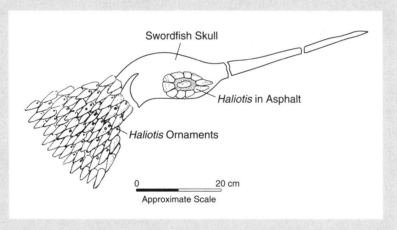

Figure 8.1. Drawing of a swordfish dancer's costume found by David Banks Rogers near Santa Barbara in 1923. The dancer wore the swordfish skull over his head, with the beak pointing upward. Courtesy of Santa Barbara Museum of Natural History.

compete. The stories unfold for hours, never losing anything in their repetition, offering wisdoms, precedents, and moral value. They are the very fabric of society.

These were societies where all information, all learning, passed from one generation to the next by word of mouth, through initiation ceremonies, chants, exhortations, and storytelling. These were societies that lived according to the unchanging verities of their world—the long, hot summer months where the grass was yellow and water dried up in the streams, the subtle signs of approaching winter in the fall when acorns ripened, the cold and rainy winter, and the fresh richness of spring, when salmon ran and plants flowered. It was a cyclical existence, tied to the passing of the seasons: to birth, growth, adulthood, and death. Human existence was unchanging, for each generation inherited from its predecessors a world identical to that of their ancestors, and expected to pass it on unchanged to their descendants. Everything depended on continuity in this cyclical world, on the regular passage of the sun, moon, and other heavenly bodies, on maintaining harmony with the spiritual world.

It was a world of powerful, yet inconspicuous, common beliefs.

A World Alive

Ancient California was a land of intensely provincial societies, tribelets with deep roots in their local environments. Trees, springs, streams, even boulders marked the finite limits of their homelands. Generation passed on knowledge of the surrounding landscape to generation, minute inventories of oak groves and plant stands, water supplies and fishing grounds, learned by recitation and description, and by first-hand observation. Before adulthood, everyone knew their environments with an intimacy that beggars a Westerner's imagination. They lived close to nature and felt part of it.

Everyone shared some common beliefs. Humans shared their existence with animals and plants, and were responsible for them. Every animal, every plant had a soul or spirit, much like that of humans, so all three were equally part of nature. Some groups believed that their ancestors became animals after death, others that their prey was immortal. Hunters thanked the spirits of their quarry for their assistance. The first salmon of the season was treated with great respect. Humans never indulged in wasteful killing, for they knew that conserving other forms of life was both respectful and the key to survival. People took what they needed and expressed their appreciation.

The world was alive—with living caves, lakes, springs, and mountains, with an unseen universe of unseen beings, who had the power to intercede in human life. Said a Nomlaki from northern California: "Everything in the world talks—the trees, the rocks, everything. But we cannot understand them."[3] The Yurok of the northwest believed that a hunter's cunning counted for nothing unless he treated his prey respectfully. Rituals surrounded every human activity, however prosaic, as the only way humans could intercede with the supernatural world, and mitigate the power of unseen forces.

From birth, people listened to creation myths and orations, recited by shamans and others, sometimes within the confines of a secret society formed by the Creator. A Maidu elder defined everyone's duty:

> Keep the sacred dance house, as I have told you, while the world endures. Never neglect my rites and honors. Keep the sacred rattle and the dances. Worship me in the night and not in the daylight. Then shall your fields be full of acorns and nuts; your valleys shall yield plenty of grass seeds and herds; your rivers shall be full of salmon, and your hearts shall be rejoiced.[4]

The ancient Californian worldview combined the physical with the mythical, sometimes an earth floating in a vast ocean, with a sky dome arching above it, sometimes a series of circles where the supernatural realm surrounds the human world. The universe was vertical, with an underworld of spirits, ghosts, and monsters, the living world in the middle, and the realm of the gods and mythic beings in the heavens above. Each human group had its own vision of the world, which almost invariably began atop the highest peak in their territory, or within a known distance. Here the Creator and other powerful gods lived, and here the world was created. The power of the supernatural world lay like a web under the surface of the earth. In some places like conspicuous rocky outcrops, caves and rock shelters, and mountain peaks, lakes, and springs, this power came close to the surface. These places were boundaries through which spirit beings entered and left the living world, and where shamans passed into the spiritual realm.

In such a living, unpredictable world, ritual was always of surpassing importance. Everywhere, the threat of cosmological instability hung over humanity. Throughout California, taboos and rituals were used to control or stabilize a dangerous environment that was peopled by animals and supernatural spirits. Eclipses of the sun and moon were moments of trauma, when a monster, perhaps a bear or a frog, devoured earth's light source. A cacophony of noises served to scare away the monster, to bring back light. World-renewal rituals such as the Kuksu bear cult of north-central California, were all-important, a continual affirmation of the forces of nature.[5]

All these life-affirming rituals must have originated in simpler forms many thousands of years back in the remote past. But in the closing centuries of ancient California, they moved to center stage in a far more crowded, competitive, and intensely political world. Ritual was a key to political power.

Formal Rituals

Ceremonial life touched on almost every aspect of ancient California life, for it provided the context for all kinds of economic and social transactions. This context was often reciprocal, a convenient way of ensuring that neighboring groups were less vulnerable to local droughts and food shortages, of sharing risk. But, especially after 1500 B.C., rituals that had once been simple mechanisms for survival became a central catalyst of society, a way of reinforcing both individual and intergroup relationships, and of stimulating the production, exchange, and consumption of foodstuffs and many other commodities. And, in time, the political authority of chiefs became more and more integrated with ceremonialism, with ritual and ancient religious beliefs. Through their alliances with religious office holders and shamans, the chiefs and aggrandizers used the forces of the spiritual world to reinforce their secular authority, and to make it stick.

Most shamans were healers, who used their powers to treat spiritual imbalances in their patients. But they could also be malevolent, inflicting spiritual disease and "shooting" magical evil into people. They were feared as much as admired. A few shamans were astronomical observers, especially among the Chumash.

As ceremonial life became more sophisticated and more pervasive, so society itself became more elaborate, more highly organized.

We have no means of knowing what forms many rituals took. All we have is a fragile skein of archaeological finds, ethnographic observations, and the rare historical document. We know, for example, that large ceremonial gatherings were of great importance in later times. Spanish friar Geronimo Boscana observed in 1822 that southern California groups "would spend days, nights, and whole weeks dancing, and it can be said that all their passion is given to dancing."[6] Such "fiestas," to use the Spanish term, endured long after European contact and were far more than religious observances. Visitors from a large area would attend, settle disputes, and trade with one another, while chiefs would throw ceremonial feasts, give lavish gifts, and generally display their wealth and power.

The annual mourning ceremony in honor of the dead assumed great significance among the Yokuts of the central Sierra foothills, a formal ritual held at regular intervals that must have had deep roots in the past. At last three tribelets cooperated in this expensive ceremony, shouldering the expense and labor on a reciprocal basis. No one made a profit, for economic reciprocity ruled the day, but the ceremony attracted as many as two or three thousand people from the surrounding area. As part of the mourning process, loose ceremonial relationships between neighbors and more distant tribelets endured for generations, sometimes marked by the exchange of strings of beads and other ceremonial gifts.

Quite apart from the larger, more public ceremonies, smaller rituals marked many of the important moments of the year, such as the catching of the first salmon (described in chapter 10), the appearance of the first rattlesnake, the naming of a child, the completion of the acorn harvest, and the passage of the solstices. Whatever its form, ritual and ceremonialism lay at the core of ancient California life, and with good reason, for everyone lived in a harsh, often capricious world (see figure 8.2).

An aggrandizer's or chief's political power depended more on his social prestige and his personal qualities as a wealthy member of society than on his ability to force people to work for him. His role was essentially paternalistic—he fed the hungry, settled disputes, and redistributed food. The chief was a powerful moral authority, with no absolute power.

Most aggrandizers and chiefs were careful to maintain close relationships with shamans, who entered the spiritual domain. Shamans were Men of Power. They entered the supernatural world in a trance, often induced by hallucinogens. Almost all of them engaged in vision quests. There they experienced visions, often called dreams. A shaman's dream could involve encounters with animals or monsters, with mythic beings or gods. While

Figure 8.2. A Chumash shaman in ceremonial regalia, including feather head-dress and milkweed fiber skirt trimmed with eagle feathers. Yokut shamans in the Central Valley wore identical costumes. Courtesy of Davidson Library, University of California, Santa Barbara.

dreaming, the shaman was often more than an observer. He would sense he was a participant, actively taking a role in the vision, moving freely and interacting with the forces of the spiritual world. His power came from his visions, his dreams. His trances and altered states of consciousness were ways to manipulate his power, to keep balance in the sacred world, and to influence events in the natural realm. It was shamans who interpreted dreams, cured the sick, and played a leading role in many important rituals.

Shamans listened carefully to the nuances of public opinion and gave advice to powerful individuals in the light of it, often in the name of the ancestors or other spiritual forces. They served as bridges between the supernatural and the living worlds, in a cosmos where there was a continuum between the two. The shaman's doings, their pronouncements, and their rituals lay behind the deeds of every aggrandizer, every chief, and every headman. In the intensely factional and political landscape of competing societies, control of ritual observance and access to supernatural power were all-important—which is why shamans preoccupy many students of ancient California.

More on Shamans

The word *saman* comes from the Tungus people of Siberia, meaning someone with unusual spiritual powers. Such people were very powerful in hunter-gatherer societies like those of California.[8] The enigmatic figure of the shaman haunts ancient California. Storyteller, healer, rainmaker, and link to the supernatural, shamans were integral to political and social life in tribelets large and small. They mediated between the living and spiritual realms, adjudicated the cross-currents of public opinion, helped achieve social harmony. Everyone respected shamans, yet feared them for their supernatural powers.

Some were benign, others malevolent. Some were chiefs, others purely religious functionaries, experts at curing, rain making, divination, or interceding with ancestors and guardian spirits. A few inherited a shaman's skills, but not necessarily the supernatural power, and they learned shamanistic expertise from early childhood. It is said that the power itself would come suddenly, unsought and spontaneously, in a dream. We have no way to verify this, but most shamans probably acquired their power from solitary, little-spoken-about, vision quests. Just occasionally, an individual, who had passed through a powerful spiritual experience, could achieve acceptance as a shaman. Shamans connected the living to the dead, the present generation to the ancestors, monitored the heavenly bodies, and presided over tribal rituals. Their power came from everyone's close relationship to the environment, to animals, plants, and the forces of nature (see figure 8.3).

Vision Quests

Nearly everywhere in the world, shamans operate through dreams seen while in a trance, or, to use a more contemporary term, in altered states of consciousness. This is certainly true of California shamans, who used datura (jimsonweed) and other hallucinogens like tobacco to enter trance during vision quests. Such experiences are common to many native American societies, typically two or three nights of isolation and prayer at a remote loca-

Figure 8.3. Dancing figures from site CA–VEN–195 in the Santa Monica Mountains, southern California. Courtesy of David Whitley.

tion, often in hills or mountains, with ritual bathing and fasting as well as prayer during daylight. Dreams came at night, often by using tobacco before retiring. Drug-induced hallucinations during sleep became powerful dreams. The shaman would awake after his dream, remain alert praying, singing, and concentrating on the vision. At daybreak, he would go to the hills to dream some more. When the dreams were sufficient, he would enter a special locale and talk to his dream helper. Full recollection of the dream was vital. If he forgot it, his spirit helper would vanish forever, or the shaman might sicken and die. Sometimes, he would engrave or paint his visions at his special place shortly after waking, usually in the morning, a time of great supernatural power.[8]

But the real visionary dreaming came at night, often with the help of native tobacco, a powerful hallucinogen. The shaman-to-be would repeat the vision quest again and again until he achieved supernatural power. He could see, hear, and feel the spirit, which he received through visual, aural, and somatic hallucinations. The shaman would now start practicing, but would renew his power through repeated vision quests throughout his life.

What form did these visions take? We have few examples, for the shamans kept their secrets well. Alfred Kroeber recorded a short Yokut dream. The dreamer

> met two strangers at dusk. They took him with them into a stream, through two doors, one formed of a snake, one of a turtle. He had become unconscious. Inside their house, the otters, for such they had become, resumed human shape. They offered *tipni* [supernatural power] to their guest, with the threat that he would not live if he refused. He took the gift, but asked for instructions concerning it. "You shall cure the sick, not kill human beings," was the naïve order he received with his song. When the man awoke, he was on land once more, and dry as if he had never left the earth.[9]

All shaman's visions shared some common patterns. The would-be shaman becomes ill with a condition that does not respond to conventional treatment. He retires to a specific place to fast and ingest tobacco. Then a spirit may or may not lead him into the supernatural world, expressed metaphorically by entering a rock, a stream, or "drowning" in the ocean. Some engaged in sexual intercourse with a supernatural being or animal. The entrance is a long tunnel, where several dangerous animals or sprits lurk. They test the initiate's resolve to acquire power. The initiate triumphs and arrives at a "large house," sometimes a rock or crystal house, where supernatural beings dwell. Among them is the being that becomes his spirit helper. Treasure, weapons, and wealth fill the house, as well as unlimited food supplies. Here the initiate resides while he eats, learns ritual curing, and receives a song and one or more talismans, his power objects. He may see ghosts and spirits of the dead and ancestors, also supernatural beings, perhaps water monsters. He learns from the guardians of the supernatural never to reveal what he has seen or learned on pain of death. Finally, the initiate emerges at a different spot from where he had entered and begins his career as a curer.[10]

The shaman's spirit helper was usually an animal. Grizzlies and rattlesnakes were deadly in life and as spirit helpers, so were black-widow spiders. Birds, water mammals, and denning species like weasels and skunks were also suitable helpers, because they moved from the earth into the sky, water, or underground. Deer were prized spirit helpers, perhaps because of their antlers.

Powerful, compelling visions of the supernatural, dreams unfolding in remote, dark places gave shamans a spiritual world view they sometimes recorded on rock walls, part of the great archive of rock art found in many parts of the state. In chapter 9, I describe some of this art and evaluate one of the great controversies of California archaeology—the role of the shaman as artist. Or were they artists at all?

Art on the Rocks

D ECEMBER 21, CONDOR CAVE IN CHUMASH TERRITORY: the winter solstice, A.D. 1200. The shaman was alone in the still winter night, oblivious to the near-freezing temperature, watching the clear sky turn gray in the predawn light. He sat cross-legged in the dark cave, his eyes fixed on the jagged mountain ridge in the distance and on an isolated sandstone outcrop on the flat alluvial plain before him. As he waited, he sang quietly. The song recalled his dream, the words echoing off the sandstone walls.

The sky lightened, turning from gray to a slight orange. Absolutely still, the shaman's eyes moved toward a small hole he had carved out in the southeastern wall of the cave. Suddenly, the sun's rays burst over the distant ridge. A ray of orange light pierced through the hole. The narrow, intense beam shone onto the sunstick set vertically into the earthen floor. The shaman sat motionless, watching the slow passage of the light beam. He felt the power of the sun flood the cave as he silently prayed, becoming briefly one with the cosmic world. Never did he feel more powerful than at the solstice, when he captures the sun in his cave.

Then the shaman moved to the cave wall and painted his spirit helper, a red and white frog, on the wall.[1] The red-legged frog was the animal that announced the coming of the winter solstice (see figure 9.1).

As the sun moved higher and the cave fell into dark shadow, the shaman added two long antennae that projected from the frog's mouth.

Figure 9.1. Painting at Condor Cave, Santa Barbara County. Courtesy of Santa Barbara Museum of Natural History.

These were the mythic powers of red-legged frog witnessed in the shaman's dream. . . .

For generations, rock art specialists have dwelt somewhat on the margins of archaeology, not because some of them are not excellent scholars, but simply because "dirt" archaeologists have found it hard to relate the images on rock faces with the artifacts and other material remains in the ground. Fortunately for science, a new era has dawned in the past quarter century, which is finally bringing California's rock art into the mainstream. Ferocious debates rage over the meaning and significance of the engravings and paintings. As this is written, the controversy remains unresolved.

Let's begin with the areas of general agreement. Everyone agrees that some carefully executed engravings and paintings may have recalled unusual events—perhaps mnemonics for now long-forgotten stories—or may have served as visual triggers for myths recited by a camp fire. Everyone also agrees that art was never a distinct entity in human life. Whatever its motivation, it was part and parcel of the fabric of existence with many significances to those who painted them. In California, some images may have served as background for initiation rites, others represent celebrated mythic beings, and still others may have been part of rainmaking rituals. There are certainly paintings, especially in Chumash country in southern California, that were astronomical markers of solstices and other heavenly phenomena. The sad conclusion is that we can never hope to understand all the roles that rock art played in ancient California life.

Rock art had many subtle nuances, which reflected the motives of the artist and the experiences he or she was undergoing, or wishing to record. Without question, too, much of it results from visionary experiences. What form this visionary experience takes is where much of the controversy lies.

Hunting Magic, Shamans, or What?

Many years ago, the artist Campbell Grant, a noted pioneer in California rock art studies, wrote: "the creators [of Chumash art] took satisfaction in a job ingeniously conceived and well executed." Art satisfied the desire of the creator "to make a pleasing image on a rock where nothing had existed before, an image that might carry part of the artist into the most distant future."[2] Grant was convinced that art for art's sake was a powerful motive, at least for some engraving and painting.

We must not fall into the trap of thinking about art through Western eyes. Undoubtedly, some carefully executed images gave considerable satisfaction to those who created them. But this begs the question of why they did so in the first place. Did ancient Californians think of engravings and paintings as art to be enjoyed, especially when they created it in small, inaccessible caverns and rock shelters—isolated places? Some ancient artists were more expert than others, which may have been a matter of aptitude and experience. They, themselves, may not have thought of themselves as artists and may have been more concerned with the symbolic meaning of the image.

Philosopher Joseph Campbell offers another perspective. He has looked at hunter-gatherer societies on a broad canvas and wrote that the typical belief system among them viewed the animal as an equivalent, not lower, form of life. All hunting cultures celebrated myths that considered animals as willing sacrifices to the spear or arrow. One particular animal—a bison, a deer, or a bighorn sheep—might serve as what he called the "Alpha Animal," "the specific animal . . . to whom the prayers and worship are addressed that are to concern the entire animal community."[3] In other words, one animal served as the mythic representative of all prey.

Campbell's mythic approach coincides with the long-held idea that much of the art was what is often called "sympathetic hunting magic," images of animals created to invoke a successful hunt.

Hunting magic theories were the mainstream interpretations until the 1970s, when rock art research on the other side of the world brought the shaman to center stage.

San (Bushmen) hunter-gatherers in southern Africa painted and engraved some of the finest rock art in the world, recorded assiduously by archaeologists for over a century. Much of the art seemed to depict straightforward hunting scenes, ceremonies, and camp life. Accordingly, interpretation stayed somewhat in the background. Then, in the 1970s, rock art expert David Lewis-Williams published the first of a series of studies of San rock art, in which he used oral traditions and nineteenth-century ethnographies to interpret numerous rock paintings, especially of hunters dancing around large antelope-like eland.[4] Lewis-Williams attributed much San art to shamanistic activities. He argued that shamans painted images soon after emerging from an altered state of consciousness, recollections of the visions they had seen while dreaming and traveling in the realm of the supernatural.

Lewis-Williams's interpretations, based on solid ethnographic observations, burst on the tiny band of California rock art experts like a thunderclap. Archaeologist David Whitley, in particular, developed interpretations of California paintings and engravings that involved shamanistic rituals and vision quests as major elements in the art. He believes that most of California's rock art resulted from shamans recording their dreams by painting or engraving them in caves and rock shelters when they emerged from a trance (see figure 9.2).

By no means do all rock art experts agree with either Lewis-Williams or Whitley. Opponents of Whitley's interpretations accuse those who use them of creating a neat shamanistic equation, which sees a culturally complex past through one simple lens, concocted in the present.[5] Clearly, shamanism is not a "one-size-fits-all" phenomenon, nor can one use a kind of generalized shamanism to interpret every image on a California rock face.

I've found it best not to think of the art as art for art's sake, rather as operating within coherent visions of living and spiritual worlds that were completely different from those of Western society. I think that most people would agree that these worldviews had powerful spiritual dimensions, whose full extent lay within the conceptual grasp of only a few members of society. Rock art is a reflection of people living in an increasingly complex and ever more crowded world, where the eternal verities of human existence pressed hard on one on every side.

Even the most ardent advocates of shamanistic interpretations would not put all California rock art in a straightjacket of shamanism. As we shall see below, there are fierce debates over the meaning of the art in different parts of the state.

How Old Is the Art?

The chronology of California's rock art is still somewhat of a mystery. Almost certainly, most of the surviving engravings and paintings date to the last two thousand years or so, most of them to the last centuries before, and even after, European contact. We know some of the art was executed after the Spanish *entrada,* simply because horses, mules, and people with hats appear in some of the art.

The earliest radiocarbon dated painting is a herringbone pattern from Tecolote Cave in the Mojave Desert, which was painted in about 7300 B.C.,

Figure 9.2. A meandering snake in red and white lies with a small rock alcove in Round Valley in the southern Sierra Nevada. The ceiling and back wall bear cupules painted red and white. The alcove is just small enough for someone to enter. Courtesy of David Whitley.

the earliest known rock painting in all of the North America.[6] Unfortunately, the ravages of weather and erosion of soft rock faces have destroyed most earlier art long ago. But most experts believe that rock art has a multi-millennial history in California. The surviving paintings and ethnographic records are the tip of a huge artistic iceberg, of cultural traditions, which go back to the earliest times—like so much else in ancient California.

Rock art specialist David Whitley has identified two major and three relatively minor, art traditions in California. We cannot possibly do full justice to them here. Anyone seriously interested in the subject should consult one of the publications cited in the Notes and References. Here, we can only visit a few sites and describe the most widely distributed art traditions.[7]

The Coso Range: Hunters or Shamans?

A rock-engraving tradition centered on the Great Basin covers an enormous area of the west, extending from southeastern Oregon, northern Utah, southern Idaho, and extreme western Wyoming south into the California deserts, and even to the eastern slopes of the central Sierra Nevada.[8] Engravings predominate everywhere including the Mojave Desert, where some paintings are also to be found. The greatest concentration of Great Basin engravings lies in eastern California's Coso Range, in Inyo County west of Death Valley, on the walls of small rock shelters, and on rocky outcrops. The densest art lies within a fifty-to-sixty square-mile area within the range, which boasted of great biodiversity and of important obsidian sources. Most of the art is out in the open, in full view of anyone walking down the canyons, in contrast with much Chumash and other art, which is much more inconspicuous.

Most of the time, the artists pecked their pictures onto the rock, occasionally using abrasion and incising or scratching outlines with fine lines. Pecking sufficed for most of the larger figures of humans and bighorn sheep and for many geometric designs—curvilinear meanders, dot patterns, grids, zigzags, and many others. No less than 51 percent of the engravings in the Coso Range depict bighorn sheep. Almost all of them are of adult males with large, curving horns and pronounced, upright tails. Spears or arrows impale some of the sheep. Other animals appear occasionally, among them rattlesnakes, depicted as a zigzag line, sometimes with a head, mountain lions, and dogs with erect tails (see figures 9.3 and 9.4).

Figure 9.3. Human and bighorn sheep from Little Petroglyph Canyon, Coso Range. Courtesy of David Whitley.

Human figures come in many forms—simply as stick figures, or sometimes horned, with feather headdresses, occasionally with prominent phalluses, or often with elaborate patterned bodies. The patterned figures invariably bear schematic heads, as simple as a solid or concentric circle. One patterned human from Petroglyph Canyon has a body filled with parallel lines and bird claw feet. The schematic head wears a headdress of quail topknot feathers. The figure carries three sticks in his left hand, another slightly curved one in the right, and may depict a shaman (see figure 9.4).

Usually, but not always, the human figures appear alone, but occasionally there are lines of dancing stick figures or a hunter shooting bighorns with bow and arrows. Almost all the humans are male, but a few females appear, with pear-shaped torsos or exaggerated labia.Sometimes, the human forms blend with the animal: the human with bird feet already mentioned, men with bighorn heads, and so on. Animal tracks abound, too, those not only of humans, but of bear, bighorn, and perhaps deer—reflecting perhaps the importance of stalking in hunting societies.

Bighorn sheep images are so plentiful that they must have occupied an important place in the symbolic world of the hunters who pursued them.

Figure 9.4. Human figure from Little Petroglyph Canyon, Coso Range. David Whitley draws attention to the clawed feet and the headdress of quail topknot feathers, which he associated with rain shamans. Human faces were commonly depicted as spirals or concentric circles. The main figure is three and a half feet tall. Courtesy of David Whitley.

Are these engravings to be attributed to shamans? David Whitley has no doubt that the Coso art was the work of such individuals, who executed them while in trance or in a state of extreme fatigue. He attributes the art to Numic shamans from the Great Basin. Whitely dates the art to later than A.D. 1300, interpreting it with the aid of ethnographic information from the Chemehuevi group of the Colorado River Valley region (people with no connection to, or territory in, the Coso area), to tell us that rock art sites in the range were places of great supernatural power, protected by powerful spirits, often guarded by grizzlies and rattlesnakes, the most dreaded of animal spirits.[9] Whitley's sources tell us that in the Coso Mountains, the sites were *pohaghani*, literally "house of supernatural power," in local Numic speech, places where the shaman would create rock art at the end of a vision quest. The engravings depicted the spirit beings seen during the trance and other visionary experiences. The art was the visual manifestation of the shaman's trance.

These places were dangerous for nonshamans. Some caves and rock shelters, like Newberry Cave in the Mojave Desert, were repositories for shaman's ritual costumes, for their ornaments and talismans. Here the shaman "would talk to the rock, which would open so that he could get his things . . . [They] would be in a basket set in a hole in the rock which he had operated by means of his power." Cracks showed where the doors lay at the shaman's command, perhaps after dancing or calling out the name of the ancestor to whom it had once belonged. The rock art sites were solitary places, where the shaman stayed in isolation, communing with his animal spirit helpers. "They gave him songs and danced with him all night. They gave him his regalia: this just appeared on him, nobody knew where it came from. . . ."[10] In the end, the animals released him and sent him home.

Whitley's thesis informs us that many shamans used important vision quest sites in the Coso Range, some traveling long distances from throughout the Great Basin, even from northern Utah, to acquire the power from these locations. Engravings of bighorn sheep are on every side there, the special spirit helpers of rain shaman. The local Numic groups such as the Coso Shoshone and Kawaiisu were renowned for their rainmaking powers. You can see the rain priests in the rock engravings, wearing the quail topknot headdresses of rain shamans. There are scenes of men killing sheep and of dead bighorns, for it was said that "rain falls when a mountain sheep is killed. Because of this, some mountain sheep dreamers thought they were rain doctors."[11] A rain shaman, himself a bighorn sheep spirit, would enter the supernatural and "die" in the form of a shamanistic self-sacrifice, thereby causing it to rain. The engravings of people killing sheep have nothing to do with "hunting magic." Rather, they are graphic metaphors of the ritual death experienced by the rain shaman.

Or were they? Back in 1962, Robert Heizer and Martin Baumhoff studied the motifs of Great Basin rock art to the east of the Coso Range.[12] They recorded hundreds of images of bighorn sheep, deer, and occasionally pronghorn antelope. Many lay near game trails and springs, or close to hunting blinds. The two experts concluded that much of the art played a role in successful hunting, but never fully elaborated the spiritual dimensions of the paintings and engravings.

In 1968, the artist Campbell Grant and others expanded on this hypothesis. They wrote that "most of the immense number of sheep drawings were connected with hunting magic." As the sheep were overhunted, so the sympathetic hunting magic and its depictions of the prey and of anthropomorphs were intensified. "With the sheep gone, the cult died out and with it, the long tradition of making rock pictures."[13] Grant dated this event to about A.D. 950, in contrast to Whitely, who dates the engravings to after A.D. 1300, to a time when Coso Shoshone and northern Paiute had settled in the mountains. According to anthropologist Julian Steward, who studied the Shoshone in the 1930s, older people among them had absolutely no recollection of the art, and no idea what it meant. Furthermore, there is almost universal agreement among Great Basin scholars that the rock art tradition of which the Coso engravings are part was created long before Numic peoples moved west. In contrast, Whitley attributes the Coso engravings to Numic rain shamans from the Great Basin, who came to the mountains on religious quests, seeking to acquire rainmaking powers there. He claims that the bighorn sheep was the special spirit helper of rain shamans.

In recent years, a major study of archaeological sites in the Coso Range has brought some much more accurate dating information and solid archaeological evidence to bear on the rock art sites.[14] No less than five hundred obsidian hydration dates from fifty archaeological deposits associated with the bighorn petroglyphs date to between about 550 B.C. and A.D. 950, a time when populations were rising sharply, and when bows and arrows replaced the ancient spear and atlatl technology of earlier times. The animal bones from these same layers show a dramatic shift from the hunting of larger prey like bighorn to a diet based on piñons and rabbits. This time span is far earlier than that claimed by Whitley, which means that we are far beyond the range of ethnographic analogy.

In chapter 7, I related how there was a sudden surge in the hunting of larger game after 2500 B.C. over much of California. Coso sites reveal a sudden rise in the use of obsidian for making projectile points after about 1550 B.C., such usage reaching a crescendo before A.D. 900. Thereafter, obsidian use was negligible. At the same time, bighorn sheep bones virtually disappear from archaeological sites. By A.D. 950, rising populations and more effective hunting technologies had decimated bighorn sheep populations, just at the end of a period when petroglyph production intensified. Perhaps, write Amy Gilreath and William Hildebrandt, there was a link between the intensity of Coso rock art manufacture and overexploitation of bighorn sheep. They believe that local groups intensified rock art production as "fervent acknowledgement of their covenant with the animal community."[15] In other words, rock art and its associated rituals were an attempt to influence supernatural forces to restore bighorn populations to a level capable of supporting many more people than in earlier times. At the same time, the highly visible art served to delineate the territories of the groups that executed it in stressful centuries when there was intense competition for game and other foods.

The Coso Range bighorns may represent not the work of shamans, but that of individual hunters acquiring power and success for themselves (see box 9.1).

BOX 9.1 Copying Rock Art

As in Europe and South Africa, rock art experts have experimented with various copying methods. Early fieldworkers traced images with florist's or tracing paper taped to the rock, or made rubbings of engravings. Then they would work up final drawings in pen and ink and water color into which, inevitably, a subjective element was introduced. These were artist's interpretations of the images, but sufficed, as did crude sketches, in an era of rudimentary photographic technology.

Today's rock art copyist has an arsenal of vastly superior materials at hand. For copying, he or she can draw on supple plastics and acetates, and many forms of pens and markers. Direct tracing is now scientifically unacceptable, so artists sometimes set up a sheet in front of the wall and trace from a short distance away, all the while checking their renderings with photographs and measurements. Today's sophisticated photographic technology has allowed systematic copying of entire caves and rock shelters in a fraction of the time required by an artist. But drawings are still of value, especially since they allow the decipherment of complicated superpositions of several figures at the same location.

Researchers today use both color and black-and-white film, diverse light sources such as lamps and electronic flash, and filters to enhance contrast. Carefully controlled light can identify faded portions of paintings. Sometimes infrared film or light makes red ochers transparent, so you can see other pigments under red figures and even identify different paint mixes. Ultraviolet light sources can highlight otherwise invisible painting detail buried under calcite and other living organisms on walls.

Other methods go hand in hand with photography. Binocular microscopes can provide ultra close-up looks at paintings. New casting technologies use elastomer silicones and polyesters that are quick and easy to apply to rock faces and produce exact, durable casts of even the finest lines. Back in the laboratory, the researcher can coat the cast surface with a mixture of ink and water that is then wiped away to expose engraved lines, a technique that is unthinkable with the original engraving.

In recent years, computers have taken a central role, both for digital enhancement of the images and to fine tune photographs for accuracy. Digital storage is the obvious solution for photographic archives of rock art.

This does not mean that shamans were inactive in the southern California desert. We know that they were active, thanks to discoveries at Newberry Cave and elsewhere.

The Shaman's Cache

Shaman's caches—the term was coined by ethnographer Anna Gayton—were often rock shelters, an isolated low ridge, most often rock art sites. Individual shamans owned their cache sites that were sometimes passed from one generation to the next. Powerful spirits protected shaman's caches—dreadful beasts, spirit helpers, even a spirit in the form of a bright light. They were dangerous to nonshamans, who avoided them, and even tried not to look at such locations, for fear of grievous harm. Here the shamans kept their costumes and paraphernalia. The cave was unimportant. What mattered was the power behind the walls, places where the shaman "could talk to the rock, which would open so he could get his things," in a hole created by his power.[16]

The caches were far more than repositories for paraphernalia. They were the place where the shaman acquired his supernatural power, where he dreamed so that his spirit helpers gathered and opened the site for him. The shaman would stay there for days at a time, talking to no one, dancing with the spirits and wearing his regalia. The interior of a rock art site served as the tunnel to the supernatural world, the door to the rock house of the spiritual world where they flew freely. Some served wider purposes, acting as locations for secret rituals and curings.

Can we prove that some painted caves and rock shelters were shaman's caches? Newberry Cave lies near the southern end of Tory Lake Basin in the Mojave Desert. Archaeologist Gerald Smith excavated the cave in 1953–1956, but it was not until 1981 that Alan Davis wrote a report on the dig. He described over a thousand bighorn stick images in levels dating to about 1080 B.C. and identified a shaman's ritual paraphernalia, stored in the dry cave sometime between 1800 and 1028 B.C.: a feather plume and tortoise shell bowls; quartz crystals; perhaps part of a wand; painting pigments; some split twig figures; miniature animal figures constructed of a single split willow sapling, bent and folded to form an animal; and weapons.[17] The cave was never occupied again. Rock art expert David Whitley studied the pictographs of bighorn sheep and possibly rabbits, motifs also found in the Coso Range to the north. He believes that the association between the shaman's regalia and the rock art at Newberry Cave cannot be fortuitous.

Under any circumstances, finding evidence of shamanistic activity in archaeological sites is very difficult. The Sally's Rock Shelter example in the accompanying box offers an intriguing attempt to do so (see box 9.2).

BOX 9.2 Sally's Rock and a Shaman's Quest

Can we identify shamanistic activity from other forms of archaeological evidence? David Whitley's researches at Sally's Rock Shelter in the Mojave Desert offer an intriguing example.[18]

Sally's Rock Shelter lies in a boulder field within the U.S. Army's Fort Irwin National Training Center (figure 9.5). The site is nothing much to look at: a small, low-ceiling rock shelter under a large boulder. A panel of rock engravings adorns a vertical portion of the large boulder, which forms the roof of the shelter. The rock engravings include no less than eighteen discrete motifs. Two are sticklike human figures, another a short zigzag that represents a rattlesnake. All the other motifs are geometric dots, as well as more complex images including gridiron patterns, which are characteristic of the mental images formed during trance.

(Continued)

Figure 9.5. Sally's Rock Shelter. The figure stands in front of the petroglyph panel. Courtesy of David Whitley.

BOX 9.2 Continued

The engravings were made in at least two episodes, the one superimposed on the other, but the interval of time between them is unknown. Unfortunately, the investigators could not date the engravings accurately, but they appear to be relatively recent. David Whitley estimates they are less than five hundred years old.

A small depression at the top of the same boulder forms another component of the site, a feature so inaccessible that Whitley and his colleagues had to bring in a sixteen-foot ladder to reach it. The depression yielded a small scatter of shattered quartz fragments. Whitley recovered a series of undisturbed quartz cobbles, which had been wedged into cracks in the boulder pile in such a way that only a human being could have put them there. Both the depression and the rock shelter contained quartz cobbles, hammer stones used to create rock engravings, all of them carried to the site from afar.

Why would someone bring quartz to a remote location and wedge lumps of it into boulders? Whitley went to other, less pristine rock engraving sites in an attempt to find an answer. He examined thirty-five samples taken from the surfaces of rock engravings from sites where white quartz did not occur naturally. Peering at them with all the panoply of modern high-tech science—electron microscopy, wavelength dispersive spectrometry and energy-dispersive spectrometry—he found tiny quartz grains embedded up to a millimeter into the surfaces of twenty-two of them, preserved by the natural rock varnish, which forms on the weathered rock surface. No other nonlocal stone fragments came from the samples, making it virtually certain almost 63 percent of the engravings were produced by white quartz hammer stones. The sample engravings date from thousands of years ago right up to the present, so the use of quartz hammer stones for rock engraving was a long-lived practice in this region.

How, then, can one explain the quartz at Sally's Rock shelter? Vision questers often left offerings at their chosen site to the spirit the supplicant wished to receive. The same sites were also places to which the shamans retired to pray for cures and for other activities when they often left offerings—normally such items as beads, seeds, arrows, even moccasins, rocks of various kinds, and in modern times, coins. Often, such offerings were placed in cracks in the rock. Modern observers have seen many instances of such offerings still adhering to rocks and protruding from cracks in them. Thus, the quartz lumps wedged into Sally's Rock shelter's boulders may have been shamanistic offerings.

Large boulders were places where the supernatural world lay close to the surface, so cracks within them were portals into the otherworld. Spirits resided inside rocks, moving in and out of the supernatural realm through the same cracks that were said to open up for shamans when they entered trance and entered the spiritual universe. Since spirits resided inside the boulders at Sally's Rock shelter, placing quartz cobbles in the cracks was a way of placing a gift at the door to the spirit's home.

Quartz was also thought to have great supernatural potency. Spirits inhabited quartz crystals, so they possessed supernatural powers that could be used for many purposes. Great Basin Yuman—speaking shamans acquired them during their vision quests, during which they created rock engravings. Yumans in the Colorado Desert would break up white quartz rock, thereby releasing the great spiritual power in them into their bodies. The scatter of quartz fragments at Sally's Rock shelter may reflect this practice, too. Quartz crystals can also produce electrical voltage when subjected to pressure, exhibiting bright, lightning-like flashes of light. This cold, luminescent glow would appear when quartz was broken during vision quests, a tangible expression of supernatural power.

Research like the Sally's example requires meticulous science, highly controlled use of ethnographic sources, and the ability to look at traditional religious beliefs as being just as logical and coherent as Western scientific thinking. It will be interesting to see if Whitley's research is substantiated by other investigations.

The California Tradition: Chumash Rock Art

Rock paintings abound in California, from the Cascade Mountains in the north, all the way to the Mexican border. They form a loosely defined California Tradition, paintings and the occasional pecked engraving, which lie under small rocky overhangs or on the walls of larger shelters. More paintings come to light in remote wilderness areas every year. Most are red monochrome depictions of geometric shapes, some are in red or white, made from pigments like red ocher mixed with animal fat, egg yolks, and other binders. There are circles, dots, disks, ladders, diamonds, zigzags, and so on. Every shape once had a meaning. Surviving informants told anthropologist John Harrington and others that zigzags and diamond chain patterns either represented sidewinder rattlesnakes moving through sand or the scales on the back of a diamondback rattler (see figure 9.6).

Some of the best-known paintings are those of the Chumash, where there are ethnographic accounts that amplify the record from the rocks, and there are clear signs of shamanistic activity.

Eyewitness accounts of painting are rare. In the Chumash region, there are firsthand descriptions of two shamans actually painting. People sometimes referred to the shaman metaphorically, as supernatural beings like water babies or mountain dwarfs, spirit helpers rather than humans. One native informant remarked that shamans "painted their spirits [*anit*] on rocks 'to show themselves, to let people know what they had done.' The spirit must come first in a dream."[19]

We have a few clues about shamanistic involvement from late nineteenth- and early twentieth-century native informants, who were anxious to perpetuate traditional knowledge for future generations. They talked about the meaning of the art with ethnographers while memories were still fresh. They did this with reluctance, for knowledge about it was restricted to those entitled to receive it. As early as 1822, Spanish missionary Fray Geronimo Boscana observed that "they [the California Indians] do not all understand the significance of their usages and customs, this knowledge being confined to the chiefs of their tribes, and the old men who officiate as priests. When they reveal anything to their children, it is only to such as they intend to rear as their successors, and these are enjoined to keep fast the secrets, and not to communicate them to anyone."[20] Even today, many Native Americans are silent about many aspects of their religious beliefs and traditional culture, which has led many researchers to conclude, wrongly, that the art is very ancient, and delinked from historic peoples. The record left by informants is spotty at best, but we know enough to be able to look at the art in a wider context. We can achieve at least some understanding of the intricate metaphors, symbolic oppositions, and principles behind the engravings and paintings.

The most elaborate paintings appear in the coast ranges near Santa Barbara, and in the southern Sierras, many of them executed by Chumash

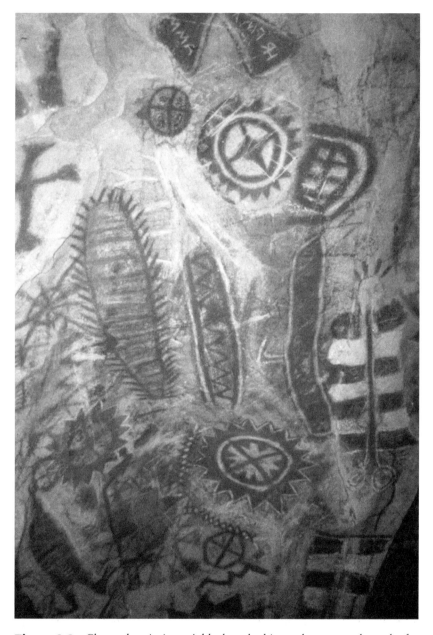

Figure 9.6. Chumash paintings: A black and white anthropomorph on the far right, two rattlesnakes to the left, and then a centipede. From Painted Cave, near Santa Barbara. Courtesy of David Whitley.

and southern Yokut artists. (The two groups were in regular contact.) Thanks to the researches of Campbell Grant, J. P. Harrington, and others, we know something of the meaning of Chumash art.

Here polychrome paintings appear in elaborate patterns in black, red, yellow, white, and other colors, but, as elsewhere, monochrome images are most common. Between 15 and 20 percent of the pictures depict animals and humans, among them bears, insects, rattlesnakes, birds, beavers, and fish. The humans are often anthropomorphic, with antlers or appendages on their heads. We see others turning into birds. Many dance, with bent knees, and arms at 45 degrees. Their hands are raised and palms open, wrists exposed to the sun. The right wrist was the seat of supernatural power. By exposing it to the sun, the dancer acquired power. Chumash paintings feature many circular and disk motifs—concentric circles, pinwheels, spider-web motifs, and endless variations of circles and dots, many of them depictions of the sun and other heavenly bodies.

Oral traditions preserved by John Harrington and others document the close involvement of shamans in this art tradition. The Chumash thought of their cosmos as dominated by powerful supernatural forces in a state of flux. There was always the potential for danger and cataclysm, which could only be averted by performing the correct rituals, and by using shamanistic power acquired from spirit beings. The heavenly bodies played a vital role in the future of the cosmos. Chumash priests believed that the Sun and Sky Coyote played a gambling game every night. Just before the winter solstice, the scores of wins and losses was calculated. If Sky Coyote's team won, the coming year would bring abundant rain and an abundance of food for humankind. But if the Sun prevailed, his prize would be human lives. The Yokut had somewhat similar beliefs.

In both societies, the astronomer-shaman, the Chumash 'alchuklash, was the man who could determine the game's count, and thereby predict food supplies for the coming year.[21] Only he could take the proper ritual steps to avert hunger. Chumash shaman-priests watched the heavens closely, for they believed that the celestial bodies were supernatural beings, endowed with great power. The universe was a complex web of interactions between humans and these spiritual entities, always unpredictable, and always dangerous.

Astronomy and cosmology touched every aspect of Chumash life. Their mythology told tales that brought together knowledge about the heavens and humanity. Myths were used to pass information from one generation to the next and defined the world. The shamans and their vision quests acquired and used their supernatural powers with the aid of spirit helpers. It is no coincidence that many rock paints depict astronomical motifs and symbols, perhaps activating spiritual power. Some of these same symbols like sun or moon signs appear on sun sticks, others on cult objects or even on painted human bodies. And public rituals balanced the forces of the cardinal directions and the powers of celestial beings.

Earth Figures

Some engravings and paintings appear on exposed outcrops, in more public places, as is the case with paintings on granite and soapstone boulders near large ancient villages in the coastal hinterland between Los Angeles and San Diego. But there are even larger examples of what one might call "public art" as well—geoglyphs on flat-topped mesas and terraces of the Colorado River in southeastern California, which are also found across the river in the Southwest.[22]

The geoglyphs occur either alone or in small clusters, some more than fifty yards long, most commonly large, anthropomorphic figures. There are snakes and other animals, as well as concentric circles and other figures. The huge figures seem to have been settings for public rituals. Human feet impressed dance circles, long lines of rocks and trails into the desert pavement, pressing pebbles into the subsoil, creating lighter, cleared areas that show up against the pavement. Most geoglyphs date to between 900 B.C. and A.D. 1200.

Oral traditions tell us that the geoglyphs commemorate the places where mythic events unfolded. They were part of ritual pilgrimages that traced the creation story. Rock alignments served a different purpose and form part of a widespread vision questing tradition.

There are rock alignments, too, some likely to be of considerable antiquity—linear and curvilinear patterns that are mere lines of stones across the desert. Sometimes those who laid them out took advantage of lighter colored rocks and the contrast between boulder surfaces coated with desert varnish to create contrasting colors in the alignments. Again, ethnography is helpful. The alignments were not strictly art. They formed part of vision quests that called for physical exertion during the quest.

Figure 9.7. Human and animal figures: the Blythe Giant Figures geoglyph site. The human is about twenty-five yards long. Courtesy of Harry Casey.

■ ■ ■

We know little of the ancient supernatural realm. A veil of silence, which surrounded their activities for thousands of years, died with the last practitioners. Occasionally, we can lift a corner of the curtain, from the isolated testimony of an aged informant, or by close study of engravings and paintings fading away on often well-hidden rock faces. We have seen enough through fleeting insights to realize that the spiritual world of the ancient Californians was infinitely more complex and sophisticated than we have often assumed. Herein lay the great complexity of their societies—not in the material realm but in the spiritual, where hunting rituals, shamanistic dreams, and other observances reflected in rock art combined to maintain cosmic balance. This balance, together with economic, social, and political interconnectedness, ensured the survival of California society for more than 13,000 years.

PART IV

A Crowded World

(C. 1500 B.C. to A.D. 1542)

You know how some men are quick and strong
and know the things to do, how people like to do
things for them, and how they have a gift for getting everyone cheerful? Well, those men are
leaders (*kwoxot*). When a man knew he had the
power to be a good leader, he told his dreams. If
his dreams were good, his plans would be followed, but if they were poor and stupid others
would tell him so and he could do nothing.
Sometimes men struggled with each other to
lead war parties and arrange daily affairs. Then
each would try to get more of the people on his
side, giving feasts to his friends and encouraging
them to speak of his wisdom. But it was not long
before we knew who was the better man and he
became leader. . . . If a leader acted stupidly, it
meant that his power had deserted him and it
was time to have another to decide things.

—PATRICK MIGUEL, a Quechan[1]

CHAPTER 10

The Northwest:
Dugouts and Salmon

A SLIGHT PINK HUE TINGES THE EASTERN HORIZON, BUT the shoreline is dark; the row of long canoes only dimly visible on the beach. The heaving Pacific is gray in the growing dawn as daylight slowly floods the bowl of the sky.

Point St. George in northwestern California, A.D. 1600, a late summer's dawn: a solitary figure stands motionless close to the endless breakers, silent, listening to the slough of the waves. The ground swell is quiet, the wind flat calm. No fog hovers over the dark rocks offshore. Wrapped in thought, the cloaked man walks up the beach to the waiting headmen clustered by the waking village. He speaks some quiet words. Within minutes, cheerful crews swarm over the great dugouts, placing clubs, paddles, and spears at their stations, hauling the long, smooth hulls down to water's edge. A chant and a solemn cry: the crews launch their canoes effortlessly through the surf, paddling swiftly clear of breaking water. Eager anticipation is in the air. Astern, elderly men, women, and children watch the canoes paddle offshore, as the sun slants across the calm ocean. . . .

With chapter 10, we begin a journey through the complicated and ever-changing political landscape of the past three millennia. These were centuries of constant climatic change, perhaps more frequent and sometimes more intense than in earlier times. There were times when acorns became a staple, fishing assumed great importance throughout coastal California, and growing webs of interconnectedness linked tribelet to tribelet, chief to chief. Our travels take us from north to south, starting in along the north and northwestern coasts, where one can detect cultural influences from the Pacific Northwest. But, for all these influences, the people of this archaeologically little-known region developed their own social and religious institutions based on wealth and prestige, which differed considerably from those to the north and west (see figure 10.1).

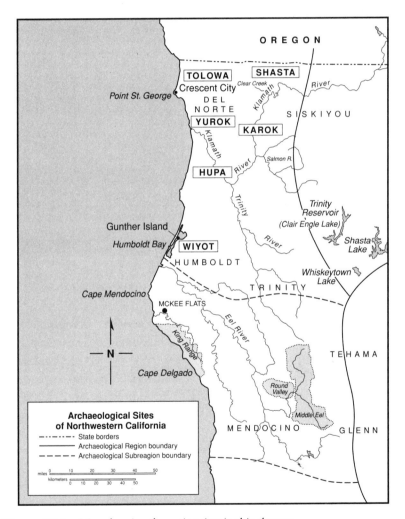

Figure 10.1. Map showing the major sites in this chapter.

We begin with a discussion of dugouts and salmon, two important ingredients of the sophisticated cultures of northwestern California. In the second half of the chapter, we look at the first settlement of the region and examine the reasons for the surprisingly late peopling of the Pacific shoreline in this rugged land of fast-flowing rivers, forests, and mountains.

By 6500 B.C., offshore voyaging was commonplace in southern California. Twenty-mile passages to Santa Catalina Island and from there to San Clemente Island were unremarkable, to say nothing of regular visits to the northern Channel Islands.

Such early seafaring was unique in California. Large offshore watercraft were nonexistent along most of the long coast of the state, where only small dugouts and tule canoes navigated estuaries and sheltered waters close inshore. Early Spanish visitors sketched tule canoes on the shallow flats of San Francisco Bay, but no local Costanoan people ventured offshore to the Farallon Islands, thirty miles west of the Golden Gate. Huge sea mammal rookeries flourished there until Aleut hunters imported by Russian traders wreaked havoc in the nineteenth century.

Only in the far northwest did ancient Californians build substantial watercraft, and these canoes, like those of the southern Californians, had specific uses. As we shall see, these imposing dugouts only came into use in the Late Period, sometime in the past five hundred years or so.

"A Thing of Beauty"

Journalist and amateur anthropologist Stephen Powers was the first outsider to record details of the large watercraft of the northwest. In 1872, he saw a magnificent redwood dugout on Humboldt Bay. Forty-two feet long and eight feet four inches wide, the huge canoe was said to be able to carry twenty-four people or five tons of freight. Underway, the twenty-four paddlers stood upright. They propelled the beautifully made vessel with long, steady strokes. Powell called the canoe "a thing of beauty," "sitting plumb and lightly on the sea, smoothly polished, and so symmetrical that a pound's weight on either side would throw it slightly out of trim."[2] The canoe was said to have proven its seaworthiness on a passage of over one hundred miles.

In Powers's day, the Yurok of the Klamath River had a near-monopoly on seagoing canoe construction. Such enormous dugouts were a direct product of the ready availability of straight-grained redwood trunks. The huge size of the redwoods allowed the builders to hollow out a deeper, more stable hull with higher sides than usual. Provided the walls were kept thin, the canoe would have been buoyant and good load carriers, but still probably dangerous in large swells and wind waves, especially when these came from the side. Two parallel rows of carved bumps on the bottom of the inside served as footholds for the standing paddlers. The builder also carved the gunwales with an interior lip, so that the crew and passengers had a convenient grip in rough water.

These canoes were so large that none other than Alfred Kroeber believed they were constructed under European influence to carry mining equipment and trade goods between coastal settlements. But he was wrong. The Yokut's neighbors, the Tolowa, did indeed build seagoing canoes, very much larger than the fifteen-foot-long river canoe with blunt ends used in smooth water.

While two men could readily build a river canoe, seagoing dugouts required much more labor.[3] The headman or a wealthy individual usually owned the boat, supporting the construction team with food and providing relatives for the heavy labor of rolling redwood logs and launching the finished boat. The canoe builders were usually close relatives, often brothers, who would work on the canoe intermittently for about a year. They would build the canoes along riverbanks, where driftwood logs were abundant, or fallen redwoods lay close to the water. Redwood being straight grained, the process of splitting logs with elk horn wedges and pounders was easy for people used to building planked houses.

The builders used fire to hollow out the split log. By moving a fire or hot charcoal backward and forward along the length of the log, they could burn deep into the timber. With good judgment, they would smother the fire carefully at intervals to control the burn. The flames or red hot charcoal excised most of the interior. Then the builders trimmed and smoothed the burnt-out hollow, using wood-handled adzes with sharp mussel-shell blades. Days of careful chipping produced a finely dimpled interior, remarkably even and thin from one end of the canoe to the other, the bottom planed to an even thickness with remarkable precision. We can imagine the careful, deliberate work, the builders eyeing the sides from every angle, debating the evenness of the finish, working with unhurried, deliberate precision. Once satisfied, they then singed the trimmed surface to remove any fuzz left over from carving and to ensure that the wood would not soften during use. This gave the canoe a gray-black color when on the water, which weathered to a lighter hue over time (figure 10.2).

Before launching, the builders repaired any cracks with pitch, then fashioned broad, heavy paddles out of ash for ocean use. The wealthy owner of the canoe owned the paddles and presided over their care and maintenance. He also took care to fill the interior of his canoe with fresh brush when it was ashore, to prevent cracks from developing in the hot sun.

None of these remarkable vessels have survived, so we can only guess at their finish and configuration. Their skippers must have been expert, conservative seamen, for they went afloat on a formidable, often windy patch of ocean. The greatest danger came not only from winter storms and the persistent strong northwesterlies of summer, but from large ground swells, generated by storms hundreds of miles offshore, which could turn beaches and estuaries into nightmarish locations with strong undertow. There are

Figure 10.2. Man and a woman in a traditional, blunt-ended Yurok dugout canoe, photographed by Grace Nicholson, between 1910 and 1920. Courtesy of The Huntington Library, San Marino, California.

rare places, like Humboldt Bay or a few relatively sheltered coves, which allow people to launch canoes or modern fishing boats off the beach even in quite severe swells, but there is always the danger of a broach, especially when landing a heavily laden craft. What made any form of offshore navigation possible was the sheer size of the local dugout canoe. And that was a direct product of the long, straight-grained redwood and of social institutions unique in California.

The Gunther Island Cemetery (After A.D. 900)

No one could build a large dugout without help—lots of it. The wealthy headman or family, which commissioned the building, had to feed not only the boat builders, who had honored skills, but the dozens of their fellow kin who came to assist with the heavy work. Everything depended on readily available food surpluses, and, above all, on individual social status and wealth. In this sense, the Yurok, Tolowa, and other northwestern California groups inherited the social institutions of their neighbors to the north, in the Pacific Northwest. Their societies were very different from the world of egalitarian tribelets elsewhere in California

Thanks to the excavations of an archaeologist and a dentist, we know that personal wealth has a long history in this region. In 1913, L. L. Loud, an archaeologist from the University of California, Berkeley, excavated a large cemetery and midden on Gunther Island in Humboldt Bay. Loud was a conscientious excavator for his day. He recovered large numbers of burials and many artifacts from the cemetery, which caused considerable interest locally. Loud did not return to the island, but a dentist named H. H. Stuart promptly leased the island from its owner and spent several summers excavating most of the undisturbed portions of the cemetery. Like so many diggers of his time, Stuart, although a relatively careful observer, never published his finds. Fortunately, his collections and notes survived. Years passed before University of California researchers Robert Heizer and Albert Elsasser were able to peruse the surviving notes and artifacts. They then produced what has become a classic account of an extremely important ancient cemetery with no less than 141 burials.[4]

Almost at once, Heizer and Elsasser spotted considerable numbers of known ceremonial artifacts in the collection, including large numbers of shiny obsidian blades, flaked on both sides. In historic times, the local Wiyot people regarded such objects as important indicators of wealth, as they had been in earlier times. Black or red obsidian blades were almost a form of jewelry, on occasion reaching twenty inches or more in length, displayed aggressively on important occasions and at major ceremonies. As Alfred Kroeber once wrote: "The Yurok concerns his life above all with property." The obsidian blades at Gunther Island hinted that this same preoccupation also flourished in earlier centuries (see figure 10.3).

The White Deerskin Dance was one of the most important ceremonies of the year. Kroeber describes how this important observance was an occasion for the wealthy to display their wealth, a time of long recitations, which served to maintain the established world, an abundance of plant foods, salmon, and game. Day after day of dances followed one on the next. The participants and spectators wore their most prized possessions, "the largest obsidian and flint blades, and the whitest deerskins . . . while the bands of woodpecker scalps are each worth more than a string of the largest shells."[5]

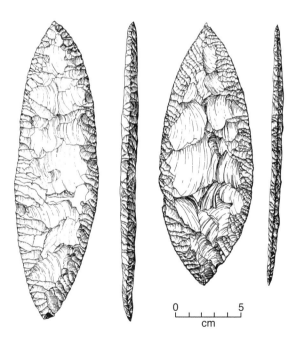

Figure 10.3. Fine obsidian bifaces from northwestern California. Courtesy of William Hildebrandt, Far Western Anthropological Research Group, Inc.

The Deerskin dancers wore richly adorned costumes and feathered headdresses, swaying in rows, the leaders and those at the end of the rows displaying obsidian blades for all to see. Such objects were compelling symbols of individual power and wealth.

The industrious Stuart excavated at least 140 skeletons from the Gunther Island cemetery. One hundred and nineteen of them were cremations, of which 84 percent were adults, and 13 percent children. There were twenty-three interments, all but one of an adult. The distribution of grave goods among the burials sent a deafening message. Only 11 percent of the dead were buried with large obsidian blades, and 14 percent with small ones. Dentalium and *olivella* shells were present in about the same percentages, while just under 40 percent were buried with abalone ornaments, perhaps a less-valued adornment. Interestingly, the same proportions of prestigious obsidian blades occur among both adults and children, but the young had more beads than their elders (see figure 10.4).

The Günter Island cemetery yielded four categories of prestigious artifact, all of them buried with only a small proportion of the cemetery sample: clearly such objects signal some form of social differentiation between members of society. The statistics are even more telling when you break down the figures even further. Only three individuals, a mere 2 percent of the population, were buried with all four categories of artifact, and only tiny numbers with any multiple combinations of prestige objects. Furthermore, both children and adolescents are found in every group except the most prestigious of all.

Few California cemeteries have yielded such definitive evidence for social ranking. Judging from the well-adorned children, such wealth, and the prestige, which went with it, was inherited at birth, long before the owners showed any ability to acquire either power or riches on their own.

These individuals, in adulthood, controlled the capital in prestige goods and food that enabled expert canoe builders to construct large dugouts. As archaeologist Richard Gould puts it: "it was incumbent upon the man who wanted the canoe built that he provide his assistants with gifts of food when they worked for him. At times when additional labor was called for (for example, when the redwood log was hauled up out of the water, or when launching took place), the headman would call together all his relatives . . . to assist."[6] He remarks that only headmen could afford to feed that many people, so the wealthy commissioned, owned, and controlled the use of the canoes.

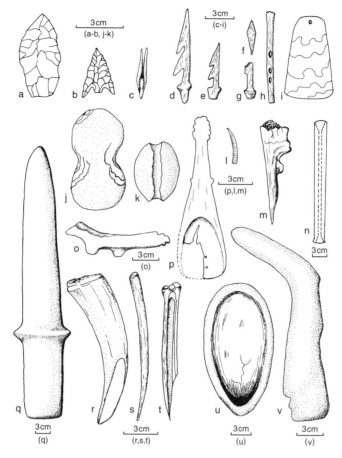

Figure 10.4. Artifacts from the Gunther Pattern of northwestern California—
projectile points, barbed harpoon points, stone net sinkers, a flanged
pestle, awls, and an adze handle. Drawing by Nelson Thompson.
Courtesy of Michael Moratto.

The same wealthy folk owned important food sources, including oak
groves, portions of offshore rookeries, and strategic rapids where salmon
were especially abundant. Such individually held wealth, usually vested in
families, was characteristic of coastal societies north of Cape Mendocino.
Further south, there was much less shoreline activity, more dispersed populations, and a far lesser degree of social ranking, even if some individuals
owned clamshell beads exchanged from as far south as Bodega Bay.

How Old Is Seafaring?

Alfred Kroeber flatly denied that the Yurok and their neighbors had built large dugouts before European settlement. One can hardly blame him, for such craft were of startling complexity when compared with the humble dugout used elsewhere in California. Nor, in his day, had any trace of maritime activity come from archaeological sites in the region.

Indian dugouts had quite a reputation in this region during the late nineteenth century, simply because of the rugged coastline. Early European settlers had to move everything by water, so much so that they turned from the slow-sailing coastal schooners owned by merchant skippers to the fast-moving Indian canoes to transport goods and mining equipment along the coast. Enterprising Indian headmen set up a regular transport service between the Klamath River and modern-day Crescent City, over twenty miles up-coast, and occasionally carried loads as far south as Humboldt Bay, some eighty miles to the south.

They picked their weather very carefully, just like the coastal schooners did, but were far faster and more reliable, simply because they relied on paddle power rather than sails, which normally had wind only a few hours a day. A canoe could slip along the shore at night or in the calm hours of early morning, while a schooner would sit becalmed until the relentless northwesterly headwinds filled in dead on the nose. According to Powers, their skippers would regularly shoot the rapids and surf at the mouth of the Klamath, "sailing boldly to sea in heavy weather and reaching Crescent City, twenty-two miles distant, whence they returned with merchandise."[7] The trade was so reliable that local newspapers called the canoes "Indian Gondolas." But the dugouts vanished rapidly with the construction of roads along the coast in 1894.

In a classic case of entrepreneurship typical of their societies, Indian canoe owners cashed in on the unexpected commercial opportunity. Their extensive kin ties and wealth enabled them to build more canoes and to expand seafaring activity beyond its earlier, somewhat more limited horizons.

It would be easy to assume that the Yurok and Tolowa canoes came into being as a result of a burgeoning European commerce. But since Kroeber's day, both oral traditions and archaeological discoveries have traced the great dugout canoes back into a far remoter past.

The people of this stretch of coast had redwood trunks in abundance to fashion large dugouts. They were familiar with the hazards of hunting on slippery, jagged rocks, both from taking sea mammals on land and from salmon fishing. At some point, long before Europeans arrived, they took the hunt a stage further and went offshore. We know that they surrounded this activity with intricate rituals. An outcrop near Patrick's Point had yielded no less than two hundred sea lion skulls, all defleshed and carefully piled together, perhaps the remains of ancient vision quests, which imbued the participants with supernatural powers.

We know that the canoes played a central role in the ancient First Sea Lion Hunt in July or August. Richard Gould collected memories of this hunt, which flourished into the late nineteenth century.[8] At least seven villages took part in the annual ceremony, which centered on the northwest and southwest Seal Rocks, about six and a half miles off Point St. George, where Steller sea lions congregated to breed. Once the headmen agreed on a date, the canoes from each village congregated at a large rock just off the point. Before dawn, a carefully selected skipper would go down to the breakers and listen carefully to the sound of the ocean, gauging the height of the ground swell and conditions offshore. He would report to the headmen, who conferred among themselves, then either postponed the hunt or gave the go-ahead.

When the signal came, the crews launched their canoes at once, paddles, spears, and clubs carefully placed in position. The dugout crews then paddled together out to the rocks, a roundabout journey of some fifteen miles to avoid dangerous reefs, often through quite rough water.

Once at the outcrops, each village team hunted on its own, the men working in pairs through the rookery. As a sea lion drew back its head to lunge forward, one hunter would ram a stick into its mouth to keep the head back. Simultaneously, the other man would club the animal from behind. Once the men had killed enough beasts, they would roll the bodies across the slippery rocks to water's edge. Loading the heavy carcasses was a hazardous task, accomplished by pulling the dead animal off the rocks, and then tipping the canoe until both water, and the sea lion, rolled into the boat. Each canoe would carry two carcasses, with perhaps a third being towed astern.

The canoes returned to a ceremonial welcome at the beach. Then the men butchered the sea lions, dividing the meat and disposing of each portion with great care, to satisfy both the dictates of social position and supernatural forces. The ceremony ended with the respectful disposal of the unused remnants of the dead sea lions, which were returned to the ocean to ensure future successful hunts.

The First Sea Lion ritual bore a close resemblance to the well-known First Salmon Ceremony practiced by many northwestern salmon-fishing groups. Such rituals commemorated the most important animals in local life, and, in the case of sea lions, recognized the dangers of hunting these large animals offshore. No one spearing from a dugout, however large, could easily take one of these large beasts, so the only effective way to hunt them was where they were most vulnerable—on land, even in calm conditions a hazardous pursuit. Quite apart from the dangers of hunting fast-moving beasts on slippery rocks, the waters around the offshore outcrops were never smooth. Landing from a canoe in any ground swell raised the specter of a smashed-in boat, dashed uncontrollably against the rocks. Loading the carcasses into tipped canoes was never easy, and very dangerous indeed in even small wind waves. And once capsized, there was no hope of righting the dugout. The best one could hope for would be a tow back to land.

All this was apart from the general hazards of navigating these waters. Strong winds and thick fogs could descend on the area without notice, even at the height of summer. Canoe crews regularly became lost at sea in zero visibility. Many never returned. Others remained at sea for days on end without food and water and came ashore miles from home, sometimes barely able to stand.

No canoes have survived in archaeological sites north of Cape Mendocino, but we know that people were visiting offshore fishing grounds inaccessible except by boat long before Europeans arrived. An archaeological site on Point St. George abandoned before the arrival of the first Western explorers contains large numbers of fish remains, among them the bones of turkey-red rockfish and vermillion rockfish. Both these species frequent rocky ocean bottoms at depths of over 180 feet. Such depths, and such fish, are found near Northwest Seal Rock, and no closer to the shore. Other fish eaten at this site included Chinook salmon, halibut, and fairly large soup-fin sharks, all of which are best taken from canoes.[9]

Everything points to canoe use centuries before European contact.

Early Coastal Settlement (? 500 B.C. to A.D. 1200)

But when did people first settle on this particular stretch of coast? For once, we have some strong clues. We can be fairly certain that the northwestern coastline was more or less deserted for thousands of years, even as southern California peoples exploited mollusks and sea mammals over four hundred miles to the south. In the far northwest, the coastline of before 6,500 B.C. is exposed to modern eyes, thanks to widespread geological uplifting north of Humboldt Bay. Archaeologists William Hildebrandt and Valerie Levulett have surveyed many areas of the shoreline and found almost no archaeological sites earlier than about five hundred years ago. As always, stone projectile points are the signposts.[10] The early Borax Lake and other projectile points of the period 9,000–2,000 B.C. are virtually unknown on the coast. Nearly all the projectile heads found there are of the highly characteristic Gunther type, named after the island of that name in Humboldt Bay.

Some conclusive evidence comes from the King Range area south of Eureka. Here Hildebrandt and Levulett discovered sites that chronicle sporadic use of the coast between 500 B.C. and A.D. 500. But it was not until after A.D. 1200 that intensive exploitation of the coast took hold. After this date, quite large groups occupied seasonal camps near Point Delgada and further north for the purpose of intensive shellfish processing.

Hildebrandt and Levulett have nailed down the chronology of coastal settlement very convincingly. Seventy-eight percent of all the radiocarbon dates from coastal sites date to after A.D. 500, whereas all the interior dates are earlier. Furthermore, the Gunther series projectile points from the coast are of a type most commonly made after that date, whereas earlier forms occur inland.

Why such late coastal settlement? As Hildebrandt and Levulett point out, the answer may lie in the food resources available in the interior. In the far northwest, where deer, elk, and other prey abounded in river valley and forest, shell middens occur no more than half a mile or so inland. As you travel southward into more arid landscapes, shell middens occur further inland—some six miles in Sonoma County, up to fifteen miles in central California and as much as twenty-five miles in the San Diego region. Mollusks assumed ever-greater importance as the hinterland became drier and land mammals were less plentiful.

The move to the coast may have resulted from population increases in the interior, which forced some groups to settle along the shore, where access to salmon runs, game, and acorns was more limited, necessitating travel inland. Exploiting sea mammals and shellfish, as well as engaging in offshore fishing, made sense to people with an expertise at canoe construction and abundant lumber for the purpose. And the technology they used offshore was merely an adaptation of familiar, and highly successful artifacts used for hunting and salmon fishing inland.

Why, then, did coastal occupation take hold far earlier in southern California than in the northwest? The answer lies in the nature of local food supplies. The northwestern region is a land of salmon runs and dense forests. There the greatest concentrations of feeds lay upstream, close to rapids and river confluences, which is where one finds the densest human occupations from the Middle Holocene onward. Here we find permanent villages and camps, widespread use of planked houses, the largest settlements closest to rapids and river confluences, where people harvest salmon in large numbers during much of the year. And here Roosevelt deer and other game could be hunted in more hilly terrain. There was little or no incentive to move downstream to the coast, where food resources were less plentiful and sea mammals bred and basked offshore—inaccessible until necessity forced the enormous labor of fashioning the large dugouts needed to paddle safely offshore.

In contrast, in southern California, the Chumash and their ancestors lived in a far more arid and much less productive terrestrial environment, where salmon runs were fewer. There was an abundance of plant foods and the fall nut harvest, but the distribution of such foods was always irregular and subject to the ravages of excessive rain or long drought cycles. For this reason, southern California peoples were forced to consume relatively predictable coastal foods such as shellfish and sea mammals far earlier than their contemporaries living north of Punta Arena. And, inevitably, deepwater canoes assumed an immediate and increasing importance early on, in environments where plentiful mollusks and sea mammals lay offshore.

Thousands of years passed before the northwesterners had sufficiently hunted out their territory. Forced to turn to coastal foods, they pursued exactly the same strategy as the southerners. They focused on the most predictable foods available, salmon, shellfish, and sea mammals, then deepwater fish. And like their southern counterparts, they developed the watercraft to do so, using the raw materials available for the purpose. In this case, redwood trunks turned into dugouts, for, like the ancestors of the Chumash, they made use of the materials available to them. As far as we can tell, the first large dugouts appeared centuries before European settlement.

There may be some linguistic clues, too. Archaeologists are always nervous of linguistics as a source of historical information, on the grounds that languages are intangibles, which change rapidly and without the kinds of tight chronological controls that excavators consider essential. But everyone agrees that the languages in the Hokan group are among the most ancient in California (see box 1.1 in chapter 1). The Chumash were Hokan speakers, which suggests that they, and their ancestors, have lived in their homeland for a very long time. In the far north, linguists are sure that the ancestors of the long-established Karok of the interior were Hokan-speakers, again suggesting a long presence in their homeland. But the Yurok and their southern neighbors, the Wiyot, who lived just north of Cape Mendocino, were Algic speakers and are said to have arrived on the coast in about A.D. 1000. These groups are believed to have originated on the Columbia River Plateau. Both moved into hitherto underexploited areas.[11]

The Wiyot settled along the coast and low-lying estuary tracts of Humboldt Bay, the Yurok along the Lower Klamath and adjacent coastal areas. The newcomers brought with them long-established expertise in deep-water fishing and woodworking, as well as in processing and storing salmon. This was when dugout canoes opened up the full potential of the coast. This was also when the first larger, more permanent coastal settlements came into being—in dramatic contrast to the Santa Barbara Channel region, where shoreline population densities began to climb—as early as 4,000 B.C. by some accounts.

Inland Settlement (Before 2000 B.C. to A.D. 500)

Hildebrandt and Levulett believe that there was no need to collect shellfish or to hunt sea mammals on the coast in earlier times, simply because there was a rich diversity of terrestrial foods inland. They excavated McKee Flats, a site on a terrace of the Upper Mattole River only seven and a half miles from the Pacific, an area with plentiful acorn-bearing oaks, deer, and tule elk, as well as bountiful salmon runs. McKee Flats dates to between 2000 B.C. and A.D. 500—long before any intensive exploitation of the coast. An abundance of mortars, pestles, and projectile points is eloquent argument for ample food supplies inland. People lived at the McKee base camp for all, or most of the year. Four small hunting camps lie within three and a half miles, probably temporary encampments used when hunting specific quarry, a classic pattern of more sophisticated hunter-gatherer societies (see figure 10.5).[12]

But the main reason why people lived inland can be given in a single word—salmon.

Figure 10.5. Excavations at the McKee site. Courtesy of Valerie Levulett, Far Western Anthropological Research Group, Inc.

Fish That Run Upstream

North of San Francisco Bay and Point Reyes, the winds blow hard along a rugged coastline battered by unrelenting Pacific swell. Magnify the dangers of the Big Sur coast several times, and you have some impression of the savagery of winter storms in the north. This has always been an inhospitable coast, even when sea levels were much lower than today. There were none of the wide coastal shelves of the south, nor the rich natural cold water upwelling like that off Point Conception, which attracted millions of fish, large and small. The shoreline was no magnet for early foragers from inland. They had little need of the shellfish or sea mammals that brought their southern contemporaries to the coast soon after first settlement. They lived in the land of salmon.[13]

In 1885, the surveyor Albert Niblack wrote of British Columbia Indians that there was little that Europeans could teach them about fishing.[14] The same remark applies to the ancient salmon fishers of northwestern California, who exploited the remarkably productive streams and rivers of the north coast.

The king (or Chinook) and silver (coho) salmon, along with the steelhead trout were the catch of choice for people living near rivers from the Klamath region in the north to Monterey Bay in the south. The only groups who caught significant numbers of other freshwater fish were those living near lakes.

The salmon's routine never varied. In the spring and fall, mature fish would swim far upstream from the Pacific to the headwaters of large rivers and their tributaries. There they would seek out clean, shallow water flowing over gravel beds, there to deposit their eggs. The adults then died. When the eggs hatched the resulting small fry matured far inland. Then the young salmon returned to the Pacific. And the cycle began all over again. The success of the run depended on adequate water flow, free access to reaches upstream, and, above all, on clean, well-aerated water and clear, gravel bottoms, with lowered temperatures in the headwaters.

King salmon ran the Klamath in the far northwest between March and June, and again in the fall. The fish were in better condition earlier in the year. They were sometimes so plentiful that nineteenth-century settlers complained that their horses would not cross shallows because they were scared of the dense masses of fish in the water. The spring run was vital. Thousands of people depended on it, from the Klamath in the north to the Sacramento and San Joaquin Rivers of the Central Valley. Harvesting the run for salmon was more productive than any acorn harvest, and certainly more profitable than cultivating the soil, so much so that other fish were usually ignored, except for eels and some trout. Since life revolved around the salmon in many parts of northern California, the rituals in its honor were of great importance.

The first salmon ritual was one of the most important ceremonial occasions of the year. While details of the ceremony varied from one group to another, they shared some important similarities. The first was the ritual consumption of the first salmon caught, the second a prohibition of any fishing until the complex ritual had ended. In the far north, the first salmon ritual involved a ceremonial fishery, in which the first fish sighted was allowed to pass to ensure a large run, while the second one was caught, cooked, and consumed by the priest in charge of the ritual and his assistants. An elaborate panoply of chants and prayers followed a set formula, telling the story of the salmon. The recited mythology was esoteric, the secrets jealously guarded by its owners. When the feast was over, the bones were returned to the river, so that the salmon would tell its companions how it had been honored. Only when the ritual was complete could fishing begin. Farther south, in the Sacramento/San Joaquin area, the rituals were in the hands of shamans, but, again, the first salmon was ritually consumed and its bones returned to the river before fishing could begin.

The rituals not only ensured the continuity of annual runs, but also reduced congestion in the spawning grounds. At the same time, the first salmon ritual controlled fishing activity until it was clear that the run was plentiful, thereby ensuring enough fish for everyone and reducing potential conflicts.

Salmon were the most intensively managed and ecologically manipulated food resource in ancient northern California. Some estimates place ancient consumption at over fifteen million pounds annually. Elaborate ritual surrounded salmon harvesting in the north, but less so in the south, where plant foods like acorns assumed a much greater importance in the diet.

Each spring and fall, salmon thronged the rivers flooded by abundant rainfall as they passed upstream to spawn. The largest communities flourished near rapids and places where tributaries joined larger rivers. Here, the people harvested salmon by the thousands during the spring and fall runs. Harvest is the appropriate word. Apocryphal stories of people walking across streams on the backs of running salmon abound, which gives one some idea of the abundance of the potential catch.

In many places, the fishers built platforms at the edge of the stream. They used simple lifting nets made of vegetable fibers to scoop the fish out of the water, then killed them with clubs, gathering their catch by the dozens in swift, effortless movements. Wealthy individuals or families owned the best spots, which could be "rented" for a portion of the catch (see figure 10.6).

Some of the best locations lay by major rapids, where the people harpooned dozens of fish with barbed spears or used harpoons with detachable bone heads. The hunter held the harpoon or spear low and thrust it into the

Figure 10.6. Traditional salmon fishing. "Little Ike fishing for salmon with a plunge net at *pame-kyá-ra-m*, Klamath River." Courtesy of National Anthropological Archives, Smithsonian Institution, negative no. 56,748.

water almost horizontally. In deeper pools, they often used three-pronged spears, the center prong being longer than the outside ones, so that the points did not shatter on a rocky bottom.

The building of large fish weirs took place in July or August, when river waters were shallow, under close ritual supervision. At strategic points, local communities constructed weirs, typically high frameworks of poles reaching across the stream, which could also serve as simple foot bridges. At intervals, the fishermen suspended long, parallel-sided wickerwork basket traps in the running water. A salmon swimming rapidly upstream encountered the shieldlike weir, turned, then swam into the trap, where it was unable to turn around. Many weirs incorporated platforms across shallow water, where dip nets made easy work of salmon milling at the fence and unable to swim upstream. At Kepal on the Klamath, the building occupied seventy men for more than ten days, with dozens more from several villages collecting the logs and stakes needed for the structure. The finished weir had nine openings, each with their pens, an industrial-scale construction that was the largest structure ever built in ancient California.

Such weirs were so effective that they caused friction between those who built and operated them and those living upstream. Accordingly, the weir was left open to allow the first of the run to pass freely upstream, not only for others to harvest, but also to allow for spawning, for the fishers were well aware of the need to maintain the fish population. Sometimes so many salmon clogged the openings that the weir was opened to relieve congestion. Once the builders had harvested a sufficiency—a tonnage established as much by their ability to process the catch as by the number of salmon—the fish were allowed to swim freely to the headwaters.

During the ten days or more of the run, entire communities worked day and night harvesting fish and processing them for later use. Salmon spoils rapidly in warm weather and must be processed almost immediately. Dehydrating fresh fish was a skillful art, but a vital one, given the major fluctuations in salmon runs from one year to the next. Improperly dried fish turned moldy and spoiled. Even well-preserved catches fell prey to insects, so much time went into inspecting stored fish.

The salmon fishers preserved fish by drying or smoking them. In drier areas like northern California, where sunny weather was a reliable commodity, the gutted fish lay on outdoor racks exposed to the wind, the rack roofed over with planks or branches to guard against direct sunlight or possible rain showers. Much depended on carefully gutting the fresh fish, normally a day after catching, when the meat was easier to slice. The butcher removed the head and fins, then cut out the backbone, tail and all. Everything was dried, even the heads.

No one knows exactly how large salmon harvests were before European contact and the days of unregulated fishing and environmental degradation. The main factor affecting the fish harvest was the ability of a community to process the catch. A modern fish cutter can fillet a thousand salmon in an eight-hour day, but it seems unlikely that ancient processors with simpler, less effective technology could match this remarkable number, even with a simple form of production line in operation.

The salmon was indeed king for the many societies that depended on it, one of the two staples that sustained many northwestern groups, the other being acorns. Accurate estimates are hard to come by, but one places the harvest as high as about 740,000 pounds in a good year, or about 240 pounds a person.

Groups living along the Klamath and its main tributary, the Trinity River, relied so heavily on fish and acorns that many of them virtually ignored forest game, especially smaller prey like rabbits, so important in the desert south. For the most part, they also left alone smaller fish like freshwater trout. Why should they bother with such small fish when they commonly netted twenty-pound salmon? Instead, they took sea-running steelhead trout, when they returned to the rivers to spawn. Lamprey eels migrated upstream in the spring, relished for their rich, greasy flesh. Once again, catches were limited not by the abundance of fish, but by the ability of the people to process them in large numbers for later consumption.

Salmon fishing was a staple of northwestern life in the closing centuries of ancient times. But when did the intensive harvesting of migrating fish begin? To answer this question, we must now step back in time, to the millennia when nomadic foragers exploited the rivers and streams behind the coast.

Living in the Interior (c. 5,000 B.C. to after A.D. 500)

Here, as elsewhere in California, the ubiquitous projectile point defines the long history of human occupation after Paleo-Indian times.[15]

From as early as 5000 B.C. until about 2000 B.C., a sparse population of hunter-gatherers occupied the region, known from their distinctive "Borax

Lake" points with their wide basal stems (see figure 2.5). We know almost nothing else about these shadowy people, who appear to have been nomadic foragers, living mainly inland, alongside rivers and streams.

The Mendocino Pattern lasted from 2000 B.C. to A.D. 500. A series of projectile points with side and corner notches came into use. This 2,500-year period witnessed major changes in the interior. About 3,000 years ago, sedentary villages appeared inland, along the banks of the major rivers, where the inhabitants harvested enormous numbers of salmon, then dried or smoked them for winter use.

By A.D. 500, large sedentary settlements were commonplace inland, in areas close to major salmon rivers. After that date, the style of projectile point changed, as bows and arrows appeared in the northwest. This is often called the Gunther Pattern, named after the island of that name in Humboldt Bay where the highly distinctive Gunther arrow point with its long shoulders and straight or contracting stem was first identified (see figure 10.3, right blade). Gunther points are wonderful cultural markers, and appear throughout much of northern California and into southern Oregon.

Projectile points tell us relatively little about the lives of those who made them, but their distributions over the landscape reveals major changes in hunting practices. For example, all the projectile forms found in the northwest, from Borax Lake to the barbed Gunther head, occur in abundance along the interior river valleys. In contrast, the interior mountain ranges have yielded Borax Lake and later forms, but Gunther Barbed points are very rare.

Why the sudden change in artifact distribution? We can only guess, but the shift may be connected with major changes both in subsistence and in local societies. Earlier groups hunted deer and Roosevelt elk in the densely forested mountains. Now, permanent, sedentary settlements appear along the major river. The salmon was always a seductive resource, but was apparently never harvested in large numbers until around A.D. 500. I suspect this was not because people were unable to catch salmon, a simple matter in the midst of a spring or fall run, but a matter of organizing the *processing* of the catch and its preservation on a large scale. And that required communal effort—and the leadership—to undertake the work. Once large-scale salmon harvesting became commonplace, hunting, and the artifacts associated with it, may have assumed lesser importance in local society.

The distribution of projectile points along the coast speaks volumes about the major changes under way. Archaeologists have combed the shoreline for

Borax Lake points, but found none of them, as if all Middle Holocene groups lived in the interior. Only one actual Borax Lake site is known from the northwestern coast and that is considered to be an elk-butchering location. Four Mendocino sites lie along the shoreline, all of them temporary camps, where the inhabitants were more interested in game or plant foods than in shellfish and other maritime foods. In stark contrast, Gunther Barbed heads form as much as 80 percent of most artifact collections from coastal settlements, reflecting a significant increase in coastal settlement.

After A.D. 500, the coastal picture changes dramatically. There are many more sites, and the artifacts found in them are much more diversified. Four major historic Tolowa villages, all permanent settlements, once flourished north of Humboldt Bay. These were substantial villages, with planked houses, square structures with an outer wall of upright redwood planks extending about fifteen feet on each side, and a square interior pit about two to three feet deep and about ten feet on each side. The dwellings had blue clay floors and, often, stone patios at the entrance. Tolowa carpenters could draw on endless supplies of straight-grained redwood from river banks and beaches. They split off long planks with stone hammers and elk antler wedges for house planks and many other uses (see figure 10.7).

These settlements flourished off sea mammal hunting and fishing. Dozens of triangular, concave-based projectile points survive, the remains of the stone tips for antler and bone harpoons, used against seals and sea lions. Smaller versions of the same artifacts sufficed for fishing.

Settlement along the Klamath River (A.D. 300 to European Contact)

We know something of the earlier inhabitants of the interior from studies of the ancient settlement pattern along the middle reaches of the Klamath River during the Late Period. Here lived the antecedents of the Karok, the Hokan-speaking people, who dwelt on the edge of the northwest coast region in historical times. The Karok themselves flourished in considerable numbers along the Klamath. In 1925 and 1936, Alfred Kroeber published two accounts of more than a hundred Karok settlements, which included both location data and information on the number of riverside settlements. Not that they lived only along the river. Much Karok territory lies in the mountainous terrain away from the river and still has not been explored for archaeological sites.[16]

Figure 10.7. Sweat house and planked house, Klamath River. Powers, *Tribes of California* (Berkeley, Calif.: University of California Press, 1976; reprinted edition edited by Robert F. Heizer), fronticepiece.

Archaeologist Martin Baumhoff once predicted that the largest number of settlements would be found below the mouth of the Salmon River, in the southern part of Karok territory, where the highest number of spawning runs would take place. According to a map published by the linguist, William Bright, in 1957, Karok settlements were densest around the confluence of the Klamath and Salmon Rivers, and were sparsest in the northern part of their territory, above Clear Creek. About 2,700 Karok lived along a sixty-mile stretch of the Klamath and twelve miles of the Salmon, with a population density of about eight people per square mile, a very high density indeed by California standards. The size of the population bore a direct relationship to the density of salmon runs moving upstream.

The Karok and their ancestors lived in a diverse homeland. Karok territory extended along the Klamath River in the Klamath Mountains region of northwest California, some forty miles east of Crescent City on the coast. Their lands covered about 1,170 square miles, a world of rugged mountains and swift-flowing rivers and streams. A very diverse fauna and flora flourished on the steep slopes and in the deep valleys of Karok territory. Of the 268 plants used by the Karok, 100 were eaten regularly, but not one of them served as a staple. Acorns were the most abundant plant food, but oaks were not nearly as abundant as they were in other parts of California.

A wide range of land mammals lived in the Klamath region, but never in large numbers, with the exception of the Columbia black-tailed deer (*Odocoileus hemionis*). The Douglas fir forest offered few plant foods to support large numbers of herbivores, with none of the rich mast found in oak groves. Rabbits and rodents were relatively abundant, and the Karok took them, but the amount of meat per square mile in their territory was much lower than in other areas.

The most abundant food source was fish, for the Klamath River was a major spawning river for king salmon, silver salmon, and steelhead trout, which ran most heavily between mid-August and early January. Smaller winter and spring runs were also commonplace. Some salmon could be caught all year. But these catches paled into insignificance when compared to the mighty spawning runs, when salmon were so abundant that they really were a staple food.

The Karok built wooden platforms over the flooding river, erected fish weirs and numerous traps. Then they harvested thousands of salmon, butchering them, smoking them, and pounding their flesh into an easily stored and transported meal. They knew of the best places for the harvest—at falls and rapids, locations where the topography made the passage of the fish upstream more predictable and less susceptible to sudden alteration by floodwaters. Salmon use river currents to help them upstream, eddies that change course without warning when severe flooding raises the water level. The best place to catch salmon was in narrow channels. Here, massive boulders and steep banks confined them within cramped defiles.

At harvest time, the Karok pressed every fishing device in their armory into service. Dip nets lifted passing fish onto wooden platforms. Seines, gaffs, hooks and lines, barbed spears, clubs, even bows and arrows helped catch salmon. Some fishermen simply waded into calmer water and caught the densely packed salmon with their hands and hurled them ashore. The technology of Karok salmon fishing was elaborate, strikingly so when compared with the simple bows and arrows used against land mammals.

As elsewhere, salmon determined the diet, the annual rhythm of life along the river, even the placement of villages. The only other fish of significance was the Pacific lamprey eel, which could be caught year-round.

In 1972, Joseph and Kerry Chartkoff located 160 archaeological sites in Karok territory, dating to between A.D. 300 and 1750. The densest concentration of ancient village sites occurs within a three-mile radius of the Klamath-Salmon confluence, either on the Salmon itself or upstream of the confluence. Furthermore, nearly all Klamath villages on the river lay near stream confluences, with the largest sites almost invariably located at falls or rapids. There were severe constraints on settlement owing to the topography, for there was little flat ground for village sites, most of it narrow river terraces. The largest sites lie at the higher terrace elevations, up to a hundred feet above the river, with smaller sites nearer the water.

The highest densities of sites lay near falls or rapids where weirs, traps, and platforms work best. At the river confluences, the flooding water would sometimes create gravel bars, diverting the fish into side streams to spawn and creating a more reliable fish supply. For this reason, the highest human populations concentrated at confluences, not above them, where fish would be less plentiful.

The people lived in circular, semisubterranean houses between ten to sixteen feet across, just like those found widely in central California. The Chartkoffs located them by identifying circular depressions on the surfaces of larger sites. They found such larger villages at higher, flood-free elevations. There were good reasons for such locations, which remained flood free, even in the wettest years. As a result, the communal investment in ceremonial structures and sweat houses was safe from destruction. The loss of the sacred artifacts and regalia housed in them would also be catastrophic. It was here that the highest status families lived, the individuals who controlled and supervised important rituals like the First Salmon Ceremony.

Most settlements dating to the past 1,500 years lie in the lower and middle reaches of the rivers, where the salmon were most abundant. The people living downstream siphoned off enormous numbers of fish, leaving many fewer for their neighbors upstream. Less than a quarter of the settlements recorded by the Chartkoff survey lay in the upstream portions of Karok territory. And those clustered near strategic falls and rapids, where the most fish were to be found.

■ ■ ■

The extreme northwest was a different world than that of the Bay Area, Central Valley, or southern California. Here, salmon ruled the people's lives; they were harvested in enormous numbers, limited only by the ability of the harvesters to process them. In many respects, the people of the Klamath and other major river valleys owed much to the ancient cultural traditions of the Pacific Northwest, where individual wealth and prestige were all-important and large permanent settlements flourished for many centuries.

If ever there were societies where aggrandizers flourished, it was these—cultures where individual ambitions had free reign and where the elaborate rituals of the first salmon and other ceremonial events of the year offered opportunities for the display of wealth, for sponsorship, and self-promotion. With wealth came prestige and social rank, just as they did in the Pacific Northwest. That such phenomena emerged and endured for many centuries was due almost entirely to the large food surpluses accumulated from the salmon harvest. And, unlike the south, coastal settlement only developed when territorial boundaries inland became so well defined that only the shoreline remained.

As we move south into the San Francisco Bay Area, we find aggrandizers as active as they were in the northwest, but operating within a very different political landscape. Here, wealth and acquiring loyal followers was closely tied to the fortunes of the ancestors. In both regions, however, elaborate rituals provided the justification and vehicle for some people being wealthier and more powerful than others, perhaps the greatest major change of ancient times.

San Francisco Bay:
A Landscape of Mounds

A.D. 500. The falling afternoon tide leaves bubbling mud in its train. A few reeds poke through the brown mire. Narrow fingers of gravelly sand and boulders extend into the marsh. Densely packed clam beds gleam in the sun. Three women and their children move slowly in a line across the exposed beds, deftly prying fresh clams from their resting places, throwing them into large baskets at their feet. At times, they are knee-deep in mud, almost at water level, grasping for mollusks in the warm, murky shallows. After an hour or so, the baskets are full. The women heft their heavy loads on their backs, steadying the laden baskets with head straps. They walk slowly to the edge of the large shell mound just above the high tide mark. Then they sit on some convenient logs and quickly shuck the clams with stone choppers, ready for the evening meal. . . .

Fifteen hundred years ago, San Francisco Bay was a landscape of mounds, of shell tumuli large and small, set in a flat landscape of mudflats and salt marshes.[1] Today, most of this unusual natural landscape has vanished under the urban sprawl of the Bay Area, buried under acres of modern landfill, highways, and housing subdivisions.

This is the story of a humanly created world, which developed around San Francisco Bay over a period of at least six thousand years, only to vanish abruptly in the nineteenth century A.D.

Before the Shell Mounds (9000 B.C. to 4000 B.C.)

People lived in the Bay Area long before shell mounds rose along its shores, but they flourished in a very different environment.

During the late Ice Age, and until about 9000 B.C., the Golden Gate was dry land, dissected by an estuary that ran fast and deep when mountain runoff cascaded to the ocean in spring. From the gate, the river emerged onto the wide continental shelf and into the Pacific.

Upstream, the estuary widened, but still flowed fast, with none of the swamps and flat mudflats that define San Francisco Bay today. Pine and redwood forests pressed on the river, mantling a hilly landscape. There were few signs of people, just the smoke of an occasional campfire, or a few spear-carrying figures walking along the bank of a tributary stream. Come spring and early summer, more people would come into sight—families, even entire bands, harvesting grasses on the river floodplain or on the continental shelf.

Back in camp, you would hear the scrape, scrape of hand stone against milling stone, as the women prepared the evening meal. Plant foods were an all-important staple at a time when the bay's rivers cascaded down to a much lower Pacific.

The Milling Stone people left few traces of their presence behind them. Such sites that remain usually lie deep below modern urban sprawl, as usual mere scatters of milling and hammerstones, of crude stone artifacts. We can only guess at their presence at a time when the bay was an estuary. They were almost certainly there, simply because there was plenty of water and many plant foods grew within a short distance, in nearby river valleys and canyons.

Even as the Milling Stone people harvested the grasses of the bay and adjacent continental shelf, their world was changing. The Pacific rose perceptibly within generational memory, shrinking the shelf and moving ever closer to the narrow, cliff-edged Golden Gate (see figure 11.1).

Between 9000 and 8000 B.C., the rising Pacific inundated the Golden Gate and flowed inexorably into the inland floodplain. Here two great river systems converged. The northern arm of the newly forming bay drained the Sacramento and San Joaquin Rivers, the southern arm Coyote Creek and the coast ranges. Enormous quantities of water moved through the expanding bay. Today, the Sacramento and San Joaquin Rivers drain no less than 40 percent of California's landmass.

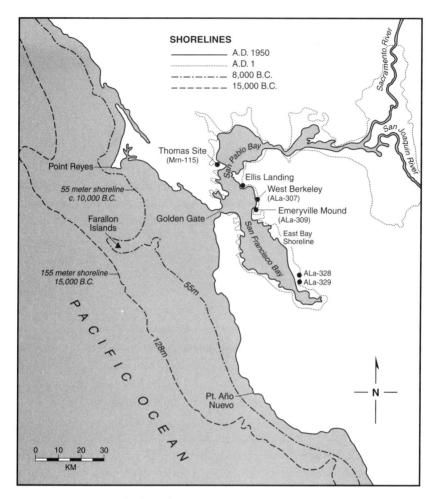

Figure 11.1. Map showing the Bay Area at the end of the Ice Age and locations of archaeological sites mentioned in the text.

The floodplain had always been of considerable size, the fast-moving river meandering past complex, long-vanished river plains, cutting down toward the shore, three hundred feet lower than today.[2] Now sea water inundated the flat lands inside the Golden Gate, ponding the rivers, forming a huge, shallow water bay. This was an entirely new world for the few people who lived nearby. For the first time, they had reliable food sources at their proverbial doorstep, not miles away at the coast.

The bay filled rapidly over the next three thousand years, as the local sea level rose by about three-quarters of an inch a year. This translated into horizontal movement of up to one hundred feet annually, an inundation guaranteed to change anyone's world. Where shallow water fingered over the flat terrain, some swamps and marshes formed.

Until about 6000 B.C., the bay marshes were narrow and discontinuous. But, as sea levels rose, sediment accumulated more rapidly in many areas, especially along the western part of the Sacramento–San Joaquin Delta, creating extensive tidal mud flats.

After 4000 B.C., the sea level rise slowed considerably, to about 0.001 inch per year. Now there was time for extensive tidal marshes to form along the shore. Shallow-water loving plants like codgrass and tules established themselves on mudflats at water's edge. These species tolerated submergence at low tide, acted as sediment traps, and encouraged the formation of dry land. Huge tracts of marsh accumulated in the bay and up the estuaries that formed it, the largest contiguous area of tidal marshland along the Pacific Coast of North America.

What had once been a large flood plain, dissected by a river gorge, now became a shallow estuary, raked by fog and strong summer winds, but with hundreds of square miles of shallow marshlands where a remarkable abundance of all kinds of animal and plant foods thrived. Here people could harvest fish and shellfish, birds and swamp-loving land mammals, and a broad constellation of edible marsh plants.

By about 3000 to 2500 B.C.—the date is mere guesswork—life along the shores of the bay was changing completely. Where once food supplies were scattered irregularly across the landscape, there were now growing marshes, where abundance was there for the taking.[3]

Within two or three millennia, the shores of the bay had become a landscape of shell mounds.

Adjusting to a New Bay (3000 to 500 B.C.)

These changes did not happen all at once. Mudflats and tidal marshes developed slowly, very much a late part of the long process of estuary formation. At first, a visit to the marshes for shellfish or waterfowl may have just been a small part of the annual round, a matter of a few weeks or months. But, as marshes became more widespread, especially along the East Bay shore between Berkeley and San Leandro, settlement became more permanent, and, if not near-permanent, certainly of much longer duration than in the first generations of estuary settlement.

Rising sea levels have buried most of the early shell mounds and estuarine settlements, which turn up only occasionally, in the lowermost levels of large shell mounds or in modern-day underground excavations far from today's shoreline. The earliest known shell mounds date to between 2000 and 1000 B.C., notably occupation layers from sites near Berkeley and in Emeryville, as well as further east along the East Bay shoreline. Their inhabitants took many bay mussels and Pacific oysters, but their tool kits included stemmed and short projectile points used for hunting, as well as pestles, presumably used to process acorns and other plant foods. There are no signs of the milling stones found on earlier sites. Clearly, the mounds were part of a much larger seasonal round, a point on a predominantly inland territory that offered easily obtainable food, especially (and here I am speculating) in the lean winter months.

The strategy may have been exactly the same as elsewhere—a hunting and gathering life way, which was based as much as possible on easily accessible and readily processed foods. Thus, mollusks and oysters must have been part of a much broader diet. Notched and grooved net sinkers occur at most of these sites, as if shallow-water fishing was already a factor in daily life.

As the centuries passed, each band tended to return to the same places, where they knew shellfish abounded and fish could be taken from tule canoes. They knew where migratory ducks and geese flocked to the mudflats in late fall and early winter, where fresh water abounded, and when it paid to move inland to harvest grasses and nuts (see figure 11.2).

Living on the lowlands posed unusual challenges. The salt marshes and mudflats were absolutely flat, infiltrated by creeping water at high tide, often ravaged by severe winter storms. Dry potential village sites were not as common as one might think, so the people started creating their own well-drained camps by piling up broken shells, mud, sand, and other debris—the matrix of so many Bay Area mounds. As the generations passed, so the people lived on increasingly large mounds of discarded fish bones, waterfowl remains and thousands upon thousands of shucked clams and oysters. Here, too, they buried their dead. The largest mounds could be seen from miles away amid the muddy flats, surrounded by mud at low tide,

Figure 11.2. Costanoan Indians ride in a tule canoe. Picture from Louis Choris (1822). Courtesy of Davidson Library, University of California, Santa Barbara.

by shallow water at high. Today, the bases of many of these ancient mounds extend feet below modern sea level, for they accumulated faster than the bay waters rose.

By 1500 B.C., San Francisco Bay was a landscape of mounds, large and small, hugging the shore, set in groups, some oval shaped, others flat topped with circular dwellings on their summits, others shallow and long deserted. This landscape was unique in California. With its tumuli and many burial places, it was also a symbolic landscape, imbued by its inhabitants with now long-forgotten spiritual qualities.

To archaeologists, this is shell mound country.

Exploring the Shell Mounds

In the early years of the twentieth century, the University of California at Berkeley was the only center for archaeological research in town. A Berkeley paleontologist named John Merriam fostered the first serious investigations of Bay Area shell mounds.[4] Merriam had a strong interest in archaeology and access to research funds. The scientific investigation of the shell mounds became the outlet for his enthusiasm at a time when collectors and looters were ravaging the mounds, digging out burials and cratering the middens with huge trenches.

One of the largest shell mounds in the entire region lay on the shore at Emeryville (known today as site Ala-309), just east of Berkeley and opposite San Francisco. This enormous testimony to ancient gastronomy covered an area nearly 100 feet long and 330 feet wide and stood over 30 feet high. The base of the mound was about 30 inches below the modern sea level. Ala-309 towered over the mudflats like a prehistoric colossus, sitting on prime real estate, and already ravaged by plunderers. Today, little remains intact of this remarkable location. Ala-309 epitomizes the tragic history of shell mound archaeology along the shores of San Francisco Bay.

Merriam cast around for a qualified excavator for the vast tumulus. He made an inspired choice in a German excavator, Max Uhle, who had trained as a philologist in Europe, but switched to archaeology and ethnography. Uhle became a curator in the Dresden Museum, where he had met archaeologist Alphons Stübel and worked with him during the 1880s at Tiwanaku, the great thousand-year-old ceremonial center close to Lake Titicaca in Bolivia, high in the Andes. The young German turned out to be a gifted excavator and carried out some of the first stratigraphic excavations on the Peruvian coast in the 1890s. He was to continue working in Peru for over thirty years. His Emeryville research was but a brief interlude in a long and successful archaeological career.

Uhle trenched into Ala-309 in 1902. He was a careful and perceptive observer, above all a stratigraphy man, an expert at excavating and recording occupation levels in archaeological sites. He also knew that the artifacts in each level were valuable markers—evidence of possible cultural change through time (see figure 11.3).

No one could excavate Ala-309 completely. It was simply too large for any excavator, let alone one on a small budget. Uhle trenched into the mound "stratum by stratum" and boldly identified no less than ten principal layers. He took his excavation down to the water table and below, until he reached sterile alluvial clay. His carefully drawn cross-section delineates his levels and even counts the number of artifacts found in each one. He wrote: "It is evident that the character of the objects in the upper strata is entirely different from that of the implements that are found in the lower beds."[5] At the same time, he recognized that there was much cultural continuity from one layer to the next.

Figure 11.3. Max Uhle's excavation of the Emeryville shell mound in 1902. The dig
was carried out on an area of the shell mound immediately to the west
of a dance pavilion and cypress hedge, seen behind the trench.
Reproduced from Uhle (1907). Courtesy of the Phoebe Hearst Museum
of Anthropology and the Regents of the University of California.

In the end, Uhle segregated two major components in the mound, each
comprising five of his ten strata. The people of the lowest component had
subsisted mainly off oysters rather than bent-nose clams. They buried their
dead in a flexed position and made their simple stone tools almost entirely
from local chert, a finely crystallized quartz. The later inhabitants cremated
their dead, consumed enormous numbers of clams rather than oysters, and
used imported obsidian for many of their stone tools.

Uhle had no sophisticated dating equipment to assist him. But he estimated that the Emeryville mound was occupied for more than a thousand years. He used changing styles in projectile points, beads, and other artifacts to identify culture change, just as he had done on the Peruvian coast, using a methodology ahead of its time.

Uhle's excavation methods were nothing to write home about by modern standards, but they were better than those of most of his contemporaries. He used picks and shovels to uncover stratified layers, but took the trouble to record the occupation levels with drawings and photographs. Unlike most others, he also took the trouble to publish his finds in a carefully prepared monograph in 1907. The wrath of the anthropological establishment promptly descended on Uhle's head. His real sin was to identify cultural change at Ala-309 instead of a static ancient California society that changed not one iota over many centuries. The all-powerful Alfred Kroeber condemned Uhle's conclusions out of hand, although he did not mention him by name:

> The one published account of a systematic though partial exploration of a shell-heap of San Francisco Bay upholds the view of a distinct progression and development of civilization having taken place during the growth of the deposit. An independent examination of the material on which this opinion is reared, tends to negate rather than to confirm it.[6]

In Kroeber's view, there were no major technological advances throughout California prehistory.

Meanwhile, John Merriam put another archaeologist to work on shell mounds, this time on a far-ranging survey of mounds large and small. He chose Danish-born Nels C. Nelson for the task. Nelson was a remarkable man by any standards. He was born to extreme poverty, bound to a farmer, and eventually was sent to an uncle in Minnesota. In 1892, he entered first grade at age seventeen, graduating from high school in 1901. Then he rode a cattle car to California and worked his way through Stanford University as a bank janitor. In 1905, he transferred to the University of California with the intention of studying philosophy, but discovered archaeology instead, under the influence of Alfred Kroeber.

Between 1906 and 1908, Nels Nelson surveyed most of the Bay Area and adjacent coast from the Russian River to Half Moon Bay. He later estimated that he walked over three thousand miles, often knee deep in mud and sea water, as well as excavated a number of important sites.

Life was easier for an archaeologist in those days. Urban sprawl and industrial development were in their infancy, so Nelson could move around more freely and observe far more evidence of human activity than we can today. Much more of the landscape of mounds that once dominated the shoreline was still intact, under plowed fields or in areas now deep under modern landfill. A few black-and-white photographs in the archives of the Phoebe Hearst Museum at Berkeley chronicle some of the large middens he recorded, which are now buried under the concrete jungle of the early twenty-first-century Bay Area.

Nelson located no less than 427 shell mounds around the bay and along the Pacific Coast. But they were in sorry shape. Lamented Nelson: "Not a single mound of any size is left in its absolutely pristine condition."[7] He mapped some mounds of considerable size, oval or oblong-shaped tumuli running parallel to the shore, some nearly six hundred feet long and thirty feet high. In places, the circular depressions left by abandoned houses could be seen.

Nelson concentrated much of his fieldwork along the East Bay shorelines of Alameda and Contra Costa counties, where salt marshes bordered dry land, extending out between two and three miles. He found no less than one hundred shell mounds in an area that once teemed with fish, mollusks, and waterfowl, but the Emeryville mound was still about the largest.

The young Nelson had never excavated a site in his life, so his methods were simple. Instead of moving slowly with trained workers armed with trowels and small picks, he trenched into the large Ellis Landing mound in a saltwater marsh near Richmond using teams of horses and agricultural scrapers to dig out 2,500 cubic yards of the site in a mere two weeks. This was excavation on a grand scale. In two years of sporadic trenching, Nelson recovered 160 burials from Ellis Landing and identified two major components, accumulated, he estimated, over a period of 3,500 years—a date reached by calculating the rate of accumulation of midden deposits. No less than sixteen feet of the mound lay below modern marsh level.

Nelson's digging had little of the relative finesse that marked Uhle's Ala-309 excavations. Nelson argued that the culture of the inhabitants changed little over the centuries. He assumed that the shifts in mollusk frequencies were the result of involuntary responses to short-term environmental change. Nelson was vaguely aware of broad stratigraphic subdivisions at Ellis Landing, but did not acquire a real knowledge of archaeological stratigraphy until he spent two years working on a well-stratified Stone Age cave in northern Spain in 1911–1912. He learned his lesson well and went on to make major contributions to southwestern archaeology.[8]

Uhle and Nelson left a jumble of artifacts and some rough stratigraphic observations behind them, but these evidences of change were dismissed by Kroeber's influential pen. He extrapolated from Uhle and Nelson's work in the Bay Area to the entire state in 1925: "Relatively little transformation and but slight succession of civilizations occurred in prehistoric California."[9] He attributed the changes noted by Uhle, Nelson, and their successors to either sampling vagaries or to local cultural variation. Ironically, Alfred Kroeber was a pioneer in the use of pottery to study ancient culture change in the Southwest. But there were no clay vessels in the Bay Area, and he did not consider stone tools such useful indicators. (For the cultural sequence as known today, see box 11.1 and chapter 1.)

Excavation of bay shell mounds, mainly by Berkeley archaeologists, continued through World War I and into the 1930s. Everyone assumed that the largest mounds resulted from hundreds or even thousands of years of continuous occupation by people exploiting the rich estuary. These were not burial mounds like the well-known Adena and Hopewell tumuli on eastern North America—the famous "Moundbuilders"—but mainly densely occupied villages, where people were also interred.[10]

The archaeological laboratories and store rooms at Berkeley rapidly filled with jumbles of artifacts, shells, bones, and other finds from mounds large and small. Few scientists ever looked closely at them, except for archaeologist Edward Gifford, who took the trouble to analyze the constituents of sixteen mounds in 1916 in a pioneering attempt to establish their use.

The Emeryville mound was on prime real estate, and did not remain undisturbed long. In 1924, a steam shovel quickly removed the uppermost twenty-two feet of the mound in preparation for the foundations of a paint factory. Fortunately, Berkeley archaeologist W. E. Schenck salvaged a staggering quantity of artifacts and shells from the midden, including over seven hundred human burials. He calculated that over 60 percent of the mound was composed of mussels, oysters, and clams, and estimated the age of the site at about one thousand years.

BOX 11.1 Chronology of Bay Area Archaeology

Although I do not discuss them here specifically, archaeologists commonly use the following subdivisions of the Bay Area cultural sequence after Milling Stone times. There is somewhat of an assumption of steady progress through time in this sequence, which is one reason why I do not use it here, apart from a desire not to use technical terms. In fact, the Bay Area's past was marked by:

Early Period (3000 to 500 B.C.)
Lower Middle Period (500 B.C. to A.D. 300)
Upper Middle Period (A.D. 300 to 900)

The Middle Period is often linked with the Berkeley Pattern. This is marked by a major emphasis on seed grinding and pounding technology, much of it devoted to acorns. Stone projectile points are commonplace, bone tools were well developed, and people were buried with no signs of social differentiation. Shellfish collecting was important near the bay.

Late Period Phase 1 (A.D. 900 to 1500)
Late Period Phase 2 (A.D. 1500 to 1700)

The Late Period is linked with the Augustine Pattern, marked by the introduction of the bow-and-arrow and the harpoon, larger, more densely occupied settlements, an increase in social stratification and widespread use of cremation for wealthier burials. Trade was more extensive than in earlier centuries. Judging from the number of bone awls used for basketry, basket weaving was important.

Three crudely excavated trenches penetrated the lowermost horizons where bones, shells, and charcoal abounded. Many years later, the basal levels were radiocarbon dated to about 850 B.C., considerably earlier than the original Schenck estimate (see figure 11.4).

Following the Kroeber line, Schenck observed that the culture of Ala-309's inhabitants was even and unchanging, that there was no stratification to be seen in the mound. As for differences in the artifacts within the mound, they could be accounted for by repeated seasonal occupation by the many groups who exploited the nearby marshes and shallows.[11]

Figure 11.4. A steam shovel removes the Emeryville shell mound in 1924. Archaeologist W. E. Schenck watched over the removal and recovered numerous burials, also artifacts. Reproduced from Schenck (1926). Courtesy of the Phoebe Hearst Museum of Anthropology and the Regents of the University of California.

By the time Schenck recovered his rich haul from Emeryville, Berkeley archaeologists had dug many other middens found by Nelson. By now, they had identified a distinctive shoreline culture in the Bay Area, with similar burial customs, patterns of subsistence, and artifacts in use over a large area, even if there were differences between many of the sites.

Invariably, even small excavations yielded large collections of broken and burnt shell and bones from all kinds of animals, but surprisingly few artifacts. Dull, very unspectacular finds to the lay person, but a treasure trove of fascinating information to the scientist dedicated enough to spend months on end poring over paper bags and boxes full of midden debris.

Bird expert Hildegarde Howard was one of the pioneers, an expert in bird bones. Even today, this is an esoteric specialty, but in Howard's day her research was truly unusual. Fortunately, she had the vision, and the detective skills, to recognize the potential of the tiny bone fragments on the table before her. She had also read the pioneering work of nineteenth-century Danish archaeologists who had identified migratory birds in Scandinavia shell mounds seventy-five years earlier.

Howard's work opened a new chapter in the study of bay shell mounds. After months of work, Howard acquired an astonishing array of information from the Ala-309 bird bones collected and excavated by Uhle and Schenck. Not surprisingly, she found that water birds, especially ducks, geese, and cormorants, were the most abundant forms, while land birds from the nearby canyons and hills were absent. She knew that the geese were winter visitors to the bay between January and April of each year. Then, in thinking years ahead of her time, she narrowed the inquiry dramatically. The cormorant bones came from immature birds between five to six weeks old, as if the inhabitants had been robbing cormorant rookeries. Howard turned to local rookery records and estimated that a date of June 28 each year would have been the best time for a successful raid.

Hildegaard Howard concluded that Ala-309 was occupied during the winter and into early summer.[12]

As the archaeologists dug, and a few scientists mulled over the finds, the mounds disappeared rapidly under a blizzard of construction and land filling, which accelerated during World War II. Dozens of sites large and small disappeared under industrial parks, housing developments, and highways. By the time serious excavation resumed after the war, only shreds and patches remained of the landscape of mounds that were so conspicuous in Nelson's day.

Since the 1940s, most research has involved much smaller excavation and cultural resource management (CRM) projects; small samples, often taken before the construction of a highway or some other form of urban development. More and more of the most important results come from intensive laboratory work, using sophisticated sampling methods, chemical analyses of midden constituents, and detailed studies of bird, fish, and other food remains (see figure 11.5).

We now know, for example, that some mound dwellers harvested their food from open bay waters, while others exploited tidal flats and beaches, or freshwater marshes. The range of animals of all kinds from the mounds is remarkable: sea otters and occasionally seals, several forms of sturgeon and salmon, surf perch and smelt, and several kinds of shark. The list goes on and on—cormorants, grebes, loons and other waterfowl, deer and wolf from inland, and so on.

Uhle, Nelson, and other early researchers remarked on the bay mussels and oysters were much eaten in earlier times, giving way to clams in later centuries. The changeover could have resulted from rising sea levels, increased

Figure 11.5. Shellmound Street, a familiar exit off US 101 in Emeryville, commemorates one of the Bay Area's largest sites, alas now largely destroyed. Courtesy of Edward Luby.

silting, or overexploitation, which caused people to focus on clam digging, a more labor intensive process. This shift is mirrored in some more recent excavations, but it's also clear that there was a great deal of variation from one location to the next.

Despite all these researches, many of the basic questions about the shell mound people remain unanswered. Why did these forager populations suddenly begin to construct shell mounds? When, exactly, did they do so? What role did such sites and the activities carried out on them play in local life as a whole? Were the mounds predominantly middens, or were they vibrant settlements, or even ceremonial places? What were the relationships between individual sites, or groups on settlements in a much wider landscape? The list of questions seems endless and, unfortunately, the answers may be long in coming, if ever at all. Not enough intact sites remain for us to find the answers.

Every surviving Bay Area shell mound has a complicated history of excavation and destruction. During the early 1970s, for example, archaeologist Polly Bickel wrote a doctoral dissertation on three shell mounds in Alameda county, which provides a chronicle of excavations over the decades. Site Ala-328, on the eastern shore of the bay, south of Alameda Creek, has a typical history. Nels Nelson recorded the site in 1909, but a test pit was not sunk into the mound until 1935, when Waldo Wedel, later a well-known Plains archaeologist, excavated several trenches and recovered some burials. Between 1949 and 1968, Ala-328 became the centerpiece of an annual field school taught by San Francisco State College (now University). Much of the southern side of the mound was excavated over the years, and partially published in 1953. 1966–1968 saw some California State University excavations. This checkered archaeological history is better than most.[13] Fortunately, the half-excavated site is now under the protection of the East Bay Regional Park District.

We are lucky to have even half of Ala-328. Most of its contemporaries have vanished without investigation, bulldozed away, covered with concrete, or looted beyond redemption. In the 1950s, Robert Heizer went out to excavate a mound first investigated before the war. The owner of the property calmly informed him that he had sold the phosphate-rich midden deposits as topsoil.

Heizer's experience is not unusual. It's a miracle that anything has survived. A new generation of data is now emerging from the surviving mounds, mainly from small-scale tests and CRM excavations. Unfortunately, much of it is little more than mindless lists of artifacts, animal, bones, and shells. Fortunately, the plethora of new data is moving us away from a minor obsession with shell mounds to larger questions. For the first time, we are looking at ancient bay societies on a much broader regional basis, where the resources of the estuary were an integral part of a complex annual round that took people inland as well.

Which brings us back to the landscape of mounds.

Base Camps, Cemeteries, and Sacred Places (500 B.C. to A.D. 900)

The man in the small tule canoe paddles slowly across the endless shallows, shivering slightly as the cold winter wind ruffles the water. Darkness is gathering, clouds mounting on the western horizon, a sign of rain by morning. The water reflects the light blue/grey of the sky, a few village mounds standing out as dark lumps on the bay. Flickering hearths shimmer on the summit of the nearest settlement as night falls. Thankfully, the paddler steers his flimsy craft toward the welcome flames, glad for a mark to steer him home. . . .

Flat, featureless, and muddy—mile after mile of the bay shoreline stretched as far as the eye could see. Rising sea levels changed this swampy world every year, with every exceptionally high tide or severe winter storm. But the people who lived off the salt marshes and flats returned year after year to familiar locations where they were assured of finding the same foods on every visit. As they visited again and again, so their camp sites rose slowly above the surrounding terrain. A natural accumulation of shells and other occupation debris accounted for some of the rise. In some cases, they piled up rocks, sand, and clay to raise their dwellings higher above storm surges. Even in Nels Nelson's day, some large mounds were buffeted constantly by wave action during major winter storms.

The mounds often occur in discrete clusters, with the largest sites closest to the bay. There are at least eight mound clusters in the East Bay alone, each consisting of four to six mounds varying greatly in size. A similar pattern occurs on the now heavily built-over San Francisco Peninsula. One hypothesis argues that since the largest sites were closest to the shore, the medium- and smaller-sized ones further away from the water are younger, but, since the uppermost levels of many mounds were removed early in the twentieth century, there is no way of proving this.

Some of the large mounded villages may have served not only as important settlements, but also as ceremonial and political centers. There are many signs of ritual activity. Condors and sacred raptors were buried in the lower levels of West Berkeley and Emeryville; clusters of charmstones appear at the Ryan Mound.[14] Traces of more elaborate, perhaps ceremonial, structures with packed clay floors and wooden uprights appear at several sites—perhaps assembly houses.

Why did people start building mounds and returning to the same places when they could simply have founded a new camp on higher ground, a safe distance from encroaching high tides? Had they done this, the archaeological sites resulting from their activities would have been shallow encampments, extending laterally across the landscape, ever further from water's edge.

We know from bird bones that most groups lived on shell mounds during the wet winter months, when both flooding streams and tidal surges caused by southeasterly storms could inundate low-lying settlements. By making the effort to raise their village sites above water level, the inhabitants created a permanent, dry base camp.

There was a good reason for such base camps. Almost invariably, they stood close to food-rich areas—good oyster beds, places where clams could be taken, or fish speared from canoes. A considerable number of these settlements were literally islands surrounded by shallow water, but easily reached in tule reed canoes. With such light watercraft close at hand, the men could easily harvest fish and take waterfowl in more open water. They could also plant nets in deeper bays, take fish like sturgeon or shark, and collect mollusks from isolated outcrops. Simple tule canoes were the automobiles of the mound people.

We still know little of the specialized activities carried out at individual mounds. Some were fishing villages, where stone net weights abounded. Sites in a cluster of mounds on San Pablo Creek yielded bones of large green and white sturgeon, some weighing nearly ninety pounds. Others were close to extensive mussel beds or canyons where deer fed on the fall nut harvest. House floors, hearths, and pits occur at most larger sites, both on the surface of the mound and often in lower levels. Few details of these structures survive, except for an excavation by Clement Meighan into a depression atop the Thomas site on the southwestern shore of San Pablo Bay. He unearthed a circular, dome-shaped dwelling of redwood poles, clay, and grass thatch, which had been burned down. A central hearth yielded the remains of four charred baskets and of numerous boiling stones. Most circular house floors are about nine to eighteen feet across, with hard-packed clay floors.[15]

Nearly all excavated shell mounds contained human burials, both inhumations and cremated remains, interred in shallow, oval pits. The early archaeologists recovered many hundreds of burials from the larger shell mounds. The great Emeryville Mound alone yielded 706 skeletons. Some of the burials lay in formal cemeteries, clusters of burials that involved more than a nuclear family. Sometimes between six and nine people lie in a discrete group, often associated with a house floor of compacted clay and the burnt hut posts. Perhaps these groups represent entire households buried near their then-abandoned dwellings. Individual burials occur in large numbers throughout the occupation levels of bay mounds, with couples sometimes buried in single graves. Only relatively few graves contain red ocher, shell ornaments, and other mortuary goods, prompting debate over whether these sepulchers were those of higher status individuals. The issue is unresolved.

From the very earliest times, the mound people buried their dead in the lower levels of their tumuli. After burial, they resided at the same location. For many centuries, people visited the same places, used the same mounds. And, in the same centuries, they dwelt on soil that contained the remains of their ancestors, an act that created a profound bond between the living and earlier generations, between the living and the landscape they exploited.

Some mounds may even have served purely as cemeteries and sacred places. Many contain very low concentrations of artifacts of any kind, often less than one per cubic yard of midden deposit, with higher numbers for sites that have been screened using more sophisticated recovery methods. These low artifact densities hint that the sites were used for other purposes, especially as cemeteries.

When Alan Leventhal excavated the Ryan Mound (Ala-329) in southern San Francisco Bay, he found that graves were the most common features, while most of the artifacts in the site were finished tools associated with burials. Such places may have served as cemeteries, set at some distance from residential sites, perhaps locations where rituals for the dead and ancestors unfolded. However, his interpretation has been called into question, as a reanalysis of the nonburial sediments yielded numerous artifacts and occupation debris, as if at least some people lived at the site.[16] In practice, most larger sites seem to have combined both residential and ceremonial functions at one location.

Landscape as Territory

Along the East Bay shoreline, the landscape was so flat that the mounds stood out against the featureless topography of mudflat and shallow tidal water. Like communal burial mounds in prehistoric Europe, the mounds became not only an integral part of the landscape, but important territorial markers—by day or night. During daylight hours, the villages stood out clearly from land or to the traveler in a canoe. By night, camp fires and flickering lights would have marked villages from a long distance away. Every mound became an important landmark to hunters, plant collectors, and fisherfolk alike. Each was associated with individual families and kin groups, with powerful shamans or other people with unusual skills. Each had a carefully preserved genealogy that linked its occupants to revered ancestral owners of the surrounding territory and the foods that could be taken from it—the original owners of the land.

The landscape of mounds was far more than clusterings of shell mounds wrought on everyone's mental map of their territory, their world. It was also a supernatural landscape, imbued with important symbolic qualities, a place where people cherished ties to living creatures of every kind. The mounds may also have served as territorial markers, which assumed much greater importance as local populations grew and the number of visitors each winter increased.

Mound Clusters (After 1000 B.C. to A.D. 500)

Quite a large population exploited the East Bay by the second millennium B.C., when at least seven large mounds flourished, spaced on an average, about two miles from one another.[17] After 1000 B.C., eight new shell mounds were founded, including Ala-309, which stood only one and a third miles apart as the shoreline was becoming more crowded. By Spanish contact, the local population density along the East Bay shore may have risen as high as 1.2–1.9 individuals per half mile—a density that certainly would have led to territorial boundaries and ownership of food sources becoming constant issues, perhaps the subject of occasional violence.

By this time, the landscape of mounds had become a powerful reality in daily life along the shores of the bay. The inexorable forces of urban industrialization mean that archaeologists will never be able to reconstruct it in any semblance of detail. But we do know that the landscape of mounds was not the signature of rich bayshore societies living in a veritable Garden of Eden made possible by an abundance of mollusks and other foods. Rather, the great mounds were used, then reused over many generations, for often as long as 500 to 1,900 years. Few were permanent villages, although some, like the well-known West Berkeley village site, may well have been.

We now have enough bones from migratory birds and other sources of subsistence data to be reasonably sure that many sites were occupied, for the most part, in late fall and winter, and sometimes even longer. Migratory duck and geese bones testify to waterfowl hunting during the rainy season, but summer occupation may have been inhibited by fresh water shortages as streams dried up. Still others yield evidence for the exploitation of Chinook salmon runs in fall and late spring/summer, and year-round harvesting of clams established by the growth rings on their shells. Hildegaard Howard established that the people of Ala-309 took young cormorants in early summer.

Finally, we know that the mounds were part of a much larger world, which extended far from the shallow waters and marshlands of the bay. By A.D. 500, Costanoan-speaking people had moved into the bay from the San Joaquin-Sacramento River system (see chapter 1: languages). They occupied many older mound sites, where their occupations represent the Late Period in strictly archaeological terms (see box 11.1). Costanoan/Ohlone tribelets supplied mussel shells, abalone shells, salt, and dried abalone upstream to the Yokuts in the Central Valley and maintained extensive contacts with other groups. There was too little territory to go around, so warfare was commonplace, both between Costanoan/Ohlone neighbors and between Costanoans/Ohlanes and the northern Yokuts and others. Every Costanoan/Ohlone group, like its ancient predecessors managed the land carefully. Spanish travelers described how the people would burn off grass to foster new growth each fall and to retard chaparral. Acorns, wild grasses and roots, and terrestrial mammals like tule elk and deer filled out the shoreline diet of waterfowl, fish, and mollusks. Here, as everywhere else, people depended on one another and on resources from throughout their increasingly small territories. And the landscape of mounds was often the anchor of their wider world.

Feasting the Ancestors

But the great mounds were much more. Yes, they were places of residence, may have been continually occupied and served as burial places, but they also attained huge symbolic importance in the lives of those who accumulated them. How can we say this? Because, for over two thousand years, hundreds, even thousands, of people were buried in the growing shell heaps. Archaeologists Edward Luby and Mark Gruber argue, on the basis of the archaeology, some ethnographic comparisons, and a few surviving oral traditions, that the shell mounds played an important role in the mythic and symbolic life of Bay Area people.[19] They were the places where the living had contact with the ancestors, those who had gone before. Of course, not all religious cosmologies revolve around ancestor worship, but a strong case can be made that the Bay Area shell mounds were places where kin connected with their forebears. They connected with them by literally feasting above the dead.

During the heyday of the shell mounds, the Bay Area was a place where large food surpluses could be accumulated with ease. Such surpluses are powerful tools in the hands of aggrandizers, the aggressive individuals who assumed such an important role in many early California societies. Aggrandizers work hard to become major players in their societies and do so by acquiring followers and giving lavish gifts. Feasts are an excellent way to display one's prestige and economic power, to enhance personal status, and establish reciprocal obligations with other players. But the feast needs a rationale, and this rationale may have lain in cosmology, in the celebration of the links between the living and the dead.

Luby and Gruber point to the close relationship between home, food, and burials as three powerful sacred associations for the shell mounds. Many societies believe that the dead need to be fed, which is why food offerings appear in so many ancient graves. Another way of feeding the departed is to feast above them, perhaps in a funerary meal where an aggrandizer may take the opportunity of death to organize a magnificent repast, to distribute some of his supplies of surplus food, and to reinforce and renew complex social obligations that extend throughout the group and beyond.

In many non-Western societies, death rituals have a profound sense of place. The places where the dead lie may be sacred places. In the case of the bay shell mounds, these may also have served as territorial markers, as points of identity on a sacred landscape. And, as Luby and Gruber put it: "The dead must be fed." The Luby and Gruber theory is just that, but it is based on close argument and careful respect for the archaeological and ethnographic evidence. I find it is extremely convincing.

CHAPTER 11

Abandonment (A.D. 700 to 1542)

After A.D. 700, most Bay Area mounds were abandoned over a period of four centuries. There's no shortage of explanations. Could population movements into the bay from the interior disrupted shell mound life? There were constant interactions between the Bay Area and the Central Valley, but no real signs of a major population shift reflected in changing tool kits in the mounds, despite the arrival of the bow and arrow in about A.D. 500.

Most likely, the explanation is environmental. The abandonment coincides with a time of warmer, drier conditions, known as the Medieval Climatic Anomaly, which affected people living over much of the west. (In dramatic contrast, the same period coincided with good harvests and the building of Gothic cathedrals in Europe.) Drought would have reduced sediment flows, while local sea level rises would have reduced food supplies along shallow bay shores.

Archaeologist Richard Gould pointed to another potential cause a generation ago—acorn-bearing oaks abounded inland from the bay and would have provided more stable food supplies that could be stored.[20] It's entirely possible that shoreline groups moved their base camps into interior valleys for a variety of reasons—drought, the need to feed more people by intensifying the exploitation of acorn harvests, food shortages, or even interband warfare. While some communities may have still flourished on the ancient mound sites, traces of occupation after A.D. 700 are rare. It is as if people adopted a more dispersed annual round, ranging over larger territories, spending less time in one place.

This is, of course, a classic ancient Californian response to drought, and there was drought aplenty during the Medieval Climatic Anomaly. During the same centuries, there was a shift from larger animals like deer and sturgeon toward sea otters and smaller fish at several well-documented sites, as if the subsistence base were changing. Large numbers of people may still have been living close to the bay, but their settlements elude us and may lie under suburban neighborhoods inland.

On the basis of survey data from the East Bay, and as far inland as Livermore, archaeologists Kent Lightfoot and Edward Luby wonder if people were now living more evenly over the landscape, visiting both bayshore and interior locations.[21] Unfortunately, many single-level sites from this period lie under modern silt and landfills, so we may never know the full extent of this more dispersed settlement. That dense populations lived around the bay is unquestionable. Early Spanish visitors commented on the numerous small communities, which housed Costanoan/Ohlone, Miwok, Patwin, and other groups in close proximity.

But the shell mounds still lay at the center of Bay Area life. The great base camps contained hundreds, if not thousands, of burials, the remains of revered ancestors going back many generations. The tumuli stood out on the flat landscape, a profoundly symbolic link between the living and those who had gone before. As local groups dispersed into reorganized societies, the mounds retained profound symbolic importance. The ceremonies that commemorated the ancestors continued at the mounds as they always had. The people buried their dead there, feasting above their graves as in former times. But their visits were more transitory, in a changed world where territories were smaller, people more restricted in their movement, and both feasting and gift giving assumed ever greater importance in societies under stress. These were the centuries that also saw cremation replace inhumation, the appearance of lavish offerings of shell beads to the dead, not only in the great mounds, but also in communities in the interior. Clam disk beads came into circulation in such volume that they became money, and obsidian no longer arrived from distant Bodie and Casa Diablo in the eastern Sierras. Rather, supplies came from nearby Napa, a primary source for Central Valley groups as well.

These shifts in Bay Area life resulted from many, still little understood, factors, among them major organizational changes in both religious beliefs and in relationships with neighbors. These were societies that lived in an intensely political landscape of small groups packed into small territories in areas where coastlines, lakes, and river valleys provided the greatest variety of reliable food supplies. These were groups where aggrandizers were active as major economic and ritual players, where prestige displayed at feasts and other public ceremonies reinforced basic values of societies under environmental and political stress. By feasting on the mounds of the dead and thereby feeding the ancestors, the people in these reorganized societies commemorated a long past and renewed the fertility of the earth for themselves.

Although abandoned, the landscape of mounds still validated a changing world, until alien newcomers disrupted the annual round of hunting and gathering forever.

CHAPTER 12

Central Valley and Foothills: Realm of the Rivers

THE SIERRA FOOTHILLS, A.D. 500. THE BROWN BEARS were fat and sluggish now, satiated with months of feasting. Days were shorter, temperatures still warm, but the leaves were turning, the sun lower in the afternoon sky. The hunter had watched his prey for hours. Now it was slowly lumbering back to its den in a small cave, the entrance dark, at the foot of a steep cliff, masked with dry grass. A huge yawn, a stretch, and the bear vanished from sight.

Next morning, soon after sunrise: the young man has returned with several friends, armed with short bows and arrows and stone-tipped spears. One man held a guttering firebrand, bright in the dark shadows of morning. Another carried a huge bundle of grass, damp with overnight dew. Everyone checks their weapons and remains close to the canyon walls, out of sight. Meanwhile, the hunter places the grass just inside the entrance of the cave, moving quietly lest he disturb the sleeping bear within. He signals to his companions, who spread out in a semicircle close to the dark hole, bows drawn, arrows at the ready. The hunter ignites the grass with the glowing brand, then steps backward when smoke billows from the damp fuel. He draws his short yew bow, strengthened with deer sinew, mounts an arrow, and hovers close to the cave.

The smoke drifts heavily into the bear's den. The men are silent, watchful, waiting for sounds within. A confused grunt, sounds of a heavy body moving. Scraping, more grunts, and the still half-awake bear shambles into the open. The hunter fires instantly, hitting the beast in the shoulder. It turns angrily toward him as he shoots a second arrow and hits a glancing blow on its chest. As the bear rises for the charge, a shower of arrows from the waiting men inflicts fatal wounds in the heart and belly. The bellowing beast collapses in its tracks.

Some hours later, the men return to camp in triumph with the quartered bear and hide. That night they feast on the meat at a meal hosted by the man who had organized the hunt, for the flesh is too greasy to dry. They have already made a wooden frame and stretched the hide, leaning it against a convenient tree. The women scraped it with stone flakes and left it to dry in the sun. One day, the hide will become a funeral shroud. . . .

Remote foothill canyons in the foothills still evoke the California of 1,500 years ago. Walking in the late afternoon hush, when shadows lengthen, you can still imagine hunters with bows and arrows slipping quietly through brush and women grinding acorns on a convenient rocky outcrop near the open country. But away from the mountains, the great Central Valley is now an organized landscape of checkerboard fields, canals, and highways. The grasslands, rivers, and marshes of ancient times have vanished in the face of modern agribusiness as if they had never been. And the ancient settlements that once crowded the banks of the Sacramento and San Joaquin Rivers lie under deep layers of detritus from industrial agriculture, irrigation, mining, and other modern-day human depredations. If there is any region of California where archaeology is a matter of slender clues, only shreds and patches of the past, this is it. In particular, we lack deep, stratified sites, where layer and layer of human occupation record the twists and turns of people adjusting to the zigzags of climatic change.

A Vanished Landscape

California's Central Valley is a vast interior lowland. Over 450 miles long and between 250 miles wide, the valley seems monotonously flat, as any traveler along Interstate 5 can tell you. In fact, the road rises and falls gently as you traverse the flatlands, starting about some sixty feet above sea level at the northern and southern extremities and descending to sea level at Stockton in the Central Valley itself. Here lies the uniqueness of this extraordinary geological phenomenon, a basin filled with deep layers of sediment that were carried downslope by mountain streams—a topography now so flat that the rivers that flow through it meander slowly with sluggish waters, even when swollen with winter rains or Sierra Nevada meltwater in spring (see figure 12.1).

Two great rivers drain the Central Valley. The Sacramento River brings water from the distant Cascade Mountain watershed far to the north, as well as from the Sierras, then flows southeastward through the valley for 150 miles. The San Joaquin River rises in the Sierras and flows west, then northwestward, in a great curve into the valley, swollen by tributaries from the adja-

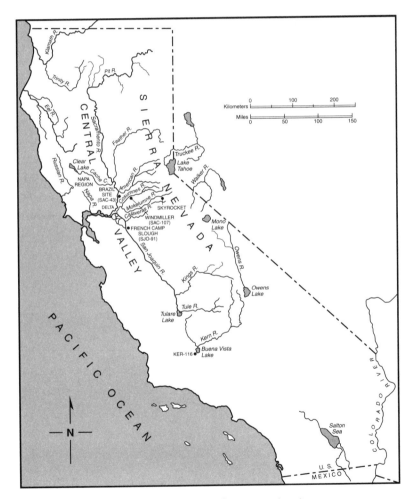

Figure 12.1. Map of the Central Valley, showing major sites.

cent foothills. Both the Sacramento and the San Joaquin swing westward in the Central Valley downstream and merge at the Mokelumne River in the narrow channels and marshes of the delta. Eventually, their waters debouch into Suisun Bay, then flow through a gap in the coast ranges at the Carquinez Strait and empty into San Pablo Bay and the heart of San Francisco Bay.

Like all of ancient California, the Central Valley was a jigsaw of dramatically contrasting environments—lush marshes, a verdant native landscape of gallery forests and grasslands, slow-moving rivers, and shallow lakes. The densest human populations flourished by stream and lake, along the edges of the vast marshes and reed-lined channels of the delta and the great rivers. Away from waterway and swamp, population densities fell rapidly and tribal territories were much larger, reflecting a quite different, much drier world, where food supplies lay across hundreds of square miles of arid terrain.

But the hub of the Central Valley world lay by the rivers and in the seemingly featureless environment of the delta. This was the land of the tule canoe, of narrow channels and rich mudflats, an edible landscape so abundant that people rarely went hungry and the rhythm of life changed little over many centuries. Had industrial agriculture and twentieth-century drainage not intervened, this would also have been an archaeologist's paradise.

When the first collectors and archaeologists dug into cemeteries and mounds near Sacramento three quarters of a century ago, the delta was already much changed from its original state. Nevertheless, many sites still lay untouched. Burial and village mounds carefully situated on higher ground and natural levees stood out above the surrounding flat terrain. Today, virtually nothing remains of the ancient native landscape.

Like the Bay Area, the delta was a landscape of mounds, built in the midst of a confusing patchwork of islands, marshes, and sloughs. Lush stands of grasses, reeds, tules, and cattails grew along the borders of freshwater marshes and backwater lakes. Each spring, meltwater from the Sierras inundated much of the landscape. As the waters receded, tule elk moved down into the marshes for the dry months. They shared the lush environment with dozens of small mammals, among them beavers, mink, otters, and raccoons. Bird life abounded—eagles, pelicans, and many other species. The sluggish waters of overflow lakes teemed with thick-tail club, perch, and sucker. Freshwater mollusks thrived on the rich, organic muds of the backwaters. Enormous numbers of coots, ducks, geese, and other migratory waterfowl wintered in the delta, as they still do today.

The lush environment continued into the heart of the valley. Upstream of the delta, the Sacramento and San Joaquin Rivers flowed through dense stands of cottonwood, oak, ash, and other trees, a riparian forest of which only small patches now survive. Bear, deer, and rabbits abounded. Huge numbers of salmon and steelhead passed through the river in spring and fall. Bands of valley oak woodland, often as much as five miles wide, passed into the native grasslands and open savanna away from the river floodplain.

Except for intense summer heat, numerous mosquitoes, thick winter fogs, and sometimes bitter cold, much of the Delta and Central Valley was a friendly, diverse environment for foragers and fisherfolk.

Unfortunately, most traces of their passing have withered in the face of industrial agriculture, and, increasingly, suburbia. Most camps, cemeteries, and villages lay on the better drained, higher ground above flood level, close to groves of oak trees and convenient fishing grounds. Modern housing tracts now stand on many of the same places, their predecessors' settlements bulldozed out of the way. Today, we work with a fraction of the sites that remained even a quarter century ago. Nearly every surviving cemetery or village has a complex twentieth-century history involving bulldozers, looting, or deep plowing. Just as with the Bay Area, much of what we know about the past comes from museum collections rather than excavations, from piecing together clues from sporadic excavations over fifty years or more, and from incomplete field notes and long-neglected bags and boxes of artifacts, human remains, and animal bones.

There are important questions to be answered. When did people first settle along the rivers and in the Central Valley? How did the river, lake, and marsh societies of later times develop and when? What long-term developments led to the densely packed hunter-gatherer bands of recent times? Finally, can we trace the origins of the Wintu and Yokut peoples who lived in the region when the Spanish arrived?

To answer these questions, we must first describe some of the early archaeological endeavors in the valley.

"Little of Positive Value"

As we saw in chapter 11, the first archaeologists to work in the San Francisco Bay Area spent most of their time searching for, and investigating shell middens. We also saw that Alfred Kroeber and others first assumed that there were no signs of cultural change over the thousands of years of shell mound occupation around the bay. By the late 1920s, a whole series of large-scale excavations, especially along the Alameda shore, proved them wrong.

The pioneer excavators assumed that the Bay Area and the Sacramento region shared a common ancient culture, which had flourished for thousands of years in an environment of waterways and swamps teeming with fish and waterfowl. Shell midden archaeology became a specialty unto itself, driven by years of searching for burials and their associated artifacts, considered to be the only data that would provide a chronology for mounds occupied over long periods of time. The professional archaeologists at Berkeley paid little attention to sites beyond the confines of the bay, and especially in the delta, until the 1930s. The archaeology of the Sacramento and Stockton areas "seemed to promise so little of positive value that the resources of the Department of Anthropology at the University of California were diverted to rescue ethnographic information from the survivors of the last aboriginal generation of California Indian groups."[1] The Berkeley folk changed their minds during the early 1930s, when J. B. Lillard, president of Sacramento Junior College, a strong supporter of archaeology, excavated a mound named the Windmiller site about four miles southeast of the town of Elk Grove, on a natural elevation above the Cosumnes River valley floor.

Lillard dug Windmiller at a time when many researchers still assumed that California Indian societies had changed little over many thousands of years. He was no professional archaeologist, but he was a good enough observer to identify at least two stratified occupation levels in the mound—the first evidence of any cultural change in the Central Valley anywhere. In 1939, Lillard and his colleagues published their work in *An Introduction to the Archaeology of Central California.*[2] Their *Introduction* outlined a tripartite subdivision of the mound sites into Early, Middle, and Late Periods, based on artifacts, burials, and stratigraphic observations. As was the custom of the day, most of the actual excavation reports on this early work were little more than dreary catalogs of their findings. But they were sufficient to identify the three broad chronological periods, the earliest dating to around 2500 B.C. Fifteen years later, Richard Beardsley further refined the delta sequence and extended it to San Francisco Bay.

When news of the Windmiller discoveries reached Berkeley, Robert Heizer, then at the start of his illustrious career, arrived to take a look. With Lillard's assistance, he excavated there in 1937 and identified a third level between the two already known. Heizer later said that he learned much from Lillard and other local diggers, who by this time had developed considerable expertise with delta sites. The lowest, and earliest, levels of the Windmiller site contained grave pits dug into a reddish brown clay, overlain by two much later occupation levels, when people actually lived on the site, as well as burying their dead there. No less than 59 human burials came from Heizer's earliest level, out of a total of 168 recovered by the University of California excavators in 1937.[3]

Heizer and his colleague Sherbourne Cook, a pioneer in the study of the soil science of mound sites, estimated that the Windmiller Pattern dated to as early as 2500 B.C., a date confirmed by radiocarbon samples from more recent excavations.[4]

With these excavations, the Windmiller site became the first archaeological site in the Central Valley excavated by modern methods. When he examined the artifacts and burials from the site carefully, Heizer realized that the lower levels of the mound contained a relatively early occupation. At first, he thought it was unique, but similar artifacts soon turned up at other locations in the area, sufficient to identify a widespread ancient culture. Twelve years later, in 1949, Heizer named this the Windmiller horizon.

At first, the Windmiller horizon was a purely local culture, defined by occupation levels in the Sacramento Valley. But its characteristic artifacts and burials now turned up over a much wider area, along both the greater rivers. The Windmiller horizon eventually became the Windmiller Pattern. This may seem like intellectual semantics, but the notion of a "pattern" gave Windmiller a much wider significance—a life way common to people living within a broad, but well-defined geographical area. The people within the Windmiller Pattern used much the same technology, subsisted off much the same foods, and enjoyed common burial and ceremonial practices. They also shared the same trade networks and handled the same exotic goods and commodities. By the same token, they seem to have had the same attitudes to social ranking and wealth.

The Windmiller Pattern has become the baseline for studying later human occupation in the Central Valley and the Delta. But the Windmiller people were not the earliest occupants of the region, whom we must now briefly describe.

The First Settlers (11,000 B.C. to 2500 B.C.)

Throughout the San Joaquin Valley, large-scale agriculture, deep plowing, and drainage have wreaked havoc with archaeological sites, especially with the deep middens and mounds that stood on natural levees and higher ground in the better watered areas. As in the delta, we have but shreds and patches of archaeology to work with. But it is here that the first signs of human occupation survive.

The earliest traces of human occupation come from the southern valley. Clovis-like Paleo-Indian points have come from a 190-foot shoreline of Lake Tulare, where they are associated with extinct bison, horse, and ground sloth. The fluted points are unmistakably Paleo-Indian, and may date to as early as 11,000 B.C.

Projectile points similar to those from Western Pluvial Lakes Tradition of the Lake Mojave region, and much of the interior, also come from Lake Tulare's shores (see chapter 4). Indeed, ties exist in projectile point designs, between the Western Pluvial Lakes tradition in the south and the long-lived San Dieguito Complex, which flourished on the southern coast and interior from at least 10,000 B.C. (see chapter 13). Some hunting and butchering tools from a deep layer in a large site (Ker-116), on the southwestern shore of Buena Vista Lake, are radiocarbon dated to as early as 6250 B.C., and are also attributed to the Western Pluvial Lakes Tradition.[5]

Two other nearby middens contain milling stones and grinders of the later part of the Milling Stone Horizon date even earlier, from 5000 to 3000 B.C. They bear a strong resemblance to those of the Milling Stone (Oak Grove) Horizon of the Santa Barbara region some fifty miles to the southwest. The same artifacts that had been used over many millennia, appear in Windmiller sites in the delta, 250 miles to the north.

In the southern Sacramento Valley, archaeologists from California State University, Sacramento, recorded traces of human occupation dating to as early as 8000 B.C. in the area now occupied by the Camanche Reservoir on the Mokelumne River. Some later human remains date to about 4500 B.C. As in the south, all these shadowy early occupations predate the later cultural sequence that starts with the Windmiller Pattern.

Acorns

From Paleo-Indian times until about 2500 B.C., the human population of the Central Valley was tiny by later standards, just as it was along the coast and in the Bay Area. Plants and rabbits were familiar staples everywhere. Then the gradual major change that affected all of a now more densely populated California, rippled though the Central Valley. The change coincides with the beginning of the Windmiller Pattern and with intensive acorn harvesting at Skyrocket.

As we saw in chapter 6, the Skyrocket people took to acorn harvesting after 2500 B.C.[6] For nearly 1,500 years, they enjoyed abundant acorn harvests in the central Sierra Nevada foothills. Local populations grew. People lived longer; infant mortality became relatively low. But the Skyrocket camps were just that—places where people gathered for the acorn harvest. They were well away from the main population centers by the larger rivers. Nevertheless, life was good in this outlying settlement, a microcosm of dozens of anonymous encampments in the Sierra foothills that came to life during the weeks of the fall acorn harvest.

Then, in about 1000 B.C., Skyrocket's fortunes changed dramatically. Unfortunately, however, there are no clear-cut occupation levels like those that document earlier times, so excavators Roger La Jeunesse and John Pryor had to work with two mass burials and their distinctive artifacts to work out what happened at a time of crisis.

In one of the mass graves, an elderly man lay with hundreds of *olivella* beads and a large projectile point, while the other five skeletons were unadorned. The second mass grave contained five people. Apparently, those buried in these graves all died simultaneously, reason unknown. But, unlike the burials of a millennium earlier, the people suffered from much poorer health, with telltale signs of malnutrition, the lowest level of life expectancy throughout the site's long history, and much higher infant mortality. The Skyrocket people were suffering through sporadic food shortages, something unknown a few centuries earlier. They had exhausted easy-to-find foods and were using slab mortars instead of bowls, which required less time to manufacture. This may reflect the processing of hard, long-stored acorns, which are harder to process than newly harvested specimens.

All this happened at Skyrocket at a time when the climate was cool and moist, a point well documented by pollen samples in sites from the New Melones Dam area nearby. But populations everywhere in the valley and foothills were now higher. There were many more mouths to support. Acorn harvests could not feed everyone, so people fell back on the cushion of other edible plant foods. The Skyrocket middens yield seeds from many more plant species, as if the inhabitants were eating a broader range of vegetable foods, including hard seeds that were less efficient to process and gave a lower caloric return. Instead of using stone bowl mortars, the women now processed acorns in shallow cups ground into stone slabs, topped by baskets with holes in their bottom. Pryor and La Jeunesse believe these may have allowed the pounding of more acorn meal.

With bad times at Skyrocket, many people moved to large settlements along the major river drainages like the Stanislaus River Valley, where, apparently, food was more plentiful and larger settlements flourished. In the valleys, aggrandizers now controlled the trade routes that linked communities over many miles.

Just occasionally, we get a glimpse of what must have been a complicated, sometimes confusing period.[7] In a more crowded world, group identity became an important issue. In the Upper Sacramento River Canyon area of Shasha County, local hunter-gatherer groups of about 3050 to 1950 B.C. made use of incised stone amulets as identifying symbols. The local pebbles and stones bear simple patterns such as cross-hatching and infilled bands, motifs somewhat akin to those used by potters—but these people did not make clay vessels. This was a time when populations were growing in the canyon, where neighboring groups were competing for food and other resources.

Two well-defined occupations occur in the same area, one labeled the Pollard Flat, a rather generalized foraging culture and the other Vollmers, where people were more specific in their exploitation of different foods. The two cultures lived alongside one another for at least five hundred years. Then Vollmers persists and Pollard Flat disappears. The more than 1,500 incised stone amulets made only by the Pollard Flats people may reflect a situation where there was a need to establish group identity at a time of intensifying competition for territory and food. Significantly, the amulets disappear abruptly when Pollard Flats artifacts vanish, as if the need for identifying symbols evaporated when their owners either moved away or were assimilated into Vollmers society (see figure 12.2).

At about the time that acorns became a staple, newcomers arrived in the Central Valley—people already adapted to marshes, rivers, and waterways. They may have been Utian speakers, remote ancestors of the Miwok and Costanoan groups who lived around San Francisco Bay and as far east as the Sacramento area at European contact (see chapter 1: languages). This much we suspect, but we do not know where they came from or why they moved into the Central Valley. Perhaps the severe drought conditions of the Altithermal in the Great Basin and on the Columbia Plateau to the north

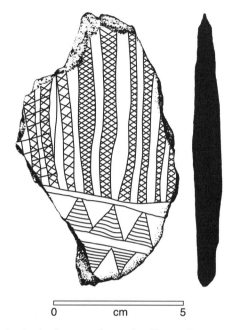

Figure 12.2. An incised stone from the Upper Sacramento River Canyon. Courtesy of Kelly McGuire, Far Western Anthropological Research Group, Inc.

and east caused wetlands to dry up and triggered a move to a region with more reliable water supplies, but this is pure speculation.

These newcomers are the Windmiller people.

The Windmiller Pattern (c. 2500 b.c. to 500 b.c. and Later)

Sometime before 2500 b.c., characteristic Windmiller artifacts and burial customs appear throughout much of the Central Valley and the delta.[8] By 1800 b.c., Windmiller artifacts and funerary rites were well established as far west as the San Francisco Bay shore, where they occur in the lower levels of the West Berkeley site. A rather generalized Windmiller culture and life way spread widely over the entire region, then developed locally, as the immigrants adapted to varying local circumstances.

This was the first time that delta and valley people made full use not only of acorns, but also of the rich and diverse fish, mollusks, and waterfowl of swamps and river valleys. For more than two thousand years, Windmiller groups exploited the full range of foods in the diverse valley environment during a period when populations rose considerably in favored locations. Base camps grew larger and more settled, many of them with their own cemeteries. Inevitably, territorial boundaries became more fixed, movement more constrained, in the areas of densest population. Away from the marshes and rivers, the harsh semiarid terrain supported much smaller hunting territories. Here small bands moved over considerable distances (see figure 12.3).

The Windmiller economy revolved around acorns, hunting, and serious fishing.

Acorn mush was a dietary staple, perhaps in the delta and other marshy areas, cooked with heated baked-clay balls, which substituted for the stones used elsewhere in more rocky environments. The large number of Windmiller projectile points testifies to the importance of deer, tule elk, pronghorns, rabbits, and waterfowl. For the first time, fishing assumed great importance in valley life, so much so that the Windmiller people developed a tridentlike fish spear, as well as using at least two forms of fish hooks and nets, weighted with small clay sinkers. Here, as elsewhere like the Bay Area and southern California coast, rising population densities forced people to exploit every food source available.

Figure 12.3. The Windmiller Mound. Photograph by Francis Fenenga (1948). Courtesy of Pheobe Hearst Museum of Anthropology and the Regents of the University of California.

But, for all these efforts, they sometimes went hungry. We know this from Windmiller cemeteries, where the dead lie in a distinctive, extended position, face down, arms lying along their sides, the head facing west. In four Windmiller sites, most bodies faced the setting sun, close to 233 degrees magnetic, which is the direction of sunset at the winter solstice. Most Windmiller people in the delta seem to have died during the winter, many children suffering from episodes of malnutrition, perhaps the result of relying more on acorns and game meat than on fish and waterfowl. Unfortunately, we lack the precise chronologies that would enable us to establish when the episodes of dietary stress occurred, but it is interesting to note that there are signs of malnutrition in Skyrocket burials dating to about 1000 B.C.

The incidence of malnutrition seems to decline as time passes, perhaps as a result of more acorn consumption, but plant foods generally were so abundant year-round that it is hard to imagine widespread starvation. Michael Moratto wonders if many Windmiller groups commuted between the Sierras in summer and the valley in winter, for Windmiller-like artifacts have come to light with skeletons in Sierra mortuary caves. There are other signs of social disruption, too, for burials tell us that people feuded, presumably over food supplies, territory, and killings. Painful, often fatal wounds are common on Windmiller skeletons, many of them healed fractures of the forearm inflicted with clubs, stone points embedded in bones, and depressed skull fractures.

More circumscribed territories meant many more contacts with neighboring groups and more distant communities. Windmiller technology and material culture was simple, but highly effective. In particular, the people excelled at making charmstones from exotic alabaster, marble, and other rocks. They made much use of fine baskets for cookery and harvesting nuts, and for many other purposes. Windmiller shell work was well developed, but much of their finer technology was based on materials acquired from afar. Their stoneworkers obtained obsidian and finished artifacts from two coast range quarries and from three sources on the eastern slopes of the Sierras. Abalone and *olivella* shells and ornaments reached them from the coast, while they traded regularly for asphaltum, quartz crystals and alabaster from the Sierras. Judging from other areas, this was an environment in which aggrandizers flourished and social ranking first developed in hitherto egalitarian societies (see figure 12.4).

By 500 B.C., change was afoot, at the same time that the complex landscape of large shell mounds described in chapter 11 developed in the Bay

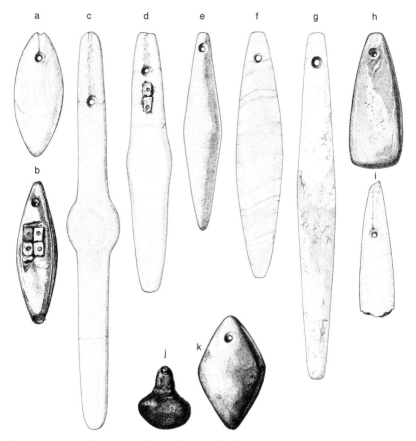

Figure 12.4. Charmstones from the Windmiller site. Courtesy of Michael Moratto.

Area. For reasons that elude us, Miwok-Costanoan groups from the bay region moved upstream, establishing new territories toward Clear Lake and eastward across the Central Valley to the Sierra foothills. Some of these groups settled around the Columnes and Mokelumne Rivers in the Sacramento region. For all these small-scale population movements, there were no dramatic changes in day-to-day ways of making a living, which were already about as effective as they would ever be. Nor were there any dramatic political convulsions, although some changes in burial customs may reflect changing social relationships. Instead of burying their dead in the ancient extended position, the newcomers interred them in a fetal pose, adorned with many fewer ornaments like shell beads than was the case in Windmiller cemeteries. Just as in the Bay Area, a small number of people were now cremated—perhaps people of higher social status.

Meanwhile, the Windmiller culture persisted, especially in the Stockton region and along the lower reaches of the San Joaquin River, in some places perhaps as late as A.D. 1000. We know this because of about 175 burials from two cemeteries at the French Camp Slough site (Sjo-91) near Stockton. One cemetery with 115 extended Windmiller bodies spanned a long period from the tenth century B.C. to the early second century A.D. The other cemetery contained 60 bodies without artifacts dating to the seventh century A.D. The French Camp Slough cemeteries were remarkably well preserved. In some cases, the actual mold of the body survived, but unfortunately the phenomenon was not observed until too late, as the excavation was conducted in unavoidable haste. The artifacts preserved with the bodies were in remarkably good condition. Some people lay wrapped in tule mats, others had once worn headdresses. One skeleton still wore fragments of fiber sandals.[9]

Writing this chapter presented a challenge, for only a few archaeological sites provide even partially complete information about their ancient inhabitants, about the ebb and flow of daily life, about people rather than just artifacts and food remains. Fortunately, the Brazil site, preserved by a conscientious farmer on the outskirts of Sacramento, paints a portrait of life on the edge of the delta two thousand years ago.

The Brazil Site, or the Case of an Enlightened Farmer (450 B.C. to A.D. 1350)

It is difficult to imagine what the Brazil site, known to archaeologists as CA–SAC–43, was once like.[10] A modern suburban neighborhood laps at the margins of a once-large village mound. The settlement of two thousand years ago lies on higher ground, at a point where the river makes a sharp bend. In ancient times, this area was close to the boundary between the flat delta landscape with its lakes and marshlands and nearby riparian woodlands, as well as the grassland beyond. If it were not for an enlightened farmer of eighty years ago, there would be nothing left.

Back in 1924, Manuel Brazil dug the foundations for his house into the dark soil of his newly purchased acreage by the Sacramento River, far from the boundaries of the then-small city. He turned up a human burial, then another, a total of seven people from a small area. At the time, he thought nothing of it, and set the bones aside, his mind on other things.

Fifteen years later, in 1939, Brazil decided to expand his residence. He was well aware that he lived atop a large ancient village, and perhaps a cemetery, and had heard stories of excavations into other such mounds. Knowing that the expanded foundations would turn up more burials, he asked archaeologists from Sacramento Junior College to make a study of the mound and cemetery on his property.

Brazil was years ahead of his time. Most landowners cared nothing about archaeology, let alone Indian villages. A young researcher named Franklin Fenenga brought a small field class to the farm. For over a month, Fenenga and his crew of students and volunteers labored on the foundation area. They recovered more than seventy burials, carefully recording the position of each body, its sex and age, the dimensions of the burial pit, and the artifacts that lay with the skeleton. Fenenga carefully boxed the artifacts and human remains, cleaned them and catalogued them, then put them in storage at the college. Eventually, they traveled to the University of California at Berkeley.

Nearly twenty years passed. Then the Brazil family dug a trench for a water pipe and found yet another grave. This time, they contacted the Lowie Museum at Berkeley, where the earlier collections lay. Archaeologists James Bennyhoff and Eugene Prince removed the skeleton and identified it as that of a woman buried in a bead-decorated cape.

By 1968, the Brazil house had burnt down and only the foundations remained. The area was still farmland, but suburban sprawl crept ever-closer to the mound. Manuel Brazil's son Francis asked archaeologists at the University of California, Davis, to excavate more of the site, as he was anxious to dispose of the acreage at a time of rapidly appreciating land values. This time, the archaeologists approached the site very differently. Their predecessors had excavated large trenches in a search for burials and grave furniture. Patty Johnson and Jack Nance spent six months of Saturdays sinking small, square pits of uniform size randomly across the mound in an attempt to document the daily life of the inhabitants and the kinds of activities that had taken place there. They excavated the site in four-inch levels and screened the soil through fine mesh.

Johnson and Nance discovered hearths and numerous artifacts. Students wrote papers and prepared notes, but nothing was published. The new Brazil collection sat neglected for twenty-five years, until 1992. Meanwhile, land values had risen rapidly, suburbia encroached still further, and a developer purchased the acreage around the mound for a subdivision. Fortunately, the developers were required by law to assess the impact of their house building on the mound and cemetery. They called in a private archaeological contractor to carry out limited excavations, to establish the size of the site and to assess ways of protecting the ancient settlement. Sterile earth fill now covers part of the site to shield it from further damage. Houses have risen all around the ancient village, but the Brazil mound remains as open space, adjacent to the levee of the Sacramento River, which is controlled by the Bureau of Land Management.

The study of the Brazil collections started from scratch. More than 9,500 artifacts alone, collected over many decades, comprised the now-incomplete original collections, which had been neglected, loaned out for study purposes, and even ravaged by thieves.

Fortunately, charcoal samples survived and allowed the dating of the site. The first Brazil inhabitants arrived in about 450 B.C. Their descendants continued to live on the growing mound for nearly two thousand years. In about A.D. 1350, the site was abandoned, for reasons that are still little understood. The abandonment coincides with a severe drought in the sur-rounding mountains, which may have caused water levels to fall dramati-cally. Alternatively, firewood and mollusks in the immediate vicinity ran short, so the inhabitants simply moved to one of the contemporary sites known to have flourished nearby. We do not know.

More than 19,000 bird, fish, and mammal bones came from the exca-vations. They tell us that the inhabitants drew on a wide range of animal and plant foods, notably exploiting the migrating fish and waterfowl that abounded in the nearby river and sloughs from fall through spring.

The twenty-one species of mammals included grassland species like the tule elk and jackrabbits, cottontail rabbits, and deer, which frequented river-side locations. Winter waterfowl such as coots and geese were common-place, as were the bones of salmon and sturgeon. Deer, elk, waterfowl, and migrating fish were most common from late fall to early spring, seasons when plant foods were least abundant. One would have expected the peo-ple to rely heavily on salmon runs, as their contemporaries did elsewhere, but the fish bones display a much greater dependence on local freshwater fish like chub and perch than one might expect, a convenient staple in lean seasons. Clams and native oysters formed a significant part of the diet, especially during the earlier phases of occupation, but whether this reflects drier conditions or a dietary shift is unknown.

Edible plants in the village included goosefoot, cucumbers, and mayberry, as well as acorns, all of which flourished in riparian woodland. Interestingly, some manzanita berries came from the site, a food now confined to the foothills and edges of the Central Valley. Either the environment was considerably drier, or people were traveling to high ground to harvest manzanitas and other edible plants.

This was a long-occupied settlement, where most food came from nearby, but there are signs that the people traveled further afield, perhaps to harvest plant foods on higher ground, and also to trade with neighbors near and far. The founders placed their camp on the boundaries of several ecological zones, which could be exploited either permanently or at different seasons of the year.

Exotic objects and commodities from some distance away abound, notably marine shells like *olivella* and abalone, and obsidian, the fine-grained volcanic rock favored for arrow and spear points. Thanks to sourcing research (see chapter 7), we know that the Brazil-site obsidian originated in two areas. Most Brazil obsidian came from the Napa Valley, where the obsidian has a higher zirconium level than that from another widely exploited source at Bodie Hills on the eastern flank of the Sierras, where strontium levels are higher. Bodie obsidian also comes from Brazil, but the dominant source was the Napa region. This is hardly surprising, for this area is easily accessible from the Sacramento River.

Here, as elsewhere in California, the basic toolkit was simple—stone-tipped arrows and spears, a variety of bone tools, including numerous pointed awls used for basket making. At Brazil, as everywhere in the valley, the women lavished great skill on finely made baskets.

The Brazil cemetery yielded numerous skeletons of children under five years old, but the average age of the dead was about forty-five. About half the Brazil burials were unadorned—a third of the men, two-thirds of the women, and all the children under five. Nine individuals, seven adults and two children, lay covered with red ocher. Bone fishhooks and harpoons came from the decorated male burials, while nearly as many women lay with spear or arrow points. *Olivella* and abalone shell beads came from some decorated burials. By the later stages of the occupation, some members of the community enjoyed a higher social status than the rest.

The convoluted history of the Brazil mound has a happy ending, while hundreds of other such sites have been bulldozed, flooded, or decimated by deep plowing. Most of the time, the archaeology of the Central Valley, like that of San Francisco Bay, is a giant salvage project, where researchers grapple with fragments of devastated sites, large and small, and with inadequately documented collections stored in museums for decades.

Brazil tells an eloquent story of people living in the heart of an exceptionally rich and varied environment for nearly two thousand years. Over more than eighteen centuries, the Brazil people survived successfully by exploiting fish and waterfowl, plant foods and game, from several environments. They lived close to other communities living in the same way, within a relatively crowded, circumscribed territory, where, apparently, there was enough food for quite tightly packed populations, so much so that they could live in the same settlement for most, if not all, the year. Here lay the great attraction of the Central Valley. Its lakes, marshes, and waterways were home to effectively sedentary groups, who also made use of outlying foods, like the acorns of the foothills. The Sacramento and San Joaquin Rivers and their tributaries were the hubs of valley life, the environments where tribelets flourished for many centuries in a closely interconnected world with tentacles that reached as far as the Bay Area and the eastern side of the Sierras.

Depletion

Let us not delude ourselves, however. Even before the rapid population increases of recent centuries, the Central Valley was never a paradise. Archaeology tells us that reality was much harsher, especially when population densities rose and closely packed villages took their toll on game, fish, and fowl. Archaeologist Jack Broughton examined the animal bones from nine sites along some 170 miles of the Sacramento Valley dating from about 2000 B.C. until recent times.[11] The people living in these settlements had access to animals from fresh water marshes, grassland, oak woodland, and forests growing along river banks. Fish like perch, suckers, and minnows teemed in the warmer waters of shallow oxbow lakes as well as in the cooler depths of the main river and its major tributaries. Ducks, geese, and pond turtles were also favorite prey.

Broughton found that the earliest sites contained the highest numbers of large and medium-sized terrestrial animals such as tule elk, which reflects a time when hunting was of considerable importance everywhere in California. The inhabitants of all Broughton's sites had ready access to migrating fish, when they moved upstream for spawning. Chinook salmon, steelhead trout, and white sturgeon could be taken at all seasons except during the summer, although the abundance varied from year to year. So plentiful were fish that all but one of his sites was occupied year-round. The one exception was a summer camp where suckers and other permanently resident fish abounded.

He also noticed that small river fish dominated the bones after A.D. 1000. The long-term trend toward smaller, resident fish was not the result of environmental shifts, or of dramatic technological innovation. It resulted from overfishing. Broughton observed the same trend in sites dating to the past five thousand years in the Pit River, a tributary of the Sacramento River in northeastern California. It was not just fish, either. Another archaeologist, James Chatters, has studied the age structures of pearl mussels (*Margaritifera margaritafera*) found in the Pitt River sites. At first, mussels were only a small part of the people's diet. During the closing centuries of pre-European times, the mussel harvest increased dramatically, followed by a sharp decline after European contact. Chatters believes the increases and declines in shellfish reflect sudden changes in local populations, ending with the decimation of the river people by European diseases. The rate of depletion varied from location to location, but there were clearly sporadic food shortages in later times as the inexorable rise of local populations put pressure on animals, fish, and plants.

The telltale signs of game depletion are not confined to the Central Valley. In archaeological sites high in the White Mountains of eastern California, Donald Grayson has observed dramatic changes in the numbers of mountain sheep through time relative to smaller animals, the direct result, he believes, of human exploitation.

To some degree, the sheer richness of the riverine environment gave the groups who lived off its bounty some protection from drought cycles, like the one that settled over much of western North America in the late first millennium A.D. The same was certainly not the case in more marginal environments like those of the Sierra foothills, where generations of drier conditions brought suffering, even to communities living along larger mountain rivers. Reliable water supplies were all-important and allowed some groups, like those who visited Skyrocket, to weather the dry cycle and short-term climatic shifts that seem to have been more volatile and unpredictable than in earlier times.

Skyrocket: Drought and Recovery
(A.D. 450 to Historic Times)

Between about A.D. 450 and 1250, intense drought again returned to Skyrocket. Much of this period coincides with what is called the Medieval Warm Period, or Climatic Anomaly, a time when very dry conditions settled over western North America.[12] Tree rings from locations like Lake Tahoe chronicle hot, dry conditions, while pollens from valley sites show a greater prevalence of drought-resistant plants. Many of the large settlements that had prospered along river drainages in earlier times were now abandoned. But people held on at Skyrocket, where artesian springs continued to seep along the banks of the creek. Excavator John Pryor believes the population had crashed during the overpopulation crisis of earlier times, but that life was better for the survivors, whose health appears to have improved dramatically. In fact, they may have done better than people living on the nearby Stanislaus and other rivers, where the trade routes seem to have collapsed, for imported obsidian now appears more frequently at the Skyrocket site.

The droughts ended by about A.D. 1250, when cooler and moister conditions returned, known from climatic evidence collected not at Skyrocket, but at other locations throughout California. The next five centuries saw newcomers settling in the Skyrocket area, thought by John Pryor to be ancestors of the Miwok who occupied the area at European contact. These were also times of population growth, when the local people processed acorns in bedrock mortars, of the type described in chapter 6. These were easier to manufacture than bowl mortars, were more productive, and also allowed groups of women to pound acorns together.

During these centuries, the way people used the Skyrocket location changed. In earlier times, they had buried their dead under the floors of their houses. Now the eastern part of the site became a cemetery, separating the living from the dead, a custom reflected in Miwok belief in historic times. Many more people were cremated, their ashes buried with numerous grave offerings, including shell beads. For the first time, status was inherited at birth, for infants as well as adults went to their deaths with distinctive ornaments. A whole segment of the population was set apart from the remainder, who lay in unadorned graves.

Skyrocket was now connected to a much wider world. A wide range of obsidian projectile points appear, of types found not only in the Central

Valley, but also in the Great Basin to the east. Not only finished heads, but the triangular, already notched, blanks for them, were traded into the site. For the first time, clam disc beads appear at Skyrocket, the common currency of the time. With well-timed opportunism, the inhabitants prospered off the salt trade.

Salt grass grew in abundance in the nearby Salt Spring Valley, easily converted into salt by boiling it. For thousands of years, the Skyrocket people had produced salt for their own use. But now extensive ash deposits cover the western portions of the site, suggesting large-scale salt grass boiling. The salt makers would collect the congealed globules of salt that dripped down during the cooking, a much-prized commodity in the valley.

People continued to live at Skyrocket until European contact. But no one was living in the valley when the first gold miners moved into the area in the 1840s. Exotic diseases may have swept across the region long before the inhabitants set eyes on a European. The survivors probably moved away into the valley or to more remote foothill locations.

Skyrocket offers an extraordinary chronicle of human occupation on the edge of the Central Valley, which spans virtually all of ancient California's history. The same profound sea changes that affected people throughout the state ebbed and flowed at Skyrocket, where the foothill environment with its limited carrying capacity reacted violently to the twists and turns of long- and short-term climatic change.

Yokuts and Wintu (Before A.D. 1400 to Historic Times)

Before A.D. 1400, Penutian-speaking newcomers expanded southward into the heart of the Central Valley, the ancestors of the Yokut and Wintu groups, who dwelt in the San Joaquin Valley at European contact (for languages, see box 1.1 in chapter 1).[13] The incursion may not have been peaceful: several cemeteries in the Lower Sacramento Valley contain skeletons with fatal wounds inflicted by stone-tipped arrows. By this time, the entire Central Valley shared in sophisticated exchange networks that carried shell beads and a bewildering array of foodstuffs and such items as ceremonial regalia from one community to the next. In the south, the Yokut maintained regular contacts with their Chumash neighbors on the Pacific coast, as well as with the eastern Sierra.

Once again, day-to-day life changed but little, for the same foods fed valley groups as they had done for many millennia. By this time, the bow and arrow were in common use everywhere, marked by dozens of small "Gunther Barbed" projectile points found the length and breadth of the valley. This was now a densely populated world, far more so than in earlier times. The first Spanish visitors described populous and well-stocked villages in the northern valley during the early nineteenth century, when as many as 31,400 people may have lived in the narrow strip of land along the main rivers and their tributaries. One authority has estimated a population density as high as ten people per square mile, a dramatic contrast to the three to four people per square mile on the nearby plains. And, of course, many environments in California could support even fewer.

An estimated 14,250 Wintu lived along the upper reaches of the Sacramento River and its tributaries, north into Shasta and Trinity counties, until a malaria epidemic introduced by Oregon trappers killed three quarters of the population in 1830–1833.

For those groups downstream, the Wintu subsisted off salmon runs in the McCloud and Sacramento Rivers. The spring salmon were too oily to dry, so the people baked them in pits lined with heated stones. They then ate some of the fish and pounded the rest into a salmon flour, which was mixed with dried roe and pine nuts. They traded this mixture downstream for salt and clamshell money. The much smaller sucker was also a common catch. Bear, deer, and rabbit hunting involved both groups and individuals. Women and children would help the hunters drive deer to the head of canyons, where the best marksmen waited for the prey. They would also drive them off cliffs and butcher them on the spot, leaving the evidence of hundreds of bones at the foot. Acorns were an important part of the diet, as they were among the foothill Yokut above the San Joaquin Valley. They were pounded into meal and sometimes made into a rich bread that stored well and was ideal for traveling (see figure 12.5).

At European contact in the eighteenth century, the Yokut to the south comprised some forty groups. Most people lived amid the sluggish water courses and sloughs of the San Joaquin River, which collected huge volumes of mountain runoff from at least six major tributaries to the east as it flowed northward. Each river supported vast tule marshes, which stretched as far as the eye could see. Beyond lay gently undulating plains, broader on the eastern side, relatively narrow and much more barren to the west, where the Coast Range provided a rain shadow.

Figure 12.5. A Nisenan village named Yupu near Yuba City, showing acorn granaries and dome-shaped, earth-covered houses. From *Gleason's Pictorial Drawing Room Companion* (Boston: Gleason, 1850–1855), 196.

The northern Yokut lived in the lower San Joaquin Valley, the northern limit of their homeland being midway between the Calaveras and Mokelumne Rivers. At least four archaeological sites near the confluence of the Sacramento and San Joaquin Valley document Yokut occupation dating back to at least A.D. 1500 and continuing into historic times, when European artifacts appear. The northern groups lived as far west as the crest of the Diablo coastal range, and across to the westernmost Sierra foothills.

Fifteen southern Yokut groups lived in the southern end of the San Joaquin Valley, from the lower Kings River to the Tehachapi Mountains, with most of the population clustered around three lakes—Tulare, Buena Vista, and Kern. Extensive tule swamps surrounded each of these lakes and the lower reaches of the Kings and other major rivers, expanding and contracting each year, depending on the extent of the winter and spring floods. These waterways provided animal and plant foods in an environment that was otherwise near-desert, with only five to ten inches of rain a year.

The rivers fed the lakes through a maze of small watercourses, over which the Yokut passed, paddling with reed canoes. Both the winter rains and the spring meltwater from the Sierra coursed into the lakes, providing two annual water surges. Except for a fringe of trees living by river channels and marshes, the entire southern Yokut homeland was treeless. Ten- to twelve-foot tule reeds and luxuriant swamp vegetation choked and covered the wetlands. Here the people could take waterfowl year-round, especially during the winter when migrants arrived by the tens of thousands. Fish, mollusks, and other aquatic foods abounded, as did tule elk and pronghorn nearby. As many as 15,700 southern Yokut clustered around these bountiful tracts of an otherwise arid land. Population densities fell rapidly away from the sloughs and water courses. In the foothills, Yokut groups lived from deer and quail hunting, off salmon runs, and, above all, on acorns.

The Yokut lived in a world of dramatic contrasts. Fish, shellfish, and pond turtles abounded in the marshes, rivers, and streams. Huge herds of tule elk and pronghorn foraged at the edge of the marshes and on the plains beyond. Plant foods of all kinds provided food and raw materials for everything from reed canoes to fine baskets. Away from the lush valley, the natural vegetation was much sparser—a grassland that came alive with wild flowers in the spring. The only trees grew along streams or in well watered valleys where oak groves could flourish. Hardly surprisingly, the greatest population densities were along the river, which formed the center of the Yokut universe. They suffered from periodic major floods, endured swarms of summer mosquitoes and intense heat, but there were sufficiently varied food supplies to feed a quite substantial population throughout the year (see figure 12.6).

And then Europeans arrived, their influence first felt through epidemics of infectious disease carried down ancient exchange routes. Over two centuries after Carrillo, the Spanish traveler Pedro Fages led a small band of soldiers through the Tejon Pass and into the southern San Joaquin Valley and Yokut territory in 1772. But the Spaniards had relatively little contact with the Yokut until the 1820s, when punitive expeditions against cattle raiders brought exotic diseases to the valley. A malaria epidemic in 1833 killed off about 75 percent of the native population of the southern San Joaquin Valley.

When the United States annexed California, a flood of gold miners and settlers overran the Yokut homelands. The people offered little resistance and their traditional culture rapidly broke down. Only a few vestiges of ancient Yokut culture survive today. What little we know about them comes from archaeology, early explorers' accounts, and the writings of missionaries and a few settlers.

The nineteenth-century traveler George Yount passed through the valley in 1833, and commented on the thousands of salmon crowding the rivers. No one was harvesting them, for the recent malaria epidemic from

Figure 12.6. A Sacramento Valley basket maker. From H. R. Schoolcraft's *Indian Tribes of the United States* (Philadelphia: Lippincott, 1858).

Oregon had killed off 75 percent of the valley population. He wrote lyrically of a now-vanished world teeming with deer, elk, and antelope:

> In herds of many hundreds, they might be met so tame that they would hardly move to open the way for the traveler to pass. . . . Wild geese and every species of waterfowl darkened the surface of every bay and firth, and upon the land in flocks of millions. . . . When disturbed, they arose to fly, the sound of their wings was like that of distant thunder.[14]

CHAPTER 13

The South and Southeast: Coast, Hinterland, and Desert

THE HUNTER CROUCHES IN THE REEDS AT WATER'S EDGE, downwind of the ducks as they feed in deeper water. They dip their heads below the surface and groom their feathers with their beaks. The hunter wears a headdress fashioned of grass and reeds into an uncanny replica of a waterfowl. The headdress pokes above the swaying reeds as he sniffs the wind and gauges his shot. The stone-tipped arrow is already notched to the bowstring, but pointed toward the ground. Oblivious to the soft mud around his ankles, the young man draws his bow with infinite care, aiming it through the curtain of reeds. The ducks look up suddenly. The hunter freezes in place, bow absolutely still. Reassured, the ducks settle down again, feet paddling gently against the afternoon wind. With practiced skill, the hunter aims his arrow at a fat mallard thirty yards offshore. There is a soft twang as the arrow impales the duck, killing it instantly. The other waterfowl take to flight, quacking in alarm. Quietly the hunter scans for other prey as the carcass floats ashore to his feet. . . .

The contrast strikes me every time I fly east from Los Angeles. You cross the hinterland behind the coast and the mountain ranges ringing the coastal. The country changes suddenly, from forest- and chaparral-covered mountains to an utterly arid landscape. Seemingly endless yellow desert stretches to the far horizon, shimmering in the midday heat, hills casting long shadows in the afternoon. Even today, the signs of human life are few—the straight lines of freeways, occasional small towns, patches of incongruously green irrigation, remote dirt roads leading to nowhere. This is a different world from that of towering redwoods, the better-watered, semiarid hinterland, or the fog-mantled southern California coast. In the desert, human life ebbed and flowed by the shores of pluvial lakes, along the occasional river, and close to rare freshwater springs.

California's southern hinterland and deserts tested human ingenuity to the limit, yet people flourished in these harsh environments for more than 13,000 years.

The Desert Pump

Deserts are living things. A few showers and spring flowers carpet the desolate landscape. A couple of years of decent rain and shallow pluvial lakes can appear in long-arid depressions. A year later, they vanish once again, victims of drought and natural evaporation. Rainfall was never predictable, never regular, but of critical import in arid environments where even two or three inches extra rain a year over a decade could trigger major change in local environments.

California's deserts were huge natural pumps. During wetter spells, they drew in people and animals to their lakes, streams, and marshlands. During drought cycles, the same pump expelled humans and their prey to the better watered periphery or to higher ground. These natural pumps drove human life in the deserts for thousands of years.

Fifteen thousand years ago, pluvial lakes abounded in the California deserts. But they soon fell prey to drier conditions and warmer temperatures, to the rain shadows, which now extended east of the coastal ranges. Today, a vast rain shadow extends eastward of the Sierra Nevada; the transverse and peninsula ranges to the south also stop moist Pacific air from moving into California's southern arid interior. The transverse ranges rise from the Pacific. Their peaks form the northern Channel Islands close offshore, meet the Sierra Nevada in the north, and end in the Mojave Desert to the southeast, a mere sixty miles from the Colorado River. The rain shadows of these mountains helped create the Great Basin desert to the north and east, the sprawling Mojave Desert in the center, and the harsh Colorado Desert to the south.

The hinterland with its sage brush and piñon-juniper and chaparral-clad traverse and peninsular ranges, provided more food for hunter-gatherers. Tracts of woodland grassland flourished in the transverse range foothills, producing abundant acorns and edible grasses. This rugged and much broken-up terrain formed slightly higher populations than the desert to the east.

The deserts comprise low, enclosed valleys, many of which once held large pluvial lakes. Low mountain ranges bisect the desert from north to south. Two major rivers, the Amargosa and Mojave, appear to be dry-water courses, except during rare periods of heavy mountain runoff. In fact, their waters flow under loose layers of gravel and sand, only emerging to the surface where the bedrock is shallow. Temporary, shallow lakes still form in arid desert playas after heavy rains, only to evaporate in the intense summer heat.

These are arid lands, with as little as two inches of rainfall a year in some places, with more precipitation at higher elevations. The Colorado Desert and low valleys are famous for their summer temperatures, which can range as high as 118 degrees Fahrenheit (the highest recorded, from Death Valley, is 134 degrees). Winters tend to be windier and often very cold at night. These are seemingly barren landscapes. Creosote scrub and saltbush extend over vast tracts of the desert, giving an illusion of desolation. Mesquite and other edible plants cluster near water courses and springs. At higher elevations, the creosote bush gives way to yuccas, agaves, and other important edible plants. Piñon pines and junipers grow on the higher mountain ranges, an important source of nut harvests for people living in the desert.

A seemingly desolate, uninhabitable landscape at first glance, but one that was a patchwork of animal and plant foods of many kinds, scattered and clumped over thousands of square miles. The California desert was an edible landscape of extremes, where variations in elevation and rainfall allowed plants to germinate and ripen in different weeks and months. Spring grasses could be harvested at lower altitudes in spring, then gathered in the mountains weeks, even months, later. Survival required an intimate knowledge of one's surroundings and constant movement from one food area to another as the seasons unfolded.

At European contact, the Gabrileño, Luiseño, Ipai, and Tipae flourished along the coast and in the hinterland. No less than twelve distinct Indian groups lived in the California deserts. They consisted of two broad linguistic divisions (for languages, see chapter 1). Between Mono Lake, the Owens Valley in the north and the Coachella Valley in the south, Shoshonean groups like the Paiute, Serrano, and Cahuilla all spoke Uto-Aztecan languages. Along the Colorado River and across the desert to the coast, the Mojave, Yuma, and other peoples spoke Yuman tongues, a branch of Hokan. Their ancestors had lived in the desert for centuries, often millennia, before them.

All hunter-gatherers, and farmers for that matter, who lived in arid landscapes, have deep-rooted traditions of movement and of aggregation and dispersal in response to constant fluctuations in rainfall, water supplies, and changing social conditions. The northern groups such as the Mono Lake and Owens Valley Paiute were more closely aligned both culturally and linguistically with the Great Basin (for tribal map, see figure 1.1). They lived like Great Basin groups—constantly on the move, foraging all kinds of foods and following the seasons of plant foods as they ripened. Only in the Owens Valley, with its diverse food resources close by, did people live in permanent villages or clusters of villages where they owned specific territories and cooperated in many activities.

To the south, the Cahuilla, Serrano, and other tribes ranged over territories that spanned both higher and lower elevations, their camps located in the best-watered locations. They lived in permanent locations, sometimes near deep wells in the desert. Come fall, foraging parties moved to higher ground to harvest corns or piñons. Throughout the southern deserts, food resources were so unevenly distributed that every group maintained trading relationships with their neighbors, and, indirectly and sporadically, as far afield as the coast. For example, the Cahuilla would trade mesquite from the low desert for acorns harvested at higher altitudes. Here, as elsewhere, survival depended on interconnectedness. In that sense, there was a continuum, between coast and hinterland, hinterland and the arid lands, even if direct contacts were rare.

Along the Colorado River, groups like the Mojave and Quechan lived in dwellings scattered along the river bank, where they lived in semisubterranean winter houses and relied on maize farming for at least half their diet. The remainder came from hunting and gathering, with bands ranging far into the desert when their crops failed. The Colorado peoples were fierce warriors, who traveled great distances to fight, visit, and trade with other groups.

Their constant movements and trading activities introduced new ideas and ritual beliefs to the desert lands in the centuries before European contact.

The roots of all these desert and hinterland peoples lay deep in the remote past, in arid environments where a close spiritual relationship with the environment sustained life and ensured survival (see figure 13.1).

Early Settlement
(?11,000 B.C. or Earlier to C. 2500 B.C.)

People have lived in the hinterland and deserts for at least 13,000 years, perhaps considerably longer. The earliest Paleo-Indian occupation clustered near pluvial lakes and streams, developing into the ill-defined Western Pluvial Lakes Tradition of Early Holocene times mentioned in chapter 4. These were diversified hunter-gatherer societies who relied heavily on plant foods, waterfowl, and small mammals—the basic life way that sustained desert peoples for thousands of years.[1]

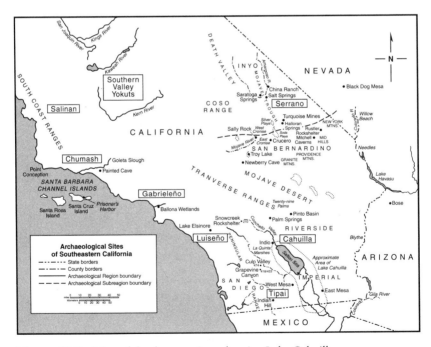

Figure 13.1. Map of the desert regions showing Lake Cahuilla.

After about 6500 B.C., the Altithermal with its drier and much warmer conditions, descended over the west. Rivers and lakes dried up, summers became much hotter, and rainfall plummeted. The vegetation changed profoundly, as creosote scrub covered the now-arid landscape. As pluvial lakes vanished, so the human population adjusted to a much harsher world, where water was at a premium and wetlands of any kind were virtually nonexistent. The desert population was tiny, reflecting the difficulties of surviving in now-extremely arid terrain. The people clustered around relatively reliable water sources, but spent much of the year on the move. By this time, coastal, hinterland, and desert bands probably followed the classic pattern of later times—they came together in larger groups during the lean winter months when they relied on stored foods, then spread out in small family units over the landscape for the rest of the year, following the seasons of plant foods. Occasionally, several groups would cooperate on a rabbit drive, herding large numbers of lagomorphs into waiting nets and clubbing them to death. Apart from the welcome meat supplies, such mass drives also exercised some control over these animals, which could literally strip the desert bare with their voracious feeding.

The details of toolkits might change slightly over the centuries, but ways of finding food in the hinterland and desert never changed (for projectile points, see box 13.1). The basic pattern of constant movement persisted. Everything depended on an encyclopedic knowledge of animals, plants, and the distribution of food across the landscape. Both the desert and hinterland were edible environments, but this edibility required not only a close knowledge of what was eatable and what was not, but also detailed information about enormous tracts of country and the foods that could be found in them. Every family gathered intelligence about animals and plants from their own observations, and from their contacts with others in a constant dialogue about food supplies and water. Every band also maintained an extremely close and intense spiritual relationship with animals, plants, and the forces that drove their natural world.

This simple, but highly effective life way survived into historic times. Unfortunately, only a handful of locations provide the all-important stratified sites, which enable us to trace the histories of desert and hinterland groups over long periods of time. All of them lie by lake shores. One of them, Lake Elsinore in the hinterland zone, chronicles over 8,500 years of survival in semi-arid terrain.

BOX 13.1 Desert Periods and Projectile Points

Changing projectile point forms chronicle cultural changes in the desert. Here is a simplified outline for reference purposes.

Pinto Period (Before 5000 to 2000 B.C.)

Coarsely made projectile points with hollow bases mark the Pinto Period, named after sites in the basin of that name in the Joshua Tree National Monument (see figure 13.2).

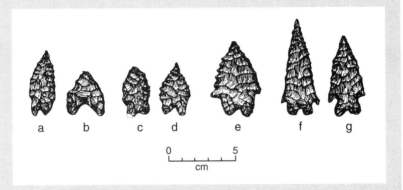

Figure 13.2. Pinto projectile points from Little Lake. Courtesy of Michael Moratto.

Pinto culture developed out of the earlier Mojave Tradition. Most known sites are extremely small, as one would expect of people constantly on the move at a time of increased aridity. About 4500 B.C., some Pinto groups moved into the southern Mojave when rainfall increased, but retreated again when drier conditions returned a thousand years later.

Gypsum Period (C. 2000 B.C. to A.D. 500)

The 1,500-year span of the Gypsum Period coincided with a brief wetter cycle, which allowed more groups to settle in the desert. This was also a time of great local cultural variation. Humboldt Concave Base, Elko eared or corner-notched points, or Gypsum Cave projectile points were in use (see figure 13.3).

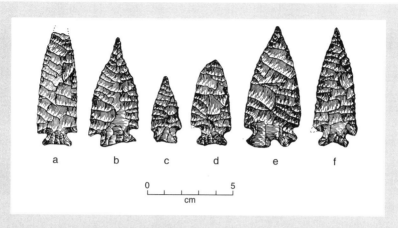

Figure 13.3. Elko projectile points from Newberry Cave. Courtesy of Michael Moratto.

Many Gypsum sites were permanent or seasonal base camps, with temporary encampments in hitherto underutilized areas such as canyons and arid uplands. Others, like Indian Hill Rock Shelter and the Oro Grande site in the southern desert, were occupied over long periods of time. The wetter conditions provided a wider variety of foods, including seeds processed with milling stones and mesquite, crushed with pestles and mortars. There are signs of sporadic trade with coastal groups (*olivella* sea shells).

Saratoga Springs Period (A.D. 500 to 1200)

The even tenor of life in the deserts ebbed and flowed with cycles of drought and higher rainfall over the next seven centuries, a time known to the archaeologists as the Saratoga Springs Period, after a site on the Amargosa River. Earlier Elko and Humboldt spear points give way to new forms, the Eastgate head and the smaller, arrow-mounted Rose Spring point. In general, the desert environment was much drier during these centuries, but the human population remained fairly high by arid land standards. Most groups camped close to springs or on low river terraces. For the first time, we can detect considerable cultural variation between groups living in different areas of the desert, much of it the result of contact with people living elsewhere (see figure 13.4).

(Continued)

BOX 13.1 Continued

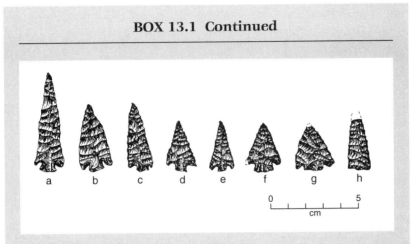

Figure 13.4. Rose Spring projectile points from Death Valley. Courtesy of Michael Moratto.

Paahashnan Tells the Story (c. 6500 B.C. to Historic Times)

Lake Elsinore, known to the local Luiseño as Paahashnan, is one of the few natural lakes remaining in southern California and lies at the eastern base of the Peninsula Range. For thousands of years, the lake provided a stable water supply, abundant fish, and water fowl and supported marshes and other shoreline environments. Oak and pine forests flourished nearby. The Elsinore site, located at the mouth of the outlet channel on the northeast side of the lake, provides a chronicle of more than eight thousand years of human settlement. In a rare break for archaeologists, these occupations are stratified one above the other over a depth of nearly ten feet.[2]

The first inhabitants arrived in about 6500 B.C., at a time of still wetter climate than in later centuries, when the lake level was stable. They occupied camps set back from the lakeshore on drier terrain, but processed rabbit and waterfowl kills at locations near the water. These people were constantly on the move, visiting the lake at specific times of the year to harvest wild grasses and to net and snare rabbits, rodents, and waterfowl. Lake Elsinore was merely one stop on a wide-ranging annual round that took the people as far west as the coast, for their artifacts resemble San Dieguito toolkits found by the Pacific rather than those of groups to the east, whose roots lay in the arid Great Basin.

By 5000 B.C., Lake Elsinore was lower, the environment more lagoon-like. Pluvial lakes throughout the desert were often dry, so locations like Elsinore with permanent water were much more in demand. At least four sites once flourished around the lake, spread around the margin of the lagoon area. Each camp lay on a terrace, where floods could not reach the dwellings. The people still subsisted mainly off rabbits and seeds, but stayed much longer, perhaps for months on end instead of a few days or weeks. They had now widened their diet to include acorns, processed with pestles and mortars, which may have relieved some of the pressure on grasses and other long-utilized food supplies. The coastal links of earlier times had evaporated, for shell beads are absent (see figure 13.5).

By 2000 B.C., at the end of the Altithermal, annual rainfall was much lower and droughts were frequent. The lake rose and fell, fluctuating with wet and dry cycles. A natural dam separated open water from a marsh fed

Figure 13.5. Excavations at the Elsinore site. Courtesy of Statistical Research, Inc.

by a hot spring, except during exceptional winter floods, which inundated the camp. The Lake Elsinore environment was still very valuable but much less stable, right into historic times—to the point that people stayed there only for shorter periods of time, perhaps drawn away to Lake Cahuilla, another fluctuating water source in the region. Once again, the visitors snared rabbits and foraged for seeds and other plant foods, often visiting in small numbers with a specific task in mind, such as netting waterfowl or gathering tule reeds. This occupation may be associated with the ancestors of historic Luiseño people, for the lake is mentioned in their origin myths.

The Elsinore site documents sporadic contacts between people living far inland and the hinterland. Another location, the Ballona Wetlands on the coast in the heart of modern-day West Los Angeles, shows how hinterland and coastal environments formed part of a single landscape.

The Ballona Wetlands

"It mixes the character of early Los Angeles architecture with modern residential concepts." Thus do the developers of Playa Vista describe their newly created urban paradise, built on the last large open space in Los Angeles, "interwoven in neighborhoods that are linked by parks, walking paths, open space, bike trails," and all the amenities of high-density urban living.[3] This huge development also lies in the heart of one of the most productive wetlands in southern California, which supported ancient hunter-gatherer groups for at least part of the year (see figure 13.6).

Archaeologists have worked at Ballona since the 1930s; some rescue work was done on sites destroyed by the building of Marina del Rey yacht harbor on the western side of the wetlands back in the 1960s and on the bluffs prior to home construction in the 1980s. Fortunately, the developers of the wetlands in Playa Vista have commissioned a long-term CRM program, which will continue for the entire duration of the complex building program. Archaeologists monitor every project within the wetlands in one of the largest archaeological projects ever undertaken in southern California. It will last at least another ten years. The developers have also preserved a wetlands area at the downstream end of Ballona Creek, where a lagoon once flourished.

Archaeologists Jeffrey Altschul, Richard Ciolek-Torrello, Donn Grenda, and their colleagues have sunk hundreds of borings in an attempt to recon-

Figure 13.6. General view of Ballona Wetlands in 1938. Courtesy of UCLA Photo Archives.

struct the history of the wetlands. The pollens, mollusks, microfossils, and other climatic data from the samples, combined with AMS radiocarbon dates, have given us a portrait of a rapidly changing environment. Rising sea levels formed the Ballona wetlands in the Early Holocene, forming a large bay that extended deep inland. By 5000 B.C., the sea level rise slowed. A spit gradually filled in across the mouth of the bay, closing off the inlet. A large lagoon had formed by 3000 B.C., which shrank gradually over the next five thousand years, becoming a freshwater wetland by about 2000 B.C. Throughout its history, Ballona was extraordinarily productive, a mixture of open lagoon, tidal flats, salt and freshwater marshes, and streams. All formed different habitats, concentrated within a very small compass, which made for an exceptionally rich environment for hunter-gatherers. Even as late as the 1870s, Ballona was famous for its fish, waterfowl, and sea mammals.

The Ballona wetlands have a human history extending back over seven thousand years. Archaeological sites abound, or abounded, both along its margins and on the Westchester bluffs that rise to the south of the once-marshy valley. Prehistorically, it was home to as many as two hundred native Californians in the centuries before European contact. The first inhabitants, Milling Stone people, arrived around 4500 B.C. Their sites lie in the upper Ballona Creek area, which was then an inland swamp. This occupation was during the height of the Altithermal, so the wetlands must have been an attractive oasis for people subsisting off plant foods in a semiarid landscape. Milling Stone people also visited the Westchester Bluffs.

The wetlands received only occasional visitors until about 1000 B.C. when people began to settle on the cliff tops and along Centinela Creek at the foot of the bluffs, as well as along the edge of the lagoon. The bluff-top sites contain Mojave Desert–style projectile points, as well as microlithic tools and casual artifacts probably used to process fish and mollusks. Interestingly, the blufftop sites yielded hundreds of shark and ray bones from prey carried up to the ridgetop, while the many contemporary sites by the lagoon yield deer and rabbits. Estuary fish are rare in both locations. Why this should be is a still a mystery. Perhaps it may be due to sudden changes in the courses of waterways, which, as a result, flooded marshes and sometimes even changed the courses of rivers (figure 13.7).

These were the centuries when the lagoon was mature. Many more sites document frequent temporary visits to the Ballona, with the sites on bluffs and by the lagoon representing many generations of visits to an area that was an obvious attraction to highly mobile hunter-gatherers exploiting large territories. The local population had not increased since Milling Stone times and was dispersed over a wide area. Nevertheless, there are some signs of more substantial, perhaps more permanent settlements, as if some people remained near the wetlands for most, if not all, the year. Or conceivably both a coastal and an inland group used the wetlands at different times of the year.

Altschul and his colleagues believe that the Ballona groups had stronger ties with the desert than with the coast, for both Gypsum and Pinto projectile points characteristic of the arid lands have come from Ballona sites of this period and the material culture generally recalls that of the desert rather than the coast. They think that these remarkable wetlands were part of a continuous ebb and flow to and from the hinterland, and perhaps even further

Figure 13.7. A house pit found at site LAN–2768 at the base of the bluffs at the east end of Playa Vista. Dates from nearby the midden lie between about 335 and 255 B.C. Courtesy of Statistical Research, Inc.

inland, to the coast and back—not just one movement, but many of them over many centuries. After A.D. 950, the bluffs were largely abandoned, and the remaining groups appear to have gathered along the edge of the now much smaller lagoon, which continued in use until European contact.

Ballona provides compelling evidence that one cannot separate the ancient California coast from the interior, for, from the very beginning of history, the two formed a continuum, with people moving from wetland and estuary deep into the dry coastal hinterland, and then returning year after year to the same favored locations along the Pacific.

Continuity and Change (Before 5000 B.C. to A.D. 1)

There are some striking continuities in the Lake Elsinore sequence over 8,500 years of sporadic occupation. Everyone who lived at, or visited the lake relied on small game, especially rabbits—as was the case at most inland southern California sites. Terrestrial foods were always the primary diet, but the lake provided waterfowl, turtles, and some fish and reptiles. The only major change was the addition of acorns after 4000 B.C., which made food supplies more reliable, if more expensive to process, year-round.

The food quest remained much the same from Paleo-Indian times until European contact, but there were striking changes in social dynamics. Before about 1500 B.C., nearly all desert and hinterland people lived in small bands, comprising perhaps no more than twenty-five people. Such a group is too small to sustain itself as a viable population, so interaction with neighbors is essential. Over areas like southern California, each band—and there were probably very few of them—must have been part of much larger social networks, which extended over very large distances indeed, sometimes linking coast, hinterland, and far interior. With such a small population, each band had its choices for base camps from one season to the next. For example, the winter would see some groups at the coast, where shellfish were abundant, while spring would find them by lakes in the interior, taking advantage of waterfowl migrations and rapidly growing wild plants.

With plenty of good locations to linger at for weeks at a time, bands tended to move when they felt a need to interact with others rather than to find more food—except on specific occasions when major rituals unfolded or people gathered for communal rabbit hunts and other activities. These were the times when major ceremonies took place, gifts were exchanged, and marriages arranged. After a few weeks, or when local food supplies were near exhaustion, each band would move out on its own and spend the rest of the year wandering in solitude, or with minimal contact with its neighbors. Anthropologist Julian Steward observed this ancient pattern of coming together and then dispersing among the Great Basin Shoshone.[4] Such forms of band organization are extremely flexible and fluid, with movements of families and individuals determined as much by hunting accidents, quarrels, and other social realities as by the availability of food and water.

This pattern of shorter-lived larger groups provided social mechanisms that made the change to living in larger groups of fellow kin much easier than it might otherwise have been. As the environment grew drier, so people became more tethered to food-rich locations, where they lived for much longer periods of time, just as they started to do at Lake Elsinore after 6500 B.C. The transition involved not only social changes resulting from more people living closer together, but also from a broadening of the diet to include acorns, a more reliable food source.

In 5000 B.C., southern California was a world of scattered oases, some at estuaries and lagoons along the coast and on the southern Channel Islands, some at permanent lakes like Lake Elsinore in the hinterland, and others around shrinking pluvial lakes in the remoter interior. As the climate became warmer and drier, a hitherto widely scattered population congregated in these oases and rose steadily. Theirs was a new social environment, but one with roots in earlier times when people came together for a few weeks at a certain season of the year. Now they lived in close juxtaposition for months on end, venturing out within well-defined territories to find specific foods like acorns. Many groups lived with small, very circumscribed territories, others, away from permanent water supplies in much larger homelands.

By 2000 B.C., territorial boundaries were, of necessity, more tightly defined, in part because each tribelet homeland was of uneven quality and areas like Lake Elsinore were in high demand. Under such circumstances, cooperation with neighbors rather than wars of conquest to acquire more land is a better long-term strategy. Cooperation leads to regular exchange of commodities unobtainable in one's own territory, also to sharing of information, and chance for assistance in lean times, when both sides know that this is a two-way street. The Newberry Cave site, famous for its shaman's regalia and described in chapter 9, was occupied during this period. Rock engravings show that the site was still occupied when bows and arrows replaced atlatls in the first millennium A.D.

The story of changing conditions is well told at the Lake Elsinore site, which provides far more than merely a sequence of hunter-gatherer societies exploiting a permanent lake in a valley landscape within reach of the coast. It paints a picture of profound economic and especially social changes that occurred together over many centuries, in response to a need to control access to valuable food resources and to greater aridity and less rainfall.

Ancestral Pueblo (Anasazi) in the Desert (?300 B.C. to A.D. 1050/1150)

We now know that these changes resulted from cultural influences from outside. In recent years, it's become apparent that the Ancestral Pueblo (Anasazi) people who settled in southern Nevada exercised a strong influence on the eastern Mojave. Why they were attracted to the eastern Mojave, we do not fully understand, but one of the reasons was turquoise, highly prized for ornaments by Indian groups throughout the Southwest.

The Black Dog Mesa site (which includes Black Dog Cave), some sixty miles northeast of Las Vegas, was home to a large Ancestral Pueblo community between A.D. 80 and 950.[5] The Black Dog deposits contain fragments of turquoise, which could only be found in the Lake Mead area or from the extensive outcrops at Halloran Springs south southeast of Death Valley. Unfortunately, no one has yet developed a technique for sourcing turquoise, as opposed to obsidian. According to archaeologist Diane Winslow, currently researching the Black Dog Mesa site, the fragments in the site most closely resemble the Halloran turquoise.

By A.D. 500, Ancestral Pueblo visitors from the east were exploiting the turquoise deposits at Halloran Springs. We know this because their "Basketmaker III" pottery comes from the springs in considerable abundance. Since the nearest pueblo lay 150 miles away across the desert, some miners must have lived near the outcrops on a permanent basis. The miners followed exposed turquoise veins as much as twelve feet into the ground, breaking and crushing the rock with stone axes and hammers weighing up to eight pounds apiece. They then threw the debris out of the open pit with a hand scoop made from a tortoise carapace or an animal shoulder blade. When a pit grew too deep or the vein petered out, they simply moved on to another location. Mojave turquoise passed far eastward into the heart of the Southwest for many centuries.

In many respects, the turquoise miners were irrelevant to the ancient desert life way, which continued much as it had for thousands of years. Certainly no turquoise passed to groups living on the Pacific coast. Only occasional innovations from outside led to more significant changes. In about A.D. 500, the bow and arrow appeared in the California desert, perhaps introduced from the Great Basin. The desert hunters adopted the new weapon without fuss and no major cultural changes, merely adding to their existing inventory of stone-tipped spears and throwing sticks. The wooden bows used in the desert were between three and five feet long, made from willow, mesquite, or palm fond stalks, and sometimes backed with animal sinew. Cane, sagebrush, and arrowweed arrows tipped with stone or wooden tips provided lethal weaponry.[6]

Bows and arrows have immediate advantages over spears, even those propelled with atlatls. As we have seen, hunting with spears with its high failure rate was an expensive way of acquiring food. The bow and arrow still required expert stalking, and a relatively close approach to the animal. But the velocity of the arrow, if shot accurately, could inflict a lethal wound on a deer when shot from as far as sixty feet away. Most hunters smeared their arrow points with vegetable poisons made from black widow spider venom, rattlesnakes, and rotten meat. The poison might not kill the animal, but it incapacitated or weakened wounded prey. If the hunter used a vegetable poison smeared on the arrow tip, he or she could then wound the beast and track it until it died from the toxic dose. Bows and arrows made hunting more efficient, especially when used in a rapid-fire way against a herd driven toward waiting hunters. The weapons also had another advantage: they could be used against waterfowl and other birds on the wing, or swimming some distance away in shallow water.

Few bows or arrows have survived the centuries, but they were used with highly characteristic projectile points. These Rose Spring points, named after a site to the west of the Coso range where they were first identified, and found mainly north of the Mojave River, had small corner notched bases, to aid in the mounting of the artifact to the arrow shaft (see figure 13.4). Some Rose Spring points are long and slender, others more triangular, but, whatever their design, they were highly effective against deer, mountain sheep, and other elusive game found at higher elevations.

By about A.D. 750, characteristic buff- and brown-colored pottery made by the Ancestral Pueblo Hakataya people of the Lower Colorado River appears in the southern Mojave. The same pottery occurs right across the Colorado Desert into the peninsular ranges far to the west. The Hakataya controlled much of the trade route in sea shells and other commodities between the southern California coast and the Colorado River for centuries—the celebrated Mojave Trail. Their influence extended as far as the Antelope Valley, whose inhabitants had traded with Pacific groups for many generations. Seashell beads and steatite objects from the coast are commonplace in Antelope Valley settlements of this period. Millions of seashell beads passed to Ancestral Pueblo and Hohokam communities in the Southwest. But no one knows what the trade brought west—perhaps salt, possibly maize and other foodstuffs—commodities that do not survive in archaeological sites. (Hohokam is the lowland desert tradition of ancient southwestern culture, centered in the Tucson region.)

The Hakataya maintained regular contacts with a remarkable desert group, whose life changed radically when a huge lake suddenly appeared in their midst. The story of Lake Cahuilla and its people epitomizes the extraordinary flexibility required of hunter-gatherers living in arid lands.

Cahuilla: The Life and Death of a Lake (A.D. 700 to 1400)

Nothing demonstrates the volatility of desert life better than the life and death of Lake Cahuilla.[7]

The great lake appeared suddenly in about A.D. 700. At its height, Lake Cahuilla extended from just northwest of the modern city of Indio, 115 miles southward, to some twenty miles south of the Mexican border. Three hundred and fifteen feet deep and up to thirty-five miles across, the great lake inundated the entire lower portions of the Coachella Valley. At times it was a single body of water, at others a string of smaller lakes. Seven centuries later, Cahuilla vanished without a trace until 1853, when a railroad geologist observed the ancient shoreline at the edge of the Salton Basin.

Lake Cahuilla formed because of the natural vagaries of Colorado River floods. The great river alternated between channels in its enormous delta, switching between them irregularly when spring floods swelled its waters. Sometimes everything flowed into the Salton Basin. At the other extreme, all the Colorado water ended up in the Gulf of California. Every spring flood season, the Colorado flooded large areas of the flat delta, carrying down tons of fine silt, more than any other major river in the world. As a result, the configuration of the delta changed constantly. Natural levees formed.

Sometime around A.D. 700, a prolonged natural shift of the Colorado River caused water to flow into the Salton Basin, which filled like a bathtub to a height of about forty-two feet. At that point, flood water overflowed across the delta near Cerro Prieto and into the Gulf of California. At its maximum, Lake Cahuilla covered 1,256,550 acres, one of the largest natural freshwater lakes in North America. The great lake survived for more than six centuries. When Cahuilla was at its high level, an estimated 16.3 million acre-feet of water entered the lake from the Colorado River each year. These estimates come from computations based on figures for Colorado River flow for the century 1866–1966, and on evaporation rates calculated from the modern-day Salton Sea. A further third of a million acre-feet accumulated from about ten inches of rain a year, a higher figure than today. Evaporation removed some seven and a half million acre-feet annually, with nine and a half million acre-feet overflowing into the Gulf of California. If these figures are correct, then less than half the volume of water that entered the lake vanished through evaporation. In addition, the amount of water lost by overflow into the Gulf of California was greater than that which vanished through evaporation. Under such circumstances, Lake Cahuilla remained relatively stable for centuries, fluctuating at the most two or three feet a year, despite major drought cycles and periods of higher rainfall.

As long as there was an overflow into the Gulf of California, the concentration of dissolved minerals in the lake water never reached the levels found in completely closed lake basins. Freshwater fish and shellfish could live in the lake. Productive marshes formed in shallow water. For this to happen, the lake level could not fluctuate more than a few feet. Otherwise, vegetation and shoreline marshes would die out, shellfish populations would be decimated, and both humans and waterfowl would find little of value in the lake. Substantial and regular overflow maintained the lake at a high, stable level.

The lake waters supported varied flora and fauna. A huge freshwater marsh once stretched from the La Quinta area north and west of modern-day Indio. Today, the undulating dunes along the former shoreline surround shallow basins that once held small ponds and freshwater marshes. Vast stands of cattail, tules, and other reeds passed into nearby mesquite-covered dunes, which still flourish in today's arid Coachella Valley. Similar environments could be found along the shores of Buena Vista and Tulare Lakes in the San Joaquin Valley. Elsewhere along the shore, the lake waters lapped on steep gravel and sand beaches, where marsh plants never flourished. In the south, the fine silt and gentle gradients of the river delta also supported extensive wetlands.

In its heyday, Lake Cahuilla was a paradise for those who lived along its shores. Freshwater clams abounded in water about two to three feet deep along the northeastern shores. The people who collected them left huge shell mounds close to water's edge. They could consume clams year-round, as there was none of the red tide that makes Pacific mollusks toxic in summer. Humpback suckers and bony tail chub, both natives of the Lower Colorado River, swarmed in deeper water. The lake became a major stopping point along the Pacific Flyway, just as the Salton Sea is today. Enormous numbers of migrating waterfowl rested here in spring and fall. Shore birds, ducks, and mudhens fed in the marshes at the northwestern end of the lake. Great blue herons, night herons, and cormorants lived on Bat Caves Buttes, a former island about four and a half miles from the northeastern shore. The ancient lakeshore dwellers used to paddle across to the island to raid nests for eggs and young birds, whose bones occur in shoreline campsites nearby.

Only a few hundred yards from the lake shore, the lush, marshy growth gave way to the creosote scrub of the virtually waterless desert, a desert so harsh that early white settlers traveled by night to avoid the heat. For more than six centuries, Lake Cahuilla served as an overflow for the Colorado River, and as a giant settling basin for thousands of tons of silt suspended in its waters. But, as the silt settled, so the entry channel from the river shallowed until it was blocked and the water once again flowed southward to the delta.

The blockage occurred sometime between A.D. 1300 and 1500. Cahuilla became a closed basin, its waters increasingly saline. Evaporation took an immediate toll. Marshes and swamps dried up. Shorelines retreated so rapidly that fisherfolk had to rebuild their traps at lower and lower levels each year. Within a half-century or so, the lake dried up completely and became a desolate playa. A few decades later, mesquite, screwbean, and other desert perennials appeared on the arid lake bed, planted by Coyote— or so Cahuilla legend proclaimed.

The sudden appearance of Lake Cahuilla had changed the lives of the local people beyond recognition. They moved from the arid northern basin to the upland plateau, where they looked down on an entirely new environment. Once the lake stabilized, marsh plants and aquatic vegetation filled in remarkably rapidly. The Cahuilla had lived in the middle of a harsh, but edible landscape for centuries, but now they had a veritable feast of different foods at their doorstep: cattails and tule, waterfowl, and many game animals that lived close to water's edge.

The Cahuilla were ultimately Great Basin people, who lacked the technology and timber to build any form of watercraft except the simplest of tule rafts. Nor were they expert fisherfolk. Much of the shoreline was shallow, unsuitable for nets, fish spears, and other weapons adapted from hunting on land. So the Cahuilla turned to fish traps instead, using the many bowling ball–sized granite stones that litter the desert floor.

Stone fish traps dating back nearly a thousand years dot the landscape around the former lake shores. They still lie intact in the arid landscape, most of them long rows of stones with a parallel shorter row in front forming a narrow canal that ends in a V. Each looks like a large check sign set at right angles to the once gently sloping shoreline. The two rows converge at a small opening, where the fish were funneled into the trap. This the Indians could block with a convenient boulder, a stick weir, or even their own hands. As the lake fell below its high point, the fishers built new traps along the receding shore, most of them between forty and eighty-five feet below sea level.

The archaeological record of the Cahuilla is as unspectacular as desert sites get: potsherds, some crude stone tools, and grinding stones for processing plant foods.[8] The granite stone circles, which once anchored their brush shelters, still lie intact on the desert sand. We still know little of life around the lake, but it seems certain that some groups lived permanently on the edges of the marshy area at the northern end of the lake, near Indio. There the people would have subsisted off fish, small mammals, and mollusks at every season of the year, taking seasonal plant foods and migratory waterfowl when they appeared.

A line of dunes extends almost ten miles from near La Quinta to well northwest of Indio. Dense mesquite thickets grew in this vicinity when the lake was full. Extensive marshlands flourished nearby. An almost continuous belt of archaeological sites lie smothered in the dunes—concentrations of potsherds, burned rocks, shell middens, and animal bones. Strong winds expose ancient land surfaces, then cover them again with sand, so it is difficult to count the number of sites. The associated Cottonwood and Desert Side-Notched projectile points date most of these sites to about A.D. 900.

The Myoma Dunes site near the Bermuda Dunes Airport yielded extensive shell mounds, also an important deposit of human coprolites, once part of a prehistoric latrine or refuse mound. Desiccated human coprolites are an exceptionally useful source of information on ancient diet. Only preserved in arid environments, they contain partly digested seeds, fish scales, small bone fragments, minute plant pollens, and evidence for parasites that once inflicted their owners. This chance find provided a snapshot of Cahuilla diet when the lake was at its high point.

The plant remains in the coprolites included hardstem bulrush (tule) seeds, which had been parched in a basketry or clay tray, by shaking and swirling them with red-hot charcoal, a widespread practice throughout North America. Softstem bulrush was not only parched and consumed, but is also known to have been used to fashion remarkably realistic canvasback duck decoys at Lovelock Cave in Nevada, where actual specimens survive. Both soft- and hardstem bulrushes could be tied together in large bundles to make tule rafts, such as must have been used to paddle across to Bat Caves Butte in search of bird's eggs and nestlings. Cattails were also abundant, the heads collected and shattered on a hard surface. Next, the women burnt off the plumes, which ignited in a moment, leaving the seeds slightly parched, a common processing method in the Great Basin. Cattails were a major late spring staple, followed by screwbean, an ancient staple in the desert, which abounded in the nearby marshes during the midsummer months.

The coprolites yielded traces of many other plant species, among them goosefoot and piñon nuts, which grew on the desert slopes of the Santa Rosa Mountains and other nearby higher ground. Fat-rich piñon harvests were never reliable, so they were a supplementary food.

The mammal bones included jack rabbits and mudhens, both taken with organized drives. Mudhens were trapped in nets while feeding in the shallows on bulrush seeds, their carcasses then dried for winter use. The people consumed humpback suckers and bonytail Colorado chub, taken close by.

Lake Cahuilla provided a fairly stable economic base for a reasonably large human population, who exploited the marshlands at the northwestern end of the lake. During piñon nut season, the people would exploit the adjacent uplands, but they lived at the lake year round. The combination of lakeside and uplands provided the Cahuilla with a subsistence base that was very similar to those enjoyed by people living in the southern Central Valley and at the effectively permanent Humboldt and Carson sinks of west-central Nevada. There, these kinds of life ways endured for more than five thousand years. They would have done so at Lake Cahuilla had its waters not evaporated suddenly, causing the people to move away. The lake dwellers adjusted rapidly to a completely arid environment, displaying the same kind of flexible behavior that was a mark of desert existence throughout ancient times.

After the Lake (A.D. 1400 to Historic Times)

The disappearance of Lake Cahuilla brought profound change to many lives. The Cahuilla now faced a very different world, similar to that faced by their remote ancestors before the lake came. They occupied some 2,400 square miles, hemmed in by the Colorado Desert to the southeast, which separated them from the Colorado River. Hills and mountains to the north and south kept them apart from the Serrano, Diegueño, and other groups. No major topographical barriers separated them from the coastal Gabrieleño to the west. Seashells and asphalt from the Pacific passed through Cahuilla hands. So did pottery and agricultural products from the Southwest. Perhaps their closest ties were with the Gabrieleño, whom they visited often, exchanging obsidian for tool making and salt for coastal commodities. (The Gabrieleño were fierce fighters and the most powerful of all the Shoshonean groups. Their easternmost villages adjoined Cahuilla territory at a carefully defined frontier.) The Cahuilla traded not only with the Gabrieleño, but with the Halcihidoma of the Colorado River, thereby creating loose-knit economic ties, which linked what is now the Los Angeles area with the Gila River Valley in Arizona.

The Cahuilla lived in areas where the climate was coolest, water most plentiful, and food close to hand.[9] Eighty percent of all food stuffs lay within two to five miles of their settlements. Cahuilla territory comprised ten or twelve areas, each claimed by a kin group, a sib. The villages within each sib clustered around springs or wells, and were occupied year-round, except when a community moved to a cooler location during the hot summer months. At some seasons, large numbers of people left camp for several days, even weeks, to collect acorns, mesquite, or piñons.

Most houses at lower elevations and in the desert were dome shaped, some as much as twenty feet across, the thatched roofs supported by upright, forked posts. Holes in the roof let out smoke from the hearth in the center of the house. In many cases, a cluster of domed houses stood close together, connected by wild breaks and brush shelters, which sheltered the inhabitants from the hot sun. The largest village structure was a dome-shaped ceremonial house, as much as fifty feet across, built in the center of the community. Here the lineage leader, the *net*, lived, protecting the *maiswat* (ceremonial bundle) and presiding over meetings, rituals, and other activities. The bundle lay in a sanctuary inside the house, where there was also a dance floor and seating area for the participants. Each village had its own sweathouse, used mostly by adult males, a place where opinions were aired and decisions made. Arrowweed or willow sapling granaries sealed with mud stood on wooden platforms or boulders close to the houses, each filled with acorns, mesquite, and other food stuffs, their lids held in place with rocks or stone slabs.

Thanks to anthropologist David Prescott Barrows, who studied Cahuilla foraging in the 1890s, we know a great deal about their use of desert plants.[10] Their practices were identical to those of people living throughout the arid lands, all of whom lived in areas of remarkable botanical diversity. The Cahuilla used several hundred plants for food, manufacture, or medicine. Acorns and two forms of mesquite were vital staples. Cahuilla groups harvested six varieties of oak, especially the black oak, coast live oak, and the canyon oak, which abounded at higher elevations. The annual yield varied dramatically from one location to the next, but the Cahuilla could harvest enormous quantities of acorns in a two- to three-week period each October and November. Large numbers of men, women, and children camped at the oaks, where they not only harvested the trees, but also processed large numbers of nuts on-site with pestles and mortars that were kept there. This reduced the weight of acorns to be carried home. While the women processed the acorns, the men stalked and hunted deer and other animals feeding on the rich oak mast. The acorn was a highly nutritious food source, if it didn't rain during the harvest, which caused mildew and the crop to rot. Oaks also provided excellent, slow-burning firewood.

Honey mesquite and screwbean (another mesquite) abounded in areas where their roots reached the water table below ground on alluvial fans and in canyons. Edible blossoms appeared in June, seed pods in July and August. An acre of mesquite trees could produce as much as a hundred bushels of beans in a good year when frosts or late rains did not affect the crop. Every summer, children would crawl among the branches to dislodge the pods, as the men plucked the blossoms and knocked ripened pods off higher limbs. Once again, the men spent much time hunting game feasting off the harvest. The honey mesquite had especially sweet and palatable blossoms and pods, which have high nutritional value—as much as 8 percent protein and 54 percent carbohydrate.

Piñons were a valuable if erratic food source found in pine-juniper habitats, usually at a considerable distance from home base. The cones were ripe in August, but had to be knocked from the trees before they dropped from them, as deer, squirrels, and other animals would eat them at once. Again, the harvesters worked with a smooth routine. The women and children gathered the cones, while the men hunted the animals preying on the harvest. Back in camp, the women baked the cones in stone-lined pits, which hastened ripening and burned off the pitch on the green cones. Once charred, the cones yielded their meat easily, which was stored in baskets until consumed. At that point, the women rolled the nuts gently on a metate, while cracking them with a mano. Piñons have a very high fat content, with about 3,170 calories per pound.

The Cahuilla collected many forms of edible cacti early each spring, the barrel cactus producing the most edible fruit. Barrels grew in large colonies on dry, rocky hillsides, each plant producing several pounds of edible buds over a period of weeks. Women and children used two sticks pressed together to extract buds and fruit and avoid the spines. They also diced, boiled, or dried the leaves, and turned the seeds into meal. Agaves were an important staple in the lower foothills, harvested each midwinter and spring, the heads and leaves baked in pits by the men, a process that took two or three days.

These were but a few of the many edible plants taken by the Cahuilla and their neighbors, who also exploited many other trees and grasses, among them the fan palm with its rich clusters of dates, and many vitamin-rich grasses and succulent greens near lakes and streams.

The Cahuilla and other desert groups were lucky to live in an environment where plant foods were rich in protein, a characteristic of vegetable foods that thrive in arid environments. Their simple technology of parching, grinding, and leaching combined with simple cooking methods such as boiling or roasting, produced a well-balanced, varied diet.

For all the abundance of plant foods, the sheer unpredictability of the environment left the Cahuilla and other desert tribes in a continual state of uncertainty. Rain could arrive too early, or not at all, or fall during harvests and ruin crops. Late frosts could decimate mesquite harvests, flash floods wash away lush plant stands, brush fires and winds destroy mesquite groves. Parasites like desert mistletoe could destroy mesquite trees, animals, birds, and insects ravage a harvest in hours. The Cahuilla never knew from season to season, or even from day to day, whether they would have enough plant foods to satisfy their basic needs. Theirs was a world of constant change, of tension caused by unexpected food shortages, even if there was enough food around in the long term. Their social organization reflected this uncertainty, like that of all desert groups.

Cahuilla social organization was based on at least seven sibs, each of which occupied a specific territory. Members of sibs cooperated in food gathering and hunting, and shared ritual activities. Each comprised several independent lineages, each with their own leader, ceremonial lodge, and sacred bundle. The people were also divided into two halves, or moieties, named Wildcats and Coyotes, membership being inherited through the father's line. Moieties served to regulate marriages and ritual obligations. Each had reciprocal obligations to the other, especially in ritual activities such as funerals and mourning ceremonies, with each being responsible for part of the ceremony. Each sib or lineage belonged to a moiety, which inhabited territory next to that of members of the other one. As a result, each moiety occupied several different ecological niches, but through marriage ties and reciprocal obligations of ritual life, the resources in all these niches were distributed through society as a whole.

The sibs were political and social units, with the *net*, the leader of the senior, or parent, lineage presiding over a council of lineage leaders. This council made communal decisions, brought people together in times of flood and other disasters, and organized communal hunts or the firing of vegetation to stimulate plant growth. Each sib had its own *maiswat*, a ceremonial bundle, consisting of feathers, shell beads used in ceremonial exchanges, a bone whistle, tobacco, and other ritual objects wrapped in reed matting. Supernatural power within the bundle communicated with the *net*. The *maiswat* symbolized Cahuilla life, connected the people with "the beginning and their creation; the time when all the good things of life came; when food was created; when their ceremonial and political structures were given to them as well as the territories they occupied; the songs they sang; and all the other things from the past."[11]

Cahuilla social organization was fine tuned to the realities of the desert environment. The distribution of sibs and lineages across the landscape ensured control over vital food producing areas from season to season, thereby minimizing conflict. By the same token, when drought brought food shortages, there was enough flexibility in the system for lineages to split off from one another to become separate economic groups. Thus, social groups could expand and contract according to the realities of survival, as well as allowing cooperative labor when needed. At the same time, the moiety served as a powerful agent of reciprocal obligation, which not only regulated marriage but created important alliances and mechanisms for exchanging food in lean times.

Ritual was central to Cahuilla life, whether a large communal ceremony or the strict taboos that regulated hunting. The *nukil* was the most elaborate Cahuilla ritual, a seven-day winter ceremony, which honored the souls of the dead, released them from the bonds of earth, and passed them into the land of the dead. Marriages were arranged, trading took place, disputes between individuals and lineages resolved. Ritual activity was most intense during the cold winters, when the people relied on stored food. The major ceremonies involved major rabbit and deer hunts, the meat being distributed to everyone present at a time of dietary stress. A constant flow of gifts and exchanges of food and other commodities both within individual communities and between lineages and moieties prevented conflict over food supplies and helped maintain a life way that had deep roots in the remote past.

Cahuilla society was flexible and governed by profoundly important rituals, based on a philosophy of life which assumed that human existence was unpredictable and subject to constant change. The Cahuilla valued reciprocity and cooperation, the sharing of food. They practiced moderation in the hunt, acting calmly, knowing that angry outbursts would cause disruption. Above all, they respected age and experience, for the knowledge and lore possessed by the elders was priceless to the survival of everyone, while providing a structure of authority in times of crisis and stress. Everything supported a highly flexible way of life, identical in most respects to that which had sustained humans in the desert for more than 13,000 years.

Memories of a Lake

In the fall of 1853, the Pacific Railroad Survey Expedition under Lieutenant R. S. Williamson traversed the San Gorgonio Pass and entered the arid Coachella Valley and the Salton Basin from the north. Williamson was surveying a railroad route to the Pacific. His geologist, W. P. Blake, described how the local Cahuilla people clustered in relatively large "rancherias," which they occupied for much of the year. They lived in a landscape where water was in short supply, camping near springs, where they sometimes impounded water in simple reservoirs, enough to grow two crops of maize and squash a year. In some places, the Cahuilla had dug deep wells, as much as twenty-five feet below the surface, complete with access steps cut into the walls. Agriculture was a sideline, learned from their Colorado Valley neighbors.

But Blake soon discovered that Cahuilla life had changed dramatically some centuries earlier. He camped near Cahuilla villages about ten miles south of the modern town of Indio. Earlier that same day, he had observed the ancient shoreline of what appeared to be a large freshwater lake at the edge of the Salton Basin. He asked the people if they had any knowledge of this ancient lake. The headman recited an ancient tradition of a great water that had once filled the basin and abounded in fish and waterfowl (see box 13.2). "Their fathers lived in the mountains and used to come down to the lake to fish and hunt. The water gradually receded [little by little], and their villages were moved down from the mountains, into the valley it had

BOX 13.2 The Salton Sea

Talk about history repeating itself—A quarter century later, in 1905, a hastily built, inadequate levee of stakes and brush on the western bank of the Colorado River downstream of Yuma broke during a high flood. A major channel of the river on the northern slope of the Colorado delta immediately eroded upstream. A cataract of water five hundred to a thousand feet wide moved upstream at a rate of about a half mile a day, carving out a channel as much as eighty feet deep. Millions of gallons of water poured into the Salton Sink, forming a lake up to eighty-five feet deep, which covered nearly five hundred square miles. The floodwaters inundated several Indian villages. Two years later, the flood ended when hundreds of frantically laboring workers dammed the levee once more, this time with thousands of tons of rubble. If the floodwaters had remained unchecked, and the deep channel cut had reached the head of the delta, a huge lake like Cahuilla would have formed rapidly, the rate of filling slowing as the surface area increased and water loss from evaporation accelerated.

The newly formed Salton Sea attracted thousands of waterfowl within a few months and is now a major congregation point along the Pacific flyway. The Salton Sink is a closed basin, which loses no water into the Gulf of California to the south. A thick section of marine and nonmarine sediments form a sill some forty feet above sea level, thereby blocking the lake waters from flowing southward. The lake is losing water from solar evaporation at a steady rate of about sixty-nine inches a year, the same process that shrank Lake Cahuilla, which once stood more than forty feet above its now-dry bed.

left."[12] Blake speculated that the lake was formed by Colorado River floods, then evaporated gradually, which would account for the local oral traditions. Another early investigator, Stephen Bowers, observed in 1888 that the Cahuilla would never harm coyotes, because the coyote had come down from the mountains and planted the mesquite bean in the old lake bed. Cahuilla ceremonial songs still commemorate water birds, which were once an important part of the lake dwellers' diet.

As we shall see in the next chapter, the same values of reciprocity and cooperation so marked among desert societies also underlay the sophisticated maritime cultures that flourished along the southern California coast. There, too, ritual played a central part in ensuring good order and continuity, and a proper world order.

Santa Barbara Channel: The World of the *Tomol*

THE MAINLAND COAST OF THE SANTA BARBARA CHANNEL, a calm fall day, A.D. 1400: The Pacific is absolutely still, mirror flat, the water blood red with the setting sun. Over twenty miles offshore, the peaks of Santa Cruz Island stand out, dark and razor sharp in the evening light. A smell of wood smoke, children's voices in the still, a dog barking—the village of grass houses is quiet in the lengthening shadows.

Two men stand on the low bluff overlooking the sandy beach by the village, where canoes lie above high water mark. They watch a small dot on the ocean, an approaching *tomol*. The shell inlay on the prow shimmers brightly in the setting sunlight. The wake from her passing ripples in a shallow V from her stern as the paddlers head for home. The canoe slows at the broad kelp bed in front of the village. The crew digs deep with their paddles, easing the heavily laden craft through the clinging seaweed. Men gather at water's edge, watching silently as the singing crew paddle hard in the shallows. The *tomol* grounds on the sand. The paddlers leap out, grasp the gunwales and drag the canoe clear of the breakers. Moments later, the crew and spectators heft the heavy planked craft on their shoulders and carry it to the side of the chief's house. Solemnly, the great man in his short bear skin cape inspects the baskets full of *olivella* bead strings and nods with satisfaction. . . .[1]

When Juan Rodriguez Cabrillo sailed into the Santa Barbara Channel in 1542, he entered a densely populated Chumash world. Some 15,000 people lived along the mainland coast and on the northern Channel Islands, many of them in permanent villages of several hundred souls. Sixteenth-century Chumash society was among the most elaborate of all hunter-gatherer societies in North America.

The Chumash impressed the Spaniards. The widely traveled Pedro Fages described them as being "of good disposition, affable, liberal." Another Spaniard, Longinos Martinez, visited a large Chumash community where "They arrange their houses in groups. The houses are well constructed, round like an oven, spacious and fairly comfortable; light enters from a hole in the roof."[2] A thick covering of grass or reeds covered a domelike sapling framework tied together at the top. Some of the houses were as large as fifty feet across and could hold as many as seventy people. Each village had semisubterranean sweat houses, covered with poles and earth, entered by a ladder through the roof (see figure 14.1).

The coastal Chumash lived in villages on high ground, where a stream ran into the Pacific, or close to the borders of a coastal slough. The cemetery lay separate from the living community, ceremonial areas, where painted boards or poles, as well as trophies such as bows and arrows, marked the graves. Sometimes whale bones lined a grave pit. The dead lay face down, the head toward the west, buried with stone bowls, charmstones, and other treasures.

Chumash artisans were famous for their *tomols,* the planked canoes mentioned briefly in chapter 5. They made fine steatite vessels and tubular smoking pipes from soapstone imported from Catalina Island. Their woodworking and basketry were of the highest order. The basket makers used both coiling and twining techniques to make fine water bottles, basinlike baskets for food preparation, olla-shaped baskets for storage, and shallow parching trays. They reserved the finest decoration and weaving for small baskets used to hold treasured artifacts and ornaments (see figures 14.2, 14.3, and 14.4).

Another Spaniard, Juan Crespi, observed in 1769 that "all the towns have three or four captains, one of which is head chief."[3] He wrote: "Among the men I saw a few with a little cape like a doublet reaching to the waist and made of bear skin." Crespi learned that these capes marked canoe owners and captains. Each village had at least one hereditary chief, inherited down

Figure 14.1. Artist's reconstruction of a Chumash village by A. E. Treganza, 1942. Courtesy of Pheobe Hearst Museum of Anthropology and the Regents of the University of California.

the male line, but subject to community approval. These *wots* could sometimes be women, and often had authority over more than one village. Public opinion limited chiefly powers, which involved serving as a war leader and presiding over rituals. They received gifts for their services.

For all its elaboration and extensive trading contacts, almost all traditional Chumash culture vanished within two centuries of European contact. A combination of exotic epidemic diseases and forced resettlement at Spanish missions wrought havoc with a society that had adapted successfully to a benign but unpredictable environment over thousands of years.

No one knows when the Chumash first settled in their maritime and inland homeland. In Cabrillo's time, they spoke a variety of dialects and lived in a great diversity of island, coastal, and interior surroundings. Unfortunately, their traditional culture had largely vanished by the time

0   5   10   15
cm (approximate only)

Figure 14.2. Chumash ground stone artifacts. The flat-rimmed mortars, which look like flower pots, are from Vandenberg Air Force Base. The pestles at bottom right are from sites Sba–126 and SNA–167 in the Santa Barbara region. Courtesy of Department of Anthropology, University of California, Santa Barbara.

anthropologists came along. Only Spanish accounts preserved eyewitness accounts of the Chumash at European contact. During the late nineteenth century, collectors and pot hunters ravaged the great shell mounds that were all that remained of their settlements. They ripped thousands of burials from ancient cemeteries, tore apart the fabric of long-abandoned villages, leaving but shreds and patches behind them. And, today, much of what remained has been bulldozed away. If it were not for Smithsonian anthropologist John Peabody Harrington (see box 14.1), we would know almost nothing of a sophisticated, vibrant hunter-gatherer society, which adapted brilliantly to a challenging and ever-changing world.

Figure 14.3. Chumash basketry. A coiled, all purpose *watik*, or bowl, probably made during the Mission period, used to carry acorn meal to be leached, and possibly also used in parching. Top diameter: 16.5 inches. Courtesy of Santa Barbara Museum of Natural History.

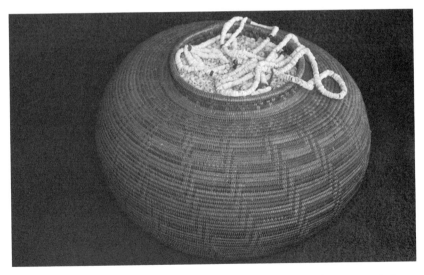

Figure 14.4. Chumash basketry. A necked trinket basket, with an unusual zigzag rattlesnake design. Height: seven inches. Courtesy of Santa Barbara Museum of Natural History.

BOX 14.1 John Peabody Harrington—
Chumash Anthropologist

Few scholars can be said to have saved an entire culture from historical oblivion. John Peabody Harrington can claim such a distinction. Harrington was the son of a Massachusetts attorney, who moved to California with his family when he was still a child. In 1902, Harrington entered Stanford University, where he majored in anthropology and classical languages. While taking a summer class at the University of California, Berkeley, he came under the influence of Alfred Kroeber, then working on his encyclopedic study of California Indians. Kroeber's lectures electrified Harrington. Almost immediately, he became obsessed with Indian languages and ethnography.

Instead of completing a doctorate, Harrington became a language teacher at Santa Ana High School in southern California. For three years, he devoted all his spare time to living with the Chumash and other southern California Indian groups. He would contact likely informants, live with them in their homes, and squeeze them dry of ethnographic information. Eventually, his work came to the attention of the Bureau of American Ethnology, the official body charged with gathering artifacts and information about Indians. In 1915, Harrington became a permanent field ethnologist for the bureau, a post he was to hold for nearly forty years.

Many government anthropologists traveled out west to work with the California Indians, but their research was always of short duration and confined for the most part to generalities. Harrington lived among people like the Chumash for years on end, acquiring data and yet more data. Tall, thin, with an abrupt way of walking and awkward gestures, John Harrington was the epitome of the dedicated scholar, who resented any form of distraction from his work. He was obsessed with detail, often working eighteen hours a day on an obscure dialect or minute ethnographic detail. For years, he dreamed of writing a grand synthesis of his work, but it was not to be. John Peabody Harrington literally drowned in data.

Harrington had a genius for Indian dialects. He is said to have spoken about forty Indian languages, developing his own orthography for recording near-extinct languages phonetically. His

(Continued)

BOX 14.1 Continued

unconventional methods preserved the phonetic accuracy of now-vanished languages, a priceless legacy for modern scholars. He would listen to "a single old man or old woman, worn out, discouraged, bewildered, clinging precariously to life," wrote Caroline Beard, his wife from 1916 to 1923. He made them repeat words again and again until he had them down correctly, as he knew they were last repositories of ancient Californian lore.

Like many obsessives, Harrington recorded everything, in his case on slips of paper cut to a convenient size. He used questionnaires, recovering information on ancient dance regalia and the process of preparing native tobacco. He experimented with spears and throwing sticks, ate Chumash food, and participated in religious ceremonies. Sparrowlike, he flitted from subject to subject. Meanwhile, the notes accumulated and accumulated. Periodically, he shipped boxes of data back to the bureau in Washington, DC, where they engulfed the archives. Absentmindedly, he also shipped old shirts, personal letters, even a bottle of prune juice at the same time.

Harrington lived alone, surrounded by dusty papers and overflowing file cabinets. He rarely talked to his bureau colleagues, refused to have a telephone, and never discussed his work, on the grounds that controversy and discussion were a waste of time. He died in lonely and reclusive poverty in 1961. No one had any idea of the extraordinary riches that lay in his yellowing papers. After his death, forgotten manuscripts and notes turned up mysteriously in warehouses all over the country. A dozen boxes turned up in the basement of a small western post office. They had lain there for more than twenty years.

In the late 1960s, some archaeologists came across some of Harrington's Chumash papers on loan to the Department of Linguistics at Berkeley. Anthropologists Thomas Blackburn, Travis Hudson, and others combed through over two hundred boxes of notes, more than 100,000 pages in all, over a period of five years. They found a remarkable treasure trove of information about the Chumash, acquired by Harrington from his informants. At times, it was as if modern scientists worked alongside Harrington, with phonetic Indian voices in the background. The obsessive John Peabody Harrington unwittingly achieved his life's ambition. Nearly all modern Chumash scholarship is based on his research. Our knowledge of the *tomol* canoe comes almost entirely from his notes.

Archaeologists love social complexity. They search for social ranking in cemeteries and shell mounds, in the form of exotic trade goods and more elaborate buildings and settlements. When Juan Cabrillo entered the Santa Barbara Channel in 1543, the Chumash enjoyed an elaborate culture. They dwelt in a world of complex rituals and intricate spiritual beliefs. Chumash bead and canoe builders were famous. Their shell beads traveled as far as the Great Basin and the Southwest. They lived under the rule of powerful, hereditary leaders who exercised taut control over economic, political, and religious life. This phenomenon alone was a clear indication of a considerable degree of social complexity.

But how did this sophistication arise? Why did the ancient Chumash develop elaborate exchange networks and trade beads by the thousands between the offshore islands and the mainland? How did they face the daunting challenge of matching growing populations with fluctuating food supplies? Generations of archaeologists have drawn on excavations and surveys, on minute studies of artifacts, and on the voluminous notes of John Harrington in a search for explanations. As so often happens, many of the answers come from fields as disparate as paleoclimatology and zoology.

Foundations of Maritime Culture (3,000 to 1,500 B.C.)

The word "Chumash" is an artificial formulation, devised by ethnographer-geologist John Powell of Grand Canyon fame in the late nineteenth century to classify an amorphous diversity of coastal, inland, and interior groups in the Santa Barbara region who shared some common culture and language. It is unlikely we will ever know when the ancestors of the Chumash first settled in their homelands. Almost certainly, however, the ancestry of these various groups goes back deep into the past, for millennia, not centuries. The people Powell called Chumash were Hokan speakers, one of the earlier ancient California languages. Most likely, also, the distinctive maritime culture of the Santa Barbara Channel developed thousands of years in the past—flexible, innovative, and fine-tuned to the realities of living in an extremely demanding and unpredictable environment.

As mentioned in chapter 1, population densities rose gradually throughout California, from first settlement to European contact, not continually, but in fits and starts, often triggering food shortages and imbalances between population and food supplies. Prolonged droughts and periodic food shortages as well as the low carrying capacity of many environments militated against steady growth.

Judging from the low density of archaeological sites, relatively few people lived in the Santa Barbara region until about 2000 B.C. Deep sea cores tell us that warmer conditions pertained along island and mainland coasts between about 5000 and 3500 B.C., during the height of the Altithermal. As we saw in chapter 2, warmer sea surface temperatures translate into reduced ocean upwelling and less productive fisheries. During these millennia, the local people subsisted off shellfish, seeds, and a wide variety of terrestrial foods, just as they had for thousands of years. They also took kelp fish and sea mammals, but with none of the intensity of later times.[4]

The first major change began in about 3000 B.C., just as ancient Egypt became a single state and maize agriculture became well established in southern Mexico. Here, as elsewhere, the changes involved basic subsistence. The pestle and mortar now appear in greater numbers, as acorns assumed greater importance in coastal diet, so did other plants such as islay fruit as well as bulrushes and tubers from coastal marshlands. At the same time, projectile point counts increase, as if people living in more permanent settlements were fabricating hunting weapons at home then venturing out on hunting trips. As we have seen, exactly the same renewed emphasis on pursuing larger game took hold elsewhere in California at about the same time.

What drove these changes? We can only guess, but I suspect that here, also, population growth was a villain. I have no really solid grounds for this sweeping statement, except for clear signs that the densest concentration of more permanent settlements lay where the greatest variety of foods were to be found.

We know this because of finds by the shores of the Goleta Slough, now occupied by the Santa Barbara Airport. Even during drier and warmer times like the Altithermal, places like this area abounded in mollusks and plant foods. At the time, the slough was an open bay, only closed by catastrophic flooding in the 1860s. A sheltered canoe landing, acres of marshlands, large mollusk beds—the Goleta Slough was a magnet for human settlement, as were other such locations, like that near modern-day Carpinteria. The first human settlers camped along its shores around 5300 B.C. Within two thousand years, more people lived at the slough than anywhere else along the mainland coast. One base camp, known today as SBA-53, was a major village between 3000 and 2500 B.C., near locations where mollusks and plant foods abounded. The village's territory extended along the neighboring shoreline, where off-lying camps also flourished.

The Goleta Slough continued to support denser than average populations for the next 4,500 years. At least three large Chumash villages flourished along the shores of this bay at European contact. In contrast, the population of the offshore islands was still very small, environments where acorns and seeds were less abundant, and shellfish such as the red abalone were the primary food source.

Until about 1500 B.C., the climate was warmer and drought prone, with relatively low marine productivity. A decrease in food productivity provided incentives for more intensive exploitation of familiar foods such as acorns. Both in the Santa Barbara Channel area and farther south, fishing and sea mammal hunting assumed much greater importance in a world where food shortages were a constant reality. The Pacific was becoming a major factor in daily life, even if fishing and hunting technology had changed little over thousands of years. By this time, people had been living on or visiting the Channel Islands for thousands of years, so offshore voyaging was a reality, although not of the intensity we witness in later centuries. The foundations of the sophisticated maritime culture of later times were in place.

The Climatic Equation (1,500 B.C. to Present)

"Will there be an El Niño this year?" I get asked this question at least twice a month in coffee shops and more frequently when the rainy season begins. At least I can turn to long-term weather forecasts and computer models as a way of giving a moderately intelligent answer. The endless seesaws of sea surface temperatures in the tropical Pacific bring both rainfall and drought to California in unpredictable abundance. Experts disagree as to how long El Niños have affected global climate. If lake sediments in Ecuador are any guide, they have been a factor in California climate for at least five thousand years.

El Niños are short-term events. They bring unusually heavy rains as part of a complicated pattern of brief and much more lasting, unpredictable fluctuations in rainfall and sea surface temperatures, which have governed life in the Santa Barbara region for thousands of years. Make no mistake. The effects of these climatic seesaws can be devastating not only on subsistence farmers, but on human societies living off fisheries and acorn harvests, in restricted territories where neighbors press on each other's boundaries, and on crowded village populations. We can pose a fundamental and legitimate question: was climate a major player in the dramatic changes in human life in the Santa Barbara region after 1500 B.C.?

Climate change is a sexy explanation for changes in human society, but it would be naive to think that a single event like, say, a series of strong El Niños "caused" major changes in local societies. We do not even know just how severe the impact of such a climatic spike, or a ten-year drought cycle, would be on a maritime culture living on the bountiful Pacific coast. As I have stressed repeatedly, hunter-gatherer societies living throughout California had all kinds of strategies for coping with drought or flood. Mobility was one such coping mechanism, falling back on less desirable foods another. Living near permanent water resources was a sound strategy in dry years, so was relying on different forms of oak trees. The maritime societies along the southern California coast were just as adaptable. For example, El Niños might bring warmer water and suppress natural upwelling, decimating anchovy populations. But the warmer Pacific brought tropical fish far north of their normal range, and the local population duly ate them. Like other ancient groups, the people of the mainland regularly burnt off dry grass to enhance new growth and improve hunting. In a real sense, they "managed" their environment, knowing that each year was different, that flexibility and conservative behavior were all-important. On these grounds, it's questionable just how much impact short-term climatic change had on local populations, even if the long-term trends are easier to observe.

For years, most archaeology in the channel region focused on individual sites, on excavations. In recent years, especially with the advent of CRM projects, the emphasis has changed toward studies of changing patterns of settlement over many centuries. Until such distributions are available both for the mainland and the offshore islands, it will be hard to assess whether, for example, people responded to long drought cycles by retreating onto coastal marshes and estuaries, or whether the dry conditions made no difference at all.

Such data are a long way off in the future.

While archaeological research lags, the study of ancient climate has made gigantic strides in recent years, especially the study of tree rings and deep-sea cores. By good fortune, the Santa Barbara Channel has yielded one of the most precise records of short-term climatic change over the past three thousand years than from anywhere in North America. The data come from a 650-foot deep sea core in the Santa Barbara Basin. Fifty-six feet of finely laminated sediments represent the Holocene, with about 5 feet of foraminifera-rich sediment accumulating every thousand years. With such a rapid sedimentation rate and a highly sensitive environmental setting, Douglas and James Kennett were able to use both marine foraminifera and AMS radiocarbon dates (described in chapter 5) to acquire a high-resolution portrait of maritime climate change in the region at twenty-five-year intervals over the past three thousand years.[5] Few ancient climatic records achieve this remarkable precision.

The Kennetts looked at both the long- and short-term record. They found that sea-surface temperatures oscillated from warm to cold and back on a millennial time scale. Cooling episodes of varying length occurred about every 1,500 years. Despite these long-term fluctuations, climatic conditions were more stable from the end of the Ice Age up to about 2000 B.C. Average sea-surface temperatures varied up to three degrees Centigrade. But after 2000 B.C., the climate became much more unstable. Sea-surface temperatures now varied by as much as five degrees Centigrade. From the human standpoint, life became more complicated, especially when the productivity of coastal fisheries could vary dramatically from one year to the next.

The Kennetts used oxygen isotope differences between minute surface-dwelling and deeper water foraminifera to measure the intensity of upwelling of nutrient-rich colder water to the surface, which dramatically increased the productivity of local fisheries. AMS radiocarbon dates on the same organisms provided a chronology for the core. They combined the core data with tree-ring records from various locations in southern California over the past 1,500 years. The end result: a remarkably accurate portrait of climate in the Santa Barbara Channel region after 1,000 B.C., over the very period when local societies changed rapidly.

The Kennetts observed major fluctuations in sea surface temperatures and marine productivity. For example, between 1050 B.C. and A.D. 450, water temperatures were relatively warm and stable. Warmer surface water means less natural upwelling and poorer fishing.

From A.D. 450 to 1300, sea temperatures dropped sharply, to between 48 to 56 degrees Fahrenheit, about 1.5 degrees Centigrade cooler than the Holocene sea surface temperature median. For three and a half centuries, from A.D. 950 to 1300, marine upwelling was especially intense, and in consequence the fisheries were very productive. After 1300, water temperatures stabilized and became warmer. By 1550, upwelling had subsided and once again marine productivity was lower.

Interestingly, the cool sea surface temperatures and increased upwelling coincide in general terms with regional droughts of less than seventeen inches a year, as is known from tree rings, from A.D. 500 to 800, 980 to 1250, and 1650 to 1750. The rings tell us that the cold interval between A.D. 450 and 1300 was a time of frequent climatic shifts, especially during the two centuries after A.D. 450 and again between 950 and 1500, both periods of persistent drought.

The Medieval Climatic Anomaly

The Santa Barbara Channel core documents several centuries of good maritime productivity in the late first millennium A.D. In sharp contrast, tree rings from the transverse ranges of central Santa Barbara County and from San Gorgonio Mountain, some 125 miles east of Santa Barbara, show a drought cycle from A.D. 650 to 800, and another one from A.D. 1120 to 1150. There are also tree-ring records of prolonged droughts in the southern Sierra Nevada between A.D. 100 and 1450. Ominously, the same record shows that the high rainfall levels of the mid-twentieth century occurred only three times in this thousand-year tree-ring record. We would be wise to pay heed to the message of history!

These droughts, now recorded at increasing numbers of locations, appear to coincide with a period known to scientists as the Medieval Climatic Anomaly (or Medieval Warm Period), which lasted from about A.D. 800 to 1350. In the North American west, this was a period of fluctuating, and decreasing rainfall. One tree-ring sequence in the Sierra records two "epic droughts," one between A.D. 892 and 1112 and another between A.D. 1209 and 1350, periods of more than 220 years and 140 years respectively.[6]

So we come to the question of questions. Can we link the climatic fluctuations, increased marine productivity, but sometimes savage terrestrial droughts with changes in the human societies on the islands and mainland? The answer, for all the inadequate archaeological data, is probably a qualified yes.

Societies in Trouble (A.D. 1 to 1150)

For years, scientists assumed that the Chumash and their ancestors lived in a veritable Garden of Eden, with a bountiful Pacific and unlimited harvests of acorns at their door steps. Early travelers inadvertently bolstered this stereotype with accounts of well-fed villagers and canoes filled with fish. Spaniard Pedro Fages wrote: "It may be said for them that the entire day is one continuous meal."[8] He should have written that "It may be said for them that they are in constant expectation of hunger." In reality, the climatic evidence tells us that the Santa Barbara Channel was no paradise over the past three thousand years.

Two thousand years ago, coastal societies were in trouble. For many centuries, warmer sea surface temperatures had reduced natural upwelling offshore. Fisheries were less productive than in earlier times. But populations on the islands and the mainland were rising. Inevitably, territorial boundaries shrank and were cast in much more rigid terms. The situation must have been worse on the islands, which lacked the oak groves and dense stands of edible plants of the mainland. The people living there relied heavily on inshore fisheries, and, judging from later times, sporadic canoe loads of crushed acorns from across the channel. But even in cycles of good years with abundant rainfall and good catches, many communities must have lived from year to year, on the edge.

What, then, happened? Here's a possible scenario. If the deep-sea core evidence is correct, sea temperatures cooled and upwelling intensified after A.D. 450. The fisheries improved. But there were now many more mouths to feed, perhaps to the point where some areas were overfished. To compound the problem, the next eight centuries were ones of very unpredictable climatic shifts and sustained, often severe, drought cycles. The effects on fisheries and coastal communities would have been relatively minor, even when periodic El Niños brought violent storms and floods, shut down upwelling, and uprooted inshore kelp beds. So coastal communities may have survived reasonably comfortably. There is certainly no archaeological evidence for a collapse of the maritime economy, which may have even peaked during these centuries.

The real trouble came in the interior, where persistent droughts played havoc with groups that relied on nut harvests and plants of all kinds, also deer and other game. Even without a growing population, inland groups everywhere always faced the constant specter of drought-induced food shortages. Now there were many more people, more fixed territorial boundaries, and inevitable competition for oak groves. Chief vied with chief for control of territory and food resources. They fought one another for food. With increased crowding and hunger came malnutrition and disease. They also competed for permanent water supplies, for, as always in ancient California, the security of perennial lakes, rivers, and springs was the measure of human life. And during the Medieval Climatic Anomaly the landscape dried up dramatically. Permanent water supplies shrank drastically.

For thousands of years, the communities of the coast and interior formed a cultural continuum, the people inland linked inextricably to the fortunes of those on the Pacific. Close reciprocal ties and social obligations knotted even widely separated communities together in ancient webs of interdependence. So food shortages and intergroup competition inland, or in the coastal hinterland, affected not just the people of the interior, but those on the coast and on the islands as well. And water shortages had an impact on everyone. In later centuries, Channel Islands communities relied on mainland villages for acorns and other plant foods in short supply offshore. No question, some plant foods crossed the channel in earlier times as well, linking even remote island camps to the general crisis.

If this theoretical scenario is correct—and it's fair to say that there is still almost no archaeological evidence to support it—then longer-term climatic events may have played a significant role in shaping coastal societies. Fortunately, some fascinating biological anthropology bears testimony to these troubled, but little known, times.

Smoking Guns from Cemeteries (A.D. 300 to 1150)

How, then, can we identify signs of stress in the societies of the day. Jeanne Arnold reports that many late first millennium sites on Santa Cruz Island were abandoned during these centuries.[9] These abandonments may be attributable to chronic water shortages on islands that never have boasted of abundant water. Then there is the evidence from the dead.

Some years ago, bioarchaeologist Patricia Lambert was particularly interested in what happened to the health of Santa Barbara Channel groups during the unpredictable climatic conditions between A.D. 300 to 1150. She studied several hundred human skeletons from eight archaeological sites on Santa Cruz and Santa Rosa Islands, from 5000 B.C. up to European contact in the sixteenth century A.D. Several "smoking guns" pointed to serious social and political problems during the mid to late first millennium A.D.[10]

Lambert searched collar and limb bones for periosteal lesions, bony plaques that form on the outside of these bones when they are exposed to infection or injury. Some bones displayed healed lesions, others active ones, still others chronic lesions. Then she studied both the severity of the lesions and the degree to which they had healed, plotting lesion frequencies against time. The frequency of them increased through time, especially during the climatically unstable centuries between 1500 B.C. to A.D. 1100, then declined somewhat in the centuries before European contact. Furthermore, the occasional small lesions from earlier times, perhaps from accidents, gave way to larger and more numerous ones during the centuries of instability. Many more of them were active or healing at the time of death, which strongly suggested that they were due to an increase in infectious diseases (see figure 14.5).

What caused the increase? Lambert knew that the subject populations enjoyed a protein-rich diet from fishing but lived off relatively few staple foods of uncertain reliability, making them potential victims of periodic malnutrition and more susceptible to infectious diseases. The first millennium A.D. was a time of rising populations and smaller territories, where people crowded into larger, more permanent settlements. Sanitation was much worse than in temporary camps, bringing the inhabitants into contact with animal and soil pathogens. At the same time, accelerating trade contacts spread infectious diseases over longer distances. Lambert believes the people were exposed to a new disease or developed increased susceptibility to an existing one. One possible culprit is endemic syphilis, a childhood disease still common in some parts of the world. For a long time, scholars denied syphilis occurred in the Americas before European contact. But four skeletons from the Santa Barbara Channel region, and others from elsewhere in North America, bear the characteristic skull lesions associated with the disease.

As health declined, so did the stature of both men and women. Lambert measured the length of thigh bones, which represent about 27 percent of a person's height. She estimated that there was a stature loss of about four inches over the period, attributable not to an influx of shorter people, but to periodic malnutrition and increased susceptibility and exposure to infection.

Some years earlier, Lambert's colleague Phillip Walker studied the dental health of skeletons from the Channel Islands and the mainland. He found frequent occurrences of dental hyperplasia, bands of defective enamel that form when a child's growth is disrupted by malnutrition and disease stress. Like periosteal lesions, hyperplasia increased significantly through time, most notably after 1500 B.C. Significantly, the highest frequencies came

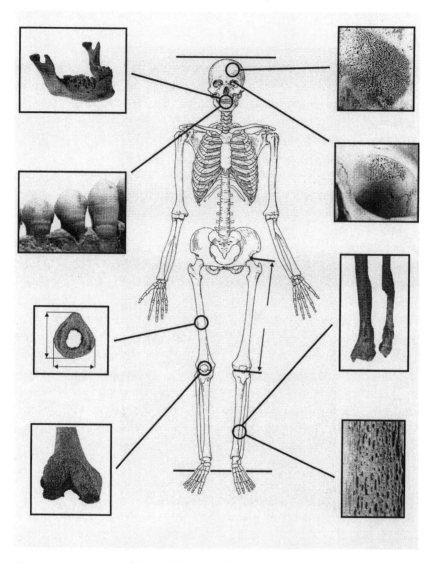

Figure 14.5. Some of the skeletal pathologies observable on human skeletal remains. Right side, from top: Porotic hyperostosis; Cribra orbitalia; Traumatic injuries; Osteoporosis. Left side, from top: Dental caries, abscesses, and tooth loss; Dental hypoplasia; Skeletal robusticity; Generative joint disease. Courtesy of Phillip Walker.

from large, densely populated mainland villages. Here, the advantages of dwelling in a sedentary settlement carried a high price: greater exposure to infectious diseases, and, probably, a decline in the nutritional quality of the diet. Malnutrition most likely advanced when the fisheries declined, or when the fall acorn harvests yielded less than usual, making it hard for a large, and growing population to feed itself.

Another condition manifested itself on ancient Chumash skulls—pitting in the eye roof socket, a condition known as *Cribra orbitalia*, which develops in children, as a response to iron deficiency anemia. *Cribra* was especially common among people living on San Miguel Island, the most isolated of the northern Channel Islands, where plant foods and drinking water were scarce. Walker found that the frequency of *Cribra* peaked between A.D. 300 and 1150, a time when the climate was unstable and droughts were commonplace. In dry years, large numbers of people depended on a few permanent supplies, which soon became polluted in an environment where more crowded villages were living under unsanitary conditions.

Walker's study was confined to the Channel Islands, but the same arguments could be applied to mainland communities, especially in a time when water supplies were shrinking—but this is a theoretical scenario. Protein-rich fish did not protect either the island or mainland people from the kinds of health declines that occur when people move into permanent settlements or have regular contact from others living afar. In this respect, the Chumash of the centuries before contact resembled sedentary farming societies, whose health declined markedly from their much more mobile hunter-gatherer predecessors.

The Dogs of War (A.D. 300 to 1150)

Long before Pat Lambert started work on human skeletons, archaeologists had found clear signs of warfare—stone projectile points embedded in the bones of the dead. Lambert looked more closely at the wounds themselves on the Channel Islands skeletons as well as excavation records and the artifacts found with burials. She conducted a series of ancient murder investigations, minute reconstructions of traumatic wounds inflicted centuries ago.

Head wounds are common when people fight, but their severity depends on the weapons used and where the blows fall. Men who settled disputes with clubs or axes, for example, often display round or elliptical depressions, which are quite easy to identify on the outer surfaces of their skulls. Injuries of this type are rarely fatal, but any wound, which penetrates the skull, is very dangerous and often lethal. Lambert and Walker examined dozens of ancient Chumash skulls. They found head wounds were most common among offshore island populations, perhaps because there was more competition for food and territory on such small, isolated landmasses. Anthropologists have observed fights in many living societies in which people resolve disputes with nonlethal force, the most famous example being the Yanomamo Indians of the Venezeulan rainforest, who settle quarrels with axes and clubs.[11]

Philip Walker extended the study to the mainland. He found that head injuries increased through time on both the islands and mainland, peaking in the centuries before A.D. 1150.[12] They then declined sharply. Lambert also looked closely at projectile injuries, which were clear evidence of violent conflict. Arrows and spears are not very accurate missiles, especially when aimed from a distance. So one might expect a high incidence of nonlethal wounds, where people walked around for years with some pieces of stone point in their flesh. Lambert found precisely those kinds of wounds—individuals whose bones displayed healing around such a wound. In contrast, those killed at short range or by an arrow hitting a vital spot display wounds with no signs of healing whatsoever. There were even some wounds where the projectile point had been removed before or after death. In one case, she found a mysterious nick in a neck vertebra. She checked the excavation records, which dated from 1928, and learned that a stone point had occupied the nick when the skeleton was dug up.

Lambert needed some precedents, not exactly easy to find when you are dealing with the pathology of arrow wounds. She turned to studies of casualties during nineteenth-century Indian wars, where she learned that the most lethal arrow wounds were to the soft tissue of the chest and abdominal cavity. No signs of such wounds survived on her skeletons, but Lambert did find one record of a male from a cemetery near Point Mugu, where a fragmentary projectile point lay in the abdominal cavity region. Many years ago, archaeologist Phil Orr unearthed a skeleton at Mescalitan Island in the Goleta Slough with no less than seventeen projectile points within his body, most in soft-tissue areas.

When Lambert tabulated her projectile wound data, she found that there were sporadic incidences of wounds as early as 3500 B.C., but such traumas were rare until about 1400 B.C. Projectile point wounds reached a peak between A.D. 300 and 1150, dropping somewhat about four hundred years before Spanish contact. She believes this peak was no coincidence. It coincides with the appearance of the bow and arrow in southern California around A.D. 500, a weapon that was the primary weapon in Chumash society when the Spanish arrived. Archers firing in groups have a major strategic advantage over spearers, because they can shoot accurately from a longer distance, whereas spears are a close-in weapon.

The spike in warfare also came at a time when populations were growing, people were congregating in much larger permanent settlements, and hereditary chiefs now controlled society. They quarreled and competed with one another at a time of climatic instability and frequent droughts. For example, the Mescalatan village lay in the Goleta Slough where fish and wildlife were abundant. This large settlement village thrived for many centuries right into mission times, but its cemetery contains more projectile point victims than any other site in the Santa Barbara Channel region. The dead date to between A.D. 700 and 1150, a time of major change in Chumash society. Not that the violence ended completely after that date. A Spanish party encountered some Indians "returning from these towns to their villages in 1783. They had been fighting and were carrying one or more scalps. One of their party had been wounded."

Sporadic warfare was part of Chumash life for many centuries. Beyond question, some of this conflict was connected with occasional food shortages and rivalry between different groups. These were not wars of conquest or battles to repel invaders. They were patterns of local conflict inevitable among people living in an area of unpredictable rainfall, highly localized food supplies, and intense social and political competition. Some of the clearest signs of violence come from the Channel Islands, an impoverished environment. I suspect that future research may also reveal a higher incidence of violence in interior communities, which must have suffered worse than those along the coast.

Nor were the Chumash unique in their belligerence. War victims lie in many ancient Californian cemeteries—in the Bay Area, in the Central Valley, and elsewhere, in areas where long-established patterns of interconnectedness broke down in the face of growing populations and increasingly fierce competition for food supplies, especially in the late first millennium A.D. The consequences of food shortages were dire, even in areas of plenty. Hunger and famine-related diseases attacked the most vulnerable members of society—the very young and the elderly. Water shortages could lead to poor village sanitation and contamination of rivers and springs. Violence would erupt without notice over prized oak groves, kelp fisheries, and other food supplies.

If Lambert and Walker are correct, the violence peaked before A.D. 1150. Then it subsided dramatically. For reasons as yet only simply understood, the Chumash may have deliberately moved away from violence and created an entirely new society in the process.

A New Way of Doing Business

An entirely new society seems like a bold statement, but it is no exaggeration. There was a major change about a thousand years ago, when the Chumash seem to have paused and made dramatic changes in the way they did business with one another. Faced with escalating violence and persistent hunger, perhaps even local population crashes, their leaders seem to have realized that they were all in the same situation, that survival depended not on competition, but enhanced interdependence.

But the damage had been done, with chronic imbalances between population and available food supplies. It seems, also, that the traditional informal exchange networks, the web of interconnectedness that had sustained coastal and mainland communities for centuries, had partially broken down in an environment of distrust and intensifying competition for food supplies. By now, the structure of society was changing. Larger settlements developed, people lived closer together. Group territories were smaller and more crowded, with hierarchies of larger settlements and smaller villages, and, above all, a changed role for the aggrandizers of earlier centuries, who had become leaders through their entrepreneurial skills and acumen at dealing with others.

For centuries, the aggrandizers' loyal followers had evaporated at their death. There was no permanent center of political power in basically egalitarian societies living in smaller settlements. But now leadership had become hereditary, vested in elite lineages headed by chiefly families, where power passed down the generations. By the time Juan Cabrillo entered the Santa Barbara Channel in 1542, Chumash society had crystallized into a more formal structure, with powerful mechanisms for controlling trade, resolving disputes, and, above all, for distributing food supplies in a world where a distance of even a few miles could mean plenty or shortage.

Ethnographic records describe a hierarchy of three types of Chumash chief—a "big chief," *wots* who controlled a group of settlements, a "chief," or head of a village, and a "lesser chief," subordinate to the others. All chiefs and members of their families were required to belong to the *'antap*, the association that supervised dances and the other rituals that validated the new social order and where shamans ensured the continuity of the world. The *'antap* may have served as a social mechanism that linked wealthy and powerful individuals throughout Chumash territory. Both the chiefly hierarchy and the *'antap* were effective in a world where social and political stability depended on the ability of a few people to control trade and food supplies, and to contain violence among a population for the islands and mainland of at least 15,000 people. Under such circumstances, public rituals and major religious gatherings assume great importance as a way of validating chiefly authority in a world where conformity and at least a degree of cooperation were all-important.

This chiefly hierarchy and the sharp division between a small, wealthy elite and commoners is well documented for historic times and the centuries just before the European *entrada*. But did such social ranking exist earlier in time, when did it develop, and how was wealth and position passed from one generation to the next? Some interesting clues come from cemeteries near Malibu at the very southern edge of Chumash country, where biological anthropology, archaeology, and ethnography have combined to provide portraits of both historic and ancient populations.[14]

The prehistoric cemetery was used between about A.D. 950 and 1150. There was also a historic cemetery at the same location, used between about A.D. 1775 and 1805, when recruitment to the missions ended. Forty-five percent of the burials in the historic cemetery had less than twenty beads. Just under half of these had no beads at all. In dramatic contrast, 9 percent of the historic graves lay in well-decorated graves with more than one thousand beads apiece. With one exception, these graves lay at the southern edge of the cemetery, with only a few relatively undecorated burials in the same area.

The richly endowed graves included people of all ages and both sexes, as one might expect with the burials of wealthy people who acquired their social status through birth rather than personal accomplishment, where only the achievers would have richly decorated sepulchers. Furthermore, the wealthiest graves lay much deeper, a phenomenon consistent with ethnographic accounts that tell of members of society who were paid with baskets and other items to dig deep graves. Eleven of the historic graves were associated with asphalt and wood fragments, as if their owners were buried with fragments of the canoes they had owned. Burial 56, a nineteen-year-old man, lay with 2,347 *olivella* beads around his head and forty-eight (European) glass beads as well as many canoe planks, as if he was buried with part of a *tomol*. Some young children were buried with canoe parts, as if membership of the Brotherhood of the Canoe was also inherited at birth.

The well-developed social divisions of the historic-period Chumash symbolically reinforced the chasm between a small number of wealthy elite and commoners. The elite inherited their wealth from their powerful families.

The Malibu cemeteries show that this was in existence considerably earlier. There were striking similarities between the historic and ancient cemeteries, so much so that 68 percent of the ninety burials in the earlier cemetery lay with fewer than twenty beads. Only 3 percent of the graves had more than one thousand beads, including a few children. At least as early as A.D. 950, Chumash buried in the Malibu cemetery were living in a society ruled by an elite who inherited wealth rather than earned it. Furthermore, studies of the bones in the cemetery showed a close correlation between utilitarian objects and physical conditions associated with hard labor and walking over arduous terrain. In contrast, the wealthier skeletons did not show similar conditions.

In the sixteenth century, Chumash society functioned at two levels. At one pole were individuals who were powerful and wealthy and who manipulated the system to their own benefit. People of elevated status controlled society, monopolized all trade, and exercised powerful influence on ritual life. At the other pole was a strong cooperative ethic, which fostered trade and exchange and evened out food supplies over larger areas. We may never know the details of how and when the reorganized society came into being, but there is no question that the change worked. In some areas, Chumash population densities before European contact rivaled those of village farming peoples.

These changes coincided with a period of cooler sea surface temperatures and more intense upwelling, with much enhanced marine productivity between 950 and 1300, but a time of intense drought on land. The signs of change are unmistakable: an explosion in the number of archaeological sites, much larger, permanent settlements, and a spectacular rise in the numbers of shell beads and other exotic artifacts on the mainland and islands. And, at about the same time, the Chumash ventured offshore in search of far more formidable and prestigious catches—swordfish and other deep water fish, speared from canoes with barbed harpoons. They had been taking the occasional swordfish for many centuries, but now their pursuit became surrounded with ritual and prestigious status. As the swordfish dancer burial reminds us (see chapter 8), the ritual surrounding the swordfish were of high importance, for the Chumash believed that the fish with its fierce attacks would drive whales ashore, a rich supply of meat for them. In his dance, the shaman-swordfish dancer would whirl around. His headdress feathers whirled like a wheel as he spun around, first in one direction and then another.[14]

This was the moment when the Chumash planked canoe, the *tomol*, came into economic and political play. Archaeologist Lynn Gamble has reviewed all the archaeological evidence for planked watercraft and makes a strong case for the appearance of the *tomol* in all its refinement by at least A.D. 650—just at the time of considerable social change and competition between neighboring groups.[15] For reasons argued in chapter 5, I believe that the planked canoe was in use, albeit in a simpler form, as early as 7000 B.C., perhaps earlier, when sea levels began their rapid climb to modern levels. I also pointed out that the individuals who built, owned, or skippered such watercraft were in a unique position to profit from their roles (see box 14.2). They had all the potential to acquire wealth and political power, to become aggrandizers in their own right. Given the great and well-documented hazards of canoe travel, we can be sure that powerful rituals surrounded offshore voyaging from the beginning.

No one doubts that the *tomol* in all its refined glory was a key artifact in Chumash life—or rather, to sharpen this statement somewhat, the building and ownership of them was. I remarked in chapter 5 that canoe builders were the rocket scientists of their day, people with unusual skills. Their expertise was not so much in woodworking, but in the classic boatbuilder's skill of visualizing and assembling the three-dimensional hull of a canoe. Such men must have enjoyed unusual prestige even in early times.

By the first millennium A.D., simpler forms of planked canoes must have assumed a powerful status in local society, as a symbol of wealth, and the ability to command the labor of others. *Tomols* were expensive to build and maintain. To skipper them required great expertise. At European contact, an influential guild, the Brotherhood of the Canoe, linked canoe builders, who were individuals of expertise, wealth, and considerable social prestige. I suspect a simpler version of the brotherhood existed long before the institution achieved its historical elaboration with the rising importance of the *tomol*.

BOX 14.2 Building a Chumansh *tomol*

Thanks to John Peabody Harrington's 3,000 pages of notes on *tomols* and *tomol* construction, we know a great deal about these remarkable watercraft. Harrington acquired a great deal of his information about the canoes from Fernando Librado, a Ventureño Chumash. Philosopher, storyteller, and keen observer, Librado had been a member of the Brotherhood of the Canoe.

"The board canoe was the house of the sea," Librado tells us. A canoe builder worked with small groups of helpers. They took their time, often between two and six months, to construct a single *tomol*. Most canoes were between twelve and thirty feet long, with a three-foot beam, large enough to carry between three and six men and a heavy load. At the same time, the vessel had to be light enough for her crew to carry and beach readily (see figure 14.6).

Figure 14.6. The *Helek*, a *tomol* replica, at sea. Such craft were a catalyst for intensive island-mainland exchange over the past 1,500 years. Courtesy of Santa Barbara Museum of Natural History.

The canoe builders began by collecting stocks of driftwood, which they seasoned, then split into planks with whalebone wedges. Then they shaped and thinned each plank with bone, shell, and stone tools, eliminating knots and cracks where possible. Once adzed to a uniform thickness, the men smoothed the planks with sandpaper made from dried sharkskin.

A long, heavy plank with a dished surface formed the bottom of the canoe, held upright with forked timbers. The hull planks usually came from a patchwork of driftwood, for longer lengths were hard to come by. The builders soaked the six planks in a clay-lined pit filled with boiling water. After a few hours, the saturated planks could be bent to shape, aligned, and fastened in position. Each grooved length rested against the edge of its neighbor, carefully beveled end to end to achieve a snug fit and the greatest possible strength.

Next, two men sealed the seams with a mixture of heated bitumen and pitch called *yop*, checking the alignment as they went along, a process that required a keen eye and speed before the caulking cooled. Finally, they gouged out and burned pairs of holes at the edge of the planks and sewed them together with waxed fiber twine made from red milkwood grass.

The only cross member was a beam that braced the hull amidships, inserted between the fifth and sixth planks. The latter formed the gunwales, which were left open at bow and stern, leaving V-shaped gaps for fishing lines or pulling ropes. Finally, the canoe builder inserted stout posts at bow and stern and washboards sewn to the gunwales at both ends. They deflected water in heavy surf and rough seas.

Now the men turned the canoe over for caulking. They hammered dry tule grass stalks into the outer seams, then sealed them with *yop*. Once the caulking was dry, the men scraped the entire hull with an abalone shell to remove surplus caulking. The faired hull was sealed with a mixture of red ocher and pine pitch, which prevented the canoe from absorbing water and becoming unduly heavy.

Raccoon tail brushes served to delineate the ties and joints with a black paint. The canoe builder then decorated the *tomol* with shell inlays on the washboards and occasionally with powdered shell thrown against the wet finish before it dried. This made the canoe glitter as it approached land.

Building a *tomol* in all its elaboration could take up to 550 hours over a six-month period, making them expensive propositions, the craft owned only by a few wealthy individuals.

(Continued)

BOX 14.2 Continued

Librado describes the sea trials of a newly completed canoe: "Once they have completed the *tomol*, they put it into the sea and row it about, seeing if there is anything wrong with it. . . . They check for leaks and whether or not the canoe is lopsided or sinks too deeply into the water." The master builder himself also ballasted the canoe, for its light structure required considerable inboard weight to achieve stability.

Each paddler sat on a pad of sea grass, paddling with an even rhythm, using his shoulders to do the work, just like modern-day kayakers do. A skilled crew would keep up the same pace all day, paddling to the sound of a canoe song repeated time and time again. Modern experiments have shown that with an eight-knot following wind and swell, experienced paddlers can make six to eight knots. But if the same eight-knotter blew from ahead, the *tomol* made no progress. Almost certainly the Chumash seafarers made their island journeys and fished offshore during early hours of the morning when winds are calm.

The *tomol* was the most important technological achievement of ancient times in the channel region, a unique craft that was crucial to settling the northern Channel Islands and to maintaining links between mainland and offshore communities.[16] By the late first millennium, the planked canoe had become far more than mere transportation. For many centuries, *tomols* had carried such commodities as pounded acorns and shell beads back and forth across the channel as part of the essential fabric of interdependence, which had existed since the earliest times. But the voyages were sporadic, the island population being considerably smaller. The incentives for regular passage making were not there.

Sometime after A.D. 500, this interconnectedness intensified and canoe owners, always influential members of society, played an important role in a burgeoning trade from island to mainland and back. If I am correct in thinking that canoes and aggrandizers went together in earlier times, then they now merely expanded their activities. Their ownership put them in a unique position to manipulate social contacts across the water, to manage information about offshore fisheries or potential trading contacts, and to monopolize load carrying between widely separated communities. They could also organize deep-sea fishing, for the prestigious, mystical swordfish and other challenging offshore fish. Judging from sporadic finds of swordfish bones, images, and regalia in earlier sites, some people had long fished away from the coast. But now the practice became institutionalized and controlled by small numbers of wealthy canoe owners.

The canoe owners could never have achieved the power they did if it were not for the constant need for acorns in island communities and the demand for shell beads on the mainland. Acorns and shell beads became the currency of surging contacts across the Santa Barbara Channel.[17]

As we saw in chapter 7, shell bead manufacture and ornament making were small-scale activities on both the islands and mainland from the earliest times. The routine contacts of interconnectedness carried such small artifacts far into the interior, as far as the Central Valley and Great Basin. In about A.D. 900, the pace of bead making suddenly intensified. Until now, the bead makers had used casually manufactured stone drills. Now the Channel Islanders developed much more formal drilling technology, using small stone microblades made from a fine local chert (see figure 14.7). At

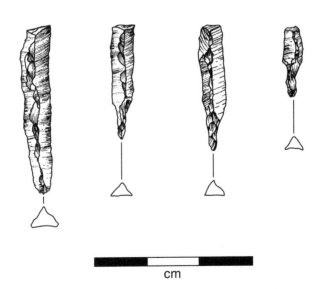

cm

Figure 14.7. Chert microdrills from Santa Cruz Island. Original from *The Origins of a Pacific Chiefdom*, Jeanne E. Arnold, ed. (Salt Lake City, Utah: University of Utah Press, 2001). Drawing by Jeanne Arnold.

first, the bead makers had produced a greater number of beads for their own use. But, after 1150, the explosion of bead manufacture, not only of *olivella* wall beads, but of undrilled forms as well, suggest an increase in their use as trade objects There was another significant change, too. Nearly all shell beads and stone drills now came from Channel Islands villages, produced on a much larger scale than in earlier times.

Bead making and stone drills were closely interconnected, so much so that bead-making villages on eastern Santa Cruz Island may have controlled nearby chert quarries. But the producers did not control the distribution of the beads themselves. To exercise such control, they would have to have owned *tomols*, which remained in wealthy canoe owners' hands. UCLA archaeologist Jeanne Arnold, who has worked on Santa Cruz Island for over two decades, believes that much of the canoe trade from Santa Cruz Island channeled through one large community with its own chief and *tomol* owners at Prisoner's Harbor on the north coast.[18] Here, permanent water supplies and a sheltered, sandy beach made for an ideal trading place, with the bead-making villages and coastal fishing grounds a short canoe ride away (see figure 14.8).

Figure 14.8. Prisoner's Harbor, Santa Cruz Island, a classic *tomol* landing. A major trading village lies close inland, behind the modern pier in the trees.

Craft specialization, if indeed bead making on the Channel Islands was that specialized an activity, involves the investment of substantial amounts of time over and above the daily routine of food gathering. Arnold believes that such specialization could only result from tight chiefly control both of production and distribution, a theory that flies in the face of numerous examples of craft specialization in different parts of the world that were not controlled by chiefs or any other form of leader. It is still an open question whether such specialization was a major activity on the islands.

There is only one difference between many of those societies and the Chumash—the logistics of transporting food and beads not over land, but over the open ocean. And the central figures in this transportation were canoe skippers—wealthier, ritually important members of society who *were* sometimes headmen or chiefs. Quite what the relationship was between these influential people and actual shell bead manufacturing or processing of acorns, we do not know, but it is likely to have involved kin ties, reciprocal obligations with relatives across the channel, and even more complex political and social nuances, which elude us centuries later.

Just how large was the scale of the expanding bead trade? You can guess at the volume of any trade archaeologically by counting the volume of such imports of beads in graves and settlements. But such calculations are, at best, inconclusive. Much depends on the part of the site you excavate, the size of your samples, and so on. General impressions are often a better guide. For instance, the number of shell beads in mainland sites jumps exponentially after A.D. 1150, not only in graves, but also in villages, to the point that isolated beads are common finds—a "bead saturation point," akin to the dropped pennies that are so common in supermarket parking lots today. As bead production increased, so the quality of both drilling technology improved. New forms such as the thicker *olivella* callus bead came into fashion. Since only one callus bead came from each shell, they were more expensive to produce. At this point, shell beads became a form of currency, especially *olivella* callus shells. This is hardly surprising, given the volume of beads in circulation and the control of their distribution in the hands of canoe owners.

The development of beads as currency in this area may have been a direct consequence of geography—the relative isolation of the islands, where tight control of both production and distribution was possible, and where acorns and other plant foods were in short supply. In the steady flow of trade across the channel, exchange was regulated by items of agreed value that were easily transported and had become a visible and countable form of wealth.

Jeanne Arnold and her colleagues examined the changing quantities of the byproducts from microdrill manufacture and bead making in several dozen Channel Island settlements. They also studied bead distributions and byproducts from mainland and island settlements to document a dramatic rise in cross-channel trade between 1150 and 1300. Arnold theorizes that as the number of people profiting from the increased exchange rose, so did their ability to finance new *tomol* construction. She believes that canoe owners on both sides of the channel seized an unusual opportunity to exchange mainland foods such as acorns and animal products for shell beads. This was at about this time that the *olivella* callus bead became a form of currency, which remained in use right up to 1782.

Huge numbers of shell beads crossed the channel, to the point that they were so common that they acquired agreed values. But does this necessarily mean that someone had to control both the production and distribution of the finished product, as Arnold and others believe? Arnold equates chiefs with craft specialization and an expanding bead trade, many of them wealthy canoe owners.

There was certainly marked social ranking in Chumash society during the last few centuries before European contact. We know this from elaborate burial goods, and from the fact that specific parts of village cemeteries were reserved for important individuals, who were buried with specific funerary markers, such as canoe planks or *tomol* models in soapstone and other materials. As the centuries pass, and we near the period of European contact, higher numbers of prestigious objects also appear, many of them of obvious ritual import—such items as raptor talon pendants, swordfish and mammal bone pins, and bone rings and tubes, as well as a wider variety of shell beads. People valued these objects because of their rarity and prestigious value.

Perhaps high-status families commissioned the manufacture such rare items, or commissioned them from trusted artisans. But it is certainly a mistake to think of Chumash society as a rigidly hierarchical organization. The greatest elaboration was not in the economic control of producers and trade routes, but in ritual—the conceptual glue that held all ancient Californian societies together. Here, as elsewhere, the intricate ties of kin, of social obligation, held society together in a highly political environment where chiefs enjoyed no absolute powers but always had to take account of the shifting tides of public opinion.

These signs of social ranking, and probably of ritual elaboration, coincide with a marked improvement in the health of both islanders and mainlanders, as if food supplies were now more evenly distributed, despite well-documented periods of intense drought. Village sanitation was still a problem, although there are signs that some settlements moved, perhaps as a result of climatic stress.

The net effect of all these changes was a dramatic change in Chumash society, from factionalism and infighting to a period when food supplies stabilized, in spite of drought cycles and other climatic perturbations. At the same time, economic interdependence and firm control of cross-channel trade in the hands of relatively few wealthy individuals, aggrandizers or chiefs meant that society was more centralized. Larger political alliances came and went, and usually failed, but there was a level of economic interdependence between far-flung communities that was unknown in earlier times. The *wots* and other wealthy families did not necessarily live in larger houses, although they may have adorned them with redwood planks or with whale bones. Rather, their status stemmed from their ownership of *tomols* and the loyalties that came from their generosity, their wealth acquired from trading and political skill and their ritual powers. In these respects, Chumash society was no different than any other, even if the range of foodstuffs and the *tomol* made for more elaborate economic, political, and social institutions.

No one knows how many Chumash chiefdoms flourished on the islands or mainland, but there are historical accounts that point to one or two major chiefs on Santa Cruz Island and some important leaders who presided over long stretches of mainland coast. To judge from the large settlement at Prisoner's Harbor on Santa Cruz Island, major chiefly villages lay at strategic points, where most trading activity and canoe shipping took place. Everywhere, the chiefly families intermarried, establishing networks of kin and marriage ties to many more communities both near and far than was normal for commoners. Such connections fostered trade relationships and helped maintain stability in a world where life expectancy was short and individual power was often transitory.

By the time Juan Cabrillo sailed into the Santa Barbara Channel, Chumash society was very different from what it had been in earlier time.

A network of powerful chiefs competed with one another for prestige and wealth, often seeking to aggrandize themselves at the expense of others. Occasional quarrels, even fighting, must have broken out over control of labor, competition for rare items, and interpersonal relations. But, in the long run, cooperative behavior prevailed between communities scattered over a large area who depended on one other. The cooperation was often for individual gain, but the presence of the 'antap brought a level of ritual integration right across society, perhaps involving greater public participation in major ceremonies.

All these changes, and the transformation of Chumash society, took place not because one or two charismatic individuals decided to take matters into their own hands. Quite the contrary: a whole range of major economic, political, and social changes occurred more-or-less simultaneously over a large area of the islands and mainland coast. This ancient society followed its own unique path toward change, interweaving specialized crafts, cross-channel trade, marine travel, and a limited degree of political and religious centralization into a truly unique hunter-gatherer society.

Their style of leadership, their emphasis on major rituals, and their means of combining both personal advancement and interdependency forged a society without rigid social ranks, warriors, or slaves. It was a brilliant solution to living in an unpredictable, sometimes violent world of climatic extremes, which flourished until Cabrillo's successors decimated Chumash society with exotic disease and forced missionization.

Entrada

I N THE SIXTEENTH CENTURY A.D., THE INHABITANTS OF
California formed a dense network of groups, large and
small, speaking over sixty languages and numbering an estimated 310,000 people. They occupied about 256,000 square miles of varied terrain, with an average population density of about 1 person per 2
square miles, a higher figure than average for the North America of five centuries ago. Then, suddenly, this world began to change rapidly.

In A.D. 1542, Portuguese explorer João Rodrigues Cabrilho (or, more commonly, Cabrillo) sailed in the Spanish service northward along New Spain's
Baja coast into California waters. He watered his three ships in San Diego Bay
on September 28, 1542, naming this "very good enclosed port" San Miguel,
then made his way slowly along an arid coastline backed with mountain ranges
into the densely settled Santa Barbara Channel. On October 13, he came to
anchor off a large Chumash village named Skuku at the back of a sandy beach
now known as a famous surfing spot, the Rincon, on the eastern side of the
modern city of Carpinteria. "Fine canoes each holding twelve or thirteen
Indians came to the ships," Cabrillo wrote. "They have round houses, well
covered down to the ground. They wear skins, eat acorns, and a white seed
the size of maize." With this fleeting visit, the Spanish *entrada* began.[1]

Cabrillo battled his way north of Point Conception, then died while
wintering over on San Miguel Island. The following year, Bartolomé Ferrelo
led the expedition before favorable winds as far north as the vicinity of Cape
Mendocino. (Despite breezes from astern, the Spaniards never spotted the

Golden Gate or Monterey Bay.) Then strong northwesterlies blew the ships southward back to San Miguel and they never returned.

The first contact was short lived. The arid, windswept California coast and its inhabitants had few attractions to gold-hungry conquistadors. It became a welcome landfall for trans-Pacific voyagers. After 1565, Spanish treasure galleons returning from the Philippines made landfall on Cape Mendocino, then coasted southward to Acapulco, keeping well offshore. The prospect of treasure brought English privateer Francis Drake to this remote land. On June 17, 1579, Drake entered "a convenient and fit harborough" on the northern California coast to repair his ships. Experts have argued over where this "harborough" was for over a century, but most likely the ships anchored in Drake Bay, in the lee of Point Reyes and north of the Golden Gate. Here Drake was in the territory of the Miwok, a group of about three thousand people who lived in some numbers around the shallow estero (coastal wetland) behind the bay and along the north side of the Golden Gate. Drake collected some Indian words during his five-week stay, which are clearly from the Miwok vocabulary.

Next morning, a man paddled out "in a canow" and delivered a long, unintelligible oration. The Miwok, like other central California groups, placed a high value on ceremonial oratory. Within a few days, a crowd of Indians had arrived from as far afield as settlements along Tomales Bay, over the coastal hills. They behaved as if the visitors were divine beings, or perhaps returning ancestors. Gifts were exchanged—shirts and linen cloth in exchange for Miwok feathers, net caps, and women's animal skins. The Indian's conical, earth-covered dwellings were "digged around in the earth," erected on frameworks of bent saplings "joyned close together at the top." The local chiefs wore clamshell disc bead necklaces (which came from Bodega Bay to the north) and net caps adorned with feathers. Common folk gathered their long hair into bunches decorated with feathers. Their faces were painted in black, white, and other colors. Drake wrote: "They are a people of a tractable, free, and loving nature, without guile or treachery."

During their stay, Drake and his gentleman journeyed a short way into the interior, where they explored the countryside. He called it "a goodlye country and fruitful soil, stored with many blessings fit for the use of man," very different from the fog-shrouded and windy coast. They saw "very large and fat" deer and large numbers of rabbits. Drake named the country Albion, "in respect of the white bancks and cliffes which lie toward the sea." Drake supervised the erection of a post bearing a brass plate claiming the land for Queen Elizabeth. Such a plate was found at Drake's Bay in 1934: its authenticity is questionable.

Almost invariably, the early explorers described the coastal people as shy and friendly folk, who brought gifts and provided hospitality, as well as water and food. California was a disappointment, a place once famed in fiction that had evolved from being an imaginary location, a land of gold and wealth, to a real place with no riches whatsoever.[3] The Spaniards did not colonize seemingly valueless Alta California for nearly two centuries, and then only in the face of perceived threats from British and Russian interests. This was the last period of peace and isolation that the coastal peoples were to enjoy. From the late eighteenth century on, they became locked in an often-violent struggle to keep their traditional way of life alive.

In 1769–1770, Gaspar Portola and Father Junipero Serra explored the shoreline from land, discovered San Francisco Bay, and looked for suitable mission sites. In 1782, a Royal Presidio rose in the heart of Chumash territory near the village of Syuhtun, a settlement of sixty houses close to a stream. A mission followed it. By 1848, when Mexico ceded Alta California to the United States, some four thousand Spanish/Mexican settlers lived along the coast from Sonoma to San Diego. They governed their new homeland using long-established colonial policies to control the native population.

Within a half century, thousands of Indians had perished from exotic diseases, or from maltreatment on the infamous *encomiendas*—near-feudal ranches modeled on prototypes developed in New Spain. Thousands more were rounded up from their camps and villages and herded into crowded and unhealthy mission barracks. They perished by the hundreds, subjected to rigid discipline and cruelty, all in the name of the One True Faith. Father President Francisco de Lasuen rationalized the harsh treatment in no uncertain words: "It is evident that a nation that is barbarous, ferocious and ignorant requires more frequent punishment than a nature that is cultured, educated and of gentle and moderate customs."[4] Word of this hellish treatment soon spread to unconverted groups.

By 1787, the missionaries were using soldiers to "recruit" reluctant communities for conversion. The Indians responded with violence and rebellion, also by passive resistance, but to little avail. Within a half century, traditional Chumash culture was in ruins, the people living in poverty and disease around local mission stations. The Miwok and other Bay Area groups resisted, then melted away in the face of Spanish settlement. The survivors became poor laborers on the margins of colonial society.

The Hispanic colonists regarded the Indians as cheap labor to acquire wealth and attempted to incorporate them into the lower end of their social order. After 1848, American settlers arrived in search not only of gold, but of land as well. The newcomers regarded Indian life as worthless, their lands for the taking. Floods of immigrants poured into the Bay Area and moved inland and along the northern coast. Many were lawless adventurers, who thought nothing of killing any Indian on sight. The Indians stood in the way of a new society, which discouraged intermarriage and met competition for land or food supplies with force and genocide, or by segregating the indigenous population in reservations. Inevitably, the native population was decimated, not only by systematic extermination, but also by epidemics, like the great malaria outbreak that killed an estimated 75 percent of the indigenous Central Valley population in 1833.

From the beginning of history, the Indians had exploited their environments with often ruthless efficiency. As archaeology shows us, at times this ruthlessness resulted in overfishing, depletion of game and fish stocks, and chronic shortages of plant foods. Undoubtedly, there were times when hundreds, if not thousands, of people died from hunger or famine-related diseases during drought or rapid population increase. After such population crashes, growth resumed or people turned to more labor-intensive crops like acorns. But the pressure on food supplies never eased. We know this because eyewitness accounts of areas like the Central Valley tell of an abundance of game and other foods but also of an absence of people, as they had been decimated by influenza and other epidemics. The natural resources had time to recover. Today, we have transformed much of California's environment, but still face the same realities of unpredictable rainfall, fire, flood, and other natural catastrophes, to say nothing of chronic resource depletion. Until the mid-nineteenth century, the interior groups had lived in peace. Now their lives were threatened and their food supplies depleted by the immigrants' total disregard for the natural environment. Mining operations destroyed fish dams and blocked salmon runs. Expanded ranches encroached on deer-hunting grounds. Farmers fenced off acorn-rich oak groves. Cattle and hogs ate huge amounts of forage and decimated wild seed yields. A frenzy of European rapaciousness destroyed the sacred relationship between the native peoples and their territories. Malnutrition and disease killed thousands of people, and group after group vanished in the face of European encroachment.

■ ■ ■

By the 1870s, only pockets of native Americans remained throughout the state, clinging precariously to the remnants of their ancient lifeways. Many were born before the Gold Rush and retained vivid memories of earlier, quieter times. Fortunately for posterity, a few individuals, like the journalist Stephen Powers and a handful of anthropologists and archaeologists from the nascent University of California, Berkeley, collected a large body of information about California Indian societies before 1900, while many survivors of earlier times were still alive. But even these accounts are from a time when the earlier world had already changed beyond recognition. And only a fraction of the enormous body of oral tradition and rich cultural tapestry of ancient times endured. Efforts to collect surviving fragments continue to this day, as part of a strong revival of native Californian culture.[5]

Today, almost nothing of the ancient California world remains. Decimated by infectious diseases to which they had no immunity, forcibly missionized, hounded off their land, sometimes hunted to death, only about 20,000 California Indians survived in 1900. Over a hundred main tribal groups or tribelets vanished during the first 131 years of European settlement.

With the researches of the first anthropologists and archaeologists, we have come full circle, back to the beginnings of the archaeologist's tale. I have told the story of the first Californians, as we know it from the testimony of anthropology, history, the trowel, the spade, and the very latest in scientific technology.[6] This is a narrative of people, individuals and groups, going about their daily business—hunting and foraging, living and dying, loving, raising children, living in plenty and in hunger, negotiating and quarreling, pondering their cosmos, and facing the unpredictable challenges of drought and El Niños. This is a book about people who showed a brilliant opportunism and ability to adapt to changing circumstances and to harsh, never predictable environments. Above all, it is a tribute to the flexible ingenuity of humanity, to people who lived successfully in a demanding world for more than 13,000 years. But they could not survive the onslaught of Europeans, with their rugged individualism, rapacious ways, and ardent religious faith. These are societies of the remote and not-so-remote past, but we have much to learn from them. And this process of learning has hardly begun, for we are still learning how to live successfully in environments as challenging and capricious as they were in ancient times.

Notes and References

Before California is a book for popular consumption, so I have made no attempt to provide complete references. The notes and references for each chapter, which follow, give information on some of the sources that I drew on and citations for quotations. Some notes define technical terms or qualify a statement in the text. Where possible, I have annotated the references, to serve as a guide to the interested reader. Most of the works here have excellent, full bibliographies, which will lead you to more specialized works. Websites are not listed here, for they change constantly and a good browser like Google will get you to them quicker than I can. Note that papers presented at professional meetings are not cited here: they are effectively inaccessible unless published.

Chapter 1: A Stream of Time

1. J. R. R. Tolkien, *Lord of the Rings* (Boston: Houghton Mifflin, 2001), 55.
2. William F. Shipley, *The Maidu Indian Myths and Stories of Hánc'ibyjim* (Berkeley, Calif.: Heyday Books, 1991), 18–30.
3. Here are some basic sources on California Indians, languages, and population:

   The Native Peoples of California. The ultimate source, if there is such a thing, is Robert F. Heizer, ed., *Handbook of North American Indians, Volume 8: California* (Washington, D.C.: Smithsonian Institution, 1978). This covers every known group as well as topics such as language and population. A copy of this work belongs on the bookshelf of everyone interested in ancient California. Fortunately, there are plenty of second-hand copies around or you can acquire it on a CD-ROM. The same author and Alfred Elsasser's *The Natural World of the California Indians* (Berkeley,

Calif.: University of California Press, 1980) is a readable account of aboriginal life, which deals with such topics as the food quest, material culture, and world views. It's an excellent starting point. Alfred L. Kroeber, *Handbook of the Indians of California* (Washington, D.C.: Bureau of American Ethnology, 1925) is a classic work, and a mine of information, if somewhat outdated. I always enjoy dipping into Stephen Powers, *Tribes of California*, originally published in 1877 and reissued a century later with an introduction by Robert F. Heizer (Berkeley, Calif.: University of California Press, 1976). It contains a wealth of esoteric and sometimes fascinating information.

Languages. I send for cold compresses when confronted with this literature, which is no reflection on those who write it. It is just plain complicated and highly technical. The best starting point for the beginner is William F. Shipley, "Native Languages of California," in the *Handbook of North American Indians*, Volume 8, 80–90. Michael J. Moratto, "Linguistic Prehistory," in his *California Archaeology* (see below), 529–74, gives a much more detailed account. He begins by describing California as the "Babel of ancient America," and he is right. Another useful volume is Leanne Hinton, *Flutes of Fire* (Berkeley, Calif.: Heyday Books, 1994). She covers many topics, among them efforts to keep the surviving fifty languages alive.

Population. Sherburne F. Cook, "Historical Demography," in the *Handbook of North American Indians*, Volume 8, 91–98, is an excellent starting point.

Indian stories and oral traditions. Herbert W. Luthin, ed., *Surviving through the Days* (Berkeley, Calif.: University of California Press, 2002) is a splendid source of traditional literature and stories, which combines Indian and scientific perspectives. Luthin also incorporates a great deal of cultural background and information as well. Many of the accounts come from old wax cylinders and recordings compiled by early researchers. Alas, this volume was published too late for use in *Before California*.

4. The two quotes in this paragraph are from Heizer and Elsasser, *The Natural World of the California Indians* (1980), 210, 216.
5. For a discussion of sources, see the Introduction to Rose Marie Beebe and Robert M. Senkewicz, eds., *Lands of Promise and Despair* (Berkeley, Calif.: Heyday Books, 2001).
6. Ethnohistorians are students of oral tradition and other nontraditional historical sources.
7. There are several accounts of human prehistory on a global basis. Brian Fagan, *World Prehistory: A Brief Introduction*, 5th ed. (Upper Saddle River, N.J.: Prentice Hall, 2002) is a brief summary.

8. Michael J. Moratto, *California Archaeology* (Orlando, Fla.: Academic Press, 1984) covers the history of archaeological research in different areas of the state in summary. I touch briefly on the subject in some of the later chapters, especially where it is relevant to today's controversies.

9. See Thomas Neumann and Robert M. Sanford, "An Introduction to Cultural Resource Management," in *Cultural Resources Archaeology* (Walnut Creek, Calif.: AltaMira Press, 2001).

10. Moratto, *California Archaeology* (1984) is essential reading for any serious student of California archaeology.

11. There are lamentably few books on the archaeology of California as a whole. Moratto's *California Archaeology* (1984) is the most thorough study, conducted at a high technical level. It is authoritative, filled with impressive detail, and somewhat outdated. However, Moratto remains *the* standard source. He has my undying admiration for pulling this book off. There is talk of a revised edition, which is needed badly. Joseph L. Chartkoff and Kerry Kona Chartkoff, *The Archaeology of California* (Stanford, Calif.: Stanford University Press, 1984) is another widely consulted work, written at a less technical level than Moratto. Both of these books are out of print, but you can find them secondhand. (For those of you who are unfamiliar with alibris.com, you are missing something!) A general account of North American archaeology, which includes California is Brian Fagan's *Ancient North America*, 3d ed. (London: Thames and Hudson, 2000).

12. Readers interested in references for the remainder of this chapter should consult the specific chapters later in the book, where they will be found.

Chapter 2: First Footprints

1. Quoted from Malcolm Margolin, ed., *The Way We Lived* (Berkeley, Calif.: Heyday Books and the California Historical Society, 1981), 124. Such song epics were performed by a ceremonial singer, the *hawaynik*, who received strict training and was much honored as preserver of these desert-living Cahuilla's sacred knowledge.

2. Brian Fagan, *The Great Journey* (London: Thames and Hudson, 1987), 7.

3. A huge and sometimes polemic literature surrounds the first settlement of the Americas. Two up-to-date sources: J. M. Adovasio with Jake Page, *The First Americans: In Pursuit of Archaeology's Greatest Mystery* (New York: Random House, 2002) and Thomas D. Dillehay, *The Settlement of the Americas* (New York: Basic Books, 2000). S. J. Fiedel, "The Peopling of the New World: Present Evidence, New Theories, and Future Directions," *Journal of Anthropological Research* 8 (2001): 39–103 offers a provocative progress report. Brian Fagan, *Ancient North America*, 3rd ed. (2000),

chapters 4 and 5, covers Paleo-Indian cultures generally. The summary that follows is based in considerable part on these works.

4. The debate about coastal settlement dates back to the 1970s and has intensified in recent years, despite an almost complete lack of evidence for it. Summaries appear in Terry L. Jones, "Marine Resource Value and the Priority of Coastal Settlement," *American Antiquity* 56 (1991): 419–43. See also D. K. Mandryk et al., "Late Quaternary Paleoenvironments of Northwestern North America: Implications for Inland Versus Coastal Migration Routes," *Quaternary Science Reviews* 20 (2001): 301–14.

5. The term Paleo-Indian is in such wide use that I make no apologies for using it in this book. Archaeologists commonly use Paleo-Indian to refer to human societies and people who lived in the Americas from the date of first settlement to c. 8000 B.C.

   The label "Clovis" comes from a Paleo-Indian site at Clovis, New Mexico, where such distinctive stone projectile points were first found. Clovis projectile heads are ideal evidence for Paleo-Indian occupation, as they are unmistakable, even when found by themselves.

6. The controversy is summarized briefly in Fagan, *The Great Journey* (1987), Part IV.

7. The discussion that follows is based on my own small boat experience of California waters. See also discussions of watercraft in chapters 3 and 5.

8. J. M. Erlandson, *Early Holocene Hunter-Gatherers of the California Coast* (New York: Plenum, 1994.)

9. Palynology, or pollen analysis, was invented by Swedish botanist Lenart van der Post in the early twentieth century to study vegetational changes in Scandinavian bogs and swamps. The minute pollens of trees, grasses, and other plants are highly distinctive when examined under a microscope, which allows scientists to study changes in local vegetation over many thousands of years. Waterlogged deposits such as ancient lake beds and marshes are ideal locations for such studies.

10. The "Fluted Point" or "Western Fluted Point" tradition is a generic label that includes sites with Clovis projectile points and other spear heads. The tradition spans a period of time from c. 11,500 to 9000 B.C. and is not a term I use widely here.

11. Jones, "Marine Resource Value" (1991).

12. Sites in these two paragraphs summarized in Moratto, *California Archaeology* (1984), chapters 2 and 3.

13. Mostin: Moratto, *California Archaeology* (1984), 99–103.

14. Borax Lake: Moratto, *California Archaeology* (1984), 82–85.

15. The latest thinking on this complex issue can be found in Donald Grayson, "The Archaeological Record of Human Impacts on Animals," *Journal of World Prehistory* 15(1) (2001): 1–68.

The word megafauna comes from the Greek megos, meaning "big." The word is commonly applied to large, now extinct animals, which flourished in the Americas until about 10,900 B.C.

Chapter 3: The First Coastal Settlement

1. Paul Porcasi et al., "Early Holocene Coastlines of the California Bight: The Channel Islands as First Visited by Humans," *Pacific Coast Archaeological Society Quarterly* 35(2&3) (1999): 1–24. Jon Erlandson and Roger Colton, eds., *Hunter-Gatherers of Early Holocene Coastal California* (Los Angeles: UCLA Institute of Archaeology, 1991) was the fundamental source for this chapter, offering essays on different areas of the coast.
2. The earth's crust adjusted to the melting of Ice Age glaciers and ice sheets, which reduced the weight bearing on it.
3. Changes summarized ably by Polly McW. Bickell, "Changing Sea Levels along the California Coast: Anthropological Implications," *Journal of California Anthropology* 5(1) (1978): 6–20.
4. "Red tide" is a harmful algal bloom, which forms when algae grow very fast and bloom into dense, visible red patches near the surface. The word "tide" is a misnomer, for the algae are not associated with tides. Certain phytoplankton species produce potent neurotoxins, which can be transferred through the food web. Such algae affect anchovies, sea birds, and certain mollusks along the Pacific Coast, rendering them toxic to humans. Red tides occur in California waters during the summer months.
5. Phillip C. Orr, "The Arlington Site, Santa Rosa Island," *American Antiquity* 27(3) (1962): 417–19. Also his "Dwarf Mammoths and Man on Santa Rosa Island." *University of Utah Anthropological Papers* 26 (1956): 74–81.
6. Nineteenth-century Scandinavian archaeologists first applied the term "midden" to piles of ancient mollusks piled up by prehistoric hunter-gatherers on the shores of the Baltic Sea. Since then, archeologists have used the word in this narrow sense as well as more generically as rubbish heaps. In this book, I tend to reserve the word for shell accumulations (such as are commonplace on the Channel Islands), while using shell mound in the Bay Area and elsewhere, where other activities beyond mollusk collecting also took place.
7. I am grateful to Dr. John Johnson of the Santa Barbara Museum of Natural History for information on the Arlington Springs site. The remark about a question mark over the date of the burial is my personal opinion.
8. J. M. Erlandson et al., "An Archaeological and Paleontological Chronology for Daisy Cave (CA–SM–261), San Miguel Island, California." *Radiocarbon* 38 (1996): 361–73.
9. J. M. Erlandson, "Maritime Subsistence at a 9,300-Year-Old Shell Midden on Santa Rosa Island, California," *Journal of Field Archaeology* 26 (1999):

255–65. I am grateful to Professor Erlandson for providing me with unpublished information on his most recent finds.

10. This section is based on Terry L. Jones. "Elkhorn Slough Revisited: Reassessing the Chronology of CA–MNT–229," *Journal of California and Great Basin Anthropology* 14 (1992): 159–79.

11. Cross Creek: Terry L. Jones et al., "The Cross Creek Site (CA–SLO–1797) and Its Implications for New World Colonization," *American Antiquity* 67(2) (2002): 213–30.

12. D. R. Gallegos, "Patterns and Implications of Coastal Settlement in San Diego County: 9000 to 1300 Years Ago," in Terry L. Jones, ed., *Essays on the Prehistory of Maritime California* (Davis, Calif.: Center for Archaeological Research, 1992), 205–16.

Chapter 4: The Mainland: A World of Milling Stones

1. Fagan, *The Great Journey* (1987), 239.
2. This passage is based on Brian Fagan, *After the Ice Age* (New York: Basic Books, in press.)
3. Windbreaks are simple brush shelters erected with sapling uprights, designed to provide shelter against the wind. They are commonplace among hunter-gatherer societies.
4. Pluvial lakes in California formed from both local rainfall and melting mountain snow pack.
5. The "Western Pluvial Lakes Tradition" dates from about 9600 to 5000 B.C. and is a generic archaeological term with little grounding in cultural reality. Specialists divide the tradition into numerous local variants marked by different projectile point forms. How meaningful these variations are in cultural terms is a matter for discussion. Readers interested in the Western Pluvial Lake Tradition should consult Moratto's *California Archaeology* (1984), which offers a technical discussion.
6. Ernst Antevs, "Climatic Changes and Pre-White Man," *University of Utah Bulletin* 38(20) (1948): 168–91.
7. Throughout this book, my accounts of Skyrocket are based on: Roger Marks La Jeunesse and John Howard Pryor, *Executive Summary of the Skyrocket Report (CA–Cal–629/630), Calaveras County, California* (Copperopolis, Calif.: Prepared for the FMC Gold Company, Meridian Minerals, 1996) and on discussions with La Jeunesse and Pryor, to whom I am grateful for checking over the Skyrocket portions of the text.
8. Roger La Jeunesse and John Pryor comment:

[Margaret Newman of the University of Calgary] did some antigen work on the surfaces of ten milling slabs and the results were positive for four of them, two showing the presence of *Pinus* [pine], dating from 7500 until 6500 B.C., and two reacting with antibodies for *Quercus* [oak] dating from 6500 until 5000 B.C. None of the specimens submitted reacted to any of the antibodies for species from common seeds. This suggests that acorns were a supplemental food stuff, a full 5,000 years before they were previously thought to have been used by pre-historic peoples in California. These people were possibly "pit leaching" their acorns in the marsh, and maybe using them as a "famine food," that they could leave and return to without having it disturbed by other people or animals, such as bears and deer. If they stuck the acorns in the ground after the fall harvest, they would be ready to eat six months later, when other foods were scarce.

The comment has been edited to conform with usages in the main text.

9. David Banks Rogers, *Prehistoric Man of the Santa Barbara Coast* (Santa Barbara, Calif.: Santa Barbara Museum of Natural History, 1929).

10. William J. Wallace, "A Suggested Chronology for Southern California Coastal Archaeology," *Southwestern Journal of Anthropology* 11 (1955): 214–30.

11. This discussion is based on the relevant passages in Moratto, *California Archaeology* (1984). Big Sur site: Terry J. Jones, "Big Sur: A Keystone in Central California Culture History," *Pacific Coast Archaeological Society Quarterly* 29(1) (1993): 1–78.

12. The classic study of Cahuilla ethnobotany is David Prescott Barrows, *The Ethno-Botany of the Coahuilla Indians of Southern California* (Chicago: University of Chicago Press, 1900; reprinted by Malki Museum Press, Banning, Calif., 1971).

13. Kelly McGuire and William R. Hillebrandt, "The Possibilities of Women and Men: Gender and the California Milling Stone Horizon," *Journal of California and Great Basin Studies* 16(1)(1994): 41–59. See also: Terry L. Jones, "Mortars, Pestles, and Division of Labor in Prehistoric California: A View from Big Sur," *American Antiquity* 61 (1996): 243–64.

14. See note 6 above.

Chapter 5: The Dolphin Hunters

1. L. Mark Raab, "The Southern California Islands during the Middle Holocene," in J. M. Erlandson and M. A. Glassow, eds., *Archaeology of the California Coast during the Middle Holocene* (Los Angeles: Institute of Archaeology, UCLA, 1997), 23–35. See also: Jeffrey H. Altschul and Donn R. Grenda, eds., *Islanders and Mainlanders* (Tucson, Ariz.: SRI Press, 2002), chapters 4 and 6.

2. Before the development of simple, then barbed fishhooks, fisherfolk commonly used baited sharp shell or bone fragments on fishing lines to catch even quite large fish, relying on such a simple gorge to stick in the fish's mouth. Fishhooks are, of course, much more effective.

3. Judith F. Porcasi and Harumi Fujita, "The Dolphin Hunters: A Specialized Prehistoric Maritime Adaptation in the Southern California Channel Islands and Baja California, *American Antiquity* 65(3) (2000): 543–66.

4. Judith F. Porcasi and Sherri L. Andrews, "Evidence for a Prehistoric *Mola mola* Fishery on the Southern California Coast," *Journal of California and Great Basin Anthropology* 23(1) (2001): 51–66.

5. Brian Fagan, "The House of the Sea: An Essay on Early Planked Canoes in Southern California," submitted to *American Antiquity*.

6. Jeanne Arnold, ed., *Origins of a Pacific Coast Chiefdom* (Salt Lake City, Utah: University of Utah Press, 2001). Also the same author's "Transportation Innovation and Social Complexity among Maritime Hunter-Gatherer Societies," *American Anthropologist* 97 (1995): 733–47. Lynn Gamble's "Archaeological Evidence for the Origin of the Plank Canoe in North America," *American Antiquity* 67(2) (2002): 301–15 offers an up-to-date summary of the archaeological evidence.

7. The comprehensive account of *tomols:* Travis Hudson, Jan Timbrook, and M. Rempe, *Tomol: Chumash Watercraft as Described in the Ethnographic Notes of John P. Harrington* (Los Altos and Santa Barbara, Calif.: Ballena Press and Santa Barbara Museum of Natural History, 1978).

8. I am grateful to Professor Mark Raab for showing me this toolkit, studied by Mr. James Cassidy, who generously provided photographs and discussed the artifacts with me. See also Jim Cassidy, L. Mark Raab, and Nina A. Kononenko "An Exploration of Early Holocene Wood Working Activities at Eel Point (CA–SCLI–43), San Clemente Island, California." Paper presented at the Society for California Archaeology meetings, Riverside, 2000. Also L. Mark Raab and James Cassidy, "Boats, Bones and Bifaces: The Early Holocene Mariners of Eel Point, San Clemente, California," *American Antiquity*. In press.

9. L. Mark Raab and Daniel O. Larson, "Medieval Climatic Anomaly and Punctuated Cultural Evolution in Coastal Southern California," *American Antiquity* 62 (1997): 319–36.

10. Little Harbor: Clement W. Meighan and Keith L. Johnson, "The Little Harbor Site, Catalina Island: An Example of Ecological Interpretation in Archaeology," *American Antiquity* 24 (1959): 383–405. For an update, see L. Mark Raab et al., "Return to Little Harbor, Santa Catalina Island, California: A Critique of the Marine Paleotemperature Model," *American Antiquity* 60 (1995): 287–308.

Chapter 6: A Changing World

1. Maidu creation myth, quotes from Malcolm Margolin, ed., *The Way We Lived* (Berkeley, Calif.: California Historical Society and Heyday Books, 1993), 125.

2. Skyrocket: La Jeunesse and Pryor, *Executive Summary of the Skyrocket Report* (1996). Also personal communication.
3. A useful survey: Sarah Mason, "Acorntopia? Determining the Role of Acorns in Past Human Subsistence," in John Wilkins, David Harvey, and Michael Dobson, eds., *Food in Antiquity* (Exeter, UK: University of Exeter Press, 1995), 112–36.

   The following was a basic source for this chapter: Mark E. Basgall, "Resource Intensification among Hunter-Gatherers: Acorn Economies in Prehistoric California," *Research in Economic Anthropology* 9 (1987): 21–52. See also: E. W. Gifford, "California Balanophagy," In Unknown editor, *Essays in Anthropology Presented to A. L. Kroeber* (Berkeley: University of California Press, 1936), 87–98.
5. La Jeunesse and Pryor comment:

   The fewer tannins removed make the acorn foodstuff less digestible. Tannins do this by complexing with proteins and carbohydrates that are part of the acorn. In effect, if you don't successfully bring down the tannin content, someone could literally eat all the acorn they could stuff into their mouth and not gain weight. In fact, vets in Africa have looked at this very same problem with sorghum and goats, finding a tannin-rich feed was problematic for successful weight gain. The technological efficiencies achieved with pulverizing the acorn first and leaching them in leaching basins is that this process removes most of the tannins, making this fat rich food more digestible. This is important, because fat in the diet is directly associated with onset of puberty and consequently rapid population growth.

6. Charles A. Du Bois, Wintu Ethnography, *University of California Publications in American Archaeology and Ethnology* 36(1) (1935): 1–148.
7. Martin Baumhoff, "Ecological Determinants of Aboriginal California Populations," *University of California Publications in American Archaeology and Ethnology* 49(2) (1958): 155–236.
8. Craig D. Bates, "Acorn Storehouses of the Yosemite Miwok," *The Masterkey* 57(1) (1978): 3–22.
9. An excellent discussion of acorn processing and acorns generally, which I drew heavily on here, will be found in Beverly R. Ortiz as told by Julia Parker, *It Will Live Forever: Traditional Yosemite Acorn Preparation* (Berkeley, Calif.: Heyday Books, 1991). This book has excellent photographs and offers an excellent account of mortars and the pounding tookit.
10. Walter Goldschmidt, "Nomlaki Ethnography," *University of California Publications in American Archaeology and Ethnology* 42(4) (1951): 303–443.
11. This passage is based on Moratto, *California Archaeology* (1984), and on Michael Glassow, "Middle Holocene Cultural Development in the Central

Santa Barbara Channel Region," in Jon M. Erlandson and Michael Glassow, eds., *Archaeology of the California Coast during the Middle Holocene* (Los Angeles: UCLA Institute of Archaeology, 1997), 73–90.

12. See chapters 2 and 4 in Erlandson and Glassow, *Archaeology of the California Coast during the Middle Holocene* (1997).

13. Discussion in Basgall, "Resource Intensification among Hunter-Gatherers" (1987).

14. Harris lines are tell-tale markings etched onto bones, which result from severe dietary deficiencies. Dental hypoplasia is a condition of reduced dental enamel growth, which results from the same cause.

15. Thomas L. Jackson. "Pounding Acorn: Women's Production as Social and Economic Focus, in J. M. Gero and M. W. Conkey, eds., *Engendering Archaeology* (Oxford, UK: Basil Blackwell, 1991), 301–25.

16. This section is based on Lowell J. Bean, "Social Organization in Native California," in Lowell J. Bean and Thomas C. Blackburn, eds., *Native Californians: A Theoretical Retrospective* (Ramona, Calif.: Ballena Press, 1976), 99–123. For the purposes of this book, a band is a small social unit comprising several families. Tribelets are village communities, small enough that a single person could exercise authority over them, sharing a common culture and language.

17. Edward M. Luby and Mark F. Gruber, "The Dead Must Be Fed: Symbolic Meanings of the Shellmounds of the San Francisco Bay Area," *Cambridge Archaeological Journal* 9(1) (1999): 95–108.

18. James T. Davis, "Trade Routes and Economic Exchange among the Indians of California," *University of California Archaeological Survey Reports* 54(1961).

19. William R. Hildebrandt, *Xonxon'ata in the Tall Oaks: Archaeology and Ethnohistory of a Chumash Village in the Santa Ynez Valley* (Santa Barbara, Calif.: Santa Barbara Museum of Natural History, 2001) is an exemplary monograph on this important site.

Chapter 7: The Seductive Glass

1. The terms "flake," "core," and "blade" have technical meanings for archaeologists. For the purposes of this book, a flake is any fragment of stone struck off from a lump, the core, to use the technical term. There are many forms of core and flake, which are described in later chapters. Flakes are different from blades, which are usually struck off from a core with some form of punch, a method used with great skill by the Aztecs of Mexico and observed by the Spanish conquistadors.

2. "Biface" is a stone tool flaked on both sides, also commonly applied to large pieces of obsidian that have been bifacially flaked either to produce a beautiful object or for potential use as a core.

3. The association maintains a website at: www.peak.org/obsidian/index/html.

4. Chert is a flintlike quartz excellent for tool making. Chalcedony is a subspecies of quartz, often with a waxy, lustrous feel. Again, it is excellent for tool making.

5. This discussion of obsidian trade is based in large part on Pat Mikkelsen, William Hildebrandt, and Deborah Jones, "Toolstone Procurement and Lithic Production Technology: California," in Michael Moratto, ed., *Archaeological Investigations PGT-PG&E Pipeline Expansion Project, Idaho, Washington, and California,* Volume 4. (Report submitted to the Pacific Gas Transmission Company, Portland, Oregon, 1994), chapter 8. Another valuable report was: Kelly R. McGuire, ed., *Boundary Lands: Archaeological Investigations Along the California Great Basin Interface* (Carson City: Nevada State Museum Anthropological Papers, 2002).

6. Mikkelsen, Hildebrandt, and Jones, "Toolstone Procurement and Lithic Production Technology" (1994).

7. Moratto, *California Archaeology* (1984), chapter 7.

8. William R. Hildebrandt and Kelly R. McGuire, "The Ascendance of Hunting during the California Middle Archaic: An Evolutionary Perspective," *American Antiquity* 67(2) (2002): 231–56.

9. Raymond Firth, *Primitive Polynesian Economy* (London: Routledge, 1939), 38.

10. An excellent anthology on adaptations to climate in California and the paradise issue can be found in L. Mark Raab and Terry L. Jones, eds., *Trouble in Paradise: Mythmaking and the Re-Discovery of California Prehistory* (Salt Lake City, Utah: University of Utah Press, 2003). The introductions offer an excellent overview for laypeople and students.

11. Kroeber, *Handbook of the Indians of California* (1925), 524.

12. Richard B. Lee, *The !Kung San* (Cambridge, UK: Cambridge University Press, 1979) is the standard account.

13. Davis, "Trade Routes and Economic Exchange among the Indians of California" (1961).

14. The literature on California's shell beads is enormous and rightly so, for it is an important, if arcane, subject. The following two references will guide you to the specialist literature: Chester D. King, *The Evolution of Chumash Society: A Comparative Study of Artifacts Used in Social System Maintenance in the Santa Barbara Channel Region before A.D. 1804* (New York: Garland, 1990) and Arnold, *Origins of a Pacific Coast Chiefdom* (2001), chapter 4.

Chapter 8: The Realm of the Supernatural

1. Chumash story quoted from T.C. Blackburn, *December's Child: A Book of Chumash Oral Narratives* (Berkeley, Calif.: University of California Press,

1975), 192–93. An account of swordfish rituals and a remarkable swordfish dancer's burial appears in Demerest Davenport, John R. Johnson, and Jan Timbrook, "The Chumash and the Swordfish," *Antiquity* 67 (1993): 257–72.

2. Robert Fagles, *Homer: The Odyssey* (New York: Viking, 1990), 487.

3. Nomlaki quote: Robert F. Heizer and Albert B. Elsasser, *The Natural World of the California Indians* (Berkeley, Calif.: University of California Press, 1980), 210.

4. Heizer and Elsasser, *The Natural World of the California Indians* (1980), 213.

5. Edwin M. Loeb, "The Eastern Kuksu Cult," *University of California Publications in American Archaeology and Ethnology* 33(2) (1933): 165.

6. John P. Harrington, ed., "A New Original Version of Boscana's Historical Account of the San Juan Capistrano Indians of Southern California," Washington, D.C.: *Smithsonian Institution Miscellaneous Collections* 92(4) (1933): 38.

7. The literature on shamans in California and shamanism generally is complex. Here are some starting points, which I relied on when writing this passage. Mircea Eliade, *Shamanism: Archaic Techniques of Ecstasy* (Princeton, N.J.: Princeton University Press, 1964); Ake Hultkrantz, *Native Religions of North America: The Power of Visions and Fertility* (San Francisco: Harper & Row, 1987); and Lowell John Bean, ed., *California Indian Shamanism* (Menlo Park, Calif.: Ballena Press, 1992).

8. Richard B. Applegate, *Atishwin: The Dream-Helper in South-Central California* (Socorro, N.M.: Ballena Press, 1978).

9. Kroeber, *Handbook of the Indians of California* (1925), 514.

10. A bibliography of shamanism and related topics will be found in David S. Whitley, *The Art of the Shaman* (Salt Lake City, Utah: University of Utah Press, 2000).

Chapter 9: Art on the Rocks

1. As paints, California rock artists used red ocher and other pigments mixed with egg whites, urine, and other bonding agents.

2. Campbell Grant, James W. Baird, and J. Kenneth Pringle, *Rock Paintings of the Coso Range* (Ridgecrest, Calif.: Maturango Museum, 1969), 115.

3. Joseph Campbell, *Transformations of Myth through Time* (New York: Harper & Row, 1990), 9–10.

4. An excellent summary of Lewis-Williams's ideas appears in his *The Mind in the Cave: Exploring Consciousness and Prehistoric Art* (London: Thames and Hudson, 2002). James L. Pearson, *Shamanism and the Ancient Mind* (Walnut Creek, Calif.: AltaMira Press, 2002) offers a useful summary in the context of what is called cognitive archaeology.

5. The debate over shamanistic approaches is, for the most part, embedded in the specialist literature. See Anne Solomon, "The Myth of Ritual Origins? Ethnography, Mythology and Interpretation of San Rock Art," *South African Archaeological Bulletin* 52 (1997): 3–13 and R. Hamayon and H-P. Francfort, eds., *The Concept of Shamanism: Uses and Abuses* (Budapest: Akadémiai Kiadó, 2001). Michael Winkelman, "Shamanism and Cognitive Evolution," *Cambridge Archaeological Journal* 12 (2002)1: 71–101 offers a discussion of shamanistic approaches to rock art with a critical analysis by several scholars.

6. Date quoted by David Whitley. *The Art of the Shaman* (Salt Lake City, Utah: University of Utah Press, 2000), 43.

7. Robert F. Heizer and Martin A. Baumhoff, *Prehistoric Rock Art of Nevada and Eastern California* (Berkeley, Calif.: University of California Press, 1962) is an oft-cited work. For rock art studies generally, Paul Bahn, *The Cambridge Illustrated History of Prehistoric Art* (Cambridge, UK: Cambridge University Press, 1998) is an excellent summary. So is David Whitley, ed., *Handbook of Rock Art Research* (Walnut Creek, Calif.: AltaMira Press, 2001). See also Christopher Chippindale and Paul S. C. Taçon, eds., *The Archaeology of Rock Art* (Cambridge, UK: Cambridge University Press, 1998).

8. Whitley, *The Art of the Shaman* (2000), chapters 4 and 5.

9. Chemehuevi shamanism: Isabel T. Kelly, "Chemehuevi Shamanism," in (no editor) *Essays in Anthropology Presented to A.L. Kroeber in Celebration of His Sixtieth Birthday* (Berkeley, Calif.: University of California Press, 1936), 139. For a recent Whitley discussion of this subject, see David S. Whitley, Joseph M. Simon, and Ronald I. Dorn, "The Vision Quest in the Coso Range," *American Indian Rock Art* 25 (1999): 1–31.

10. Whitley, *The Art of the Shaman* (2000), 82–83.

11. Kelly, "Chemehuevi Shamanism" (1936), 139.

12. Heizer and Baumhoff, *Prehistoric Rock Art of Nevada and Eastern California* (1962).

13. Grant et al., *Rock Paintings of the Coso Range* (1969), quotes from pages 42 and 113.

14. In writing this section, I drew on Amy J. Gilreath and William R. Hildebrandt, "Coso Rock Art within Its Archaeological Context," unpublished paper, 2001. I am grateful to the authors for their permission to use and quote from this important article.

15. Gilreath and Hildebrandt, "Coso Rock Art" (2001), 18.

16. Anna H. Gayton, "Yokuts and Western Mono Ethnography," *University of California Anthropological Records* 5 (1948): 169.

17. C. Alan Davis and Gerald A. Smith, *Newberry Cave* (Redlands, Calif.: San Bernardino County Museum Association, 1981).

18. David S. Whitley et al. "Sally's Rockshelter and the Archaeology of the Vision Quest," *Cambridge Archaeological Journal* 9(2) (1999): 221–47.

19. Chumash rock art. Campbell G. Grant, *The Rock Paintings of the Chumash* (Berkeley, Calif.: University of California Press, 1965) is the standard work. For a survey, see Whitley, *The Art of the Shaman* (2000), chapter 4, and the series of volumes edited by D. Travis Hudson and Thomas C. Blackburn, *The Material Culture of the Chumash Interaction Sphere* (Santa Barbara, Calif.: Santa Barbara Museum of Natural History, 1982 onward), quote from Whitley, p. 71.

20. Harrington, "A New Original Version of Boscana's Historical Account" (1933), 17.

21. Travis Hudson and Ernest Underhay, *Crystals in the Sky: An Intellectual Odyssey Involving Chumash Astronomy, Cosmology and Rock Art* (Santa Barbara, Calif.: Ballena Press and Santa Barbara Museum of Natural History, 1978). This monograph also describes Condor Cave.

22. Whitley, *The Art of the Shaman* (2000), chapter 4.

Chapter 10: The Northwest: Dugouts and Salmon

1. Quoted from Malcolm Margolin, ed., *The Way We Lived,* 2d ed. (Berkeley, Calif.: California Historical Society and Heyday Books, 1993), 56.

2. Powers, *Tribes of California* (1976), 69. (Reprinted version of the original 1877 book.)

3. Richard A. Gould, "Seagoing Canoes among the Indians of Northwestern California," *Ethnohistory* 15(1) (1968): 11–42.

4. Robert. F. Heizer and Albert B. Elsasser, "Archaeology of Hum-67, the Gunther Island Site in Humboldt Bay, California," *University of California Archaeological Survey Reports* 22 (1964): 1–122.

5. Kroeber, *Handbook of the Indians of California* (1925).

6. Gould, "Seagoing Canoes" (1968).

7. Powers, *Tribes of California* (1976).

8. Gould, "Seagoing Canoes" (1968).

9. Richard A. Gould, *Archaeology of the Point St. George Site and Tolowa Prehistory* (Berkeley, Calif.: University of California Press, 1966).

10. William Hildebrandt and Valerie Levulett, "Middle Holocene Adaptations on the Northern California Coast: Terrestrial Resource Productivity and Its Influence on the Use of Marine foods," in J. M. Erlandson and M. A. Glassow, eds., *Archaeology of the California Coast during the Middle Holocene* (Los Angeles: UCLA Institute of Archaeology, 1997).

11. Ethnographic accounts of these groups can be found in *The Handbook of North American Indians,* Volume 8: *California.*

12. William Hildebrandt and Valerie Levulett, "Late Holocene Emergence of Marine Focused Economies in Northwest California," in J. M. Erlandson and T. L. Jones, eds., *Archaeology of the California Coast during the Late Holocene* (Los Angeles: UCLA Institute of Archaeology, 2002), pagination unknown. I am grateful to the authors for sharing this paper with me in manuscript form.

13. Kroeber, *Handbook of the Indians of California* (1925), 54.

14. Gould, *Archaeology of the Point St. George Site* (1966), 121.

15. Area discussion by David Fredrickson in Moratto, *California Archaeology* (1984), chapter 10. This section is based on several sources: George J. Gmoser, "Co-Evolution of Adaptation and Linguistic Boundaries in Northwest California," in G. White et al., eds., *There Grows a Green Tree, Papers in Honor of David A. Fredrickson* (Davis, Calif.: Center for Archaeological Research, 1993), 243–64; Joseph L. Chartkoff and Kerry K. Chartkoff, "Late-Period Settlement of the Middle Klamath River of Northwest California," *American Antiquity* 40(2) (1975): 172–79 (where full references will be found); William R. Hildebrandt, "Late Period Hunting Adaptations on the North Coast of California," *Journal of California and Great Basin Anthropology* 6(2) (1984): 189–206; and R. Lee Lyman, *Prehistory of the Oregon Coast* (New York: Academic Press, 1991).

Chapter 11: San Francisco Bay: A Landscape of Mounds

1. The word *tumulus* from the Latin meaning "mound" is not often used in California archaeology. In Europe, it often refers purely to burial mounds. Here, I use it in a generic sense, to mean more than a mound used purely to bury the dead. This was partly a literary decision, as I needed another word other than "mound." I hope that it is clear that I am not referring to mounds used purely for burial purposes!

2. A floodplain, the flat area over which a river meanders, is distinct from an estuary, which is the area through which a river enters the ocean, typically defined by the limits of tidal flow.

3. Bickell, "Changing Sea Levels" (1978).

4. A paleontologist is a student of fossil animals such as dinosaurs. The early history of Bay Area archaeology appears in Kent Lightfoot, "Cultural Construction of Coastal Landscapes. A Middle Holocene Perspective from San Francisco Bay," in J. M. Erlandson and M. W. Glassow, eds., *Archaeology of the California Coast during the Middle Holocene* (Los Angeles: UCLA Institute of Archaeology, 1997), 129–41. I relied heavily on this important paper for this chapter.

5. Max Uhle, "The Emeryville Mound," *University of California Publications in American Archaeology and Ethnology* 7(1) (1907): 39.

6. Alfred Kroeber, "The Archaeology of California," in Editorial Committee, eds., *Anthropological Essays Presented to Frederic Ward Putnam in Honor of His Seventieth Birthday, April 16, 1909, by His Friends and Associates* (New York: Stechert, 1909), 15.

7. Nels C. Nelson, "Shellmounds of the San Francisco Region," *University of California Publications in American Archaeology and Ethnology* 7(4) (1909): 12.

8. Nels C. Nelson, "The Ellis Landing Shellmound," *University of California Publications in American Archaeology and Ethnology* 7(5) (1910).

9. Kroeber, *Handbook of the Indians of California* (1925), 931.

10. For a summary of the so-called moundbuilder cultures of the Midwest and eastern United States, see Brian Fagan, *Ancient North America*, 3rd ed. (London: Thames and Hudson, 2000), chapters 18 to 20.

11. W. Egbert Schenck, "The Emeryville Shellmound Final Report," *University of California Publications in American Archaeology and Ethnology* 23(3) (1926).

12. Hildegaard Howard, "The Avifauna of Emeryville Shellmound," *University of California Publications in Zoology* 32 (1929): 301–94. Later research into the Emeryville shell mound is described by Jack M. Broughton, "Resource Depression and Intensification during the Late Holocene, San Francisco Bay: Evidence from the Emeryville Shellmound Vertebrate Fauna," *University of California Anthropological Records*, 32 (1999). More recent work remains unpublished, being the result of intensive CRM investigations. Numerous human remains were recovered, and are being reinterred. Radiocarbon dates establish the base of the mound at about 850 B.C., with later occupation at different locations dating to as recently as A.D. 1600. I am grateful to Dr. Sally Morgan for information on this research. A report will be posted on the City of Emeryville's website in due course.

13. Polly M. Bickell, *San Francisco Bay Archaeology: Sites ALA-328, ALA-13 and ALA-12* (Berkeley, Calif.: Contributions of the University of California Archaeological Research Facility 29 (1981).

14. Charmstones are carefully shaped stones, usually found with burials, usually in interments dating to after 2500 B.C. Some are spindle shaped, others phallus-like, and may denote a life force. They were often made from exotic, attractive-looking rocks, and were perforated to be suspended around the neck.

15. Clement W. Meighan, "Reexamination of Early Central California Culture," *American Antiquity* 52 (1987): 28–36.

16. Alan Leventhal, "A Reinterpretation of Some Bay Area Shellmound Sites: A View from the Mortuary Complex from CA-ALA-329, The Ryan Mound" (M.A. Thesis presented to California State University, San Jose, Calif., 1993).

17. This section is based on Lightfoot, "Cultural Construction of Coastal Landscapes" (1997) and on Luby and Gruber, "The Dead Must Be Fed" (1999). It is also based on Kent G. Lightfoot and Edward M. Luby, "The Late Holocene in the Greater San Francisco Bay Area," in Erlandson and Jones, eds, *Archaeology of the California Coast* (2002). I am grateful to Ed Luby for much stimulating discussion on this subject.

18. The culture history of the Bay Area is summarized in Moratto, *California Archaeology* (1984). See also David A. Frederickson, "Spatial and Cultural Units in Central California Archaeology," in R. E. Hughes, ed., *Toward a New Taxonomic Framework for Central California Archaeology* (Berkeley: Contributions of the University of California Archaeological Research Facility 52 (1994): 25–47, 91–103.

19. Luby and Gruber, "The Dead Must Be Fed" (1999) covers this section.

20. Richard A. Gould, "Exploitative Economies and Culture Change in Central California," *Reports of the University of California Archaeological Survey* 62 (1964): 123–63.

21. Lightfoot and Luby, "The Late Holocene in the Greater San Francisco Bay Area" (2002).

Chapter 12: Central Valley and Foothills: The Realm of the Rivers

1. Richard K. Beardsley, *Temporal and Areal Relationships in Central California Archaeology* (Berkeley, Calif.: University of California Archaeological Survey Reports 24 and 25, 1954), 3.

2. Jeremiah B. Lillard, Robert F. Heizer, and Franklin Fenenga, *An Introduction to the Archaeology of Central California* (Sacramento: Sacramento Junior College, Department of Anthropology, Bulletin 2, 1939).

3. All of this research is summarized in Robert F. Heizer, "The Archaeology of Central California, I: The Early Horizon," *University of California Anthropological Records* 21(1) (1949): 1–84.

4. Robert F. Heizer and S. F. Cook, "The Archaeology of Central California: A Comparative Analysis of Human Bone from Nine Sites," *University of California Anthropological Records* 12(2) (1952): 85–111.

5. Moratto, *California Archaeology* (1984), chapters 3 and 5.

6. Skyrocket: La Jeunesse and Pryor, *Executive Summary of the Skyrocket Report* (1996).

7. See Mark C. Basgall and William R. Hildebrandt, *Prehistory of the Sacramento River Canyon, Shasta County, California* (Davis, Calif.: Center for Archaeological Research at Davis Publication 9, 1989).

8. Windmiller literature is diffuse. A descriptive starting point, beyond the references in Notes 3 and 4, is: Sonia Ragir, "The Early Horizon in Central

California Prehistory," *University of California Publications in American Archaeology and Ethnology* 15 (1972).

9. French Camp Slough: Moratto, *California Archaeology* (1984), 210–11.

10. A popular summary of the Brazil Mound appears in Sharon A. Waechter, *The Brazil Mound: Archaeology of a Prehistoric Village* (Davis, Calif.: Far Western Anthropological Research Group, 1995). It has a useful bibliography.

11. See Jack Broughton, "Late Holocene Resource Intensification in the Sacramento Valley, California," *Journal of Archaeological Science* 21 (1994): 501–14, for references to the Grayson research.

12. La Jeunesse and Pryor, *Executive Summary of the Skyrocket Report* (1996).

13. This section is based on Moratto, *California Archaeology* (1984), chapter 5 and on the relevant chapters in the *Handbook of North American Indians, Volume 8: California*.

14. Charles Lewis Camp, ed., *The Chronicles of George C. Yount, California Pioneer of 1826* (Sacramento, Calif.: California State Library, 1963), 52.

Chapter 13: The South and Southeast: Coast, Hinterland, and Desert

1. A synthesis of desert archaeology by Claude Warren appears in Moratto, *California Archaeology* (1984), chapter 8. My account is based in considerable part on this account. For the relationship to the Great Basin see: Claude N. Warren and R. H. Crabtree, "Prehistory of the Southwest Area," in Warren L. D'Acevado, ed., *Handbook of the North American Indians, Volume 11: The Great Basin* (Washington, D.C.: Smithsonian Institution, 1986), 183–93.

2. The Lake Elsinore excavations are described in Donn R. Grenda, *Continuity and Change: 8,500 Years of Lacustrine Adaptation on the Shores of Lake Elsinore* (Tucson, Ariz.: Statistical Research Technical Series 59, 1997). Dr. Grenda very kindly critiqued this account.

3. The Ballona Wetlands Project is an enormous undertaking. Publications will continue to appear for many years. An initial synthesis appears in Jeffrey H. Altschul, Richard S. Ciolek-Torrello, and Jeffrey A. Homburg, *Life in the Ballona: Archaeological Investigations at the Admiralty Site (CA–LAN–47) and the Channel Gateway Site (CA–LAN–1596–H)* (Tucson, Ariz.: Statistical Research Technical Series 33 (1992). See also Jeffrey H. Altshuhl et al., "Ballona Archaeology: A Decade of Multidisciplinary Research," *Proceedings of the Society for California Archaeology* 14 (2002). And see also Altshuhl and Grenda, *Islanders and Mainlanders* (2002) for a discussion of Ballona's wider context. This

book is important because it treats the interior and coast as a single continuum. In press. I am grateful to Dr. Grenda for checking this section of the chapter, for showing me around the wetlands, and for sharing unpublished articles with me.

4. Julian Steward's Shoshone monographs are classics. See: "Ethnography of the Owens Valley Paiute," *University Publications in American Archaeology and Ethnology* 33(3) (1933): 233–350 and "Basin-Plateau Aboriginal Sociopolitical Groups." *Bureau of American Ethnology Bulletin* 120 (1938).

5. The Ancestral Pueblo of southern Nevada: Margaret M. Lyneis, "The Virgin Anasazi, Far Western Puebloans," *Journal of World Prehistory* 9(2) (1995): 199–241.

   I am grateful to Ms. Diane Winslow for information on the Black Dog Mesa site and for checking this portion of the chapter. Ancestral Pueblo people were responsible for the "Basketmaker II and III" occupations at Black Dog Cave—to use the technical label that archaeologists use for the artifacts in these levels. Black Dog Mesa is described in: Diane L. Winslow, *Mitigation Black Dog Mesa Archaeological Complex (26CK5686/BLM 53-7216. Volumes I to IV.* Draft n.d. (Report prepared for the Bureau of Land Management, Las Vegas District Office and the Nevada Power Company. Las Vegas, Nev.: Harry Reid Center for Environmental Studies, Marjorie Barrick Museum of Natural History, University of Nevada-Las Vegas), Report No. 5-4-26[1-4]).

   Halloran Springs: N. Nelson Leonard, III. "Prehistoric Turquoise Mining in the Halloran Springs District, San Bernardino County, California," *Journal of California and Great Basin Anthropology* 2 (1980): 245–56.

6. Robert M. Yohe, II, "The Introduction of the Bow and Arrow and Lithic Resource Use at Rose Spring (CA–INY–372)," *Journal of California and Great Basin Anthropology* 20 (1998): 26–52.

7. Philip J. Wilke and Harry W. Lawton, "Early Observations on the Cultural Geography of Coachella Valley," *Ballena Press Anthropological Papers* 3(1) (1975).

8. For a popular account of fishing in Lake Cahuilla, see: Rick Dower, "Fishing in the Desert," *American Archaeology* 4(4) (2000–2001): 20–26.

9. Lowell J. Bean, *Mukat's People: The Cahuilla Indians of Southern California* (Berkeley, Calif.: University of California Press, 1972) is the authoritative source on the Cahuilla.

10. Barrows, *The Ethno-Botany of the Coahuilla Indians of Southern California* (1900).

11. Bean, *Mukat's People* (1972), 89.

12. Wilke and Lawton, "Early Observations on the Cultural Geography of Coachella Valley" (1975), 5.

Chapter 14: Santa Barbara Channel: The World of the *Tomol*

1. This scenario is based on a scene described by Fray Juan Crespi in 1762. Herbert E. Bolton, ed., *Fray Juan Crespi: Missionary Explorer on the Pacific Coast 1769–1774.* (Berkeley, Calif.: University of California Press, 1927. Reprinted by AMS Press, New York, 1971), 252–59.
2. Lesley Byrd Simpson, *Journal of José Longinos Martinez: Notes and Observations of the Naturalist of the Botanical Expedition in Old and New California and the South Coast, 1791–1792* (San Francisco: J. Howell-Books, 1961), 7.
3. Bolton, *Fray Juan Crespi* (1927), 38.
4. Glassow, "Middle Holocene Cultural Development" (1997).
5. Douglas J. Kennett and James P. Kennett, "Competitive and Cooperative Responses to Climatic Instability in Coastal Southern California," *American Antiquity* 65 (2000): 379–95.
7. The Medieval Climatic Anomaly is the subject of intensive research. For an initial summary of its impact, see: L. Mark Raab and Daniel O. Larson, "Medieval Climatic Anomaly and Punctuated Cultural Evolution in Coastal Southern California," *American Antiquity* 62 (1997): 319–36.
8. Bolton, *Fray Juan Crespi* (1927), 37.
9. Arnold, *Origins of a Pacific Coast Chiefdom* (2001) is essential reading for anyone interested in culture change among early Chumash societies. Chapter 14 is relevant here.
10. This section is based on two important papers: Patricia M. Lambert and Phillip L. Walker, "Physical Anthropological Evidence for the Evolution of Social Complexity in Coastal Southern California," *American Antiquity* 65 (1991): 963–73 and Patricia M. Lambert, "Health in Prehistoric Populations of the Santa Barbara Channel Islands," *American Antiquity* 58(3) (1993): 509–22.
11. Napoleon Chagnon, *The Yanomamo,* 5th ed. (New York: Wadsworth, 1996).
12. Phillip L. Walker, "Cranial Injuries as Evidence of Violence in Prehistoric California," *American Journal of Physical Anthropology* 80 (1989): 51–61.
13. The most comprehensive account of Chumash culture comes from John Peabody Harrington's notes, which form the basis for Hudson and Blackburn's series of volumes *The Material Culture of the Chumash Interaction Sphere* (1982–1987). See also Hudson and Underhay, *Crystals in the Sky* (1978), and Travis Hudson et al., eds., *The Eye of the Flute: Chumash Traditional History and Ritual as Told by Fernando*

Librado to John P. Harrington, 2d ed. (Banning, Calif.: Malki Museum Press, 1981). For Chumash archaeology on Vandenberg Air Force Base, see Michael Glassow, *Purisimeño Chumash Prehistory* (New York: Harcourt Brace, 1996).

14. The all-important Malibu cemetery study appears in Lynn H. Gamble, Phillip L. Walker, and Glenn S. Russell, "An Integrative Approach to Mortuary Analysis: Social and Symbolic Dimensions of Chumash Burial Practices," *American Antiquity* 66(2) (2001): 185–212.

15. Davenport, Johnson, and Timbrook, "The Chumash and the Swordfish" (1993).

16. Gamble, "Archaeological Evidence for the Origin of the Plank Canoe in North America" (2002).

17. Hudson, Timbrook, Rempe, *Tomol* (1978). The quotes in this box are from this seminal work.

18. The section that follows is based on Arnold, *Origins of a Pacific Coast Chiefdom* (2001).

19. This discussion is based on Arnold, *Origins of a Pacific Coast Chiefdom* (2001), chapters 4 and 5.

Chapter 15: *Entrada*

1. An excellent source book is Rose Marie Beebe and Robert M. Senkewicz, eds., *Lands of Promise and Despair: Chronicles of Early California, 1535–1846* (Berkeley, Calif.: Heyday Books, 2002). See also: Luthin, *Surviving through the Days* (2002).

2. Robert F. Heizer, "Francis Drake and the California Indians, 1579," *University of California Publications in American Archaeology and Ethnology* 42(3) (1947): 253.

3. The name "California" first appeared in Garci Rodríguez de Montalvo's *The Labors of the Very Brave Knight Esplandián*, published in Seville, Spain, in 1510. For a fuller account and extract, see Beebe and Senkewicz, *Lands of Promise and Despair* (2002), 10.

4. Sherburne F. Cook, "The Conflict between the California Indian and White Civilization," 2 vols. *Ibero-Americana* 21 and 22 (1943): 124.

5. Luthin, *Surviving through the Days* (2002).

6. There is a rich literature on the historic archaeology of California, which lies outside the scope of this book. An excellent example of such complex research is Thomas N. Layton's compelling *Gifts from the Celestial Kingdom: A Shipwrecked Cargo for Gold Rush California* (Stanford, Calif.: Stanford University Press, 2002).

Index

About the Author

BRIAN FAGAN IS ONE OF THE LEADING ARCHAEOLOGICAL writers in the world and an internationally recognized authority on world prehistory. He studied archaeology and anthropology at Pembroke College, Cambridge University, and then spent seven years in sub-Saharan Africa working in museums and in monuments conservation and excavating early farming sites in Zambia and East Africa. He was one of the pioneers of multidisciplinary African history in the 1960s. Since 1967, he has been Professor of Anthropology at the University of California, Santa Barbara, where he has specialized in lecturing and writing about archaeology to wide audiences.

Professor Fagan has written a series of well known textbooks, including *In the Beginning* (10th edition, Prentice Hall, 2001) and *People of the Earth* (11th edition, 2003). His general books include *The Rape of the Nile* (Scribners, 1975), a classic history of Egyptology; *The Adventure of Archaeology* (National Geographic Society, 1985); *Time Detectives* (Simon & Schuster, 1995); *Ancient North America* (Thames & Hudson, 3rd ed., 2000); *The Little Ice Age* (Basic Books, 2001). He was also General Editor of the *Oxford Companion to Archaeology* (Oxford University Press, 1996). In addition, he has published several scholarly monographs on African archaeology and numerous specialized articles in national and international journals. He is also an expert on multimedia teaching and has received the Society for American Archaeology's first Public Education Award for his indefatigable efforts on behalf of archaeology and education.

Brian Fagan's other interests include bicycling, sailing, kayaking, and good food. He is married and lives in Santa Barbara with his wife and daughter, four cats (who supervise his writing), and last but not least, a minimum of four rabbits.